Chicago Whispers

# Chicago Whispers

## A History of LGBT Chicago
### before Stonewall

## St. Sukie de la Croix

THE UNIVERSITY OF WISCONSIN PRESS

The University of Wisconsin Press
1930 Monroe Street, 3rd Floor
Madison, Wisconsin 53711-2059
uwpress.wisc.edu

3 Henrietta Street
London WC2E 8LU, England
eurospanbookstore.com

Printed in the United States of America

Library of Congress Cataloging-in-Publication Data
De la Croix, St. Sukie.
Chicago whispers : a history of LGBT Chicago
before Stonewall / St. Sukie de la Croix.
p.     cm.
Includes bibliographical references and index.
ISBN 978-0-299-28694-1 (pbk.: alk. paper)
ISBN 978-0-299-28693-4 (e-book)
1. Gays—Illinois—Chicago—History.
2. Homosexuality—Illinois—Chicago—History.
3. Transgenderism—Illinois—Chicago—History.
I. Title.
HQ76.3.U52I443     2012
306.76′60977311—dc23
2011041961

———————————————— For Ian ————————————————

my candle on the water

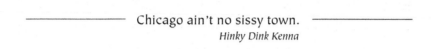

Chicago ain't no sissy town.
*Hinky Dink Kenna*

# Contents

# Contents

---------------- *Foreword* ----------------

## JOHN D'EMILIO

Over the last generation a substantial body of scholarly literature has appeared on the history of sexual and gender identity. We have accounts of social movements and of urban communities; biographical studies; explorations of how medicine and science have shaped common understandings of sexuality and gender; investigations into the role of the state in enforcing sexual norms and hierarchies; studies of popular culture and the arts; and much more.[1] Lesbian, gay, bisexual, and transgender history now reaches across long stretches of time and broad swaths of geography. It is a field of research that, in the twenty-first century, has gained legitimacy in the academy. Graduate students are able to write dissertations on LGBT topics and thus add to what we know, while courses in the undergraduate curricula of many colleges and universities transmit that knowledge to the next generation of students.

Need I say that it wasn't always so?

If I had to identify a moment when this new field of historical research was born, I would pick the fall of 1976, when Jonathan Ned Katz published his groundbreaking study, *Gay American History*.[2] While others had made some forays into writing about the history of same-sex relationships and identities, Katz's work stood apart. It was unlike anything that had appeared before. A massive volume, it defied the common belief that LGBT history would be impossible to write because, in the past, the oppression was so intense and the silences in the archival record so profound. Putting the lie to those beliefs, Katz presented several hundred pages of documents, stretching from the period of European exploration through the post–World War II era. He grouped the documents by topic—"Trouble," about the different forms of oppression that the violators of sexual and gender norms faced; "Treatment," about the role of the medical profession in defining and trying to cure homosexuality; "Passing Women," about the extraordinary lives of those who, today, we might describe as transgender men; "Native Americans/Gay Americans," which presented the long history of sexual and gender variation within many Native American cultures; "Resistance," which chronicled the many ways that queer people have fought back against oppression; and "Love," a section about same-sex romance and intimacy. Within those sections Katz provided some interpretive commentary, and he arranged his documents chronologically, so that a reader could detect patterns of both continuity and change.

When I finished the book, I could not help but feel thrilled at these new and unimagined worlds that opened on every page. More to the point, Katz's book inspired me. It confirmed for me that the decision that I had made—to write a dissertation in this undefined field—was not an act of foolishness; rather, there was a gay history out there to be uncovered and written. I also know I was not the only one who responded this way. Katz motivated quite a number of his readers to go beyond what he had done. They took particular stories evoked by one document or another and fleshed them out with research of their own.

I mention *Gay American History* in this foreword because Sukie de la Croix strikes me as being very much in this founding tradition of LGBT history. In writing *Chicago Whispers*, he chooses to stay very close to his sources. He provides, of course, some structure and narrative, but he also displays great respect for the documents. As much as his materials permit, he has them speak to us directly. As readers we get to encounter the evidence in a way that gives us a great deal of freedom to draw our own conclusions, to ask our own questions, and to imagine the lives and the worlds that produced these written records.

*Chicago Whispers* reminded me of *Gay American History* in another important way. For all the LGBT history that has been written in the last three decades, Chicago remains woefully understudied. Because of that, *Chicago Whispers* is very much a pioneering work. By the time I reached the end, I felt that it had opened up for me new and unexplored worlds. As someone who has recently made some research forays into Chicago's queer past, I came away eager to do more. I felt motivated to take what Sukie has offered as a starting point, and run with it.

Interestingly, within this chronological framework, the themes and topics that structured Katz's account a generation ago are still relevant. "Trouble" is never far away in the pages you're about to read. The police are a ubiquitous presence in the history of queer Chicago. They seem always ready to make arrests and disrupt the lives of ordinary people who were simply searching for love, companionship, and pleasure. Present also are the acid-drenched pens of the journalists and editorial writers who whipped up popular hostility to the sexually different and the gender crossers of the past. Doctors, too, have a part in defining and making public this new queer world that was emerging in late nineteenth-century Chicago. Transgender experience surfaces again and again in *Chicago Whispers*. Whether by performing on stage or displaying their bravado on the streets, gender crossers provided visibility, claimed public space, and opened up opportunities for collective life. At the same time, the historical record is filled with examples of individuals, like Albert Cashier, who successfully transitioned from one gender to the other and remained invisible. Sukie also reminds us that Native Americans whose cultural traditions involving gender and sexuality challenged European views of a proper social order were the original residents of the land that is now Chicago. "Resistance" repeatedly surfaces as a theme. Resistance is explicit in the work of activists like Henry Gerber in the 1920s and the members of Mattachine in the 1960s. But it can also be found in the bravery of those who risked arrest by patronizing bars on weekend nights or by publishing physique magazines and pulp novels that authorities might declare obscene. Finally, "Love" weaves its way through the documents and the historical narrative, as we learn about the relationships of many of the individuals whose stories fill these pages.

This contribution to LGBT history—focused on a particular place, organized chronologically, and told through original documents—also allowed certain themes to emerge clearly. I came away from my reading of *Chicago Whispers* noticing connections across time that speak beyond the Chicago experience to the larger field of LGBT history.

One of these themes is the vital role of artistic and cultural production. It surfaces in lots of ways and at so many different points in Chicago's history: the wildly popular gender-bending performances of male and female impersonators and, later, drag queens; the blues and jazz singers whose lyrics touched upon same-sex love and desire; the work of bohemian writers who were willing to challenge social convention; the authors of lesbian pulp novels and the photographers for male physique magazines. Not only was their work a form of personal self-expression that often violated social norms. It also provided visibility. It offered settings for collective experience. It allowed countless individuals to identify their own desires and name themselves. The audiences who came together at performances and the readers who consumed culture in the privacy of their own home were members of an inchoate community, connected in both tangible and imagined ways.

Oppression is another inescapable theme. This is not a new idea, of course. It has been a central and continuing feature of the history that has been produced. But Sukie's focus on Chicago and the chronological structure of the narrative puts the insidious role of the police into sharp focus. With their actions stretching across a century, the police function as the primary agents of oppression. At times they seem to operate independently; at times they are carrying out the orders of politicians; at times they are goaded into action by the exposés of journalists. But, whatever the cause of a particular set of arrests, the police reach was wide, and the damage that they did to individual lives was profound.

I noticed in particular one recurring phenomenon that had never before caught my attention. Again and again, a newspaper article states, or Sukie informs us directly, that the criminal charges filed against those arrested by the police were dropped. In other words, the police regularly exceeded their authority. Even with statutes about disorderly conduct, lewd behavior, and public indecency (laws, by the way, that give police enormous latitude), they could not make the charges stick. The arrests were harassment pure and simple, and they were an abuse of law enforcement authority.

In this matter of oppression, *Chicago Whispers* makes it abundantly clear that the police were not alone in their distaste for sexual and gender nonconformists. The United States has a long history of moral purity campaigns, and Chicago was not exempt from this tradition. Sometimes ministers stoked these crusades. Sometimes civic leaders and the business community propelled them forward. Sometimes a newspaper took up the cause. But whoever instigated them, these movements allowed the police to take action. At different points, they had wide appeal. And these crusades are not a thing of the past. In more recent decades, purity campaigns have continued to affect state policy and the social climate.

This collection also allowed me to think differently about LGBT history in relation to issues of periodization. If there has been one more or less consistent goal in the studies produced since the 1970s, it has been the effort to push further and further back into the past the story of queer identities and communities. In other words, all of us have tried to demonstrate that "it didn't start with Stonewall." In writing about the homophile movement, for example, I was demonstrating that there was a meaningful history of movement organization and activism in the 1950s and 1960s. Allan Bérubé pushed the story back further by demonstrating that World War II was a critical moment in which a broad sense of identity and commonality took hold, with an almost national reach.[3] Elizabeth Kennedy and Madeline Davis for Buffalo and Nan Alamilla Boyd for San Francisco wrote urban studies in which they offered clear evidence of community that stretched from the 1930s to the 1960s. In writing about New York, George Chauncey argued that a visible gay male life had emerged by the 1920s.[4]

The evidence in *Chicago Whispers* gave me a more nuanced take on this. In some ways, one could certainly argue that the content of *Chicago Whispers* very much continues in the mold of pushing back in time the existence of queer social worlds. For instance, the authors of *The Social Evil in Chicago*, a report compiled by a special vice commission, make reference to "a definite cult," a phrase that suggests the existence of social networks, or what today we would call community, even before World War I. Writing in 1932 in *Modern Thinker*, W. Beran Wolfe says that "homosexual clubs are known in every large American city." But, at the same time, there is an abundance of evidence in the documents to warn us against romanticizing some golden age in the past or to caution against overstating the depth and breadth and stability of these imagined communities. There are the words of Sam, who reminds us that in the 1930s, "you were scared to death . . . it was always dangerous." Or consider the fact that, while Henry Blake Fuller might be thought of as a gay novelist, he had to erect a "high wall of secrecy" around himself, and his novel was not only self-published but sold only a couple of hundred copies. Finally, reading many of the documents from the early decades of the twentieth century, I could not help but notice how tentative the language of sexual and gender difference was. This was not a well-developed and robust discourse. Whether commenting from the outside or the inside, writers displayed awkwardness and uncertainty about how to talk about their subject matter.

The last theme I will mention is the centrality of gender-crossing behavior not only to what we might call transgender history but to gay, lesbian, and bisexual history as well. In the 1970s and 1980s, when the first LGBT histories were being written, the interpretive framework went something like this: In the nineteenth century, doctors wrote about gender, or sexual, "inversion": men and women behaving as if they were the other gender. Eventually, they came to understand that it was "really" homosexuality—love for, and sexual attraction to, members of the same sex. As the twentieth century wore on, a self-conscious gay and lesbian community emerged. Implicit in this—and sometimes articulated in the rhetoric of political activists—was the sense that "gay" and "lesbian" was the real thing, while "drag" and transsexuality was a form of false consciousness, a reflection of internalized homophobia. In the last two decades, transgender activists have vigorously challenged these presuppositions, and transgender historical research has emerged. As with virtually every kind of identity-based scholarship, some of this has been a reclamation project, a process of finding historical evidence to lay claim to a history and a tradition.

Reading *Chicago Whispers*, I found it hard not to notice how pervasive gender-crossing has been. It stretches across the time span covered by the book. It exists on stage and on the streets, in public and in private, as drama and as comedy, as a form of mocking social norms and as a means of finding one's true self. It is both individual and collective. It is something that individuals can turn on and off, and something that simply is. Gender crossing—as social role and as identity—seems more encompassing and enduring than homosexuality. Is it possible, I wonder, that fifty years from now, the reigning wisdom will argue that gay and lesbian proved to be relatively short blips on the historical screen and that transgender—or what I am referring to as gender crossing—provides the more robust framework for historical understanding?

Finally, let me finish with what I most enjoyed about *Chicago Whispers*. What makes me keep reading history, and what kept me reading this volume to the end, is the magic of wonderful stories. It is exciting to encounter the life of Albert Cashier, who successfully lived as a man for decades, or to imagine the pleasure of Annie Hindle as she openly married her female partner with the blessing of a minister. I could hardly believe the amount of detail that Sukie uncovered about the life of Henry Gerber, whose efforts in the 1920s anticipated the fight for gay rights by a full generation. In the end, this is what makes history so satisfying to read and to write. I love learning about lives and events that challenge common assumptions about what the past was like. In this regard, *Chicago Whispers* more than met my expectations.

## Notes

1. On social movements, see, for example, my own *Sexual Politics, Sexual Communities: The Making of a Homosexual Minority in the United States, 1940–1970* (Chicago: University of Chicago Press, 1983; 2nd ed., 1998); and Marcia M. Gallo, *Different Daughters: A History of the Daughters of Bilitis and the Rise of the Lesbian Rights Movement* (New York: Carroll & Graf, 2006). On urban communities, see Elizabeth Lapovsky Kennedy and Madeline Davis, *Boots of Leather, Slippers of Gold: The History of a Lesbian Community* (New York: Routledge, 1993); Marc Stein, *City of Sisterly and Brotherly Loves: Lesbian and Gay Philadelphia, 1945–1972* (Chicago: University of Chicago Press, 2000); and Nan Alamilla Boyd, *Wide-Open Town: A History of Queer San Francisco to 1965* (Berkeley: University of California Press 2003). For a biographical approach, see Lillian Faderman, *To Believe in Women: What Lesbians Have Done for America—A History* (Boston: Houghton Mifflin, 1999). On science and medicine, see Jennifer Terry, *An American Obsession: Science, Medicine, and Homosexuality in Modern Society* (Chicago: University of Chicago Press, 1999); and Joanne Meyerowitz, *How Sex Changed: A History of Transsexuality in the United States* (Cambridge, Mass.: Harvard University Press, 2002). On the state, see David K. Johnson, *The Lavender Scare: The Cold War Persecution of Gays and Lesbians in the Federal Government* (Chicago: University of Chicago Press, 2004); and Margot Canaday, *The Straight State: Sexuality and Citizenship in Twentieth-Century America* (Princeton, N.J.: Princeton University Press, 2009). On culture and the arts, see Michael S. Sherry, *Gay Artists in Modern American Culture: An Imagined Conspiracy* (Chapel Hill: University of North Carolina Press, 2007); and Richard Bruce Nugent, *Gay Rebel of the Harlem Renaissance*, edited and with an introduction by Thomas H. Wirth (Durham, N.C.: Duke University Press, 2002).

2. Jonathan Ned Katz, *Gay American History: Lesbians and Gay Men in the U.S.A.* (New York: Thomas Crowell, 1976).

3. Allan Bérubé, *Coming Out Under Fire: The History of Gay Men and Women in World War II* (New York: Free Press, 1990; 20th-anniversary ed., Chapel Hill: University of North Carolina Press, 2010).

4. For Kennedy and Davis and for Boyd, see above, note 1. See also George Chauncey, *Gay New York: Gender, Urban Culture, and the Making of the Gay Male World, 1890–1940* (New York: Basic Books, 1994).

# Acknowledgments

I've interviewed and consulted with hundreds of LGBT Chicagoans over the several years this book was in production, far too many to name here. I give my greatest thanks to those who shared their memories with me, some still hidden in their closets, others out and proud. I thank the bulldykes and the femmes, and I lift my glass to those crapulent old queens propping up bars, sipping cocktails and regaling me with their sometimes humorous, often heartbreaking, tales of life before Stonewall. What do you do when an eighty-year-old man tells you that in the 1950s he was repeatedly picked up by the police and forced to perform oral sex on them, before being beaten and tossed out of the car? What do you say when someone tells you they haven't seen their family since they were rejected by them in 1956? ANSWER: You buy them another beer. God Bless the Queens.

Although I could complain ad nauseam about Chicago's bitter winters or about the potholes, and I could ponder the criteria for hiring staff at the CTA—one has to have graduated from the No Manners School with honors—I cannot find one bad word to say about the librarians and other workers at the libraries in the Windy City. They helped me navigate the rough seas of Law, Medicine, Science, and other areas of learning that I don't pretend to be an expert in. My special thanks go to the staff at the Library of Health Sciences, Cook County Law Library, Chicago History Museum, University of Chicago Library and Archives, Northwestern University Archives, University of Illinois at Chicago Library, Loyola University–Chicago Library, Sulzer Regional Library, Harold Washington Library, Roosevelt University Library, and Gerber/Hart Library.

## Acknowledgments

Thanks to my partner and to friends and colleagues who helped me through this long process, to Corey Black for reading my early drafts, to Bruce Kamsler for his knowledge and support. A special thank you to John D'Emilio for advising me in the early stages, Karen Sendziak for her continuous support and expertise, and Rick Reed for his knowledge of publishing. A special thank you to Tracy Baim at *Windy City Times*: without her support this book never would have happened. And thanks to Gregg Shapiro and Rick Karlin for helping me overcome the naysayers.

Chicago Whispers

# Introduction

---◆---

The Chicago El screeches overhead and rains down a firework display of electrical sparklers, while below ground in the belly of the city the bloated trains rumble hungrily to their destinations. The human cargo could be anyone: Women in business suits riveted to Stephen King, men reading newspapers while clenching briefcases between their knees, homeless bundles of rags, and the ranting, raving, and twitching of the ubiquitous crazy person. All this amid an aromatic cocktail of Yves St. Laurent's Opium, Contradiction by Calvin Klein, and the ever-present smell of imminent chaos. A twice daily—or should that be DALEY—rush-hour movie played out to a soundtrack of faint buzzing and crackling of iPods on shuffle. Chicago swells with people, pregnant with anticipation: Marshall Field's—for Chicagoans it will always be so named—spewing out and sucking in customers, tourists turning digital cameras up the walls of skyscrapers, at cops, cab drivers, musicians, newspaper vendors, and fiery street preachers.

It's easy to slip into purple prose when you love Chicago, and I've loved this city since the bitter cold day I arrived in 1991; the city Carl Sandburg described as a "Stormy, husky, brawling, City of the Big Shoulders." Chicago is a cacophony of sound. A local once told me that if you stand on a corner in Chicago and close your eyes, you can hear the past: the rat-tat-tat-tat of Al Capone's machine guns, the Haymarket Rioters, and the screams of the passengers on the SS *Eastland* capsizing into the Chicago River in 1915. Stand on the corner long enough, peel away those cries of the past like the layers of an onion, and underneath you'll hear the whispering of ghosts as they tell their untold stories. These voices belong to lesbians

3

and gay men locked in the closet of Chicago's past. Men and women who lead double lives, lying to the world by day, then turning up their collars to hide their frightened faces as they dart down litter-strewn alleys into unmarked bars at night.

I started listening to these "Chicago Whispers" in the summer of 1997. I had arrived from Britain six years before, a writer, author, playwright, and photographer, but mostly just another pilgrim, an immigrant. I began writing a column called "A Letter from America" for the *Pink Paper* in Britain; a wry, humorous look at gay life in a large American city. A couple of years later I started working for Tracy Baim, editor and publisher of gay paper *Outlines* (later *Windy City Times*), and reported on various aspects of the gay community in Chicago. I started listening to people talking in bars, and noticed the past was a popular topic. I tried to buy a book about the history of lesbians and gay men in Chicago and was told there wasn't one. There were books about New York, and San Francisco, but nothing about this midwestern metropolis I'd adopted, though it was yet to adopt me. I started taking a microcassette recorder to bars and interviewing the customers. My first question was always the same: "What was the name of the first gay bar you went to in Chicago?" I began collecting stories about drag bars in the 1960s owned by the mob, about raids on lesbian bars; I learned where to pick up men in the 1930s, and the meaning of phrases like "don't drop your hairpins"—useful tips should I ever build a time machine. And so I started writing the weekly column called "Chicago Whispers." The *Windy City Times* column ran for six years and spun off into a ten-week series for the *Chicago Tribune*, bus tours with Chicago Neighborhood Tours, and lectures and talks all over the city. In the spring of 2004 I burned out and moved on to pursue other forms of writing.

I began writing for the *Chicago Free Press*, and my gay history project was a thing of the past. While clearing out my computer files I began to see the amount of information I'd gathered over the years. A list of over eight hundred gay bars in Chicago going back to Diamond Lil's in 1928, a thousand-page timeline, and my office crammed with hundreds of documents, newspapers, books, and memorabilia I'd collected. I started rereading my notes. There were a few leads I hadn't followed up on: What was the connection between gay piano player Tony Jackson and lesbian singer Alberta Hunter? Was there really a link between the police raid on Louis Gager's bar and the tax evasion case of mobster Tony Accardo? I became hooked again, and it was soon clear to me that I was destined to write this book. But where would I start and end?

At the time I was listening to a song called "Before Stonewall" from the musical *Ten Percent Revue*, music and lyrics by Tom Wilson Weinberg:

> There was a time before demonstrations,
> When the queens and fairies were shy and fearful.
> We ran and we hid from the fist and the knife,
> And we still found each other, the ones "In the Life."
> Do you know Dorothy?
> Do you have the time?
>
> Have you got a light, dear?
> Change for a dime?
> Do you come here often?
> I see what you mean.
> I know a tavern,
> Where we won't be seen.

Before Stonewall pushed us into activism, gay men and lesbians in Chicago were quietly fighting for gay rights back in the 1920s with Henry Gerber, then in the 1950s and '60s through pioneering groups like the Mattachine Society and the Daughters of Bilitis. Those groups only existed because, like the song says, "We still found each other, the ones 'In the Life.'"

I've focused the book on Chicago before Stonewall. In fact, the book begins pre-Chicago itself, with a chapter on homosexuality among the First Americans. It ends with a chapter on Mattachine Midwest and Chicago on the night of Stonewall. One thing I decided early on was to indulge myself on some subjects, while skimping on others; for example, Jane Addams is barely mentioned as her story is already well documented, while the virtually unknown African American female impersonator Gloria Swanson gets special attention.

I can remember all those years ago visiting People Like Us Bookstore—now sadly gone—and asking, in vain, for a book on the history of LGBTs in Chicago. Well, here it is, the book I tried to buy back then. In the end, I had to write it myself.

# 1

# The Explorers

Before the birth of Chicago, the land upon which it now stands was the home of the Illiniwek Indians, and through the writings of French Jesuit and Spanish explorers, we learn about the role of "feminine men" in the Indian tribes. Later, in the nineteenth century, Hastiin Klah, a twin-spirit Navajo weaver, brings First American culture to the 1893 Chicago World's Fair.

More than any other city in America, Chicago was and still is a city of neighborhoods. After its incorporation in 1837, the remainder of the nineteenth century saw waves of immigrants arriving clutching bare essentials and precious heirlooms from the Old Country. On arrival the huddled masses set out across the city, taking refuge in cultural pockets celebrating the language, cuisine, religion, and mores of their homelands: the Norwegians created Logan Square; the Irish fled poverty to settle in Canalport, now Bridgeport; and the Russian Jews escaped marauding Cossacks to punctuate Devon Avenue with synagogues, bookstores and kosher delis.

Another piece in the jigsaw puzzle of diversity in Chicago are the lesbians and gay men who have also created neighborhoods for support, though their inclusion in the list of "minority groups" is due to sexual orientation not nationality, albeit both circumstances of birth. While most minority groups came through Ellis Island, or were bundled chattels aboard slave ships, homosexuals were already established among the First Americans.

The earliest anthropological studies of homosexuals in the Chicago area were written over a hundred years before Haitian fur trader Jean Baptiste Pointe du Sable, the son of a slave woman and a French pirate, built the first non–Native American house and rooted the city.

As far back as the seventeenth century, French Jesuit explorers wrote in their journals of the existence of "feminine men" among the Illiniwek who performed the duties of women. The French called these men "berdache," a term first applied to them in 1702 by fur trader Pierre de Liette. He lived in the Illinois area for thirty years and noted in his memoirs that "the sin of sodomy" prevailed among the Miami and that some men were raised from childhood for the purpose. The word "berdache" comes from the Persian "bardaj," a derogatory term meaning a passive homosexual partner, or a feminine young boy. The earliest accounts of bardaj as "sodomite heretics" were written in the Middle Ages by Christian Crusaders invading Persia.

Gender roles within the Illiniwek were strictly adhered to: the women dealt with affairs in the village, while the men were warriors and hunters. The Illiniwek also practiced polygamy, with a man sometimes marrying several sisters, though the reverse was not true: a woman accused of adultery was punished with the loss of an ear or nose. "Illiniwek," in the Ojibwe-Potawatomi-Ottawa language, means "those who speak in the ordinary way." The French Jesuits changed the word to "Illinois." The Illiniwek were a loose-knit association of tribes making up the Algonquin family, comprising the Tamaroa, Kaskaskia, Peoria, Cahokia, and Michigamea who shared a similar culture, language, and ancestry. The tribes lived along the rivers in Illinois, Wisconsin, Iowa, Missouri, and Arkansas, and as the French explorers came in small numbers, the Illiniwek traded with them. While living among them the French colonists recorded their lives in words and images. The French artist Alexandre de Batz was the first to produce drawings of the Illiniwek Indians in 1735, and along with the writings of Jesuit missionary Father Jacques Marquette in 1673, a picture emerges of the lives and culture of these First Americans, albeit through judgmental European eyes.

The earliest account of feminine men among the First Americans was written by the Spanish explorer Álvar Núñez Cabeza de Vaca, who landed in Florida on April 15, 1528, and traveled across country with three hundred men to join compadres in Mexico; only four survived the journey. While observing the Indians in Florida, Cabeza de Vaca wrote in his journal about "soft" men who dressed and performed as women, and that marriages between two men were commonplace. Later, in 1552, the Spanish historian Francisco López de Gómara documented the travels of Conquistador Hernán Cortés, who led the expedition that caused the fall of the Aztec empire. In his book *Hispania Victrix; First and Second Parts of the General History of the Indies* López de Gómara noted that Cortés also witnessed men marrying men, describing the feminine partners as "impotent or castrated" and as men who "cannot carry or use a bow."

In 1564 the French painter Jacques Le Moyne de Morgues traveled through Florida and wrote this account, published in 1591:

> Hermaphrodites, a mixture of both sexes, are common there, and the Indians use them instead of beasts to carry loads because they are robust and strong, even though they are odious to the Indians themselves. When a chief goes out to war, the hermaphrodites carry the provisions. When an Indian dies of wounds or disease, two hermaphrodites take a pair of stout poles, fasten crosspieces on them and attach to them a mat woven of reeds. The head rests on a fur; a second fur is wound around the stomach; a third around the hips; a fourth is placed around the calves. I did not ask the reason for this custom, but I suppose it is for show, for sometimes they do not do all this and simply bind one leg. Next they take strips of leather, about three or four fingers wide, and fix them at both ends of the poles and put them on their heads, which are very hard; then they carry their dead to the place of burial. Persons affected by contagious diseases also are carried on the backs of hermaphrodites to appointed places, where they are given necessities and cared for by them until they are fully restored to health.

The first accounts of feminine men in the Illiniwek tribes came in 1673–74, when Father Marquette and French Canadian explorer Louis Joliet embarked on two explorations down the Mississippi River. Joliet was born in Quebec in 1645 and attended a Jesuit seminary, and in 1667 he studied cartography in France. King Louis XIV sent Joliet back to Canada with a mission to map a path to where the Mississippi emptied; at the time it was hoped the river ran into the Pacific and would provide a western trade route to China.

On Joliet's return to Quebec, Louis de Buade Frontenac, the governor of Canada, advised him to seek the help of Father Marquette, who had experience with Native Americans. In 1668 Marquette and Father Claude Dablon built the Jesuit mission of Sault Sainte Marie at Chequamegon Bay in northern Wisconsin to minister to the Huron Indians. In 1673 seven men set out in two canoes: Joliet, Fathers Marquette and Dablon, an oarsman called Jacques Largillier (known as "The Beaver"), and three hired men. They paddled down the west shore of Lake Michigan observing over forty villages along the way. Joliet wrote two volumes on the journey, one that was lost in a cabin fire, the other in an overturned canoe accident, which left Marquette's journal the only surviving record. On the second trip a year later, the Jesuit explorers arrived at the mouth of the Chicago River and ministered to a nearby Illiniwek village.

Marquette writes that some of the male villagers dressed as women from an early age, never married, and glorified "in demeaning themselves to do everything that the women do." Their guise as women extended to the use of female tattoos and language patterns. Marquette wrote: "They go to war but can only use clubs and not bows and arrows, which are the proper weapons of men. They are present at the solemn dances . . . at these they sing. They are summoned to the councils and nothing can be decided without their advice. Through their profession of leading an extraordinary life, they pass for manitous, that is to say, spirits, or persons of consequence."

In the Algonquin family, manitous are shamanistic figures, supernatural beings with the power to inhabit human form, as well as plants and animals. These twin-spirits are both male and female and have the power to see into the future. Twin-spirits have been recorded in 155 First American societies and feature in folklore and myths. One Ho-Chunk story says that a dedjâ'tcowîga, a "blue ocean woman" as they call a twin-spirit, is created when a young man transforms during his fasting vision quest and is blessed by Moon and told by his spirit to adopt the work of a woman. Another story in the Potawatomi tribe says that if a twin-spirit grooms the hair of a warrior going out to hunt, that hunter gains a spiritual advantage and protection against harm.

In 1721 Pierre Charlevoix, a Jesuit traveler and historian, visited the area around Lake Michigan and wrote a detailed account of his travels in *Histoire de la Nouvelle France.* Of the Illiniwek he wrote: "It must be confessed that effeminacy and lubricity were carried to the greatest excess in those parts; men were seen to wear the dress of women without a blush, and to debase themselves so as to perform those occupations which are most peculiar to the sex, from whence followed a corruption of morals past all expression . . . these effeminate persons never marry, and abandon themselves to the most infamous passions, for which cause they are held in the most sovereign contempt."

These biased Jesuit accounts of the berdache were a far cry from how the First Americans viewed twin-spirits. Though attitudes varied from tribe to tribe, the Algonquin, who called these feminine men Ikoneta, held them in high esteem. British sexologist Havelock Ellis wrote in the preface to his book *Studies in the Psychology of Sex: Sexual Inversion* (1897): "If we turn to the New World, we find that among the American Indians, from the Eskimo of Alaska downward to Brazil and still farther south, homosexual customs have been very frequently observed. Sometimes they are regarded by the tribe with honor, sometimes with indifference, sometimes with contempt; but they appear to be always tolerated."

The Spanish and French explorers saw twin-spirits as further evidence that the savage barbaric lifestyle of the First Americans needed to be Christianized. This attitude was still prevalent two to three hundred years later, when in 1893 the Woman's Building at the World's Colombian Exposition hosted an exhibition of First American arts and crafts called "Woman's Work in Savagery." On the landing of the southwest staircase of the Woman's Building was an "Indian Alcove" where a Navajo woman sat before a backdrop of blankets weaving rugs and applying the sacred designs of the Navajo sandpaints. The woman was most likely Hastiin Klah, a twin-spirit weaver, chanter, and medicine man/woman chosen from her tribe to appear at the fair, though it's unlikely her true gender identity was known.

Klah was born in New Mexico in 1867 to father Hoskay Nolyae and mother Ahson Tsosie soon after the Navajos returned home after their "internment" at Fort Sumner in Bosque Redondo. As a child Klah was fascinated by Navajo ancient ceremonies, and under the tutelage of an uncle he studied to become a Singer (Medicine Man). Then, as a young adult, Klah decided he was twin-spirit, a sacred state in the Navajo tradition as it meant he would excel in both male and female pursuits. While still studying to be a medicine man, Klah also took up the traditionally female skill of weaving, and his/her expertise was with rugs depicting the designs of sacred Navajo sandpaintings.

Sandpaintings were integral to the complex Navajo healing rituals that sometimes lasted nine days and nights. After each day of chanting, the Singer/Medicine Man created designs from ground earth on the floor outside the hogan (home) of the patient. The design is swept away by morning or harm befalls the Medicine Man. Having witnessed the United States government destroying Navajo traditions, forcing children into Christian boarding schools and barring them from speaking their own language, Klah took the controversial step of preserving the sacred sand-painting designs in a permanent form for future generations of Navajo by weaving them into rugs.

Hastiin Klah, a twin-spirit, both male and female, died at age seventy on February 27, 1937, in New Mexico. A permanent exhibition of Klah's rugs is housed at the Wheelwright Museum of the American Indian in Santa Fe.

# 2

# The Chicago Doctors

Three Chicago doctors in the nineteenth century studied homosexuals: Doctor Frank Lydston had some odd theories about male inversion; Doctor James Kiernan studied lesbian barbers and killers; and Doctor Denslow Lewis prescribed cocaine on the labia as a cure for lesbianism.

Doctor G. Frank Lydston was born in 1858, and in 1879 graduated from Bellevue Hospital Medical School in New York. He was the resident surgeon at the city's Blackwell Island Penitentiary, then became a professor of genito-urinary surgery and venereal disease at the State University of Illinois and a professor of criminal anthropology at Chicago-Kent College of Law. Lydston also wrote extensively on sexual vice and crime, race problems, and the treatment of sexual criminals. His medical books include *The Diseases of Society (The Vice and Crime Problem)* (1904) and *Addresses and Essays* (1892). Aside from medical writing, he wrote such fiction books as *Over the Hookah: Tales of a Talkative Doctor* (1896), *Poker Jim, Gentlemen, and Other Tales and Sketches* (1908), *Trusty Five-fifteen* (1921), and a play called *Blood of the Fathers* (1912).

On September 7, 1889, Lydston delivered a lecture titled "Sexual Perversion, Satyriasis and Nymphomania" to the Chicago College of Physicians and Surgeons; it was published later in his *Addresses and Essays*. It began: "Gentlemen: The subject of sexual perversion (*Contrare Sexualempfindung*), although a disagreeable one for discussion, is one well worthy the attention of the scientific physician."

The lecture came at a time when medical attitudes toward "sexual abnormalities" were changing, from being treated as a moral weakness to being regarded as a mental disorder with social, legal, and medical implications. "There is in every community of any size a colony of male sexual perverts; they are usually known to each other, and are likely to congregate together," wrote Lydston. "At times they operate in accordance with some definite and concerted plan in quest of subjects wherewith to gratify their abnormal sexual impulses. Often they are characterized by effeminacy of voice, dress and manner. In a general way, their physique is apt to be inferior—a defective physical make-up being quite general among them, although exceptions to this rule are numerous."

Lydston wrote that "sexual perversion is more frequent in the male; women usually fall into perverted sexual habits for the purpose of pandering to the depraved tastes of their patrons rather than from instinctive impulses." Lydston was referring to woman-on-woman sexual sideshows, a common feature in Chicago brothels at the time. In his lecture he concedes that some lesbians are not prostitutes, noting that some move in high social circles, and mentions one woman in particular he knew, who "has a fondness for women, being never attracted to men for the purpose of ordinary sexual indulgence." He goes on to say that cases of perverted women are rarely seen by doctors in the medical profession, and "when evidence of their existence is placed before him he is apt to receive it with skepticism. He regards the subject as something verging on Munchausenism, or, if the matter seems at all credible, he sets it aside as something unholy with which he is not or should not be concerned."

Another of Lydston's theories was that men who occasionally taste the forbidden fruit of homosexuality may "stamp their nervous systems with a malign influence which in the next generation may present itself as true sexual perversion. Acquired sexual perversion in one generation may be a true constitutional and irradicable vice in the next."

Another theory reads: "Carelessness on the part of parents is responsible for some cases of acquired sexual perversion. Boys who are allowed to associate intimately are apt to turn their inventive genius to account by inventing novel means of sexual stimulation with the result of ever after diminishing or even perverting the natural sexual appetite. Any powerful impression made upon the sexual nerve centers at or near puberty when the sexual apparatus is just maturing and very active, although as yet weak and impressionable, is likely to leave an imprint in the form of sexual peculiarities that will haunt the patient throughout his after-life."

Lydston suggests that in large cities homosexuals have been taken under the wing of the demimonde, that upper strata of mistresses kept in luxury by their rich patrons. He also writes of houses in Chicago catering to the taste of sexual inverts. "Were the names and social positions of these patrons made public in the case of our own city, society would be regaled with something fully as disgusting, and coming much nearer home, than the *Pall Mall Gazette* exposure." The mention of the London newspaper was in reference to their recent exposé of an establishment in Britain's capital where the aristocracy procured young men for the purpose of passive pederasty. One of the paper's contributing writers at the time must have felt these scandalous revelations were a little near to home; the *Pall Mall Gazette*'s book reviewer was Oscar Wilde.

In his *Studies in the Psychology of Sex* Havelock Ellis cites several cases of sexual inversion provided by Lydston and another Chicago doctor, James G. Kiernan. The latter informed Ellis that in Chicago, homosexuality was especially prevalent among barbers, and that he knew of two female barbers who were inverts. Kiernan also wrote on the subject of lesbians and crime. In one article he refers to the case of the Tiller Sisters, a double act of quintroons (an archaic word meaning the offspring of an octoroon and a white person), entertainers in the cheap theaters of Chicago. The Tillers, who were most likely not sisters in the familial sense, were sexually involved with each other, but when one ran off with a man, the jilted Tiller, in a fit of jealousy, shot the man dead. In court the killer pleaded insanity. She was sent to prison.

Kiernan wrote of another Chicago case in *Medicine* (June 1899) and the *Alienist and Neurologist* (October 1899). This time it was an attempted homicide by another jealous lesbian. Charles L. Seibert was shot and wounded by Nettie A. Miller; Seibert's wife, Hattie (née Leonard), had once been Miller's lover. Seibert claimed he was standing on the sidewalk several doors down from Miller's store when she came out and shot him. Miller's version was that Seibert entered her store and threatened her. The court sided with Seibert as Miller's previous jealous behavior unfolded.

In court Hattie Seibert admitted living with Miller for fourteen years in what she described as "a hypnotic relationship," claiming to be the reluctant recipient of Miller's obsessive infatuation; Miller barred Hattie from even speaking to men. Hattie managed to escape Miller's clutches four times over the years, but each time she returned, succumbing to the woman's hypnotic spell. Hattie couldn't explain the hold Miller had over her but could only say it was irresistible.

This was not Miller's first brush with the law, a few months earlier she had assaulted Hattie for consorting with a male drug clerk, whom she also threatened to kill. In the course of that investigation it came to light that Nettie A. Miller was a trained nurse who had married twice and never lived with either of her husbands. Also, her mother died in an asylum and her brother committed suicide. For the attempted homicide of Charles L. Seibert, Miller was charged with disorderly conduct and fined.

In another Chicago case quoted by Kiernan, Anna Rubinowitch, a twenty-two-year-old Russian immigrant, shot dead her female childhood sweetheart and then shot herself. "We love each other on a higher plane than that of earth," Rubinowitch was apt to tell friends. That was until her sweetheart showed an interest in men and Rubinowitch was gripped by an "uncontrollable jealousy."

Another Chicago medical practitioner who studied women's sexuality was Denslow Lewis, MD, professor of gynecology at the Chicago Polyclinic. In 1899 he delivered a lecture at the Fiftieth Annual Meeting of the American Medical Association in Columbus, Ohio. Titled "The Gynecological Consideration of the Sexual Act," his lecture touched on the subject of "women for whom the sexual act is not only devoid of pleasure but positively repugnant. In certain instances, these women have been accustomed to find gratification in abnormal practices from their earliest girlhood." He suggests that because girls are taught to avoid impropriety with boys, "they think no harm can come from any form of intimacy with one of their own sex."

He says in the lecture:

> With the awakening of sexual appetite there too often develops an objectivation of affection toward a congenial girl friend. No warning has ever been given against the dangers of such an intimacy. The parents look with approval on the growing friendship between their daughter and the daughter of worthy neighbors. They are thankful, perhaps, that their daughter shows no inclination to associate with boys. The young girls, thus thrown together, manifest an increasing affection by the usual tokens. They kiss each other fondly on every occasion. They embrace each other with mutual satisfaction. It is most natural, in the interchange of visits, for them to sleep together. They learn the pleasure of direct contact, and in the course of their fondling they resort to cunnilinguistic practices. I do not mean to be alarmist, but I can positively assert

the existence of these pernicious practices to an extent that is not imagined by most physicians, simply because they have given the subject no thought.

Lewis goes on to suggest these "pernicious practices" were mostly limited to the affluent: "The poor, hard-working girl is not addicted to this vice. The struggle for life exhausts her capabilities. The girl brought up in luxury develops a sexual hyperesthesia that is fostered by the pleasures of modern society. She indulges in these regular and detrimental practices, perhaps for years, and when she assumes the responsibility of a wife, the normal sexual act fails her."

Lewis's cure for women with "sexual abnormalities" included applying a cocaine solution to the external genitals, and prescribing large doses of bromides combined with cannabis indica. In one severe case he amputated a lesbian's clitoris "with gratifying results."

"The result in fifteen of the eighteen patients thus treated by me was satisfactory," he told his audience. "The intense reflex excitability subsided. By moral suasion and by intelligent understanding of the duties of the marital relationship the patients became in time proper wives. Thirteen of these became mothers. Of the three unsuccessful ones, two of the patients never experienced any gratification during the sexual act, but they both became mothers and their family life has been undisturbed. In one instance the patient, a marked neurotic, finally became insane and is now in an asylum."

Kiernan's cure for lesbianism was more down-to-earth: he recommended cold sitz baths, essentially cooling off the vagina by sitting waist deep in an icy hip bath—in other words, a cold shower.

When it came time to publish "The Gynecological Consideration of the Sexual Act" in the *Journal of the American Medical Association* (*JAMA*), Lewis met with rigorous opposition from his peers. The problem was that women's sexuality was a taboo subject. George H. Simmons, the journal's editor, flatly refused to publish the article. In a 1983 *JAMA* article, Marc H. Hollender discusses the letter exchange between Lewis and Simmons. When Lewis wrote and asked when his article would be published, Simmons replied: "I will candidly say that I do not want to publish your paper. There is much in it that I would like to print, but there is more that I believe would be out of place in the *Journal* . . . There is nothing in it that is not true, and possibly it ought to appear in the *Journal*, but with my personal views in reference to this class of literature, I hardly think so."

Lewis fired back:

I wrote my paper after very careful study and close observation during twenty-one years. . . . I know the extent of ignorance and apathy which exists in the profession in regard to sexual matters. I recognize the amount of injury which is done our women by the thoughtlessness of their husbands. I know how young girls are degraded and outraged by the egotism of men. I felt it my duty to try to bring about some amelioration of this unfortunate situation by calling attention to the truth. . . . If you still see fit to decline my paper, kindly inform me. . . . I shall appeal to the Trustees and, if necessary, to the membership at large.

The publication committee also turned the paper down. One member said: "I am opposed to the publication of the article in the *Journal*, as it will lay the Board of Trustees open to the charge of sending obscene matter through the mail." Lewis sought the opinion of five eminent Chicago lawyers, and one, Clarence Darrow, issued a statement: "Any physician who did not have the courage to deliver such a paper before an association of scientific men, when he believed it was for the purpose of making people better and happier, and who hesitated for fear that some law might be construed to send him to jail, would not be worthy of the profession to which he belongs."

Lewis took his case to the AMA membership at the 1900 national convention in Atlantic City, New Jersey, taking along hundreds of copies of his article published in pamphlet form. A *Chicago Tribune* headline from June 9 read: "Doctors Vote Paper by Denslow Lewis Unfitted to Publish . . . Chicago Man's Pamphlet Is Unsuitable for Insertion in Journal."

Lewis's protestations fell on deaf ears. After a heated discussion, the majority of doctors voted to exclude Lewis's paper because "it treated a purely scientific subject in a way which rendered it unsuitable for general perusal." The *Chicago Tribune* reported Lewis's paper was denounced by Doctor Howard A. Kelly from Johns Hopkins in Baltimore, who said the discussion of sex "is attended with more or less filth and we besmirch ourselves by discussing it in public." Lewis reasoned that only physicians of the association would read *JAMA*, but AMA president William Williams Keen insisted he had witnessed women and nonmembers perusing it. During the debate, Kelly read out loud passages he considered women should not read. A Doctor Myers of Pittsburgh defended Lewis, saying that as a scientific paper it should be "entitled to scientific consideration." A vote was taken and Lewis lost by a large majority.

Lewis then rented a store on Tennessee Avenue, just off Atlantic City's Board Walk, where he handed copies of "The Gynecological Consideration of the Sexual Act" to any doctor who asked for one. "A string of men sought the place in a few minutes after the news had spread that copies were to be had," declared the *Chicago Tribune*, "and the big box full was soon in the hands of physicians."

The militant action was condemned by most of the physicians attending the convention. "The Gynecological Consideration of the Sexual Act" was finally published in the *JAMA* in 1983, eighty-four years after Denslow Lewis first read it at the 1899 AMA national convention in Columbus, Ohio.

It's easy to write off the theories of Lydston, Kiernan, and Lewis as snake oil hooey and bunkum conjured up in the infancy of psychiatry, but as recently as the spring of 1973 Sara Charles, assistant professor of psychiatry at the University of Illinois, wrote a letter to advice columnist Ann Landers that read: "I have worked with many homosexuals and, in my opinion, they are individuals whose emotional development was arrested at a pre-adolescent level. When a massive lack of development in the maturation process occurs in any area, it can be referred to as an illness in psychiatric terms."

On December 15, 1973, the American Psychiatric Association (APA) voted to remove homosexuality from its list of mental disorders. The front-page headline in the January 1974 *Chicago Gay Crusader* read: "20,000,000 Gay People Cured!"

# 3

# Chicago's Cesspools
# of Infamy

From the Civil War until the *Vice Commission Report* (1911), Chicago was infamous for its debaucheries, orgies, and all manner of vice: the secret rooms at Roger Plant's Under the Willows sex complex in 1861, through the "nauseating spectacle" of female impersonators at Alderman "Bathhouse" John Coughlin and "Hinky Dink" Kenna's annual First Ward Ball, to the Levee "Red Light" District and the sins of Riverview amusement park.

Chicago became a major manufacturing center for the Union army during the Civil War, supplying meat, leather, and weapons to grease the cogs in the modern military machine. Job opportunities attracted thousands of single men to the city, and coupled with off-duty soldiers from Camp Douglas on the South Side, this led to an increase in brothels, saloons, cheap theaters, and opium and gambling dens. The most infamous of these vice dens was on the corner of Wells and Monroe Streets.

Roger Plant opened his resort at the onset of the war in 1861, and with the characteristic whimsy of this diminutive Englishman from Yorkshire he named the establishment Under the Willows. Local Deputy Superintendent of Police Jack Nelson called it "Roger's Barracks" because with its tunnels, secret rooms, and alleyways, it was impenetrable. Not that he made any serious effort to bust it, however. In January 1868 Nelson became embroiled in a bribery scandal, and when Plant was called before the Common Council appointed to investigate the corruption, he refused to answer the question, "Did you ever give Deputy Superintendent Nelson any money?" The case was dismissed.

Under the Willows opened as a two-story building, but as the war progressed it grew to sixty rooms and stretched half a block. It comprised a saloon, private cubicles and rooms, and at least three brothels. "The wickedest place in the world" provided every vice, including "male degeneracy"—male prostitutes rented cubicles to perform the "infamous crime against nature."

While Plant lorded over the saloon, his 250-pound amoral Liverpool-born wife held court over the brothels, which included a room where kidnapped teenage girls were "broken-in," that is, gang-raped, then sold to bordellos around the city. Barely five feet tall and weighing a hundred pounds, Roger Plant never shied away from a brawl; he was known to use his teeth and anything else that came to hand. And yet he was no match for his overbearing wife, who, during marital disagreements, would hold him by the throat at arm's length while his fists flailed in midair.

Plant was rarely out of the news. In April 1864 he was arrested, along with his wife, a Mrs. Filkins, and Josephine Neary, for running a disorderly house. There were between eighty and ninety others arrested at the barracks that night. Plant was fined a hundred dollars, brothel keeper Neary forty dollars, and the others between five and fifteen dollars; those who couldn't pay were sent to crush rocks at the Bridewell, a one-story 100-by-24-foot wooden prison built in 1851.

The exact number of children the Plants sprouted is unknown, but it's thought to be around fifteen, all of whom were seasoned thieves from an early age. In 1868, having raked in a considerable fortune, Plant closed Under the Willows, bought a country house, and retired to a life of respectability as a landed proprietor, claiming it was a better moral environment for his children. It seems the rural life and pious climate failed for at least three of his offspring. British journalist William T. Stead noted in his book *If Christ Came to Chicago* (1894) that Roger Plant Jr. owned three saloons and two brothels, while two of his sisters, Daisy and Kitty, ran adjoining brothels on South Clark Street.

Vice in Chicago showed no signs of abating after the Civil War, and by the late 1870s prostitution was so established that gossip sheets about the brothels appeared on the streets. These were published by Shang Andrews, and in his *Chicago Street Gazette* one intriguing item from September 15, 1877, read: "Ada Huntley is now happy—she has a new lover—Miss Fresh from Pittsburg." Andrews also published *The Sporting Life*, a paper that in June 1878 was taken to court for indecency because it reputedly contained same-sex personals.

In 1882 vice eclipsed religion in Chicago, host to 300 churches and 5,242 saloons. Boy houses catering to pederasts were common, and regular brothels also retained a young man or two for their homosexual clientele. The area around Randolph and Dearborn Streets was infested by "viperous dives" catering to all manner of "perversions," including lesbian "freak" shows, midget sex, and forms of sadomasochism like flagellation. It was called Bryant's Block, and in *Chicago: An Intimate Portrait of People, Pleasures, and Power: 1860–1919* (1973), Stephen Longstreet writes of the area's Sodom and Gomorrah orgies, of "lesbians, dildoes, 'nameless ecstasies,' flagellation, and soixante-neuf," and also of the female impersonators along a strip of twenty-seven panel houses on one block of Clark Street between Harrison and Polk.

Not all homosexuals frequented houses of ill-repute; one cruising area was the subject of a letter to the editor in the *Chicago Tribune* of May 18, 1879, headlined "Look under the Bridges, Officers" and signed by "DECENCY": "Would it not be a good thing if the Mayor, among other reforms, would call the attention of the police to the night habitués of the regions under some of our bridges? The one at Randolph Street is infested with a set of men who would have been cleaned out even in Sodom."

## First Ward Ball

Alderman "Bathhouse" John Coughlin and his sidekick Michael "Hinky Dink" Kenna instigated the outrageous orgy known as the First Ward Ball. Every year around Christmas between 1896 and 1908 the ball was held to raise funds for the spring campaign. Before entering the murky waters of Chicago politics, Coughlin had worked as a "rubber" in the steam rooms of the Palmer House Turkish Baths at 36 Monroe Street, the most exclusive bathhouse in the city. Coughlin was so successful in stimulating the guests with salt and sand that in 1882 he opened his own bathhouse at 169 Wabash Avenue and another in 1887 at the Brevoort Hotel, 143 East Madison Street. Coughlin was not gay himself, even though bathhouses in nineteenth-century Chicago were notorious for same-sex activities, especially at the Lafayette Baths at 180 Wabash Avenue.

In his book *The Intersexes: A History of Similisexualism as a Problem in Social Life* (1908), Xavier Mayne (real name Edwin Irenaeus Stevenson) writes: "A special factor in homosexual uses of vapor-bath establishments in larger cities is the fact that in America these are kept open, and much patronized, during all night hours, and first morning ones; indeed some are never closed at all; in many examples a double staff of attendants being employed. In most such baths, each client has always a separate dressing room, usually with a couch. What 'goes on' is under the guest's own lock and key, and without surveillance: New York, Boston, Washington, Chicago, St. Louis, San Francisco, Milwaukee, New Orleans, Philadelphia are 'homosexual capitals.'"

It was in the bathhouses that Coughlin familiarized himself with the machinations and intrigues of political life in Chicago. He ran and was elected alderman in the First Ward, which included the notorious Levee "Red Light" District. Coughlin and Kenna had a gift for making money. They created the annual debauchery known as the First Ward Ball, or the Derby, as a means of extracting cash from those who had acquired it by nefarious means. It was the perfect scam; owners of every brothel, gambling den, and saloon operating in the First Ward were "invited" to buy a block of tickets to the ball with profits siphoned into Coughlin and Kenna's campaign coffers. Not surprisingly, nobody refused.

The First Ward Ball was a colorful and outrageous affair, as were Coughlin's outfits. At the 1900 ball he wore a green swallowtail coat, lavender trousers, and a white silk waistcoat brocaded with heliotrope rosebuds and saffron carnations. Thousands of revelers turned out for the annual event, making upwards of $70,000 for its two organizers. In *Lords of the Levee: The Story of Bathhouse John and Hinky Dink* (1943), authors Lloyd Wendt and Herman Kogan write that at midnight Coughlin and Kenna led a grand march through the main hall, followed by "madams, prostitutes, strumpets, airily clad jockeys, harlequins, Diana's, page boys, female impersonators, tramps, panhandlers, card sharps, mountebanks and pimps, owners of dives and resorts, young bloods and 'older men careless of their reputations.'" The balls continued until 1908, the year one newspaper threatened to name respectable citizens seen at the event. This resulted in notables sneaking in wearing false beards or masks.

One pious observer that year, attending for the purposes of research only, was the reformer Walter T. Sumner, dean of Saints Peter and Paul cathedral. The following day Sumner railed against the ball: "It was an everlasting disgrace to Chicago," he said. ". . . The most disgusting spectacle I ever witnessed." He described the female impersonators as "unbelievably appalling and nauseating." A campaign was launched to prevent the First Ward Ball from ever shaming the city again, and a month before the 1909 ball, Mayor Fred A. Busse severely limited their liquor license. Also, the *Chicago Tribune* of December 4 reported police warning "the first male who appears in dresses will occupy a patrol wagon all to himself for a swift ride to Harrison Street. In expectation of a large harvest . . . adjacent police stations will be prepared for the revelers." To acquire a "special" license required the organizers to convince the mayor of the "good character and reputable standing of the society conducting the dance and the respectability of the gathering." That wasn't going to happen, so the ball was canceled.

## The Vice Commission

Throughout 1909 the reformers gathered strength, taking aim at not only the First Ward Ball and the Levee District but also the amusement parks, including Riverview. Among the children's water chutes, the "catastrophic thriller" moving picture show "Kansas Cyclone," tattooed ladies, and minstrel shows, there were other attractions like "Salome" and "The Dance of the Seven Veils." Even after the Chicago Law and Order League convinced the police to clamp down on these immoral performances, the managers of the parks rebelled against them. The *Chicago Tribune* reported that barkers at the parks were openly mocking the new rules.

One barker at "The Streets of Cairo" sideshow was heard to announce: "Ladies and gentlemen, before I start I want to say a few words regarding this show. This is an oriental dancing show to the limit. This is not a bible class. We don't have them here. The management of the park does not pay for the privilege of holding bible classes and Sunday school. I have never heard of a bible class being held in Riverview. If you are looking for such things you are in the wrong place. You ought to be at a Salvation Army hall or at a church. An amusement park is no place for you." One Law and Order League investigator reported that at one park a female impersonator, who had recently been arrested and found not guilty—presumably for lewd behavior—was again doing his "sensational dance" on stage.

In October 1909, Rodney "Gypsy" Smith, a fire-and-brimstone evangelist, led a crowd of over fifteen thousand pious souls into the Levee District, where he preached the gospel. The inhabitants of the district laughed and jeered, but it was the beginning of the end for the largest commercialized vice district in the country. The Juvenile Protection Association also called attention to the newsboys gathered in an alley near the courtyard of the Hearst Building. Born into impoverished families, many youths were left to fend for themselves and would sell newspapers on the streets. At midnight the boys returned to the Hearst Building to be paid for their labors; some would stay in the alley overnight, smoking, playing cards, and making themselves available for older men who offered them money and a bed for the night.

It was in this atmosphere of moral decline that on January 31, 1910, the Federation of Churches (FOC), comprising representatives from six hundred Chicago churches, met at the Central YMCA building to discuss what they called "The Social Evil Problem in Chicago." Dean Sumner led the meeting, which concluded that Mayor Busse be asked to appoint a commission to investigate vice in the city and present solutions. The mayor agreed to their demands, and a thirty-member vice commission was formed, with Dean Sumner as chairman. The reformers sent undercover investigators out onto the streets of Chicago to study vice. The following year the commission published the results in book form. *The Social Evil in Chicago* sent shockwaves through the city. While the study's primary aim was to study female prostitution, investigators were surprised to find large numbers of homosexuals. One investigator was propositioned twenty times when he wore a red tie, a homosexual symbol, and walked down State Street. The British sexologist Havelock Ellis quotes an American in *Sexual Inversion* (1897): "It is red that has become almost a synonym for sexual inversion, not only in the minds of inverts themselves, but in the popular mind. To wear a red necktie on the street is to invite remarks from newsboys and others—remarks that have the practices of inverts for their theme. A friend told me once that when a group of street-boys caught sight of the red necktie he was wearing they sucked their fingers in imitation of fellatio."

The vice commission noted perversion was prevalent among the "counter jumpers"—dry goods salesmen—working in department stores like Marshall Field's. The commission also noted its failure to gain access to women perverts, although they were made aware of them. One commission investigator observed:

It appears that in this community there is a large number of men who are thoroughly gregarious in habit; who mostly affect the carriage, mannerisms, and speech of women; who are fond of many articles ordinarily dear to the feminine heart; who are often people of a good deal of talent; who lean to the fantastic in dress and other modes of expression, and who have a definite cult with regard to sexual life. They preach the value of non-association with women from various standpoints and yet with one another have practices which are nauseous and repulsive. Many of them speak of themselves or each other with the adoption of feminine terms, and go by girls' names or fantastic application of women's titles. They have a vocabulary and signs of recognition of their own, which serve as an introduction into their own society. The cult has produced some literature, much of which is incomprehensible to one who cannot read between the lines, and there is considerable distribution among them of pernicious photographs.

In one of the large music halls recently, a much applauded act was that of a man who by facial expression and bodily contortion represented sex perversion, a most disgusting performance. It was evidently not at all understood by many of the audience, but others wildly applauded. Then, one of the songs recently ruled off the stage by the police department was inoffensive to innocent ears, but was really written by a member of the cult, and replete with suggestiveness to those who understood the language of this group.

The commission also noted that female impersonators often performed on the vaudeville stage and in saloons. In the latter, they solicited drinks from men and invited them upstairs for "pervert practices." The commission suggested reinforcing the 1845 law prohibiting "the infamous crime against nature" by consulting contemporary scientists and emphasizing society's condemnation of perversion. It also supported loss of citizenship, a reference to a law passed in 1827 when Illinois became the first state to prohibit voting and jury service by anyone convicted of sodomy. At the same time the commission seemed to brush the topic of homosexuality under the carpet: "It would appear very doubtful, however, whether any spread of the actual knowledge of these practices is in any way desirable.

Probably the purity and wholesomeness of the normal sexual relationship is all that is necessary to dwell on."

In 1911, the year *The Social Evil in Chicago* was published, Mayor Busse retired and was succeeded by Mayor Carter Harrison II, returning to serve his fifth, and final, term. The reelection of Harrison sent a chill down the spine of reformers, as he was known to be a strong advocate of "personal liberty." Harrison believed that vice should be "segregated" and was an unfortunate, but necessary, compromise toward human weakness. The reformers believed that yet again their efforts to clean up the city would be stymied.

In June, the *Chicago Daily News* reported that the Reverend Joseph A. Vance, a member of the delegation who set up the vice commission, chastised Mayor Harrison II: "Conditions are rapidly becoming worse and Chicago is today, with the possible exception of San Francisco, the most wicked city in the world. When you send a committee to him he acts like a man who is worn out with office seekers and anxious to go fishing." Under pressure, and as a symbolic gesture, Harrison raided and closed down the notorious Everleigh Club, the most luxurious of the brothels, which was run by sisters Minna and Ada Everleigh. But it wasn't until a year later that the Levee District was hit by a week of nightly raids. The final brothel was padlocked in 1914.

# 4

# Mannish Women

In the second half of the nineteenth century, some women freed themselves from male bondage by throwing off their corsets and bicycling. Other women cross-dressed as men and fought in the Civil War, and then there was the strange case of Nicholai de Raylan, secretary to the Russian consul in Chicago, who duped two wives into thinking she was a man.

In 1889 the *Chicago Times* published an article headlined "Masculine Corsets," about a new craze, mostly among "dandies and actors," for wearing the feminine garment. "It was at Mme. G's on Broadway," stated the paper, "that the pink haired dude returned a pair of baby blue satin corsets trimmed with lace, after they had been fitted three times, to have them made a half inch smaller, and his anxious perplexity was very amusing to the mischievous merry maiden who fitted them on."

At the time, men in women's clothing was rarely mentioned, but cross-dressing women proved a more abiding subject. One women's emancipation movement then was for dress reform, from skirts to pantaloons. Many women campaigned to break free from the constraints of corsets and heavy skirts, claiming they were injurious to one's health and symbolic of women's slavery to men. The most famous exponent of dress reform was Amelia Bloomer, who popularized "bloomers," sometimes called "Turkish" or "Syrian" trousers, though the original design was by Elizabeth Smith

Miller. Bloomer first wore trousers with suffragist Elizabeth Cady Stanton in 1851, and her outfit comprised a short dress worn over oriental-style pantaloons. The fad was short lived. The negative male attitude toward women's rights was shown in 1869, when Sorosis, a group founded a year earlier in New York by Jane Cunningham Croly, held its first convention in Chicago. One Chicago newspaper described the event as "the best argument for woman suffrage, the men being ladylike and effeminate, and the women gentlemanly and masculine."

It was the bicycling fad that brought bloomers into the mainstream. Toward the end of the nineteenth century, when the sport became popular with women in Chicago, the *Daily Inter Ocean* solicited opinions from their readers: "There is no reason why women should not wear any becoming and useful garment," wrote Bayard Holmes, MD. "The bloomer is certainly useful. It is a matter of opinion whether or not it is becoming. In this matter each woman is likely to be the best judge for her self. I like bloomers, and I hope the ladies will allow the men to put on short skirts whenever they have occasion to wear them. If the wheel makes women and men independent of the fashion it will have accomplished a couple of centuries of evolution."

Amelia Weed Holbrook wrote: "Any man who conscientiously desires to know why women wish to adopt a new style of dress for the bicycle should borrow from his cousin, his sister, or his aunt, two long, full petticoats and take a turn round the back yard on his machine, and lo! He is answered! I should deplore its advent anywhere else, but I am open to conviction."

Women viewed bicycle bloomers as an issue of comfort and independence, but the male establishment treated them as a threat to the status quo. One critic suggested that if women were mobile they might stray to unsavory parts of the city and take to vice. Shopkeepers insisted the bicycle would drive them into bankruptcy because women could seek cheaper goods in other neighborhoods. Articles began appearing in medical journals suggesting bicycling would lead women into masturbation and sexual inversion.

The *Chicago Tribune* of May 25, 1896, reported on a parade of Chicago's all-male bicycle clubs, gathering at Washington Park; forty groups were represented with 2,936 members, but the final tally of 3,200 bicyclists included the nonaffiliated "women's auxiliary" and "bloomer brigade." Two other rather homely "female" bicyclists are depicted in a cartoon with the caption "A Tandem of Female Impersonators." The bicycle did get the thumbs-up from some prominent women, like actress and singer Lillian Russell, who reputedly rode a gold-plated bicycle around Chicago. But Russell did not like masculine women; in the *Chicago Tribune* of April 29, 1915, she wrote:

> There is no more reason to laugh at the effeminate man than at the masculine woman. The one cuts the same sorry figure as the other. In the lines of business and professional endeavor women are meeting men on an equal plane. Some women seem to believe that to hold a position on a parity with men they must neglect their personal appearance, wear harsh and plain clothing, ignore the powder puff, and abandon gentleness for the crudities and rough mannerisms of men. Not at all. They will make more progress as women than as "would-be" men. Remember: The masculine woman is rated just about as high as the effeminate man.

## Women Warriors in the Civil War

A pall of mystery hangs over the early life of inscrutable soldier Jennie Hodgers, who served as Private Albert D. J. Cashier in Company G of the 95th Illinois Infantry Volunteers during the Civil War. Cashier was born female in 1843 in the fishing village of Clogher Head on the west coast of Ireland, the daughter of Sallie and Patrick Hodgers. One story goes that she arrived in New York as a stowaway or cabin boy; another that she immigrated with her poverty-stricken parents, who dressed her as a boy and sent her to work in a shoe factory; a third version romanticized a lost love left behind in Ireland, waving her off at the docks, unable to pay for the trip himself.

Nobody knows for sure. After President Abraham Lincoln called for more volunteers in the war effort, nineteen-year-old Albert Cashier signed up on August 3, 1862, at the recruiting office in Belvidere, Illinois; being illiterate he signed the necessary forms with an X and claimed to be a farmer. An article in the *Pike County Republican* of May 14, 1916, published after his death, reads: "The story goes that the cause of Cashier's enlisting in the war was a broken heart due to the death of a lover in one of the early battles." Cashier's basic training was at Camp Fuller in Rockford and he went on to fight bravely in forty battles and skirmishes, including some of the bloodiest clashes in the Civil War in Nashville and Vicksburg. During the latter, he was captured by a Confederate outpost, overpowered his captors, stole a gun, and escaped. In another act of bravery, when rebels shot down a Union flag, the nimble Cashier climbed a tree and hung it from a limb in midbattle.

Even though Cashier was only five feet three inches tall, the shortest soldier in his regiment, and had small hands and feet, his gender remained undetected during the time he served. He had a light complexion, blue eyes, and auburn hair; other soldiers described him as quiet, never joining in with the games, preferring to sit separately smoking a pipe and observing. At the end of the war, when the 95th Illinois Infantry Volunteers were mustered out on August 17, 1865, Cashier moved to the village of Saunemin, Illinois, and continued to live as a man. He chewed tobacco while herding sheep and cows, and also worked as a janitor, groundskeeper, church bell ringer, and village lamplighter; he ignited the kerosene street lamps at dusk and snuffed them out at 10:00 p.m. One of Cashier's employers built him a twelve-by-twenty-one-foot one-room house, which the secretive soldier secured with several locks; if he was away overnight he nailed the doors and windows shut. Cashier also voted in elections, possibly the first woman to vote in Illinois.

An aging Cashier joined the Grand Army of the Republic, the largest organization of Union veterans, marched in parades, and in 1899 applied for a military pension, which he received after three doctors examined him; somehow the secret of his gender remained intact, especially surprising considering his medical papers filed in the Pension Bureau Records of the U.S. National Archives states the doctors diagnosed chronic hemorrhoids "so sensitive as to bleed on slight touch."

In November 1911 State Senator Ira M. Lish backed his car out of his garage, hit the old soldier (who was working as his handyman), and broke his leg. During examination by Doctor C. F. Ross, it was discovered the diminutive Civil War veteran was a woman. That's the story as told, but the truth is that Ross had been Cashier's doctor for years and must have known already. In the *Peoria Journal Star* of December 10, 1995, seventy-year-old Syd Smith, Ross's grandson, noted that Cashier "might even have had some problems with her females." Whatever the details of who knew what and when, Ross and State Senator Lish agreed to keep Cashier's secret, but as the Civil War veteran's health deteriorated Lish arranged for him to enter the soldiers' and sailors' home at Quincy, Illinois. Crippled and bed-ridden, his true sex came to light when two male nurses tried to bathe him. Cashier was sixty-eight years old. When his mental state also deteriorated he was committed to Watertown State Hospital for the Insane at East Moline, Illinois, where he was put in the women's ward and required to wear dresses, though they allowed him to pin the skirts between his legs to fashion pants. One soldier he served with visited him in the hospital and said: "I left Cashier a fearless boy of 22 at the end of the Vicksburg cam-paign. . . . When I went to Watertown, I found a frail woman of 70, broken because, on discovery, she was compelled to put on skirts. They told me she was awkward as could be in them. One day, she tripped and fell, hurting her hip. She never recovered."

Cashier died at the hospital on October 10, 1915, and his comrades at the Grand Army of the Republic honored him with a full military funeral at the Angevine Funeral Home in East Moline. Dressed in full uniform and in a flag-draped casket, "The Little Soldier," as he became known, was laid to rest at the Sunnyslope Cemetery in Saunemin. The grave was marked with a simple tombstone that read "Albert D. J. Cashier, Co. G, 95 Ill. Inf."

In 1977 the town of Saunemin erected a larger monument at the gravesite that reads "Albert D. J. Cashier Co. G, 95 Ill Inf. Civil War. Born: Jennie Hodgers, in Clogher Head, Ireland. 1843–1915."

Although an estimated 750 women masqueraded as men and served as soldiers in the American Civil War, Albert Cashier was the only one to go full term undetected and receive a pension. Another Illinois woman who fought was Frances Hook, who enlisted in the 65th Illinois Home Guards as Frank Miller, then later rejoined as a private in the 90th Illinois. Hook and her brother—his first name is lost—were orphaned in Chicago when she was three years old. Their means of survival is unknown, but at the age of twenty-two, Hook, along with her brother, signed up for military service. As Frank Miller he served three months in the Home Guard and was mustered out with no suspicions of his true sex. He went on to join the 90th Illinois, where his brother was shot and killed April 6 or 7, 1862, in the Battle of Shiloh (Pittsburg Landing). In early 1864 Miller was shot in the right calf and captured by Confederates near Florence, Alabama. While in custody it was discovered he was a woman; a doctor described Miller as of medium height, with dark hazel eyes, dark brown hair, and feminine voice and appearance. While incarcerated in Atlanta, Miller was shown the due respect afforded a Victorian lady—a member of the "weaker sex"— and given a separate cell. His bravery was duly noted, his captors even offering him a commission as a lieutenant in the Confederate Army; he turned it down, preferring to be a regular soldier for the Stars and Stripes.

Miller was released in a prisoner exchange at Graysville, Georgia, on February 17, 1864, after which he was treated in a military hospital in Tennessee before being returned to Illinois and discharged. Having no family to return to, it's thought that Frances Hook signed up again and continued to serve. Hook later married, and on March 17, 1908, her daughter wrote to the Records and Pension Office, a division of the Adjutant General's Office, to confirm her mother's military service, which they did.

## The Strange Case of Nicholai de Raylan

In December 1906, Nicholai de Raylan, the private secretary of Baron Albert A. Schlippenbach, the Russian Consul in Chicago, died of tuberculosis in Phoenix, Arizona. An autopsy revealed that de Raylan was really a woman, and to aid her deception she had worn an artificial penis made of chamois leather and stuffed with duck down hanging from a belt around her waist. De Raylan's personal physician, the elderly W. C. Rowe of Chicago, who was in attendance at the time of death, was "astounded and mystified" to find out he was a she, as were de Raylan's current and former wives. Schlippenbach told the *Chicago Tribune* that de Raylan, who was supposedly the "son" of a Russian admiral, had lived in Chicago for twelve years as an employee of the Russian government. "I do not know of his antecedents," Schlippenbach told the paper. "Whether he is of noble birth or not, I do not know. If there is any mystery attached to his identity I cannot solve it." De Raylan's coworkers at the Russian bureau office at 50 West 5th Street insisted she was male and called the accusations a "falsehood."

Accompanied by Rowe, de Raylan had recently moved to Phoenix because of his ailing health, his body weakened by consumption, while his wife, Anna, stayed at their Chicago home at 592 South California. When informed of her husband's death, Anna said: "I received a message from him within the last day or so, in which he said he was ill, but not dangerously so. I did not think there was anything serious in his illness." Even more surprising than his untimely death was the news that he was a woman. Anna de Raylan insisted the person she lived with was a man. In some respects de Raylan was masculine: he smoked, drank, stayed out all night chasing chorus girls, and rode a horse like a Cossack; but in other ways he was feminine: he had narrow shoulders and broad hips, and wore high-heeled shoes. He was also unable to grow a mustache, and one paper reported he scratched and slapped his wife's face like a girl when he was angry.

De Raylan's former wife was equally shocked by the news. "A woman, a woman," said Mrs. Eugene Bruchulis of 3112 South Halsted Street. "That is absurd. He was a man." Her new husband backed her up, "I can testify to that, too," he said. "I can positively say that I know he was a man."

De Raylan was born female in Russia in 1873 in Ivadnoy near Saint Petersburg; it's possible her birth name was Anna Racznowicz, though nothing concrete has ever been established. According to the *Chicago Tribune* he was "forced to flee Russia . . . under urgent necessity for disguise." He was eighteen years old when he sailed from Odessa; his parents lived in the nearby town of Elizavetgrad. According to one rumor, he was smuggled out of the country because of a secret he learned about his father, who was a lawyer. Though he may have first visited Mexico, it was in New York that he settled and gained employment with Baron Schlippenbach, as his personal secretary at the Russian consulate in Chicago. According to both his wives de Raylan received constant communications from Russia, which he destroyed after reading; other immigrants arriving from Odessa came under his special scrutiny; presumably, he feared someone he knew from the Old Country blowing his cover.

In 1902 Lucy Kwitschoff of Paterson, New Jersey, lived in the Chicago household of de Raylan and his first wife for nearly a year; she was hired to do "fancy sewing." Kwitschoff said:

> I am convinced Mrs. De Raylan never knew that her husband was a woman. It was her belief that his neglect of her was due to his infatuation for other women. She loved him with a passion that only Russian women can display.
>
> One thing I noticed was that De Raylan never took his wife out with him. They never appeared in public together. Mrs. De Raylan told me that during their married life they never had been companions as husband and wife usually are. With tears in her eyes

she one day took me to her husband's room, and throwing herself upon the bed, cried out between sobs that in reality she never had been a wife to the man she loved above all others in the world.

When her grief had subsided, Mrs. De Raylan confided to me that before the marriage ceremony her husband told her he was a sufferer of consumption. He compelled her to agree that she would never incur the danger of contracting the disease by becoming any more than a wife in name only.

Kwitschoff also said Mrs. de Raylan was a large woman and that she beat her little husband frequently; the marriage ended in divorce on the grounds of cruelty. Before his marriage de Raylan lodged with Charles Tanner and Martin Kastle in bachelor apartments at 3500 Rhodes Avenue. Although Tanner suspected de Raylan was an assumed name, both men were convinced the Russian was a man, although they sometimes kidded him about his feminine looks. Most of the evidence in this cloak and dagger mystery of disguise and subterfuge pointed to de Raylan being mixed-up with Russian insurgents. On hearing of his death, his second wife, Anna, blurted out: "This is the work of his enemies. He was connected with the revolutionists." It was suggested that by day de Raylan took stenographic dictation from Baron Schlippenbach and at night passed the secrets back to the revolutionists in Russia.

De Raylan left eight thousand dollars and diamond jewelry in his estate, which under normal circumstances would have passed to his wife, but as bride and groom were both female the marriage was illegal. And yet, Anna de Raylan was so convinced her husband was male that in May 1907 she ordered his body exhumed and examined by coroner J. M. Burnett and a jury; they confirmed Nicholai de Raylan was female, as did Baron Schlippenbach, who also identified the body.

Presumably de Raylan's wife did not inherit her husband's money, and in June 1907 their home on California Avenue was sold for a thousand dollars. One year later Anna de Raylan sued Baron Schlippenbach in the municipal court for taking one diamond ring, one diamond shirt stud, and one gold chain belonging to her husband. The outcome of the court case is unknown to the author, but Anna de Raylan disappeared after that and was never heard from again.

# 5

# The *Little Review*

Margaret Anderson's intolerance for the mundane brought her from Indianapolis to Chicago, where she lived in what Emma Goldman called a "strange ménage" and started the *Little Review* literary magazine with Harriet "Deansie" Dean and Jane Heap. Like many bohemians of the period she migrated to New York and then Paris, searching for a new ism.

Even as a child Margaret Anderson shunned the rules, was fiercely independent, and valued "ideas" above all else. Her entire life was a constant flight from mediocrity. In *Chicago's Left Bank* (1953) author Alson J. Smith describes her as "volatile, unpredictable, brilliantly imaginative, impatient, and stubborn" and notes that Gertrude Stein called her "an hysteric, pure and simple." Friend or foe, nobody could argue with the impact Anderson had on the arts.

Margaret Caroline Anderson was born on November 24, 1886, into a wealthy Indianapolis family, but she rejected the bourgeois trappings when she left the Western College for Women in Oxford, Ohio, and headed for Chicago; she had to sell a calfskin-bound book by Henrik Ibsen and two silk negligees to raise money for the train fare. On arrival Anderson worked for Clara Laughlin, the literary editor of *Interior*, a Presbyterian weekly, reviewing books. Her next job was as a clerk in the Frank Lloyd Wright–designed bookstore in the Fine Arts Building, run by Francis

Fisher Browne, who also published the *Dial*, a Chicago-based literary journal he founded in 1882.

While at the bookstore, Anderson also reviewed books for the *Dial*, where she learned the skills of publishing a small magazine. A seed was planted for the *Little Review*, so named because the little theater movement was in vogue at the time. Among Anderson's talents was her ability to extract money from advertisers and donors for her ideas. On a visit to New York she raised $450 in advertising revenue for the first issue of the *Little Review*. She set up office in room 917 of the Fine Arts Building with the assistance of her lover, Harriet "Deansie" Dean, and published her magazine. In August 1915 Dean, who like Anderson came from a prominent Indianapolis family, wrote a piece for the *Chicago Tribune* about why she joined Anderson's colony of writers: "I became a reader of Miss Anderson's magazine and because I found in her writings an expression of my ideals. I came to her to give all that I could for her cause."

Articles in the premier issue of the *Little Review* included Anderson's thoughts, "Life and Art," and a piece on the Cubist literature of Gertrude Stein contributed by George Soule, an editor for the *New Republic*. The *Little Review* was among the first publications to embrace Dada. Anderson praised the Baroness Elsa von Freytag-Loringhoven, the American Dadaist who created sculpture from trash, performed sexual sound and music events on stage, and sometimes wore a tomato can bra, teaspoon earrings, and black lipstick. Most people thought the baroness was insane. Anderson hailed her as a genius.

Anderson adopted "isms": Futurism, Bergsonism, the New Paganism, Imagism, Dadaism, Surrealism, and Anarchism all found a home in the *Little Review*. She adored the British bisexual poet Rupert Brooke. On a visit to Chicago, Brooke visited the offices of the magazine with Maurice Brown, a pioneer of the city's Little Theatre. Anderson later described Brooke as "shy as a girl, an English girl. His beauty was a girl's beauty." Brooke was on the periphery of the Bloomsbury Group, the British literary circle that included homosexual writers James Strachey, his brother Lytton Strachey, John Maynard Keynes, E. M. Forster, and Duncan Grant, all spinning satellites around the real star, the bisexual Virginia Woolf.

Among others, the *Little Review* introduced the work of Ernest Hemingway to the world, also gay and bisexual writers like Witter Bryner, Hart Crane, Djuna Barnes, Max Bodenheim, the Imagist poet Amy Lowell, and black poet Mark Turbyfill. After attending a lecture by political agitator

Emma Goldman, a longtime advocate for the rights of homosexuals, Anderson converted to anarchism on the spot, which led to her first blip on the radar of the authorities; when labor activist Joseph Hillstrom was executed in 1915, Anderson wrote in the *Little Review*: "Why didn't someone shoot the governor of Utah before he could shoot Joe Hill?" This inflammatory editorial resulted in a visit from two Bureau of Investigation detectives. The *Little Review* lost advertisers, and publishing the next issue proved difficult as rich donors headed for the hills, fearing hordes of Industrial Workers of the World and a ragtag of other revolutionaries trampling their manicured lawns.

Eventually Goldman visited Anderson's home, and the world's most infamous anarchist wrote of the "strange ménage" at the sparsely furnished apartment:

> Besides Miss Anderson, the latter's sister with her two children, and a girl named Harriet Dean, the entire furniture consisted of a piano, piano-stool, several broken cots, a table, and some kitchen chairs. . . .
>
> Harriet Dean was as much a novel type to me as Margaret, yet the two were entirely unalike. Harriet was athletic, masculine looking, reserved, and self-conscious. Margaret, on the contrary, was feminine in the extreme, constantly bubbling over with enthusiasm.

In Goldman's letters to her lover, Ben Reitman, she hinted her friendship with Anderson went beyond platonic. In one missive she wrote: "The stirrings as a result of my friendship with Margaret were expressive of my previous theoretic interest in sex variation."

As the magazine's fortune declined, the cigar-smoking lesbian author Amy Lowell offered a large donation to the *Little Review* in return for supervising the poetry department. Anderson, wary of Lowell's domineering nature, declined the offer, fearing she would take over the magazine completely. One time, when she was unable to pay the rent, she spent a summer living in three tents with her sister and friends on the shores of Lake Michigan, cooking over a campfire and washing clothes in the lake. In August 1915 the *Chicago Tribune* wrote: "Two weeks ago a Lake Bluff landlord, unappreciative of the spirit of the Greeks, not a believer in art for art's sake, forced Miss Margaret Anderson, editor of the *Little Review*, a magazine devoted to New Hellenism, to vacate her house. The colony decided to move down to the beach near Ravinia Park, where Uncle Sam charged no rent. But the newspapers found them out and the 'people' came to look at them and to wonder at their 'queerness.'"

On September 2, 1915, the *Chicago Tribune* wrote: "Miss Anderson was seen yesterday in the tent to which she and her assistant have repaired pending a readjustment of the periodical's finances. 'The magazine will come out,' she said, 'but perhaps it will be a little late. We need money for the paper and the press work.'"

Harriet Dean's comments in the August 1915 *Chicago Tribune* article explained her newfound freedom camping out on the beach:

> Yes, I knew all the conveniences of life, of the pretty little dressing bureau trimmed in pink, of the cozy corner, of the supplying of every artificial want, of all the human perverted ideas of elegance but this is the real way to live. I don't miss these things because I have learned not to concentrate on the trivials.
>
> I can swing a hammer and drive stakes for the tents; I can cut wood; I can put on an old sweater and work right in the heart of nature. I bobbed my hair because it is easier to take care of, and because I am not vain.
>
> If I found pleasure in doing it up I would let it grow. The essence of this life is pleasure of doing as one wishes. Perhaps if I find skirts in the way I shall design a robe or trouserettes that will permit free expression of limb and mind. Who cares? Who should care? It is entirely my own affair.

On February 4, 1915, Edith Mary Oldham Lees Ellis, the openly lesbian wife of British sexologist Havelock Ellis, delivered a lecture at Chicago's Orchestra Hall comprising two papers, one written by her husband and titled "Masculinism and Feminism," and her self-penned "Sexuality and Eugenics"; the lecture is considered the first in America to call for equal rights and tolerance of homosexuality. Ellis departed Britain for America in the fall of 1914 planning to earn much-needed funds from her lecture tour. It was an ill-fated trip; not only did she suffer from seasickness, but she was "highly-strung," a situation exacerbated by her husband's dalliances with other women.

The lecture proved a great success, however, except in the eyes of Margaret Anderson, who lambasted it in the *Little Review* for not going far enough. In the talk Ellis cited the accomplishments of homosexuals like Oscar Wilde, Michelangelo, and Rosa Bonheur as examples of what "deviants" could do. The lecture was sponsored by Doctor Effie Lobell, a "Miss Cook," and the Medical Women of Chicago, and was originally a woman-only event, until Ellis insisted men should be allowed in. The event was advertised "For Men and Women Only." The *Chicago Tribune* report of February 5, 1915, titled "300 Brave Men Hear Mrs. Ellis," noted:

> Three hundred fearless representatives of the now obscure sex on which expectant, triumphant feminism pins its hopes for the evolution of superman sat at the feet of Mrs. Ellis in Orchestra Hall last night and listened to her uncensored views on the subject of "Sex and Eugenics."
>
> The little English novelist, satisfied she had done her duty when she gave men warning they entered the hall at their own risk. . . . Not one of her masculine hearers, however, was seen to leave the hall or to cover his ears.

Ellis began her lecture: "This is the proudest moment of my life. It is my first chance to say what has been in my heart since I was 18. I have studied woman and I have loved her. I have been afraid of man. I have tried to understand him and I have been married to a man for 23 years."

Ellis exhorted her sisters to shy away from prudery. "The time is at hand," she said, "when supermen and superwomen will see nothing but beauty in the world and when the prude will be regarded as abnormal." She encouraged women to begin "organizing a new love world." "It's our duty," she maintained, "to see to it that equality of opportunity . . . is given alike to the normal and the abnormal men and women in our midst."

The arrival of Ellis in Chicago was much trumpeted. A month earlier her occult novel *Love-Acre* was published to good reviews; the *Chicago Tribune* noted her fascination with whimsical Cornish characters. At the same time more of these Celts appeared in three one-act plays collectively titled *Love in Danger* and produced by Maurice Brown and his company at the Little Theatre. The evening before the lecture at Orchestra Hall, Ellis spoke to several hundred women at the Women's Athletic Club with a lecture called "Olive Schreiner and the Woman Movement." A week later she discussed her lecture at an informal gathering of a dozen women at the home of Lolita Ogden Armour, the wife of the meatpacking magnate; every Thursday morning Armour invited a person of prominence to speak to a salon of her select group of friends.

Margaret Anderson was unimpressed by Ellis's lecture and wrote an editorial in the *Little Review* (March 1915) titled "Mrs. Ellis' Failure"; it was the first printed, and certainly the most militant, defense of homosexuality ever published in America. "There was one great fault to be found with Mrs. Ellis' lecture: it was not illuminating," charges Anderson. In Anderson's opinion Ellis had not come through with her promise to tell the truth about sex. Ellis had said: "I have read all my husband's manuscripts before they were published and I know he has never told anything but the truth about sex. . . . I shall tell the truth as I know it, if I am sent to jail or put out of Chicago for it."

Fighting words.

Anderson writes that Ellis promised to "talk of those people who, through perverted or inverted sexual tendencies, faced the problem of having to turn their abnormality—perhaps their gift of genius, if we understood these things better—into creative channels." Anderson adds: "Because of all this it was only natural to expect a message from Mrs. Ellis." No message was forthcoming. Anderson describes Ellis's lecture as "beautifully written and charmingly delivered, and which said nothing at all." Anderson also accused Ellis of treating the audience as if they were untutored and unsophisticated about sex, and of skirting around certain subjects by declining to give an opinion on "free love, free divorce, social motherhood, birth-control, the sex 'morality,' of the future, or any of these things." Anderson ended her critique with: "Mrs. Ellis knows the workings of our courts; she knows of boys and girls, men and women, tortured or crucified every day *for their love*—because it is not expressed according to conventional morality. All this was part of her responsibility on February 4th; and this is why I say she failed."

The lecture tour proved too punishing for Edith Lees Ellis. After returning to Britain she attempted suicide and subsequently suffered a nervous breakdown. She died in 1916.

The *Little Review* was saved from bankruptcy in 1916 with the arrival of artist Jane Heap, who became Anderson's lover and coeditor of the magazine. Heap, often overshadowed by Anderson's dynamism, contributed immensely to the flagging journal, first by redesigning it with a modern Cubist motif, then with her crisp writing, signed with the lowercase "j.h."

Heap was born in Topeka, Kansas, in 1887, and spent her formative years residing in the grounds of an insane asylum where her father worked. She once wrote that as a child she read books and observed her father's patients, often joining him on his rounds. After graduating from Topeka High School, she entered the Art Institute of Chicago, before continuing her studies at the Lewis Institute and then in Germany. It was at Lewis that Heap befriended Marie Blanke, and together they created the Blanke and Heap Nickel Theatre. This was not Heap's only connection with the performing arts, as she later acted and designed scenery for Maurice Brown's Little Theatre. On May 12, 1908, a musical comedy burlesque called *Modern Arabian Nights* was staged at the Art Institute, performed by the young women of the life class. Heap's paintings appeared in numerous exhibitions, including the 1911 23rd Annual Chicago Water Color Exhibition.

It was through her friendship with Marie Blanke and a group of artistic women called the Chicago Group that in 1908 Heap met Florence Reynolds, who became her lover, mentor, and lifelong friend. Reynolds's father was a prosperous businessman who had moved his family from Stanton, Michigan, to the salubrious Edgewater neighborhood in Chicago. Heap referred to Reynolds as "mother," and their friendship is celebrated in Holly A. Baggett's *Dear Tiny Heart: The Letters of Jane Heap and Florence Reynolds* (2000). Reynolds not only gave financial support to the *Little Review* but also translated the work of French writers. When she died in Los Angeles on December 2, 1949, she bequeathed everything to Jane Heap.

Heap was by all accounts a striking figure strutting the streets of Chicago; a large woman, she wore her hair short and preferred men's clothing, including tuxedos and bow ties. Heap's brilliant mind complemented and grounded Anderson's pretentious flights of fancy. One of their first joint decisions was about the content of the famous September 1916 issue of the *Little Review* when, in Anderson's opinion, contributions from authors so lacked literary merit they published two pages of cartoons and twelve blank pages. In 1917, through the *Little Review*'s association with writer Ezra Pound, who was the magazine's foreign correspondent in London, more European writers contributed their work, including T. S. Eliot, Ford Maddox Ford, Wyndham Lewis, and W. B. Yeats.

In the *Chicago Literary Times*, a caustic magazine launched by Ben Hecht and Max Bodenheim, New York was described as the "National

Cemetery of Arts and Letters." For years Chicago's literati had scorned and ridiculed New York as bourgeois and hailed the blue-collar realism of their own hog-butchering town. And yet, in the late 1910s and early 1920s an exodus of Chicago's writers and artists began to trickle east to New York, with most moving on to Europe; the editors of the *Little Review* were no exception. Anderson and Heap relocated to New York in 1917 and threw themselves into the lesbian and feminist art scene in Greenwich Village, while still publishing the *Little Review*. It was around this time that Ezra Pound sent the *Little Review* the first installment of James Joyce's *Ulysses*. Pound warned Anderson that the explicit nature of the text could put them on the radar of the U.S. Post Office, but when she read it she cried over its brilliance. Heap agreed and the *Little Review* published the book in monthly installments. Reader reaction to *Ulysses* was mixed, with one describing it as "the most damnable piece of filth ever published." The post office burned copies of the magazine, and the Society for the Suppression of Vice hauled Anderson and Heap into court. This fired up the arts community and protests against censorship took place in Greenwich Village and London; Pound raised $1,600 in Europe for the defense fund.

The trial was farcical; for example, the judges refused to allow obscene passages to be read aloud in court in the presence of the editors because they were women. Anderson and Heap were fined a hundred dollars and deemed "subversive" in the eyes of the Bureau of Investigation; the two editors were overjoyed. As a parting shot Anderson told a clerk waiting to take her fingerprints that she would not "submit to such an obscenely repulsive performance," until they produced soap, a bottle of eau de cologne, and a clean towel. After the trial Anderson drifted away from the magazine; the flowing rivers of new art movements and isms were drying up, and she was artistically parched. She also had a new love interest, the French soprano Georgette Leblanc, once married to Belgian dramatist Maurice Maeterlinck. On December 16, 1923, Leblanc, "the great French lyric tragedienne" as the *Chicago Tribune* called her, sang songs and played scenes from her ex-husband's plays in Chicago at the Blackstone Theatre. The paper described her performance as "precious."

In May 1923 Anderson, Leblanc, and Heap left New York for Paris. Anderson had minimal involvement with the *Little Review* after that, though Heap continued to publish it until 1929. In July of that year the *Chicago Tribune* reported on the magazine's final issue, with the two editors giving their reasons for its demise. Anderson's statement read: "Even the artist doesn't know what he is talking about. And I can no longer go on publishing a magazine in which no one really knows what he is talking about."

Anderson and Leblanc settled into a quiet life in Le Cannet, a small gothic village on the French Riviera. When Leblanc died on October 27, 1941, her obituary in the *Chicago Tribune* read: "She once wrote that having come across a volume of Emerson's essays with a preface by Maeterlinck she read and reread that preface all night and when day dawned she was convinced 'he was the only one I could ever love.'" No mention of Margaret Anderson, the other great love of her life, who was with her until she died. After Leblanc's death Anderson returned to the United States, where she met and lived with Dorothy Caruso, widow of opera singer Enrico Caruso, for thirteen years until she too died, on December 16, 1955, in Baltimore. Again there was no mention of Anderson in Caruso's obituary. Anderson returned to Le Cannet, spending her twilight years writing and listening to music. In 1973 she died of heart failure at age eighty-two in the Clinique Beausoleil hospital in Cannes; she is buried next to Georgette Leblanc in the Notre Dame des Agnes Cemetery.

Anderson condensed her long life into three volumes of autobiography: *My Thirty Years' War* (1930), *The Fiery Fountains* (1951), and *The Strange Necessity* (1962). She also wrote *Forbidden Fires* (1996), a novel of lesbian love, reputedly about her relationship with Leblanc. In the *Chicago Tribune* of November 4, 1951, Fanny Butcher reviewed *My Thirty Years' War* thus: "Margaret Anderson, the recorder of Margaret Anderson, 'the greatest literary figure of her day,' as she tacitly labels her on every page, is, up to a certain point, perfectly frank. There is nothing more alluring than watching a human being take itself apart to see how it ticks, if that human being is really interested in how the wheels go round."

Margaret Anderson spent her whole life interested in "how the wheels go round," and the last ism she adopted was Gurdjieffism; along with Jane Heap and Georgette Leblanc she became a devotee of Russian philosopher Gurdjieff after meeting him in New York. In France all three studied at Gurdjieff's institute, but it was Heap who made the man's mysticism and the teaching of his sacred dances her life's work. On October 18, 1935, she moved from Paris to London to teach Gurdjieffian philosophies and to be with her new love, the British clothing designer Elspeth Champcommunal, the first editor of *Vogue* magazine. Heap died in London on June 22, 1964.

# 6

# Kings and Queens
# of Burlesque

The heyday of burlesque was between 1870 and 1910, and the theaters of Chicago hosted many performers who cross-dressed: women who played the sailor, the English "Bobby," and the swell, and female impersonators like Francis Leon, who sang as an opera diva in a blackface minstrel show. The most successful of Chicago's burlesque performers was Loïe Fuller, "The Electric Fairy."

In the late-nineteenth century, burlesque and minstrel shows often featured cross-dressing performers. In September 1877 Annie Hindle appeared at Cotton's Opera House in Chicago. Hindle was one of the most successful male impersonators of her day; born in England in the mid-to-late 1840s, she first sang on stage at age five. She went on to become the star of London's Music Hall as a male impersonator, a "nattily-dressed swell," who went as far as shaving her face to entice a mustache. In late August 1868 Hindle sailed to New York, where she became the first woman on the city's stage to use male impersonation as her whole act. On September 16, 1868, she married Englishman Charles Vivian, a ballad singer, in Philadelphia. The marriage was short-lived and the couple split, though they stayed married. Vivian told friends the honeymoon lasted one night, but Hindle claimed they were together "long enough to black both eyes and otherwise mark me; yet I was a good and true wife to him." Vivian died on March 20, 1880, in Leadville, Colorado.

Six years after her husband's death Hindle remarried, this time to a woman, her dresser Annie Ryan. The ceremony took place in Grand Rapids, Michigan, officiated by the Reverend E. H. Brooks, a Baptist minister. Hindle gave her name as Charles and wore men's attire. The best man was female impersonator Gilbert Sarony, a regular on the Chicago stage, either playing "Old Maids" or in his character sketch "The Giddy Girl." The same-sex wedding caused a storm in Grand Rapids. Reverend Brooks told one paper: "I know all the circumstances. The groom gave me her—I mean his—name as Charles Hindle, and he assured me that he was a man. The bride is a sensible girl, and she was of age. I had no other course to pursue. I believe they love each other and that they will be happy."

Hindle's wedding confused her fans, and some doubted her female gender and suspected the "male impersonator" had been a man all along. Her stage career came to an end. Hindle and Ryan settled in Jersey City, New Jersey, living openly as a lesbian couple until Ryan's death in late 1891. She was in her early forties. After Ryan's death, Hindle revived her career, performing until the end of the century. On June 26, 1892, Hindle married again and became, as the *Chicago Tribune* put it on July 18, "the lawful husband of Louise Spangehl." The wedding took place in Troy (state unknown to author) and the ceremony was officiated by the Reverend G. C. Baldwin. "The oddity of her recent marriage is increased by the fact that Miss Hindle has three times been married," wrote the *Chicago Tribune*. "Once she was a bride and twice she has been a groom. Once she had a husband and twice she has had a wife, once she was a widow, once a widower, and now she is a husband again."

Another of Hindle's dressers was Ella Wesner, who became a male impersonator herself. Wesner's lover was Josie Mansfield, the infamous "harlot" who was the love interest of two men, Edward S. Stokes and James Fisk Jr. In a sensational crime of passion over Mansfield, Stokes fatally shot Fisk in the lobby of New York City's Grand Central Hotel in 1872. On October 18 of that same year, the *Chicago Tribune* reported that Wesner had eloped with Mansfield: "She [Wesner] broke an engagement here to accompany Miss Mansfield to Europe a fortnight ago, an unnatural attachment existing, it is said, between the two women."

In 1874, back in the United States, Wesner starred in Chicago burlesque shows at Hooley's Theatre, and in 1894 she was at Frank Hall's Handsome Variety Theatre and Casino. A *Chicago Tribune* review of November 15, 1874, read: "Miss Ella Wesner has been playing to fair business at the

Academy of Music during the past week, exhibiting her ability to counterfeit the lords of creation in the proper use of the masculine uniform—an art in which she excels."

Other impersonators followed in Hindle's and Wesner's footsteps, including Blanche Selwyn, described by an ad in the *Chicago Tribune* on November 10, 1872, as a "brilliant and dashing protean change artist" who strutted the stage in masculine attire in several shows in Chicago, including one at the Coliseum in April 1876. A later male mimic was Hetty King, like Annie Hindle an Englishwoman. Born Winifred Emms, she started in music hall and cross-dressed on stage for over seventy years. King entertained the troops in World War I and II with songs like "Bye Bye Bachelor Days" and "All the Nice Girls Love a Sailor." In December 1907 King was the featured attraction at the Auditorium in Chicago. "She gives impersonations of the sterner sex," wrote the *Chicago Tribune* on December 1, "and in the quality of her offerings and the general artistic effects obtained is more on the order of Miss Vesta Tilley than any other London music hall entertainers who have come to these shores of late. She gave four songs last evening, appearing as a 'Piccadilly Swell,' a London 'bobby,' a gilded youth of convivial habits and a jolly little jack tar. All the songs were free of vulgarity. At the conclusion of *I'm Going Away* she danced a sailor's hornpipe neatly and gracefully." King's last show in Chicago was at the Palace Theatre on Randolph and LaSalle in October 1929. She died on September 28, 1972, and is buried in London.

The most successful Victorian male impersonator was the aforementioned Vesta Tilley, yet another Englishwoman, born Matilda Alice Powles on May 13, 1864, in Worcester. In an interview with the *Chicago Tribune* of June 9, 1895, Tilley recalled that she was five years old when she first performed at the Crystal Palace Theatre in Birmingham, and at sixteen she took the boy's role in the pantomime *Robinson Crusoe* in Portsmouth. Tilley told the paper she was more comfortable in male clothes, but she was no feminist. She told the *Chicago Tribune*: "I don't believe much in the New Woman. I think women should be womanly and sweet, and bloomers are dreadful."

On August 16, 1890, Tilley married Walter de Frece, her manager and songwriter. He was later a Conservative Member of Parliament and was knighted for his war work, which made Tilley Lady Walter de Frece. On her first visit to Chicago in June 1895 the *Chicago Tribune* gushed: "Vesta Tilley, with her sailor hat, her tan half-shoes, her colored shirts with

white-edged collars and cuffs, her stunning street suit with its severely
correct silk hat, her Prince Albert coat with long skirts, her trousers of ideal
fit, and her black ribbon bows in place of cuff-buttons—the dashing, fascinating, fetching Vesta Tilley and her fifteen trunks of the very finest and
properest male attire ever seen on or off the stage, her dozen character
songs, and a special costume to go with each one—the idol of the swells,
the darling of the dudes—Vesta Tilley is to appear tonight for a brief engagement in *Aladdin Jr.* at the Chicago Opera House. Among the original
songs in her repertoire are, *My Friend the Major, The Ricketty Racketty Boys,
Half-Past Nine, The Smile, End of the Song, Our Sea Trip.*"

Tilley was fastidious in her dress and considered an expert on male attire.
In 1903 Tilley was named Best Dressed Man in Chicago. She told the
*Chicago Tribune* on June 5, 1895: "You asked my opinion as to correct
wearing apparel for the man who has the means and the taste to dress well.
First of all, simplicity. I think the Englishman excels in that, for he sticks
to serviceable, simple clothes. Simplicity in a man's clothing is a sign of
good breeding."

Tilley returned to Chicago several times; in March 1898 she was at the
Haymarket Theatre, and on October 4, 1903, "Miss Vesta Tilley and her
Company" opened at the Garrick Theatre in a three-act farce called *Algy*,
in which she took both male and female roles. Tilley's last performance
was in 1920 at the Coliseum Theatre in London, when she was fifty-six.
She lived the rest of her life in quietude, with her husband in Monte Carlo
until his death in 1935, and then in England. *Recollections of Vesta Tilley*,
her autobiography, was published a year earlier. She died on September 16,
1952, aged eighty-eight, and is buried next to her husband in Putney Vale
Cemetery in London.

## Francis Leon and the Minstrels

In the latter half of the nineteenth century, three female impersonators
dominated the stage in Chicago: Burton Stanley, Burt Shepherd, and
Francis Leon. In May 1875, the *Chicago Tribune* described Stanley as "a
male soprano" and "the greatest of all the female impersonators." Little
is known of Stanley's life, only that his last show in Chicago was at the
Olympic Theatre in November 1879, after which the "lady" vanishes. A
contemporary of Stanley's was Burt Shepherd, a regular with Haverley's

New Orleans Minstrels. Shepherd performed "under cork," that is, in blackface. Minstrel shows, popular from the 1830s, often featured white men cross-dressing as black women, whom they portrayed either as mannish or oversexed. Black men were lazy buffoons or dandified "niggers," out of their depth in society.

In July 1876 Shepherd played Simmons' Hall in Kenosha and was met by "hearty bursts of laughter." The *Chicago Tribune* noted: "He looked and acted the prima donna to perfection, his flexible voice possibly reaching the extreme high notes peculiar to a lady's voice of high range." In June 1879, after a performance at Hooley's Theatre, the *Chicago Tribune* was less complimentary: "Burt Shepherd, a female impersonator, opens the second part. We never liked his species, and we cannot say that we tackle kindly to Mr. Shepherd. Unless it be in broad burlesque, there is something nauseating in seeing a man in petticoats." Shepherd's final show in Chicago was at the Casino Theatre in 1896, after which he too vanished.

Burt Shepherd and the other Chicago minstrel female impersonators were all copying Francis Leon's creation of the opera "Prima Donna" in blackface. Leon was born Patrick Glassey on November 21, 1844. At the age of eight he debuted as a boy soprano in Mozart's Twelfth Mass at Saint Stephen's Church in New York City. When he was fourteen he ran away from home and joined the Wood's and Christy's Minstrel shows as a female impersonator. His first appearance in Chicago was most likely with the Wood's Minstrels on July 18, 1860, at the Kingsbury Hall. The *Chicago Tribune* review read: "This excellent corps of negro funniests give another recherché entertainment tonight, where the lovers of amusement can while away two pleasant hours and gain ten pounds of laughing flesh thereby."

Leon's portrayal of a mulatto opera diva was enhanced by his collection of over three hundred dresses, some costing as much as four hundred dollars. He refused to call them costumes. In a 1902 interview Leon told the *Chicago Tribune*: "I always went on the theory that the public wanted the best, and I never failed to give them the best. What is more, I never wore 'stage' jewelry. My jewelry always was the real thing." In his later career he was billed as just "Leon" or "The Only Leon." The press loved him; in 1870 the *New York Clipper* enthused: "Leon is the best male female actor known to the stage. He does it with such dignity, modesty, and refinement that it is truly art." Another reviewer wrote, "He is more womanly in his by-play and mannerisms than the most charming female imaginable."

On June 6, 1863, Arlington, Leon, and Donniker's Minstrels, starring singer/composer Edwin Kelly, opened for a short run in Chicago at the

Opera House on Randolph Street, after which they briefly toured the country. In September they were back to "settle down" and open the Academy of Music, their own minstrel hall at 91 Washington Street. On January 18, 1864, the theater opened with *Peter Pipes, or Man About Town*, an Ethiopian farce. One skit, *Miss Lucinda's Lovers*, starred Leon as Miss Lucinda. So successful were Arlington, Leon, and Donniker's Minstrels that in February 1864 they staged a benefit to raise money for "Relief for Soldier's Families." Later that year Arlington and Donniker left the company. Kelly and Leon continued with their "Africanized opéra bouffe," spoofs of comic operettas, like Jacques Offenbach's *The Grand Duchess*, produced as *The Grand Dutch S*, and *La Belle Hélène* as *La Belle L. N.* Leon always played the female lead.

In 1867 Kelly and Leon opened a theater in New York. On December 11 of that year, while attending a show at the 5th Avenue Theatre on 24th Street, an incident occurred. It was 4:00 p.m. and as the audience left the matinee a pistol shot rang out, followed by others in quick succession. One man lay on the floor dead, while two others were wounded. On one side of the altercation was Edwin Kelly and Francis Leon, on the other Samuel M. Sharpley of the rival Theatre Comique, his brother Thomas, and a man called Allison. According to Sharpley, Leon told Delehanty and Hengler, a clog-dancing act, that his Theatre Comique was bankrupt and therefore they shouldn't work for him; presumably, Leon wanted the cloggers in his own show. Sharpley heard about the slight and quite by accident walked into the 5th Avenue Theatre to find Kelly and Leon in the audience. Sharpley waited outside, and when they came out he tapped Leon on the shoulder, balled his fist, and punched him in the face. Kelly stepped between them, but was beaten to the ground by Sharpley, his brother Thomas, and Allison. As Kelly struggled to his feet he pulled out a Sharp's repeater and fired three shots. Two shots hit Thomas; one ball entered his heart and the other his right side. He fell dead. Other shots were fired, and a bullet struck Kelly above his ear and lodged itself above his eye; Sharpley fired once more but only managed to shoot off his own finger.

Kelly, Sharpley, and Leon were arrested. Thomas Sharpley was taken to the morgue at Bellevue Hospital. On August 8, 1908, decades later, Franklin Fyles wrote in the *Chicago Tribune* that Thomas Sharpley died because he defamed Leon for being a female impersonator, a "falsetto freak." The outcome of any court case, if it ever got that far, is unknown, but Leon and Kelly's Minstrels toured until 1900, even though Kelly sold his half of the company to Leon in 1895.

In January 1875 Kelly and Leon's Minstrels were back in Chicago at the Grand Opera House in *The Crimson Scarf,* followed by *Belles in the Kitchen* in March. The troupe toured for the next fifteen years, in between stints in New York and Chicago. On November 10, 1890, they stunned the Windy City with the British pantomime *Babes in the Wood,* which employed four hundred in the cast, including a ballet with a hundred dancers. The 1895 split between Kelly and Leon occurred when a plan to build a theater in Australia failed and they lost a fortune. Kelly tried to return to legitimate theater with little success and died in Australia in 1899.

In 1900 Leon opened his own Burlesque Opera Co. in Chicago, but it was short-lived after the opening show received a bad review in the *Chicago Tribune* on October 17: "Some persons who attended the opening of the Kelly & Leon Opera-House last night may have thought they were back in an earlier day. The Only Leon did not appear until the second division of the program was reached. It consisted of a burlesque, *Ill-Fed-Dora,* of Sardou's *Fedora.* The black-face was employed, and every woman's role was taken by a man. Mr. Leon was Princess, and with more attention to costume his take-off would have been fairly good. As a specialty he sang a burlesque on grand opera having almost a feminine tone." The show lasted nine days.

After forty years of female impersonation Leon retired and bought a four-story house at 144 North Kedzie Avenue, where he took pride in his roof garden. On June 22, 1902, the *Chicago Tribune,* in an article titled "Chicago Man Satisfied on a Roof: Home of Leon, Once Famous Female Impersonator," wrote of Leon's life of simple quietude: "His home itself is an exceedingly remarkable place, but the crowning feature of the retreat is the garden . . . the roof is a tangled mass of small trees, climbing vines, blooming flowers, and trailing foliage which completely hide the bare brick walls. In one corner is an artistic little Japanese tearoom. In another is an old-fashioned well, lacking in depth, but marvelously realistic . . . scattered throughout the garden are cages holding canary birds, nightingales, and a garrulous parrot."

Leon told the paper: "I have nothing to regret; nothing to look forward to; nothing to do but enjoy my plants, my flowers, and my birds. I get up every morning during the summer at 7 o'clock, take the paper out into the garden, read until 11, and then eat my breakfast. Perhaps I am lazy—in fact, I will not deny this imputation—but I want nothing better than to enjoy the luxuries of my garden. I take great pleasure in looking after my trees and plants and caring for my birds. I have had enough activity. I worked hard for thirty years and this is my reward, and it is great enough to satisfy me. I go about little and I am contented to live here just as you see me. I still cherish memories of the stage as you will observe."

Leon opened a closet door to reveal a dozen trunks: "These are the remains of my costumes and the manuscripts of plays in which I figured. I should not want to part with any of them although I never expect to use them again. They are just interesting as keepsakes."

Francis Leon died in August 1922 at age seventy-eight and is buried in Mount Carmel cemetery.

## Loïe Fuller, the Electric Fairy

Loïe Fuller was born Marie Louise Fuller in the barroom of the Old Castle Inn in Fullersburg, Illinois, on January 15, 1862, now the Chicago suburb of Hinsdale. When Loïe Fuller was two her parents, Reuben and Delilah, left Fullersburg to open a boarding house in Chicago at 164 West Lake Street. After the Great Chicago Fire in October 1871, Reuben was restless and the Fuller family upped and moved again, this time to run the National Hotel in Monmouth, Illinois, a small town famous for being the birthplace of Wyatt Earp.

It was in Monmouth that tomboy Fuller threw herself into "good works" by performing recitations at benefits raising money for abstinence groups like the Monmouth Temperance Reform Club. In April 1896 Fuller told the *Chicago Tribune*: "I remember when I first appeared as an actress. It was when I was a tot 2½ years old. I was taken by my brothers to a spiritualist Sunday-school. There had been a long and tedious program and after they had finished reciting 'At Midnight in his Guarded Tent,' and 'Curfew Shall Not Ring Tonight,' I felt called upon to contribute my mite towards the happiness of the occasion. So I trotted up the steps of the platform, but I was so small I could not go up in the usual way, but had to crawl, and my little short dress bobbed up and the Sunday-school was highly entertained at my lavish display of red flannel petticoat. But I finally reached the center of the stage and then I shut my eyes and clasped my little chubby hands and recited: 'Now I lay me down to sleep.'"

After two years in Monmouth, the family moved back to Chicago, where Fuller signed up and toured in minor roles with the Felix A. Vincent

Comedy Company. One production was *The Two Orphans*, a melodrama in four acts and six tableaux at Hooley's Opera House. Her first major role came when William F. "Buffalo Bill" Cody rode into town, and Fuller ran off with his cowboy circus as a "skirt dancer"—skirt dancing was a vaudeville dance with ballet steps and high kicks. In December 1880 Fuller was back in Chicago in a burlesque variety show called *Blunders: Or, the Maid, the Mimic, and the Spinster.* Her next big role was in Fred Marsden's *Humbug* at New York's Bijou Opera House, an old "sporting" saloon turned theater. This play introduced her to the king of burlesque, Nat C. Goodwin, who offered her the cross-dressing lead role in *Little Jack Sheppard.* Fuller's male impersonation was such a hit she was cast as Aladdin in *Arabian Nights or Aladdin's Wonderful Lamp* at the Chicago Opera House, followed by leads in *Sinbad the Sailor* and *Ali Baba.*

It was while playing Aladdin that Fuller first grasped the potential of stage lighting effects that would one day earn her the moniker "The Electric Fairy." When Aladdin rubbed his lamp, through lighting, optical illusions, colored prisms, and backstage wizardry, the scenery changed. Fuller's ideas crystallized further with her next role in *She*, an adaptation of H. Rider Haggard's "Lost World" subgenre adventure novel. In the final scene, "She-Who-Must-Be-Obeyed" bursts into flames, shrivels up, and magically transforms herself into an old hag. Experimenting with textures, costumes, colored lighting, silhouettes, and phosphorescent materials, Fuller created and debuted her highly original *Serpentine Dance* at her one-woman show at New York's Madison Square Theatre. It was so successful that in March 1891 she took it to the Avenue Theatre in London, and then Berlin and finally Paris, where she became the darling of the Art Nouveau movement, inspiring works by Henri de Toulouse-Lautrec, Auguste Rodin, and the father of the modern poster, Jules Chéret. In 1899 James A. M. Whistler painted her portrait.

Artistic studies of Fuller suggest a tall slender woman of great beauty dancing in swirls of fabrics, but in truth she was short, stocky, and rather plain. Fuller's charisma captivated not only artists but scientists too. She held patents for the chemical gels used in her luminescent lighting effects and was an active member of the French Astronomical Society. A canny businessperson, she patented not only *The Serpentine Dance* but the skirt she wore decorated with squirming serpents, and also the sequence of stage lights used in the dance.

In a 1906 interview with the *New York Dramatic Mirror*, Sada Yacco, a Japanese actress and dancer whose Kawakami Theatre Company appeared at the Théâtre Loïe Fuller at the 1900 Exposition Universelle in Paris, described Fuller: "I learned a great deal from her. She was wonderfully young for her age. She must be more than fifty. Her house was such a wonder with four or five carriages and fifty horses . . . she danced, too. She was a great manager herself. Our company was paid three thousand dollars a week, but afterward she begged us to cut down the salary."

The Théâtre Loïe Fuller was not a success; in fact the fin de siècle as a whole proved troublesome for the dancer. According to the *Chicago Tribune*, Paris had grown tired of Fuller, and Fuller had grown tired of Paris. The theater opened June 26, 1900, with a new fantasy called *La Chinoise*, and the July 8 *Chicago Tribune* described Sada Yacco's Japanese Kawakami Theatre Company as "a rather puerile Chinese pantomime." After canceling several performances Fuller announced—in her signature dramatic and sweeping fashion—that she was leaving Paris for good. The *Chicago Tribune* suggested the French public had "failed to give her the enthusiastic reception she thinks she is entitled to."

Fuller was a fixture in the gossip columns. The *Chicago Tribune* of July 15, 1900, reported an incident in Paris: "Gossips are busy rehearsing the details which led to the final snub inflicted by Loïe Fuller on the Duke of Manchester, who had been pursuing her attentions for several weeks. At first, she accepted his company with pleasure, and they were often seen dining together at fashionable places. Whether or not he proposed marriage cannot be ascertained, but the two parted company definitely on Friday, the dancer leaving the luncheon table in the pavilion at D'Armensville somewhat noisily without waiting for the repast to end."

The paper failed to mention Loïe Fuller was a lesbian.

In 1896, Fuller's *Serpentine Dance* was captured on film by brothers Auguste and Louis Lumière, and shows the Electric Fairy in all her spectacular glory. In 1908 Fuller opened her own school of dance in Paris with fifty students. She also published her memoir, *Quinze Ans de Ma Vie* (1908), which was translated into English five years later as *Fifteen Years of a Dancer's Life*. During World War I Fuller entertained the troops, but afterward she rarely danced in public. She focused instead on sending her student dance companies on tours of Europe and the States. In November 1910 the company appeared in *Loïe Fuller's Ballet of Light* at Chicago's Majestic Theater.

In 1926 Fuller returned to the United States for the last time, accompanied by her friend Queen Marie of Rumania. This was a dual-purpose visit: Fuller's company was touring with *The Lily of Life*, and Queen Marie was to open the Maryhill Art Museum in Washington State. The museum was dedicated to Mary Hill, the wife of businessman, entrepreneur, and art lover Samuel Hill. Mr. Hill was a close friend of Fuller's, and she had talked him into converting his mansion into an art museum.

The visit drew national attention, more for Queen Marie of Rumania, the eccentric granddaughter of Britain's Queen Victoria, than for the notoriety of Loïe Fuller. *Time* on November 1, 1926, noted that Fuller donated a collection of plaster casts of the hands of famous people like Voltaire to Maryhill Museum of Art, and solicited donations from artists and sculptors like Rodin. Queen Marie's visit was not without drama; by the time her whistle-stop tour arrived in Chicago, Loïe Fuller had been ejected from the train after a contretemps with the queen. Fuller and Miss Birkhead, her press secretary, were accused of stirring up trouble among members of the queen's entourage. The queen's four-day stopover in Chicago was in a twenty-three-room suite at the Drake hotel where M. Czerwinski, the hotel's *confectionare*, built a "wondrous sugar crown, to sit on a red sugar cushion."

Fuller's final stage appearance was in *Shadow Ballet* in London in 1927. The Electric Fairy died on January 1, 1928, from breast cancer in her suite at the Plaza Athénée hotel in Paris. Her ashes are interred in Cimetière du Père Lachaise. In the last few hours of her life, Queen Marie of Rumania sent her a message: "Good-by, Loïe, 'La Belle Loïe,' my best beloved. Marie." The *Chicago Tribune* wrote on January 3: "Her colored lights were said to be inspired by the nuances dropping from the great rose windows of Notre Dame upon her handkerchief, spread (since in her discouragement she had been weeping) upon her knees to dry."

The French newspaper headlines read: "A Magician Is Dead" and "A Butterfly Has Folded Its Wings." During her life Fuller had many lovers, most notably a twenty-year relationship with Gabrielle Bloch, whose stage name was Gab Sorère, a Jewish French banking heiress who wore men's clothes and dared to enter the male-dominated world of filmmaking and set design. Bloch/Sorère inherited Fuller's dance school and in 1934 reconstructed some of Fuller's dances for a George R. Busby film called *La Féerie des Ballets fantastiques de Loïe Fuller*.

In her 1927 autobiography *My Life*, Isadora Duncan wrote of Fuller:

> Before our very eyes she turned to many colored, shining orchids, to a wavering, flowing sea flower, and at length to a spiral-like lily, all the magic of Merlin, the sorcery of light, color, flowing form . . .

I went every night to see Loie Fuller from a box, and I was more and more enthusiastic about her marvelous ephemeral art. That wonderful creature—she became fluid; she became light; she became every color and flame, and finally she resolved into miraculous spirals of flames wafted toward the Infinite.

# 7

# Towertown

In fairy town, Chicago's "Quartier Latin," the "snuggle-pupping" and radical goings-on at the Wind Blew Inn were too much for the police, as were the visiting men in corsets at the Green Mask Tearooms. But even the police couldn't silence the hobos and hecklers at the Dil Pickle Club.

In 1914 Margaret Anderson and Chicago-born poet Harriet Monroe ignited the flame of the Chicago Renaissance by launching two magazines that gave venues for writers and artists to publish their work: Anderson with the *Little Review* and Monroe with *Poetry: A Magazine of Verse*. Monroe lived in an artists' colony called Towertown at 543 North Cass Street where she established her magazine, enticing gay author Henry Blake Fuller onto the Poetry Advisory Committee. The Cass Street salon buzzed with artists and poets, and Monroe's poetry readings at the Petite Gourmet restaurant were a magnet for local writers and others passing through the city. Two regular readers were homosexual poet Witter Bryner and the "It Girl" of poetry, the bisexual Edna St. Vincent Millay.

Author Harvey W. Zorbaugh, in his book *The Gold Coast and the Slum* (1929), writes: "If one gets off the bus at the water tower and rambles the streets within a half-mile radius of it one discovers, however, tucked away in dilapidated buildings, quaint restaurants, interesting art shops and book stalls, tearooms, stables and garrets with flower boxes, alley dwellings, cards in windows bearing the legend 'Studio for Rent.'" Towertown was

Chicago's equivalent of Paris's Latin Quarter, and Zorbaugh described it as predominantly a "woman's bohemia": "In New York and Chicago, with changing mores and emancipation of the younger generation of America women, Greenwich Village and Towertown have become women's bohemias. It is the young women who open most of the studios, run most of the tearooms and restaurants, most of the little art shops and book stalls, manage the exhibits and little theaters, dominate the life of the bohemias of American cities."

Harland Rohm wrote in his "Breezes from the Lake" column of February 6, 1927, in the *Chicago Tribune*: "Striding through Lincoln Park on almost any afternoon is a tall woman who swings along with a schoolboy's wholehearted zest for life. She wears tightly fitting trousers and a jersey coat, and many are the amazed stares at her. The story is told that for years she was a hopeless invalid, condemned to be pushed around in a chair the rest of her life. Then a miraculous cure brought back the use of her legs and again she could walk. The regained sense of freedom was so great she never since has permitted her stride to be hampered by skirts."

Emma Goldman's lover Ben Reitman, the anarchist, syphilis doctor, and "King of the Hoboes," looked back on Towertown in an article in the *Chicago Times* on August 22, 1937: "In 1917 came war, high wages, prohibition, and a transition in the Near North Side. The girls in the neighborhood rose up in arms against the old landladies. They demanded the right to live their own lives and many of them established studios in the neighborhood."

At a time when respectable women didn't smoke cigarettes, the women of Towertown strutted through alleys smoking cigars and openly advocating "free love." In *The Gold Coast and the Slum*, Zorbaugh quotes from the diary of a student who visited Towertown:

> Distorted forms of sex behavior also find a harbor in the "village." Many homosexuals are among the frequenters of "village" tearooms and studios. B—— L—— keeps a vermillion kitchenette apartment, with a four-poster bed hung with blue curtains and an electric moon over it. When he has his loves he gets violently domestic, tailors, mends and cooks. S—— was married, but indifferent to her husband, and lived in a "village" studio, posing as a homosexual and having a succession of violent affairs; when she finally "fell" for the blond lion of the "village" she went around and

bade her former "flames" dramatic farewells featured by long, passionate kisses and embraces. A number of times I have followed a cab through the "village," the lights of my car revealing the occupants, two men or two girls, fondling each other. A nurse told me of being called on night duty in an apartment in the "village" and of being entertained every night by the girls in the apartment across the well, some of whom would put on men's evening clothes, make love to the others, and eventually carry them off in their arms into the bedrooms.

A friend of mine was asked by an acquaintance to accompany him to the studio of a well-known "villager" to Sunday afternoon tea. There was a large group there. The men were smoking and talking in one end of the room, the women in the other. There was a good deal of taking one another's arms, sitting on the arms of one another's chairs, and throwing an arm about one another's shoulders. But he thought that it was merely that the group were old friends. He was asked to tea again a few weeks later. This time he remained in the evening. Soon the men were fondling one another, as were the women. A man he had met that afternoon threw an arm about him. He got up, went over to the acquaintance who had brought him, and said, "I'm leaving." When they got out on the street he asked, "What sort of a place was that, anyhow?" "Why, I thought you knew," his companion replied, "The best-known fairies and lesbians in Chicago were there."

There used to be a group of male homosexuals who frequented the "village" known, after their leader, as the "blue birds." Warm summer evenings they would distribute themselves along the benches on the esplanade. The leader would start walking by, down toward the Drake. From bench to bench would go the whisper, "here comes the blue bird!" They would flirt with him as he passed by until he selected a partner for the night. Then the rest of them would pair off and seek their "village" haunts.

Doctor Frank O. Beck, a Methodist minister, wrote about the "sexual depravity" in Towertown in his *Hobohemia* (1956). He mentions Professor Lant, who ran a club for homosexuals called the Pit: "Here, night after night, huddle the sexually distorted and perverted, the uncouth forms, the pathological misfits: that mélange of middle sex which nature started but never finished. Prepare for consummate disgust for, in such vile and loathsome spots the 'stripper' is omnipresent and there are everywhere evidences of grossly radical sex practices."

Another feature of Towertown were "open houses," where creative souls dropped in and discussed art and politics. One was at the home of Jakob Loeb, who lived with his wife, Claire, two daughters, Esther and Sara-Jo, and a son, Myndiert, at 8 West Walton Place. Loeb, though from a wealthy family, lived a modest lifestyle as an insurance broker. He was also a patron of the radical arts and his door was always open for visitors like Margaret Anderson, D. H. Lawrence, Isadora Duncan, and Sergei Prokofiev. Two notable attendants at Loeb's salon were his nephew Richard Loeb and Nathan Leopold, the lovers who committed the "crime of the century" when they murdered fourteen-year-old Bobby Franks in 1924.

The poet Kenneth Rexroth, not homosexual himself, was an important figure in the modernist poetry movement, later joining the beat poets in San Francisco. He died in 1982, and during the 1920s he was a fixture at Towertown's poetry readings, a frequent visitor to the Dil Pickle Club and lesbian tearooms, often run by ex-circus acts. Rexroth explains in *An Autobiographical Novel* (1964): "Like Gaîté Montparnasse, North Clark, Dearborn, and LaSalle Streets were lined with cheap hotels, the winter quarters of carnival and cheap circus people, burlesque queens and comics, stars of the Chautauqua circuit and pitch artists and grifters."

Towertown had its detractors. In Ione Quinby's book *Murder for Love* (1931), reprinted in the *Rise and Fall of the Dil Pickle Club* (2003), edited by Franklin Rosemont, Quinby describes the Towertown community:

> It was just about the time that the young sophisticates, amateur artists, and would-be writers began to splash a bit of red and yellow paint over an alley garage and call it a studio—to sprawl queer letters or flip names such as "The Crazy Parrot," "The Green Bottle," and "A Little Bit of Turkey" across a wobbly board and make it a bohemian eating place. . . .
>
> Life in Towertown wasn't so modern physically as it was mentally. The garage living-room might be a colorful spot with its bookcases of volumes (suppressed rather than repressed) and its penciled nudes (badly done), but the bathroom was often

windowless and unsanitary: while the delicatessen salad sometimes grew stale in the kitchenette as the residents worked out
some new problem of sex.

## The Wind Blew Inn

The Wind Blew Inn at 116 East Ohio was a bohemian gathering place run
by circus performer Lillian Colley and her "aid" [*sic*] Virginia Harrison. In
February 1922 the Wind Blew Inn was raided by police and forty people
were arrested, four of them students from Evanston. The *Chicago Tribune*
of February 13 claimed one of them, Theodore Strehlow, was a sophomore
at Northwestern University and "prominent in dramatic circles at the university, having taken the leading feminine role in last year's annual play of
the *Hermit and the Crow.*"

Judge Lawrence B. Jacobs dismissed the charges after hearing weak
evidence of alcohol sales and incidents of petting at the Wind Blew Inn.
The inn's next-door neighbor, Albert Otto, a rooming house proprietor,
told the court his patrons were moving out because of the "syncopated
blues piano" coming from the establishment at all hours. The *Chicago
Tribune* of February 15 wrote: "Police officers testified that the hall, when
they entered, was of Stygian darkness; that only candle stumps guttered on
the tables; that under the stairs and in the corners sat couples cuddling
amiably and holding hands." As evidence of alcohol consumption, the
police produced "one empty gallon jug, one square bottle, formerly containing the fruit of the juniper, and a flock of pint flasks of liquors of varied
hue."

Wearing a demure pink-checkered gingham blouse, Colley denied the
charges, claiming the Wind Blew Inn was a simple restaurant serving tea.
Virginia Harrison, her "aid" [*sic*], insisted there was no "snugglepupping"
in dark corners of the café. After the raid, some male students at Northwestern University affirmed their manhood by forming an "anti-effeminacy"
club. A week later the Wind Blew Inn was raided again, this time with
Colley warning the police she would speak to Mayor William "Big Bill"
Thompson, a friend of hers. Again, a month later the inn was in the news
when an ugly brawl broke out and three men were arrested and fined.

A headline in the *Chicago Tribune* on April 23, 1922, read "Hobohemia's
Temple Burns" and noted: "Art treasures, the work of a coterie which finds

its mission in life to be 'self expression,' were destroyed yesterday morning when the Wind Blew Inn went up in smoke. The place was a rendezvous for long-haired and bobby haired real and near bohemians."

The fate of the burned out Wind Blew Inn hung in the balance as Colley took out an injunction restraining the police from harassing the café. Chief of Police Charles Fitzmorris and Captain Morgan Collins had been enforcing a 1:00 a.m. closing license that was repealed three months earlier. Fitzmorris commented in the *Chicago Tribune* of March 5: "What's the use of trying to enforce the law in a case like this? That stinks. If the courts want to open up these places, why should I care? No one else does." In May 1922 a legal opinion written by First Assistant Corporation Counsel James W. Breen and delivered to Mayor Thompson backed up the Wind Blew Inn and halted Fitzmorris's attempts to govern cabarets by "police regulations."

It was too late to save the Wind Blew Inn, however; the premises were sold, and in September the Marie Antoinette gown shop opened in its place with the respectable Little Southern Tea Shop upstairs.

## The Green Mask

After a relative died, the poet Kenneth Rexroth received a small inheritance that he invested in the Green Mask tearoom. The Green Mask was in an English basement situated under a Greek syndicate–owned brothel at 8 East Grand Avenue. The tearoom, managed by Agnes "Bunny" Weiner and her lover Beryl Boughton, drew an eclectic crowd. Weiner had been a burlesque queen, chorus girl, and snake charmer, and Boughton a silent movie actress. The two women were also artists and writers, and they were friends of Emma Goldman and the editors of the *Little Review*, Margaret Anderson and Jane Heap.

Rexroth describes Weiner as "a slightly plump girl with a black Dutch bob, a large white nose, a rather beautiful face, and a most harum-scarum manner." Of Boughton he writes: "Her partner, Beryl . . . had been the leading lady of the famous old heavy Frank Keenan. They had made a Garden of Allah–type movie, perhaps that very picture, in which she had ridden a camel on a treadmill all day into an airplane propeller at which two men continuously shoveled sand. This had removed the skin from her face, and she lived the rest of her life on the damages." On this detail

Rexroth is mistaken, as Frank Keenan never made a Garden of Allah–type movie; the accident was more likely to have occurred during the filming of *The Long Chance* (1918), a Wild West movie with desert storms.

On the decor and clientele of the Green Mask, Rexroth writes:

> Around the walls were blue nudes dancing with silver fauns under crimson trees and shelves with books of free verse and books about the sexual revolution, and all the current little magazines. These in the course of time withered away as the customers stole them. The place was a hangout for bona-fide artists, writers, musicians, and people from show business. June and Beryl seemed to know everyone of importance from Mercedes the Strong Woman to Little Mercedes, the Strong Woman for Singer's Midgets, and from Eva Le Gallienne to Bert Savoy. After the shows the place filled up with headliners from the Follies and the Orpheum circuit as well as people from the burlesque shows. The girls had a friend, Gertrude, who was a concert pianist devoted to modern music, and she brought everyone in serious music who came to the city—composers and performers. So in a couple of years I met everybody in show business and in music who was of the slightest importance, and in addition the great female impersonators Bert Savoy, Julian Eltinge, who was not supposed to be gay but who had huge natural breasts, and Carole Normand, "The Creole Fashion Plate."

Another habitué at the Green Mask was hermaphrodite violinist Aldebaran, whom Rexroth describes as "a tall yellow-faced youth with slit eyes, a prognathous jaw and a shock of hair that looked like a wig. He played the violin while his mother and father did a contortionist turn in carnivals and cheap vaudeville."

When the Ziegfeld Follies rolled into town, vaudeville drag star Bert Savoy entertained the denizens of the Green Mask with ribald jokes that were far too risqué for stage. Savoy worked in a "boy and girl" act with his lover, Jay Brennan, a former drag queen himself. Brennan was the "straight man," and Savoy played Marjorie, a New York "dame." In August 1916 the *Chicago Tribune* published a column called "Vaudeville Wit" that often featured Savoy and Brennan jokes. One exchange starts with Brennan:

Marjory and I were on the top deck of the ship when it stopped in the middle of the ocean. The captain then came along and Marjory asked, "What's a matter?"

"The rudder's broke."

"O, that's all right; it's underneath and nobody will notice it."

In November 1921 the *Greenwich Village Follies* arrived at the Schubert Garrick. "The Bohemians Inc. Present A Panorama of Silken Tights and Subtle Lights and Swift and Comic Escapades" ran the ads in the *Chicago Tribune*. "That supremely artistic and exquisitely designed pageant of exotic splendor, reflecting in satiric and antic vein the gay commotions, the purple ethics, the full-blossomed emotions, and the amorous notions of the impressionistic and radical folk who ply their devious and nocturnal wiles in Greenwich Village, New York's heralded Quartier Latin—that fanciful colony where verse and love are equally free, where genius sprouts and dissipates and adventurer rub elbows in attic tearooms."

The stars of the *Greenwich Village Follies* were Bert Savoy and Jay Brennan. The vaudeville team was so popular in Chicago that local acts were compared to them. In 1922 one duo at the Palace was Liddell and Gibson. The *Chicago Tribune* of February 1 described them as "a pair of female impersonators, one of whom emulates Bert Savoy, while the other denotes femininity by emitting a noise like that of the whistles on the mail trucks."

In 1923 Savoy and Brennan recorded two songs on Vocalion, "You Don't Know the Half of It Dearie" and "You Must Come Over." Later that year Savoy met an untimely death while strolling with Brennan along a New York beach in a thunderstorm. The story goes that he turned to Brennan and said, "Mercy, ain't Miss God cuttin' up something awful!" after which he was fatally struck by lightning. Harpo Marx famously commented later: "On the following day, so the legend goes, all the pansies at Coney Island were wearing lightning rods." Jay Brennan went on to a successful career as a Hollywood scriptwriter and died in 1961.

Massachusetts-born female impersonator Julian Eltinge first appeared in Chicago in 1908 with three personas, "The Sheath Gown Girl," "The Bathing Girl," and in his own version of the "Salome" dance at the Auditorium. He most likely frequented the Green Mask in late 1922 when he was in a show at the Palace, where he elicited much sympathy and laughter

63

from the women in the audience when he confided that his corsets were hurting him. Eltinge also cross-dressed in seven movies, including *An Adventuress* (1920) with Rudolph Valentino, later rereleased as *The Isle of Love*. Valentino and Eltinge were thought to have been lovers, and Eltinge is rumored to be the mysterious veiled woman in black who brought flowers to Valentino's grave every year. Eltinge died in New York in 1941.

Cross-dressing in vaudeville was an accepted comedic device, but not everyone appreciated drag. In 1915 *Variety* launched a stinging attack on female impersonators: "The offensive, disgusting, effeminate male or 'fairy' impersonator is now in line for expurgation. And the same influences that banish the 'cooch' may be relied upon to kick this odious creature through the stage door into the gutter, where it belongs."

In Towertown's Green Mask café these "odious creatures" were welcomed with open arms, and that annoyed the cops. Chief of Police Fitzmorris and Captain Morgan Collins were still smarting from their dealings with Lillian Colley and her Wind Blew Inn. The *Chicago Tribune* of July 22, 1922, declared the Green Mask the successor to the Wind Blew Inn for outrageous behavior. This was proved when Agnes Weiner called police that month about someone "wrecking the place." The police arrived to find the patrons had solved the problem by tossing the" wrecker" through a window. Sometime later, a bleeding man staggered into the police station asking for a doctor. As with the Wind Blew Inn, neighbors complained about the "bohemian atmosphere." Two months later the police raided the premises and arrested sixteen "mostly artists and young society folk." Weiner was charged with keeping a disorderly house. The café was raided again in January 1923, and this time twelve women and twenty-three men were loaded into paddy wagons and driven away after police posted outside the café overheard obscene poetry read by George Lexington.

Towertown's decline began soon after the Green Mask raids. The more ambitious artists answered the siren call of New York and Europe. The romance of debating Freud and Marx over flasks of illicit hooch was no match for the reality check of Al Capone's machine guns and dodging a hail of bullets. By 1932 Towertown was a shadow of its former self. The North Loop League turned it into a must-see tourist spot for visitors to the upcoming 1933 Century of Progress Exposition. One ad read: "This Little Paris of Chicago seems to be a combination of Park Avenue and the Latin Quarter on the left bank of the Seine. There are art centers, the radical stamping grounds such as Bughouse Square, the curiosity shops, the strange little eating places in which one can get food in any style from Arabian and Syrian to Swedish and German dishes, and some of the strangest industries imaginable are located right here."

## Dil Pickle Club

The only venue for radical thought and progressive sexual politics that maintained its integrity through the turmoil of prohibition was the infamous Dil Pickle Club, often misspelled as Dill with two Ls. The Dil Pickle Club was located at 18 Tooker Alley, but to enter its portals, patrons were urged to squeeze "Thru the Hole in the Wall Down Tooker Alley to the Green Lite Over the Orange Door." After navigating the trash cans between two four-story buildings at 858 North State Street, adventurers were met with a sign reading: "Step high, stoop low, and leave your dignity outside." The Pickle was a rambunctious forum where hobos, poets, artists, rebellious academics, college kids, opera stars, scientists, prostitutes, psychoanalysts, revolutionaries, and con men debated, argued, performed plays, and lectured to a chorus of hecklers. The three minds that guided the Pickle through its turbulent existence were Industrial Workers of the World (IWW, also called the Wobblies) veteran Jack Archibald Jones; Jim Larkin, an Irish radical; and anarchist, hobo, and clap doctor Ben Reitman. But Jones was its heart and soul and stayed with it until the bitter end. And it was a bitter end. Jones's history is somewhat nebulous, as he never bothered to deny any scurrilous rumors about himself; in fact, he actively encouraged them. He had several fingers missing, which he lost as a radical bomb maker, or as a criminal safecracker, depending on which story you believe.

Jones was a regular soapbox orator at Bughouse Square, an open-air free speech forum properly known as Washington Square. The Bugs comprised all manner of crackpots who cajoled, lectured, persuaded, and insulted crowds of up to ten thousand on the weekends. The speakers included suffragists, Druids, single-taxers, free-love advocates, speakers who claimed the Earth was flat, and one eloquent soapboxer delighted the crowds by waxing lyrical on the joys of oral sex. One popular subject was homosexuality, referred to as "third sex" or "sex variants."

The Dil Pickle opened in 1917 when it was chartered as a nonprofit organization for the promotion of arts, crafts, literature, and science. Its roots, however, go back further, and the Pickle is thought to have had its origins in a weekly radical discussion group at the home of Howard and his blind wife, Lillian Udell, who ran the Radical Bookshop at 817½ North Clark Street. In *The Damndest Radical: The Life and World of Ben Reitman, Chicago's Celebrated Social Reformer, Hobo King, and Whorehouse Physician* (1987), author Roger A. Bruns describes the birth of the Dil Pickle: "Jones opened a small coffee shop on Locust Street and invited labor leaders, street corner orators, and hoboes to share food and fellowship and to plot direct action and sabotage against capitalist swine." Whatever the Pickle's origins, it was in Tooker Alley in 1917 that Jones converted an old barn and opened the orange door with a program of lectures and other diversions that continued until it closed in 1933.

Although the club was a venue for plays, poetry readings, dances, and music events, the highlights were the lectures and riotous debates. Some people stepped high, stooped low, and left their dignity outside just to hear the hecklers. When Lucy Page Gaston of the Anti-Cigarette League spoke on the perils of smoking, one heckler shouted that she was ugly enough to scare Christ off the cross. Another called: "I never smoked a cigarette in my life. I've always been a snuff user. But after hearin' this woman and lookin' into her face I'm gonna start smoking. Has anybody got a cigarette?" During a debate between Reitman and the Reverend Lewis Aronson on the existence of God, the anarchist repeatedly referred to the Old Testament as the Old Testicle, prompting the outraged minister to shout "blasphemy." The audience loved it.

In Franklin Rosemont's book on the Dil Pickle Club (2004), he writes that in August 1920 Jack Ryan gave a lecture called "The Third Sex." Whether Ryan was a homosexual is not known, but he was a Dadaist and also involved in Dil Pickle theatrical productions. An item in one issue of the *Dil Pickler* reads: "Jack Chomondley Ryan, hobohemian prize athlete and model of virile beauty is cast as a gentleman in the Dil production 'Gentlemen All.'" Ryan was also in charge of the lighting affects for the musical revue *Tooker Alley Sillys*. Another lecture at the Pickle was advertised as "Miss Elizabeth Davis will read her paper from Lesbos. 'Will Amazonic Women Usurp Men's Sphere?'" Davis was "Queen of the Hobos," a Wobbly, a Bughouse soapboxer, and a notorious Pickle heckler. Ben Reitman described her in an August 22, 1937, *Chicago Times* article: "Lizzie would spend her winters around the Dil Pickle, but summer she would hitch-hike to Florida, New York, California—anywhere and everywhere. She always came back with more money than she had when she left."

In 1931 Magnus Hirschfeld, founder of the German Scientific Humanitarian Committee in 1897, the first gay rights organization in the world, lectured at the Dil Pickle "In Defense of Homosexuality." While in the city he granted an interview to *Earth*, a small literary magazine published by young radicals in the Chicago suburb of Wheaton and edited by Joseph Niver. Hirschfeld talks about his work: "In 1928, the World League for Sexual Reform on a Scientific Basis was founded by Havelock Ellis, August Forel and myself. This took place directly after the second congress for sex-reform in Copenhagen." He continued: "We are fighting for the most precious possessions of men and women—justice, freedom and love. Our enemies are powerful, but not invincible."

Hirschfeld lists the chief planks of the league's platform:

1. The same economic, political and sexual rights for men and women.
2. The liberation of marriage and especially divorce from the present Church and State tyranny.
3. Control of conception, so that procreation may be undertaken only deliberately and with a due sense of responsibility.
4. Race betterment by the application of the knowledge of eugenics.
5. Protection of the unmarried mother and the illegitimate child.
6. A rational attitude towards sexually abnormal persons and especially towards homosexuals, both male and female.
7. Prevention of prostitution and VD.
8. Disturbances of the sexual impulses to be regarded as probably a pathological phenomenon and not, as in the past, as a crime, vice or sin.
9. Only those sexual acts to be considered criminal which infringe on the sexual rights of another person. Sexual acts between responsible adults, undertaken by mutual consent to be regarded as private concern of those adults.
10. Systematic sexual education.

In the late 1920s the Dil Pickle declined. The Great Depression, complaints from churches, and raids by corrupt police contributed to its fall, as did gangsters trying to muscle in on the club. In January 1932 the *Chicago Tribune* reported that five henchmen working for "king of the bombers" Jimmy Belcastro were charged with disorderly conduct after attempting to seize control of the Dil Pickle, the "resort of parlor pink radicals." After the Pickle closed, Jack Archibald Jones never gave up hope of reviving the club, but he never succeeded. On December 12, 1940, he died in a rooming house and is buried in Graceland cemetery.

During its decline the club spawned dozens of competitors, each vying for the Dil Pickle crown. One group that splintered from the Pickle in 1927 was the sex-oriented Seven Arts Club, later run by Edward Clasby, an open homosexual who once started a lecture with: "Oscar Wilde was a sodomist. A sodomist is one who enlarges his circle of friends." Four of the "Arts" at the Seven Arts Club were Vice, Vulgarity, Sacrilege, and Midnight Slumming—the remaining three are lost to history. A typical meeting would be a discussion of Havelock Ellis's *Studies in the Psychology of Sex*, or Miss Polly La Couche debating "Free Love or Marriage." Myriad topics were discussed: for example, on October 29, 1927, "The Philosophy of James Joyce" at 55 West Goethe Street. Meetings were also held at the St. Clair and Bismarck hotels. On March 7, 1931, Ben Reitman lectured to the group on his book *The Second Oldest Profession* (1936).

In November 1930 twelve members of the Seven Arts Club were arrested and stood before Judge Charles McKinley in Morals Court charged with being inmates of a house of ill repute. It was likely Madame Block's place at 3549 South Park Way. She was a black medium, spiritualist, and tarot reader who ran a gay whorehouse. Edward Crane, the Seven Arts president, explained in court that they were at the brothel to study "the Negroid temperament and mysticism." Another arrested member, Doctor Charles A. Lapin, added: "Our club is devoted to the study of psychology, sex, and other modern problems and we thought this was a psychological mixing place." The judge dismissed the case on condition the Seven Arts Club were more prudent in their future choices of study venues.

It's not known when the Seven Arts Club folded, but on October 12, 1940, June Provines mentioned them in her *Chicago Tribune* column "Front Views and Profiles": "Probably the last outpost of Bohemianism in Chicago is an organization called the Seven Arts Club, which meets weekly on the third floor of a hall on North Dearborn street. The Bohemian era in Chicago during which poets read their works in tearooms and speakeasies, young women wore smocks and long, dangling rings, young couples moved into garage and carriage house apartments, painted the floor red and invited friends in to sit on the floor and listen to poetry by candlelight has long since gone. The Seven Arts club carries on in the Dil Pickle club tradition, with speakers and hecklers, and a varied audience of members and novelty seekers from conservative neighborhoods."

Ed Clasby still shepherded the motley collection of habitués, which Provines lists as "E. Buckland Plummer, an Englishman, who rarely is heckled, so dazzling is his oratory; the Sheridan brothers, Jack and Jim, both of them soap box orators and experienced hecklers; Triphammer Johnson, with a walrus moustache, a north Minnesota accent, and a booming voice; Bert Weber, red-cheeked poet laureate of Bughouse square, who shouts his poems to audiences, and Box Car Bertha, other name unknown, are among the figures at Seven Arts Club meetings, Morris Levin, blind, gray-haired orator of soap box fame, is another frequenter."

Provines notes that the Seven Arts Club meetings all begin with the singing of the club's theme songs: the hymn to the auto industry "Oil in My Lamp" and the old Irish ditty "The Pig Got Up and Slowly Walked Away":

> One evening last October, when I was far from sober
> And dragging home a load with manly pride
> My feet began to stutter and I fell down in the gutter
> And a pig came up and parked right by my side
>
> Then I mumbled, "It's fair weather when good comrades get together"
> Till a lady passing by was heard to say,
> "You can tell a man that boozes by the playmates that he chooses"
> Then the pig got up and slowly walked away.

Another splinter group from the ailing Dil Pickle Club was a women-only discussion group called the Mary Garden Forum chaired by "Red" Martha Biegler, a German Marxist who would open each session with: "This is a woman's forum. Mere man, however, is always welcome." Beigler often referred to men as low-grade morons.

The last vestige of the Dil Pickle is the College of Complexes, founded in 1933 by Slim Brundage, a regular Pickler, and Jack Ryan, the man who once lectured there on "The Third Sex." The college is still hosting lectures and debates in various restaurants around Chicago.

# 8

# Henry Gerber and the German Sex Reformers

Germany was at the forefront of gay rights, with Magnus Hirschfeld campaigning against the German Criminal Code Paragraph 175. One man he inspired was Henry Gerber, who emigrated from Germany and founded the first gay rights group in the United States in Chicago in 1924. It lasted six months.

On May 15, 1871, the German Criminal Code was revised to include Paragraph 175, a law that made sexual acts between males illegal. The first challenge to the law came in 1897 when Magnus Hirschfeld founded the gay organization Scientific Humanitarian Committee (Wissenschaftlich-humanitäres Komitee). One of their first actions was to draft a petition against Paragraph 175 with six thousand signatures from prominent people in the arts, politics, and medical profession. In 1898 it was presented to the Reichstag, but it failed to have any effect. Another attempt to change the law was made in 1929, but the rise of Adolf Hitler and the Nazis ensured its failure.

Homosexual physician and sex reformer Magnus Hirschfeld was born into a Jewish family on May 14, 1868, in Kolberg in the Prussian province of Pomerania (now Kołobrzeg, Poland). Hirschfeld studied modern languages in Breslau, then philosophy, philology, and medicine in Strasbourg, Munich, Heidelberg, and Berlin, earning a doctoral degree in 1892. After college he traveled throughout the United States, visiting Chicago for the

1893 World's Fair, returning to the city in 1931 to speak at the Dil Pickle Club. On his return to Germany after his trip to the fair, Hirschfeld published his first writings on homosexual love, a pamphlet called *Sappho and Socrates*. A year later he cofounded the Scientific Humanitarian Committee, with lawyer Eduard Oberg, writer Max von Bülow, and bookseller and publisher Max Spohr, to undertake scientific research of homosexuality and work toward the repeal of Paragraph 175.

In 1919 Hirschfeld cowrote with Richard Oswald *Anders als die Andern* (*Different from the Others*), a film starring Conrad Veidt as Paul Körner, a homosexual violinist who falls in love with a male student, but their love is discovered by a blackmailer. Körner pays up at first, but then takes the extortionist to court. After his sexuality is made public, Körner is shunned and his career is over. In desperation he commits suicide. Hirschfeld plays himself in the film and delivers the final speech: "You have to keep living . . . live to change the prejudices by which this man has been made one of the countless victims . . . restore the honor of this man and bring justice to him, and all those who came before him, and all those to come after him. Justice through knowledge!" The film closes with Paragraph 175 being crossed out of a German law book. The movie was banned in Germany.

In India Hirschfeld was lauded as "the modern Vatsayana of the West," in America "The Einstein of Sex"; the latter was used as the title of a 1999 Rosa von Praunheim film about him, his Institute for Sexual Research, and the rise of Nazism. Hirschfeld penned an article for the *Chicago Tribune* on January 6, 1901, with the headline "Marriage Will Continue to Decrease." Though homosexuality was not mentioned, Hirschfeld gave his view of "marriage" and glorified the state of bachelorhood; Hirschfeld considered marriage unnatural, merely a financial contract treating women as property. In the *Chicago Tribune* of January 31, 1927, a headline read: "Girl Slayer of Two Babes Stirs German Science." Hirschfeld was one of the top three psychiatrists consulted in the case of a double child murder in Duisberg, Germany, "strongly reminiscent of the Loeb-Leopold case in Chicago," except this thrill-killer was an eighteen-year-old lesbian. Kaethe Hagedorn confessed to killing, in "an irresponsible frenzy," six-year-old Katie Gelsleighter and nine-year-old Friedrich Schaefer. "Kaethe worked in her father's grocery store, and was described by the neighbors as modest, exceptionally bright in music, and with a passion for Chopin," the article read. "She seems to have been awakened to a craze for sensationalism through a woman circus acrobat, much older than herself, with whom she some time ago began a friendship which is believed to have been her undoing."

Another case Hirschfeld advised on was reported in the *Chicago Tribune* on March 30, 1930, under the headline "Berlin Youth, 22, Wins Right to Dress as a Girl; Herbert Is Now Hertha and Student Nurse." The influential Berlin Social Welfare Committee, "whose decision in social welfare matters has the legal force of a court decree," decided that Herbert Haase can "openly wear the girls' clothes he has yearned to wear all his life." The committee went further, finding him a job as a student nurse in a hospital. The *Chicago Tribune* noted that Haase is "already cheerfully launched as a member of the weaker sex."

Hirschfeld wasn't averse to product endorsement, including an early Viagra-style male enhancement pick-me-up. Ads in the *Chicago Defender* in the fall of 1932 read: "Dr. Magnus Hirschfeld, the world-known authority on Sexology and Director of the Institute of Sexual Science of Berlin Germany, created TITUS-PEARLS . . . Start regaining your youthfulness now! To-day! In 2 weeks time you will be aware of the new, virile force within you."

Hirschfeld opened the Institute for Sexual Research in 1919 as a center for the study of sexuality with a library and medical services. Many of the books housed there Hirschfeld had written himself, including *The Trans-vestites* (1910); *Homosexuality in Men and Women* (1914), which contains descriptions of Chicago's homosexual community; *Sexual Pathology* (1917); and five volumes of *Sexual Science* (1926–30). In 1930 he toured the world for two years, and on his return to Germany he found himself on Hitler's hit list. He fled to Switzerland, then France, first Paris and later Nice. On May 10, 1933, the Nazis destroyed the Institute for Sexual Science in Berlin, burning the "Un-German" books. A headline in *Time* on May 22, 1933, read "Germany: Bibliocaust": "Pride of the book burners was the seizure and destruction of the files of famed Sexologist Dr. Magnus Hirschfeld, who has analyzed many an abnormal Nazi leader in his Institute for Sex Science. Heir to Krafft-Ebing's theories, Dr. Hirschfeld put over the door of his Institute the motto of Hitler's hero Frederick the Great, 'I intend in my state that every man amuse himself in his own way.'"

Magnus Hirschfeld died of a heart attack in Nice on May 14, 1935, on his sixty-seventh birthday. His estate was left to his lover, Li Shiu Tong, a sexology student from Hong Kong.

## Henry Gerber and the Society for Human Rights

One American inspired by the writings of Magnus Hirschfeld was Henry Gerber, who in 1924 was granted an official charter by the State of Illinois for the Society for Human Rights, the first gay rights organization in the United States, which he ran from his home on Crilly Court in Chicago. Gerber was born Josef Henry Dittmar on June 29, 1892, in Passau, Bavaria, Germany; coincidentally, it was the same year a three-year-old Adolf Hitler and his family moved there from Braunau, Austria. On October 27, 1913, Gerber (still called Dittmar at the time), arrived at New York's Ellis Island on the SS *George Washington* and then traveled west to Chicago, where he worked briefly for Montgomery Ward's department store; his first known address in the United States was 507 Stone Street, Joliet, Illinois, where he enlisted in the army on January 26, 1914. In his military documents, he described himself as 5 feet 7½ inches tall, 180 pounds, with blue eyes and brown hair. He changed his name to Gerber soon afterward. On April 2, 1917, the United States declared war on Germany, and the newspapers filled with lurid tales of German spies. "GERMAN INTRIGUE: Trail of Vast Spy System Maintained by Ambassador von Bernstorff's Agents in the United States" was a typical *Chicago Tribune* headline. As a result, the United States opened prisoner-of-war internment camps; fifty thousand unnaturalized aliens of German birth were now "alien enemies," and eight thousand were detained using presidential arrest warrants. Those arrested in Chicago were sent to Fort Oglethorpe, Georgia. Gerber was "offered internment," which he accepted, as it guaranteed three meals a day. After the war he reenlisted in the army on October 2, 1919, at Jefferson Barracks in Lemay, Missouri, a training and recruitment center for soldiers being sent to fight in Europe, or, in Gerber's case, to join the Illinois American Forces in Germany (AFG) regiment AMAROC News Company of the U.S. Army of Occupation in Koblenz, Germany.

In December 1919 Gerber arrived in Koblenz to work as a printer and proofreader on *Amaroc*, a military daily newspaper serving the AFG. In *The Amaroc News: The Daily Newspaper of the American Forces in Germany, 1919–1923* (1981) by Alfred E. Cornebise, the author writes that the first issue was published on April 21, 1919, with an editorial that began: "Lest we forget—the paper will not refight the war." The "issue," as the paper described World War I, "is closed." As inconspicuously as possible, the

U.S. Army insinuated itself into the lives of the defeated citizens of Koblenz. One of the complications of publishing *Amaroc* lay in the fact that it was produced in English by American soldiers, and then printed on German typesetting machines and presses operated by locals. Gerber was one of the few German speakers on the paper's fluctuating staff of between ten and twenty. At the time, the only other English-speaking paper available to the AFG was the Paris edition of the *Chicago Tribune*.

The *Amaroc* published a mixture of local news pertaining to military life, and news from home, that is, the United States, especially sports; the career of legendary baseball player Babe Ruth was followed avidly, as were boxers like Jack Dempsey. There were also short stories by O. Henry and poems composed by the readers; on March 4, 1921, *Amaroc* published Warren G. Harding's inaugural address only hours after it was given. The most lively feature of the *Amaroc* was the letters page, an ink-stained battleground for GIs to share opinions and counter-opinions, often in poetry, on any given subject; the new prohibition law that passed in their absence produced a hot and heated debate, as did the merits of opera, Charlie Chaplin films, and subjects like the misuse of hard liquor and drugs and the scourge of syphilis.

One issue that filled the pages of the *Amorac* was the way the AFG presented themselves to the German locals. Cornebise writes in *The Amaroc News* of one amusing letter in the *Amaroc* of October 10, 1919, from a concerned soldier on the subject of dress: "Today when I walked into a barber shop that I patronize . . . I noticed something unusual. . . . A soldier was having his hair curled, yes I think he wanted it all fluffy and nice, it wasn't so much of this one thing that I noticed but besides this he had Rouge on his face and his eyebrows blackened. When he left the shop I heard several remarks about him and in the end it reflected upon the soldiers of the army."

The last of the AFG left Koblenz in January 1923; the final issue of *Amaroc* was dated Wednesday the 24th. According to Cornebise, Captain McMahon, the editor, wrote in his final report that after the last issue was published the staff returned to the States, except for himself and one enlisted man who remained to liquidate the paper. It was Private Henry Gerber.

It was while serving in Koblenz that Gerber found Hirschfeld's Scientific Humanitarian Society. He wrote in *ONE* magazine in 1962:

In Coblenz on the Rhine I had subscribed to German homophile magazines and made several trips to Berlin, which was then not occupied by American forces. I had always bitterly felt the injustice with which my own American society accused the homosexual of "immoral acts."

What could be done about it, I thought. Unlike Germany, where the homosexual was partially organized and where sex legislation was uniform for the whole country, the United States was in a condition of chaos and misunderstanding concerning its sex laws, and no one was trying to unravel the tangle and bring relief to the abused.

Gerber returned to Chicago, took up residence at 1710 North Crilly Court, and began work for the U.S. Postal Service. His records say he was employed on July 10, 1923, as a "temporary sub. clerk" at the Lakeview Station. Then he was hired full time August 23 in the same position and assigned to delivery. He could speak "German fluently, French and Esperanto well," and "some Spanish." He said he had "fair speeds" at "stenography and typing." In March and April 1924, during the period he was forming the Society for Human Rights (SHR), Gerber was off sick, possibly with tonsillitis and definitely syphilis. On April 1, 1924, Gerber wrote to Chicago's Superintendent of Mails asking to use eleven days of annual leave, saying he needed a tonsillectomy and a few days to recuperate. On April 2 the superintendent responded by asking him to complete an "application for sick leave for five days beginning March 31." The letter further stated Gerber could take an eleven-day vacation beginning April 5 and concluding April 17. It's not known if the operation took place, but April 19, the day after Gerber would have returned to work, a doctor's certificate with the diagnosis "secondary syphilis" was executed. The document states Gerber was to be off work April 18, 1924, "for an indefinite period." A week later, a letter dated April 26 and signed by Bernard Roloff of the Illinois Social Hygiene League, 950–954 North Clark Street, a clinic where Gerber sought treatment, was sent to the Chicago post office. Roloff's letter, located in the Gregory Sprague Collection at the Chicago History Museum, reads: "Gentlemen: Henry Gerber, who came here for treatment for a venereal disease which he probably acquired accidentally, has already had nine successive treatments and in our opinion is not contagious nor infectious and could safely be taken back to work. He should continue treatment however, to prevent a recurrence of his disease. This man came quickly after his infection was noticed and this enabled us to gain quick control over his infection."

Gerber returned to work April 28 and focused his attention on forming the SHR with a handful of friends. Gerber's strategy was to network and gain support from other "sex reform" leaders; he even met with Margaret Sanger, the American birth control advocate, but they didn't like each other at all. He tried contacting others, but nobody seemed interested. Undeterred, he decided to go it alone. Through a lawyer, SHR applied for and received a charter from the State of Illinois on December 10, 1924. The stated objectives were:

> To promote and to protect the interests of people who by reasons of mental and physical abnormalities are abused and hindered in the legal pursuit of happiness which is guaranteed them by the Declaration of Independence, and to combat the public prejudices against them by dissemination of facts according to modern science among individuals of mature age. The Society stands only for law and order; it is in harmony with any and all general laws insofar as they protect the rights of others, and does in no manner recommend any acts in violation of present laws, nor advocate any matter inimical to the public welfare.

Years later, Gerber reflected in *ONE* magazine: "No one seemed to have bothered to investigate our purpose." It's thought SHR never had more than ten members. Gerber elected himself secretary; president was the Reverend John T. Graves, "a preacher who preached brotherly love to small groups of Negroes"; vice president was Al Meininger, an "indigent laundry queen"; and treasurer was Ralph (Ellsworth Booher), whose job with the railroad was threatened when his homosexuality became known. Throughout the rest of his life Gerber lamented that SHR failed to attract "men of good reputation." In Germany the homophile movement included enlightened politicians, doctors, scientists, as well as those in the arts; in the United States nobody in those professions was willing to stick a neck out for homosexuals. "The only support I got was from poor people," Gerber wrote in 1962. Some friends warned against him "doing anything so rash and futile" as starting a homosexual rights group. He explained:

"The average homosexual, I found, was ignorant concerning himself. Others were fearful. Still others were frantic or depraved. Some were blasé." Gerber also wrote: "Many homosexuals told me that their search for forbidden fruit was the real spice of life. With this argument they rejected our aims. We wondered how we could accomplish anything with such resistance from our people."

Gerber produced two issues of the SHR newsletter *Friendship and Freedom*, of which sadly no copies exist; it was the first known homophile publication in the United States. In *Homosexuality: Lesbians and Gay Men in Society, History and Literature* (1975), James Steakley discusses a German photograph of a collection of 1920s gay periodicals with *Friendship and Freedom* at the center, the only known image of the newsletter. In *Paris Gay 1925* (1981), a French book coauthored by Gilles Barbedette and Michael Carassou, is a review of *Friendship and Freedom*, written by Clarens, published in *L'amitie* in 1925 (excerpt from pages 246, 263–64):

> Within the New American newsletter Friendship and Freedom (Amitié et Liberté) I find admirable simplicity in this minister's statement:
>
> "There are," he states, "two types of people: those who believe in the fraternity of men and who do all they can for the good of each, independently of questions regarding race, religion, belief, social class—and the others who only have at heart their own self-interests."
>
> These last, not less than the heterosexuals (although, I swear it, are not only among them) are the majority of the world. However the first type (not all homosexuals certainly! but all well-wishing, due to homosexuality) are not a minority so weak that one is able to silence them easily for a long time. A government can suppress a newsletter, a book, a man. But men of good intentions are standing. They close ranks. It will produce a strange migration of souls. And the just, noble, necessary Belief will bring forth, probably larger numbers, better disciplined where the adversary least expects them.
>
> Is this what he wants? . . .
>
> Friendship and Freedom, of which we receive the first issue, is a moral, homosexual American newsletter. I'm not embarrassed to associate these two words: but it seems to me much more difficult

to justify their individual usage. In order to express my thought, if I knew the most beautiful and best way of stating it, rest assured I would never have recourse to those which don't satisfy me. At the very least I'll attempt to explain what I intend by "moral."

There is a moral code which is the study of the mores in a place at a given moment. (This sense is the only good one but it isn't in agreement with my sentence.)

What one intends the most often by "moral code" is popular opinion, and even below popular opinion—in the same manner as certain spectacles, so-called "artistic," and which only have the goal of flattering popular opinion, on which quite often, God have mercy! their promoters deceive themselves, losing almost as much money as they counted on gaining.

Should there be another "moral code" which, taking into account (inevitably) the general movement away from the actual opinion, would choose the most noble tendencies, and attempt to surpass it, to guide it towards a personal ideal. Here then, for me, is true art and ethics.

The first page of Friendship and Freedom is composed of an article on "Self-control" (isn't this the oldest and perhaps most lasting virtue?), a poem by Walt Whitman, and an essay "Green Carnations" (translated moreover from Die Freundschaft [Friendship]) of which here is the opening:

"Oscar Wilde wore a green carnation in his buttonhole. His friends and admirers did likewise. Society was quite unjust towards him, and this injustice is more than a crime because the well-known Wilde was a great poet.

"When a canary escapes from its golden cage, and invigorated by the feeling of freedom, vanishes into the street—the sparrows attack the overly confident bird and, with their sharp beaks, peck it to death.

"The common grey sparrows don't wish to see brilliant plumage mixed with theirs. And likewise, it's not accepted carnations are green . . ."

Friendship and Freedom is the issue of the Society for Human Rights which proposes, by subscriptions, to establish an assistance fund. The members' intent to use this money for helping their fellow homosexual friends (whom they call "intermediates"—of

the intermediate sex—according to the word usage of Carpenter*).
They also propose to find positions for their friends, to assist them
with every possible means. Finally, but with all sorts of precautions
("We don't publish under this heading what has already appeared
in other newsletters, etc.") what they wish above all, is to lead the
way towards modifying the unjust law which oppresses them.
Free America!

"One of the reasons why one acts contrary to the laws in our
country than elsewhere is that we have more laws."

(Translated by Bruce Kamsler)

[Je trouve admirable admirable de simplicité, dans le nouveau
journal américain Friendship and Freedom (Amitié et Liberté) cette
phrase d'un Pasteur:

"Il y a, dit-il, deux sortes de gens: ceux qui croient à la fraternité
des hommes et qui font tout ce qu'ils peuvent pour le bien de
chacun, indépendamment des questions de race, de religion, d'idée,
de caste—et les autres qui n'ont à coeur que leur propre intérêt."

Ces derniers, non moins que les hétérosexuels (bien que, je
l'avoue, pas uniquement parmi eux) sont en majorité dans le
monde. Pourtant les premiers (non pas tous homosexuels certes!
mais tous bienveillants, fût-ce à l'homosexualité), ne sont point en
minorité si faible qu'on puisse les bâillonner aisément ni pour
longtemps. Un government peut supprimer un journal, un livre, un
homme. Mais les homme de bonne volanté sont debout. Ils serre-
ront les rangs. Il se produira d'étranges migrations d'ames. Et
l'Idée juste, noble, nécessaire, surgira, probablement plus nom-
breuse, mieux disciplinée, où l'adversaire l'attendait le moins.

Est-ce là ce desire? . . .

Amitié et Liberté don't nous recevons le premier numéro est un
journal américain, homosexuel et moral. Il ne me gene point
d'associer ces deux mots: mais il me semble bien plus de justifier
leur emploi individuel. Pour exprimer ma penseé, si j'en savais de

---

*A reference to Edward Carpenter, the British socialist poet, philosopher,
anthropologist, homosexual rights activist, and author of The Intermediate Sex: A
Study of Some Transitional Types of Men and Women (1908).

plus beaux et de meilleurs, soyez sûrs que je n'aurais pas recours à ceux-ci qui ne me plaisant guére. Au moins tenterai-je d'expliquer ce que j'entends par "moral."

Il y a la morale qui est l'étude des moeurs dans un lieu à un moment donne. (Ce sens est le seul bon, mais il ne convient pas à ma phrase.)

Ce qu'on entend le plus souvent par "morale" est l'opinion vulgaire, et meme en dessous de l'opinion vulgaire—ainsi qu'il en est souvent de certain spectacles, dits "artistiques", et qui n'ont pour ideal que de flatter l'opinion publique, sur quoi bien souvent, Dieu merci! leurs promoeurs se trompent, perdant prsque autant d'argent qu'ils en comptaient gagner,

N'y aurait-il pas un autre "morale" qui, tenant compte (forcé-ment) du movement general de l'opinion actuelle, choisirait ses tendences les plus nobles, et tenterait de le devancer, de le guider vers un ideal personnel. Voilà, selon moi, l'art et l'éthique véritables.

La première page d'Amitié et Liberté se compose d'un article sur "Le contrôle de soi" (n'est-ce pas la plus ancienne vertu et peut-être la plus durable?), d'un poéme de Walt Whitman et d'un essai, "OEillets verts" (d'ailleurs traduit de Die Freundschaft), dont voici le début:

"Oscar Wilde portait un oeillet vert à la boutonniere. Ses amis et ses admirateurs en firent autant. L'humanité fut trés injuste envers lui, et cette injustice est plus qu'un crime, car le nommé Wilde était un grand poéte.

"Quand un Canari s'échappe de sa cage dorée et, enivré par le sentiment de sa liberté, s'envole dans la rue—les moineaux attaquent l'oiseau trop confiant et, de leur bec aigu, le frappent jusqu'à la mort.

"Les vulgaires moineaux gris ne veulent pas voir de plumes brillantes parmi eux. Et de meme il ne convient pas que les oeillets soient verts . . ."

Amitié et Liberté dépend de la Société pour les Droits humains qui se propose, par cotisations, de fonder une caisse de secours. Les sociétaires comptent se servir de cet argent pour aider leurs camarades homosexuels (qu'il nomment des "intermediates"—de sexe intermédiare—selon le mot de Carpenter). Ils se propsent aussi de trouver des situations à leurs amis. De les secourir par tous les moyens possibles. Enfin, mais avec toutes sortes de pre-cautions (Nous ne publierons sous cette rubrique ce qui a déjà paru dans d'autres journaux, etc.") ce qu'ils veulent surtout, c'est amener à modifier l'injuste loi qui les opprime.

Libre Amérique!

"Une des raisons pour lesquelles on contrevient aux lois plus souvent chez nous que dans les autres pays, c'est que nous avons plus de lois."]

Gerber was an inveterate letter writer, and he often directed his condemnation at those who attempted to restrict human nature with moralistic claptrap. He wrote in *ONE* magazine: "It is hard to believe that Mother Nature needs our police to protect her from her creatures." His earliest known published work is dated February 20, 1925, and appears in the *Chicago Tribune* of March 2, 1925. It reads: "Are Indecent Shows Realistic?":

Although you never published any of my letters before, because, I am sure, you reject everything that is against your policy. I try again to reach your Voice of the People column. I may have funny ideas, but I believe I am not as stupid as some of your contributors, as, for instance, the one who says that in Kansas grass grows when farmers say prayers. Why not give me a chance, too, for I am sure my views are not as stupid as some of your contributors.

There were a number of articles in your paper recently in which Vox Populi lauds your commendation on "indecent" theaters. There is no good or bad, because all things are relative. "Indecent" means simply "not in accord with some people's brand of views." But the same intolerance which you fight in your paper when it takes the form of "moral intolerance" you seem to uphold as some-thing "decent."

My reason why I admit that many people go to "indecent" shows—I never go to a show because I have more altruistic occu-pations to kill my time with—is that the majority of people just simply are sick and tired of that 'decent' hypocritical stuff which is served patrons. If I want to hear "spiritual" things I go to the Salva-tion Army and get an hour's "inspiration" free or for buying a copy of the War Cry. But if I want to spend two or three dollars in going to a show, do you not think that I am entitled to some portrayal of life as it in reality is? Doubtlessly numerous people of the neurotic class call THE TRIBUNE an "indecent" newspaper, but nevertheless it is the World's Greatest Newspaper.

Gerber's description of his arrest and the demise of SHR has always been the accepted and only version; however, I recently uncovered a different account. It was thought that in the spring of 1925, Gerber moved house, taking rooms at 34 East Oak Street. The story he told was that on July 12, 1925, at 2:00 a.m., a detective, accompanied by a reporter from the *Chicago Examiner*, arrested him at this address. The trouble started when SHR vice president Al Meininger, the "indigent laundry queen," turned out to be married with two children. After Meininger's wife found a copy of *Friendship and Freedom*, she informed her social worker, who, in turn, told the police. When they raided Meininger's apartment, he was caught in flagrante delicto with another man; both were arrested. During questioning Meininger named the other members of SHR, who were promptly rounded up and held in a cell overnight. The following morning, in a pretrial hearing, the judge ordered the defendants be charged with sending obscene material through the mail. According to Gerber, the *Chicago Examiner* headline read: "Strange Sex Cult Exposed." The article accused Meininger of bringing men home and performing "bizarre sex acts" in front of his wife and children. Also, it claimed *Friendship and Freedom* "urged men to leave their wives and children." (Note: none of Chicago's libraries have a copy of this issue of the *Chicago Examiner*. In fact, the *Chicago Examiner* ceased publication on May 1, 1918, and became the *Chicago Herald-Examiner*.)

It was always thought the *Chicago Examiner* had a second edition the day after Gerber's arrest and that Chicago libraries had failed to save a copy. Not true. Neither is Gerber's memory of being arrested at 34 East Oak Street. The article concerning Gerber's arrest appeared on the front page of the *Chicago American* on July 13, 1925, under the headline "Girl Reveals Strange Cult Run by Dad":

Police of the East Chicago av. Station today began investigation of a weird cult brought to light when 12 year old Betty Meininger, 532 N. Dearborn st., appeared and asked the policemen to find out "why her father carried on so."

She described afternoon and night meetings in the Meininger home, attended by men and devoted to séances at which strange rites were performed by her father and men who came to take part. Her description led to a raid.

SEE FEDERAL ACTION

They found Meininger, who is 37, married, and the father of four children; the Rev. John Graves, self-declared pastor of a church, and one Henry Gerber, 1710 Crilly Court, publisher of the cult paper, *Friendship and Freedom.*

Meininger, Graves and Gerber, arraigned in court today, were given continuances until Thursday. Meantime the police intend to see if federal action can be taken as a result of sending the paper through the mails.

The pretrial judge also presided over the first trial, at which two postal inspectors were present, one insisting the three accused deserved heavy prison sentences "for infecting God's own country." Gerber later wrote in *ONE* magazine: "In the Chicago Av. police court, a detective triumphantly produced a powder puff, which he claimed he had found in my room. That was the sole evidence of my crime. I have never in my life worn rouge or powder." Things were looking bad for Gerber after "I love Karl," an excerpt from his confiscated diaries, was read in court by, in Gerber's words, "a hatchet-face female." Gerber recalled in *ONE* magazine: "The detective and the judge shuddered over such depravity." Gerber, Meininger, and Graves were released on bail at a thousand dollars each. In the third and last court appearance, there was a new defense lawyer and judge. The case took an unexpected turn, when the accused were informed that all charges were dismissed and everything had been "arranged." After reviewing the evidence, or lack of it, the new judge reprimanded the prosecution: "It is an outrage to arrest persons without a warrant." He ordered the return of Gerber's property—he received his typewriter, but not his diaries.

After his arrest, Gerber was suspended from the post office. On August 10, 1925, John H. Bartlett, the First Assistant Postmaster General in Washington, D.C., wrote the Hon. Arthur C. Leuder, Postmaster in Chicago:

The Department is in receipt of a report from inspectors, in which they recommend the removal of Clerk Henry Gerber for conduct unbecoming a postal employee.

> After careful consideration of the evidence submitted, the Department believes that Mr. Gerber is not a suitable person for retention in the service. You are therefore authorized to remove him, effectively August 13, 1925, and directed to inform him in writing of the reason for the department's action, reporting his separation on Form 1532, in triplicate.
>
> Mr. Gerber has been carried on the rolls as suspended from duty without pay. In the event that he has not already exhausted his annual leave, he may be carried on the rolls as absent on account of vacation during the time that he is actually entitled thereto, and the reminder of the time he should be carried as suspended without pay.

Gerber briefly took a room at 34 East Oak Street. On August 13 he wrote to the Honorable Arthur C. Leuder: "I have to respectfully advise that I have changed my address of residence from 34 E. Oak Street (formerly 1710 Crilly Court) to Room 374 Lexington Hotel, Twentysecond Street and Michigan Avenue . . . my present status on your roster of postal clerks is 'Suspended.' Apropos I also wish to report that I have lost my Post Office badge, number 9336, Mailing Division."

After the demise of the Society for Human Rights, Gerber became despondent with homosexuals; later in life he uttered such choice phrases as "Most bitches are only interested in sex contacts, not challenging legal and social stigmas of homosexuality" and "I have absolutely no confidence in the Dorian crowd, mostly a bunch of selfish, uncultured, ignorant egoists who have nothing for the ideal side of life." On a visit to New York in 1927 he became reacquainted with an associate from his days with *Amaroc*, who encouraged him to move to the city and reenlist in the army. This he did, serving another seventeen years, working on Governor's Island as a proofreader; in 1945 he retired with an honorable discharge and a hundred-dollar-a-month pension.

In spite of his cynicism, Gerber hadn't entirely given up. In 1930 he ran a pen-pal club called *CONTACTS*, a mimeographed monthly newsletter that, although not exclusively gay, served as a meeting place for homosexuals. Gerber also published a literary magazine called *Chanticleer*, in which he espoused his views on priests and politicians. One of his essays in defense of homosexuality, written under the pseudonym Parisex, was published in the *Modern Thinker*. He also fired off letters to newspapers.

In 1939 Gerber's own ad for pen pals appeared in *CONTACTS*. It began: "NYC Male, 44, proofreader, single. Favored by nature with immunity to female 'charms,' but does not hate women," and continued:

> Introvert, enjoying a quiet evening with classical music or non-fiction book. Looking at life, I understand why monkeys protested Darwin's thesis. . . . Brought up Catholic, now an avowed atheist. (God loves atheists because they do not molest him with silly prayers). . . . Religion is a racket and one who believes in supernatural powers is ready to swallow anything, including Jonas' whale.
>
> . . . Believe in French sex morality: that it's not the state's business to interfere in the sexual enjoyment of adults so long as rights of others are not violated. . . . Like cats, men and women create children, which in the case of cats are drowned every time a litter appears. It is still against the law to drown unwanted children. . . . Religious racketeers realize that man's emotions, if freely expressed by sex activity, would leave nothing for religion. But sex repressed and inhibited leads to religious hysteria, and priests get rich thereby.
>
> . . . Brainless people fear being alone with their empty selves and run from party to party and from the many amusements offered such unthinking people. I am fond of reading non-fiction books and have quite a library of selected volumes. Very fond of classical music. Have about 1000 gramophone records (all classical) and a radio-combination, also play the piano. Fond of outdoors in summer. Like foreign, especially French, films, and the few worthwhile Hollywood pictures, but am disgusted with the hypocrisy and 'goody-goody' film ware which shows all men honest and all women 'pure.' Firmly for realism even if it shakes a few pious spinsters out of their "Alice-in-Wonderland" reverie.
>
> . . . Rather particular about correspondents. Not interested in smut or "obscenity," not because it is a "sin" but believe my private affairs personal and sacred, not to be divulged to gossip. Not interested in the gossip mongering of the average Contacts female nor inclined to waste time on brainless male "old wives" who are too lazy or cowardly to solve their own problems. Consider myself civilized and self-sufficient, but always welcome people of like

minds who can discuss life intelligently, and can share the simple pleasures of discussion, music, and travel.

Given the disagreeable tone of the ad it's surprising anyone wrote back to him, but one did: Manuel Boyfrank, the future ONE, Inc. president, who at the time described himself as a sailor and office worker. Boyfrank was upfront about his homosexuality and suggested forming an organization. On January 17, 1940, Gerber answered him: "I was surprised to find you a homosexual, too, but let me tell you from experience it does not pay to do anything for them. I once lost a good job in trying to bring them together. Most men of that type are too scared to give their names or to join any association trying to help them; the other half are only interested in physical contacts and have not the slightest interest to help their cause. I found that out to my own sorrow." Gerber suggested that if Boyfrank wanted to start an organization, he would pass on the relevant information to the homosexual members of *CONTACTS*. This he did, but nothing came of it. While the two corresponded regularly, the topic of forming a gay organization didn't crop up again until a letter dated March 19, 1944. This time it was Gerber who brought it up. Frank McCourt, a friend of his in New York, had recently started "a camouflaged society for homosexuals" that masqueraded as a chapter of the American Rocket Society, a group founded in 1930 by science fiction authors like G. Edward Pendray, David Lasser, and Laurence Manning; they published their own journal and conducted experiments with rockets. Gerber suggested Boyfrank join with him and McCourt to form an organization called the "Society Scouting Sex Superstition, An International Movement Fighting Fascism in Sex." By way of explanation, Gerber added a note: "The word homosexual would nowhere appear, we fight any kind of sex superstition."

This idea came to nothing, as the three main players had widely different visions: Gerber fell out with McCourt when he held a prayer service for GIs being sent off to the war in Europe—this didn't suit Gerber's devout atheism—then Boyfrank wanted to organize groups of homosexuals in different cities by using a correspondence club, while Gerber envisioned a group of enlightened leaders whose mission was to educate the public on all sexual matters. In 1942 Gerber spent several weeks in the guardhouse on suspicion of being homosexual. "They put me before a Section VIII board and tried to get me out of the army on that. When I told the president of the board I only practiced mutual masturbation with men over 21, the psychiatrist told me 'You are not a homosexual.' I nearly fell out of my chair! Imagine me fighting all my life for our cause and then be told I was not a homosexual!"

Throughout the 1940s Gerber continued his letter writing. On July 18, 1947, he penned a thirteen-page missive to Doctor Leopold Wexburg, chief of the Mental Health Division of the Bureau of Disease Control in the Department of Public Health, after the Washington, D.C., *Time-Herald* reported the physician was calling for longer jail sentences for homosexuals. In July 1947 the *American Mercury* published a letter from Gerber adding his thoughts to an ongoing discussion about homosexuality. The editor subsequently invited Gerber to contribute an article on the subject, but rejected the two he sent: "Is Homosexuality Inborn or Acquired?" a long, rambling piece at 3,100 words that covered several topics, but in no discernable order; and "Can Homosexuality Be Cured?" In 1949 Gerber translated into English several chapters of Magnus Hirschfeld's *Die Homosexualitait des Mannes und des Weibes* (*Homosexuality in Man and Woman*), later published in *ONE Institute Quarterly*, the journal of ONE Inc.

Gerber maintained contact with both ONE Inc., and New York Mattachine, though only as a letter and article writer. He was now a cranky old man. In his last letter to Boyfrank on June 18, 1957, Gerber wrote: "I am now 65 and my libido has gone. So I no longer worry much what the lot of other homosexuals may be." In September 1962 *ONE* magazine published an article by Gerber recounting the story of the rise and fall of the Society for Human Rights in 1925. His last contact with the editors of *ONE* was a letter dated January 24, 1966.

Henry Gerber spent his twilight years in the U.S. Soldiers' and Airmen's Home in Washington, D.C., where he died from pneumonia on December 31, 1972, at age eighty. According to his record card at the home, Gerber retired from the U.S. Army as a staff sergeant after serving twenty-one years, eight months in World War I and World War II. His army serial number was 6423386. His place of birth is typed "Barvaria" [*sic*] but this is scratched out and "Illinois" written in. He is buried in section Q, grave 833 at the cemetery next door to the Soldier's Home.

In 1981, the Midwest Gay and Lesbian Archive and Library honored Henry Gerber and lesbian attorney Pearl Hart by changing its name to the Henry Gerber–Pearl Hart Library: The Midwest Lesbian and Gay Resource Center; it's now called the Gerber/Hart Library. Gerber was posthumously inducted into the Chicago Gay and Lesbian Hall of Fame in 1992 and the Henry Gerber House, located at 1710 North Crilly Court, was designated a Chicago Landmark on June 1, 2001.

# 9

# Some in the Arts

Starting in the late nineteenth century, Chicago's literary circles and salons were numerous, but three artists who made an impact were J. C. Leyendecker, who created the Arrow Collar Man; Henry Blake Fuller, the author of the first gay play and novel in the United States; and Carl Van Vechten, author, photographer, and "Negrotarian."

Although the heyday of the Chicago Renaissance spanned from 1912 to 1924, the city's rich history of literature and the arts didn't begin and end with the bohemians of Towertown. In 1888 the morbidly bizarre Whitechapel Club was formed by a group of writers who were no strangers to the occasional cocktail. The club was founded by Opie Read, George Ade, Finley Peter Dunne, and Ben King, and aspired to raise the literary consciousness of the general populace. The Whitechapel Club was named after the area of London where Jack the Ripper plied his murderous trade. The entrance to this literary tomb was down an alley at the back of the *Chicago Daily News* building, and the funereal decor included a huge coffin as a center table, walls adorned with knives and pistols, and a collection of skulls with colored-glass eyes lit by gas jets. One of the Whitechapel Club's leading lights was Doctor G. Frank Lydston, who studied and wrote extensively on the subject of homosexuality.

Three years before the formation of the Whitechapel Club, the Fine Arts Building opened as Chicago's official center for the arts. One of the homosexual artists who rented a studio there was Joseph Christian Leyendecker, who shared the space with his brother Frank Xavier, an aspiring illustrator himself. J. C. Leyendecker was born in 1874 in Montabour, Germany, and in 1882 immigrated with his parents and brother to the United States, where he attended the Chicago Art Institute. In 1896 the Leyendecker brothers studied in Paris at the Académie Julian. On their return to Chicago, J. C. Leyendecker held the first exhibition of his work in a restaurant at Monroe and LaSalle Streets. The *Chicago Tribune* art critic wrote: "The designs are spirited, suggestive, free from sameness, and executed in a broad, dexterous manner, which makes them strikingly attractive. In some of them, executed in Paris, there is a suggestion of French training and French surroundings."

In the summer of 1898 the Leyendecker brothers opened a studio in the Stock Exchange Building. J. C. Leyendecker soon found a lucrative niche creating covers for *Colliers* and the *Saturday Evening Post*. In 1900 he moved to New York and went on to become the most popular illustrator of his time, with Norman Rockwell naming him as an inspiration. Leyendecker painted more than 400 magazine covers, 319 for the *Evening Post* alone. His most famous creation was the Arrow Collar Man, a commission from Cluett, Peabody & Co., of Troy, New York, to produce an ad for their detachable shirt collars. Leyendecker's image of a well-dressed sophisticated man, masculine and undeniably fey in equal measure, became the new model of American manhood. The Arrow Collar Man was a sensation, driving sales of Arrow detachable collars through the roof. In 1918 they earned Cluett, Peabody & Co. $32 million. The fictional character also received up to seventeen thousand fan letters a week from women, some offering marriage, others threatening suicide if they didn't meet him.

The Arrow Collar Man ad campaign also inspired a Broadway musical comedy called *Helen of Troy, N.Y.* that opened at the Selwyn Theater on June 19, 1923, with a libretto by George S. Kaufman and Marc Connelly and music by Bert Kalmar and Harry Ruby. The story is set amid a backdrop of rivalry between two shirt collar manufacturers in Troy, New York. Stenographer Helen McGuffey is fired from her job at one of the factories after her boss discovers his son has fallen for the lowly office girl. When McGuffey designs a new, improved, softer collar and sells it to the rival company, it forces the two factories to merge and she wins her beau. The musical was a moderate success; one reviewer wrote: "There wasn't a dry collar in the house when the audience joined in the fun with shouting and laughter." Unbeknownst to most of the audience there were a few in-jokes; for example, the male character who models the shirt collars, who is a mincing queen, is based on Charles A. Beach, the real-life model for Leyendecker's Arrow Collar Man ads. He was also the artist's longtime lover. Leyendecker first met Beach in 1901, and they lived together until the artist's death on July 25, 1951. Beach followed him three years later.

## Henry Blake Fuller

Henry Blake Fuller was born in Chicago on January 9, 1857, on the site of what later became the LaSalle Street station, 414 South LaSalle Street. He lived in the city his whole life, though he traveled and became enamored with Europe and its culture. He attended Moseley School, then Chicago High School, the Allison Classical Academy boarding school in Wisconsin, and finally Chicago's South Division High School. Throughout his childhood he kept a journal, in which he planned meticulous itineraries for his future trips abroad. Methodical, his early writings also confirm his reputation for being a fastidious and private person. In one journal entry, while at Allison, he bemoans the fact that he has to share a room with another student, and an untidy one at that.

Fuller made his first trip to Europe in 1879, sending some of his journals home to be published in the *Chicago Tribune*. His life changed when his father, successful banker George Wood Fuller, died in 1885, and Henry took over the business, while at the same time continuing his literary pursuits. Fuller resided in the family home at 2823 Prairie Avenue until his mother died in 1907, when he moved out and spent the rest of his life in a series of cheap boarding houses, though he was not without funds. Though reclusive by nature, Fuller was charming and amiable in social situations, but the high wall of secrecy he built around his private life kept him from entertaining guests, or even telling his friends where he lived. After his death the *Chicago Tribune* on July 29, 1929, described him as "always a shy, lonely boy, a shy, lonely young man; a shy, lonely old man, but a man always for whom every one had a special deep affection; for he had a lovely, gentle kindness for youth." It was said that Fuller was so shy that if he saw an acquaintance walking toward him he would cover his face with a handkerchief until the person passed him by. Fuller was a prolific writer who dabbled in short stories, poetry, and even opera librettos, before finding a measure of success with his first novel, *The Chevalier of Pensieri-Vani* (1892), set in Italy. But it was *The Cliff Dwellers* (1893) that cemented him in the national consciousness as a writer of "realism."

Appropriately for a city of skyscrapers, *The Cliff Dwellers* is a reference to the ancient Native Americans of the Southwest who built their homes on cliff sides in canyons and on mesas. The novel, set in Chicago, examines the lives of people who populate the Clifton, an eighteen-story skyscraper—tall for the time—and of the uneasy relationship between the city's nouveau riche and its aspiring artists.

Fuller wrote two gay-themed pieces: a short tragic play, *At Saint Judas's* (1896), originally written for marionettes; and a novel, *Bertram Cope's Year* (1919), which is the first work of fiction by a U.S. author to treat homosexuality in a sympathetic manner. *At Saint Judas's* was published in a collection of twelve short plays collectively titled *The Puppet-Booth* (1896). On Fuller's original handwritten manuscript the title is *The Puppet Booth: 12 Plays for Marionettes*. It's unlikely that Fuller intended the plays to be staged, as they read more like notes, character sketches, and scenes for inclusion in upcoming novels. A *Chicago Tribune* review read: "They are not acting plays, they are too literary for that, but they are good reading and will set people to thinking." In February 1896 Anna Morgan started a series of Sunday afternoon studio teas in her rooms at the Auditorium Building; they were titled "High Bohemia." The salons were a mix of talks and music, and at one such event Henry Blake Fuller read a paper on Belgian playwright Maurice Maeterlinck called "Maeterlinck and the Symbolists," followed by a musical interlude of piano selections by Mrs. A. O. Mason and songs by the delightfully named Minnie Fish Griffen.

Maeterlinck was an important influence on Fuller's plays. In the *Chicago Tribune* review of *The Puppet-Booth*, Jeannette L. Gilder writes: "If I had taken up this book without seeing the author's name on it I should say at once that it was by Maurice Maeterlinck. After reading a few of the plays I should still say that they were by Maeterlinck, but that he was writing in a new vein, for there is humor in them and humor is a quality that has been denied to Maeterlinck." Another *Chicago Tribune* review reads: "Best of all these strange dramas, perhaps is *At St. Judas's*. If here be any cryptic meaning to all this it does not lie upon the surface. But one need not read beyond the first page to perceive that the style of the author is as fine and polished as his ideas are grotesque and unique." The *Chicago*

*Evening Post* wrote: "It might be argued that a suspicion of decadence attaches to 'At St. Judas's' and it is a little unfortunate that Mr. Fuller did not emphasize the purity of his meaning."

While not breaking new ground on the literary front, *At Saint Judas's* does have historical importance, as it is the first known gay-themed play written in the United States. The play is a short dialogue between the groom and the best man at a wedding, with the latter harboring a secret love for the unsuspecting former. While the groom ponders who has been sabotaging the nuptials with scurrilous rumors about him and his bride-to-be, the best man eventually admits his guilt and confesses his undying love. At the climax of this Victorian melodrama the groom, drenched in chivalry and honor, draws his sword, the lights dim, and we learn that one of them is dead; which one is unclear. *At St. Judas's* was never performed, but two other plays from *The Puppet-Booth* collection were staged on May 18, 1897, when Anna Morgan selected *Afterglow* and *The Stranger within the Gates* to be presented at the last matinee of the season of the Chicago Conservatory dramatic department. The plays were not a success. The *Chicago Tribune* on May 19 described *The Afterglow* as "a dull and commonplace little story" and suggested it "might be recommended as a drawing room piece for amateurs."

Considering *Bertram Cope's Year* was published in 1919, when homosexuals were expected to die or go insane in the last chapter, the gay characters in Fuller's novel walk away remarkably unscathed, with the exception of dinged egos from lessons hard learned, and one character who is expelled after an indiscretion. Reviews were mixed. Burton Rascoe of the *Chicago Tribune* wrote on November 8: "I confess that I have been unable to reach the end of this satirical chronicle of a Socratic episode, even though its scene is academic Evanston. I have tried on five occasions. I have gone to sleep each time."

The book traces a year in the life of Bertram Cope, a young yellow-haired English instructor at a thinly disguised Northwestern University in Evanston. Cope's beauty and charming demeanor ignites passion and interest in both men and women alike, notably Basil Randolph, an older man who desires nothing more than to have the young knight occupy his spare bedroom. However, Randolph's plans are thwarted when Arthur Lemoyne, an old "friend" of Cope's, arrives to share his life, but Lemoyne doesn't fit in with Cope's new circle of friends, and is possessive and protective.

Lemoyne is the flighty fly in everyone's ointment. An aspiring actor, he lands a part in the college amateur theatrical show: a female role in *The Antics of Annabella*, a musical comedy. The performance is a success, but Lemoyne fails to discard his feminine camp when the play is over, and backstage wearing wig and lingerie he attempts to seduce the leading man. Lemoyne is banished from the college and leaves town. At the end of the school year, Cope himself takes a better post at an Eastern University, where we suspect he is reunited with the disgraced Arthur Lemoyne.

*Bertram Cope's Year* with its "delicate theme" was rejected by every publisher it was sent to, and Fuller ended up self-publishing the novel through Ralph Seymour Fletcher, a designer and publisher based in the Fine Arts Building in Chicago; it barely sold two hundred copies. Opinions vary, but some felt the poor sales were due to its subject matter, while others judged the book to be dull. *Outlook* magazine described the character of Bertram as "flabby of purpose" and commented that "he gives nothing in return for the friendships he inspires, and escapes all love entanglements. The study of this weak but agreeable man is subtle but far from exciting."

*At St. Judas's* was reprinted by Routledge in a book called *Lovesick: Modernist Plays of Same-Sex Love, 1894–1925* (1999), and *Bertram Cope's Year* was reprinted by Turtle Point Press in 1998 with a cover photograph of a young man sailing, taken by Fuller's friend Carl Van Vechten.

Fuller continued writing until his death on July 28, 1929, when he suffered heart failure at age seventy-two at the home of Wakeman T. Ryan, 5411 Harper Avenue, where he lived for the last three years of his life; he died quietly, sitting in a chair looking out the window. His *Chicago Tribune* obituary notes that Fuller's name was never listed in a telephone book and the author never married.

## Carl Van Vechten

Though he married two women, author, critic and photographer Carl Van Vechten was homosexual and also what the African American author Zora Neale Hurston called a "Negrotarian"—a white patron of a black artist. With his Nordic good looks, Carlo, as his friends called him, left his hometown of Cedar Rapids, Iowa, where he was born on June 17, 1880, to attend the University of Chicago from 1899 to 1903. In 1906 he moved to New York, but it was Chicago that nurtured Van Vechten's enthusiasm for the art, music, and literature that shaped and inspired his life's work. His writing career began with the *University of Chicago Weekly*, then continued as a street reporter for the *Chicago American*, where he developed his skills as a photographer.

In 1906 he was working for the *New York Times*. A year later he took a leave of absence to visit Europe and indulge his passion for opera, and it was while in England that he married his first wife, Anna Snyder, an old friend from Cedar Rapids; the marriage lasted five years. On returning to New York and the *New York Times* in 1909, Van Vechten became their dance critic during the heyday of the mother of modern dance, Isadora Duncan, who was bisexual, and lesbians like Russian ballerina Tamara Karsavina and Art Nouveau muse, the Chicago-born Loïe "The Electric Fairy" Fuller.

In 1914 Van Vechten remarried, this time to Russian-born actress Fania Marinoff, whose stage and movie career is almost forgotten, overshadowed as she was by her husband; she was often referred to as "Carlo's wife." Marinoff, who was born to a Jewish family in Odessa in 1890, played dozens of lead and supporting roles in plays, and made eight silent movies. Her first performance in Chicago was in November 1914 in *Consequences* by H. F. Rubenstein, a comedy about intermarriage between Jews and Gentiles. Though Van Vechten was openly gay, their marriage was a happy one, more an emotional love than physical passion, and it lasted over forty years. Marinoff was not naïve about homosexuality; in 1917 she appeared in a New York production of *Spring Awakening* by the controversial German dramatist Benjamin Franklin Wedekind. The author describes the play as "a tragedy of childhood." The play concerns turn-of-the-century children ignorant of sexual matters and explicitly examines subjects like sadomasochism, masturbation, suicide, abortion, and homoerotic love. Not surprisingly it lasted only one performance. *Spring Awakening* was forgotten until a musical adaptation of the play opened off-Broadway in 2006 and went on to win eight Tony Awards, including best musical.

Van Vechten published many books on music, ballet, and cats—furry felines were another of his passions. He once wrote: "As an inspiration to the author, I do not think the cat can be over-estimated. He suggests so much grace, power, beauty, motion, mysticism. I do not wonder that many writers love cats; I am only surprised that all do not." His first novel, *Peter Whiffle: His Life and Works*, was published in 1922 and was a semi-autobiographical account of a young man's time in Paris. Over the next few years Van Vechten immersed himself in the culture of Harlem, frequently visiting and photographing the writers, artists, and other creative people he met there; he was also generous in his financial support of gay black artists, including Langston Hughes and Countee Cullen. Another way he helped was by introducing African American authors to his friend Margaret Anderson, the lesbian anarchist who cofounded Chicago's *Little Review* magazine; she promptly included them in the publication's repertoire of contributors. Through his articles in the *New York Times*, his books of art and music criticism, and his novels, Van Vechten promoted the "New Negro" movement, sometimes amid controversy, as with his novel *Nigger Heaven* (1926).

The perceived problem with *Nigger Heaven* was that a white writer had the audacity to create realistic African American characters living in the good, the bad, and the ugly culture of Harlem, and also used the provocative "N" word in the title. The controversy fueled generational disagreements within the African American community about racial separatism, with the old guard lambasting the book as having no merit, and younger intellectuals like Hughes and Cullen who judged *Nigger Heaven* an important contribution to black literature. In support of Van Vechten, poet and Chicago resident Donald Jeffrey Hayes wrote in the *Chicago Defender* in 1928: "*Nigger Heaven* came unheralded and without precedent—the first real passionately throbbing novel of contemporary Negro life—a careful timely study; a sympathetic portrayal of that which before had known only the jester's touch. But America was not ready for it. America in general and the Negroes in particular." Hayes goes on to accuse African American critics of being racial prudes, judging the book by its title alone.

In the 1930s Van Vechten was introduced to the 35-millimeter Leica camera, and he began a second career as a photographer. Among his subjects were Gertrude Stein, Mahalia Jackson, W. Somerset Maugham, F. Scott Fitzgerald, Paul Cadmus, Marc Chagall, Georgia O'Keeffe, Marlon Brando, Orson Welles, Norman Mailer, Ella Fitzgerald, Gore Vidal, Truman Capote, Tallulah Bankhead, and Sir Laurence Olivier. Van Vechten became the most famous celebrity photographer of the twentieth century, and his photographs are still used to illustrate books and magazines to this day. During World War II Van Vechten volunteered at New York's Stage Door Canteen, founded by the American Theatre Wing and the United Service Organization (USO) as a servicemen's nightclub featuring the big band sounds of Tommy Dorsey, Benny Goodman, and Count Basie among others. It was there he met a busboy, Saul Mauribar, who became Van Vechten's life partner, his assistant in the dark room, and after his death the executor of his estate.

Carl Van Vechten died on December 21, 1964, in New York City at age eighty-four. Two years later Mauribar donated 1,400 of Van Vechten's photographs to the Library of Congress.

# 10

# The Blues and All That Jazz

Jazz and blues developed as sexually explicit voices of slavery and represent a musical document of African American lives in the first quarter of the twentieth century. Bessie Smith's "Foolish Man Blues," Ma Rainey's "Sissy Blues," and George Hannah and other "freakish men" sang the blues. Tony Jackson and other jazz musicians left the South for the Chicago area, and crowds enjoyed performances by Alberta Hunter, Ethel Waters, and the "shimmies and shivers" of Ethel Williams in the Darktown Follies.

On February 14, 1920, Mamie Smith walked into the Okeh Record Company's New York studio and sang "That Thing Called Love," the first known recording of an African American female vocalist. For months the disc sold some 7,500 copies a week, revealing an untapped African American market the record companies were quick to exploit. In Chicago, Paramount's Mayo Williams, the first black executive to work for a white record company, signed Alberta Hunter in 1921, and Ma Rainey and Ida Cox in 1923. After that, ads for "race records" began appearing weekly in the *Chicago Defender*. Mamie Smith's first record gave a voice to the black women of America, and they used it to document the brutality of their lives, as victims of men, poverty, and racism. Performing was one of the few ways that African American women, especially lesbians, could be financially independent and escape the preordained timeline of marriage and children.

Armed with a newfound independence, many singers adopted a rebellious stance; the "arrogant and bragging" woman who can fend for her self and make a fool of her man became a popular blues theme. Sexual variance also featured in many songs, as both male and female singers acknowledged sexual fluidity and offered alternative options, the same option that Shug, the blues singer, offers Celie in a tender, powerful encounter in Alice Walker's book *The Color Purple*:

> There's two things got me puzzled,
> There's two things I don't understand;
> That's a mannish-actin' woman,
> And a skippin', twistin' woman-actin' man.

So sang Bessie Smith in her self-penned "Foolish Man Blues," a critique of butch dykes and effeminate men, recorded in 1927. Yet this daughter of a Baptist preacher, born in 1894 in Chattanooga, Tennessee, was no stranger to the ways of Sappho; she bedded as many female members of her performing troupe as she could, including Boula Lee, one of her lesbian back-up singers when she toured with the Harlem Frolics in tent shows through the "Sunny South" in 1926. Smith also visited a gay buffet flat in Detroit; a buffet flat was a resort for all manner of vices. Smith surrounded herself with gay men and lesbians; she was a close friend of male impersonator Gladys Fergusson, and her pianist was Porter Grainger, a man so shrouded in mystery that neither his dates of birth or death are known, though we do know he lived in Chicago prior to working with "The Empress of the Blues."

A young Bessie Smith was introduced to the world of blues by singer Gertrude "Ma" Rainey. Rainey was eight years her senior, stout in stature with a gold toothy smile and a down-to-earth charm. She was the first female singer to sing in the less polished style of the male blues minstrels who roamed the back roads of the southern states of America. Rainey was born Gertrude Pridgett on April 26, 1886, in Columbus, Georgia, the second child of Thomas and Ella, two veterans of vaudeville and minstrel shows. At the age of fourteen she first took the stage in *A Bunch of Blackberries*, a local black revue at the Springer Opera House. Two years later she married William "Pa" Rainey, and they toured the southern states as Ma and Pa Rainey and Assassinators of the Blues in shows like Tolliver's Circus, the Musical Extravaganza, and the Rabbit Foot Minstrels.

Ma Rainey's first appearance in Chicago was in April 1924 at the Grand Theatre as "Madame 'Ma Rainey,'" though some of the shows had to be canceled as a result of the shooting death of her brother Essie P. Pridgett in Detroit. Throughout the 1920s Rainey toured extensively as a solo artist, always returning to Chicago, where most of the hundred songs she recorded were made in the Paramount studio. It was Paramount who gave her the title "Mother of the Blues," although she was also known as the "Paramount Wildcat," and "Gold Necklace Woman of the Blues."

Rainey made no secret of her love for women, and she mixed freely in the homosexual circles of the time. In August 1926 she recorded "Sissy Blues" in Chicago with her Georgia Jazz Band:

> I dreamed last night I was far from harm
> Woke up and found my man in a sissy's arms.
>
> "Hello, Central, it's 'bout to run me wild.
> Can I get that number, or will I have to wait a while?"
>
> Some are young, some are old.
> My man says sissies got good jellyroll.
>
> My man got a sissy, his name is Miss Kate
> He shook that thing like jelly on a plate.
>
> Now all the people ask me why I'm all alone.
> A sissy shook that thing and took my man from home.

In June 1928 Rainey was back in the studio recording "Prove It on Me" with her Tub Jug Washboard Band, a tease song about her cross-dressing and lesbian love-life:

> It's true I wear a collar and a tie,
> Make the wind blow all the while.
> They say I do it, aint nobody caught me.
> They sure got to prove it on me.
>
> . . . I went out last night with a crowd of my friends,
> They must've been women, 'cause I don't like no men.

Wear my clothes just like a fan,
Talk to the gals just like any old man;
'Cause they say I do it, aint nobody caught me.
Sure got to prove it on me.

The Paramount ad for this song appeared in the *Chicago Defender* on September 22, 1928, and depicted Rainey, wearing a man's hat, waistcoat, jacket, and tie, soliciting the attentions of two slender, feminine women, while in the background a cop with a flashlight looks on suspiciously. Ironically, three years earlier, Chicago cops did "prove it" on Rainey, when they answered a noise complaint and found the "Mother of the Blues" in an orgy with several naked chorus girls. The story goes that after spending the night in jail she was bailed out the next morning by Bessie Smith.

Playwright August Wilson's Pulitzer Prize–winning comedy *Ma Rainey's Black Bottom* is set in the Paramount recording studio in Chicago, and features Rainey and her band members in conflict with one another and the white management who made money from her records. The play was first performed at the Yale Repertory Theater in 1984, before opening on Broadway at the Cort Theater in 1985.

Although Rainey's recording career ended in 1928, she toured for another seven years. After her mother and sister died in 1935, she retired to her hometown of Columbus and bought a house and two theaters, which she operated. She was also an active member in the Congregation of Friendship, a Baptist church where her brother was the deacon. On December 22, 1939, Rainey died of heart failure; an obituary in the local paper described this great blues singer and businesswoman as a "housekeeper."

## Lucille Bogan

Lucille Bogan was born Lucille Anderson in Amory, Mississippi, on April 1, 1897. She married Nazareth Lee Bogan Sr.; bore a son, Nazareth Bogan Jr.; and inherited a daughter, Ira Betty, through her husband's first marriage. In 1916 Bogan's family moved to Birmingham, Alabama, where she became active in the vibrant music scene. In 1923 she recorded her first songs, "Lonesome Daddy Blues" and "Pawn Shop Blues," with pianist Eddie Heywood Sr., on the Okeh label in Atlanta, but it wasn't until she moved to Chicago in 1927, where she recorded for Paramount and Brunswick, that she had her first big hit, "Sweet Petunia."

Bogan, who also recorded under the name Bessie Jackson, was a tough cookie, and her songs tackled taboo subjects head on: abusive men, alcoholism, drug addiction, prostitution, and lesbianism all featured in her repertoire. Often she would sing from the point of view of the prostitute, as in "Tricks Ain't Walking No More"; "Baking Powder Blues" is about her cocaine dealer.

In her famous raunchy song, "Shave 'Em Dry," which she recorded more than once, one version starts with the lyrics:

I got nipples on my titties, big as the end of my thumb,
I got somethin' between my legs that'll make a dead man cum,
Oh daddy, baby won't you shave 'em dry?

Even though she was not a lesbian herself, Bogan recorded the classic "B. D. Woman's Blues" in Chicago in 1935 with Walter Roland on piano; B. D. stands for "bulldyke" or "bulldagger":

Comin' a time, B. D. women, they'n't gon' need no men.
Comin' a time, B. D. women, they'n't gon' to need no men . . .

B. D. women, B. D. women, you know they sure is rough.
They all drink up plenty whiskey, and they sure will strut their stuff.
B. D. women, you know they work and make their dough.
B. D. women, you know they work and make their dough.
And when they get ready to spend it, they know just where to go.

Like many other women blues singers, Bogan's recording career ended in the late 1930s, when the times and musical tastes changed, although she still wrote songs and had them recorded by others until she died in Los Angeles in 1948.

## Sissy Man Blues

Among the male blues singers who made reference to homosexuals in their songs were "Peg Leg" Powell in "Fairy Blues" and Bert "Snake Root" Hatton in "Freakish Rider Blues." In another hokum song, "Garbage Man (The Call of the Freaks)," sung first by the Harlem Hamfats and covered by several artists, the chorus goes: "Stick out your can, here comes the garbage man." And Rufus "Speckled Red" Perryman in his song "Dirty Dozens" sings:

Now I liked your mama, liked your sister too
I used to like your daddy, but your daddy wouldn't do,
I met your daddy on the corner the other day,
You know about that, he was funny that way.

Several artists recorded the song "Sissy Man Blues," but it was the straight Josh White who is probably the most famous. In the song he complains about losing his "gal," so he sets out to find another one with little success: "The good book tells me I've got a woman in this world somewhere," he sings, and then in a state of heightened sexual frustration:

I woke up this morning with my "poor kinda business" in my hand.
God, if you can't send me no woman,
Then send me a sissy man.

One blues singer whose life story seems to have been lost in the mists of time was the hermaphrodite Guildford "Peachtree" Payne, a man gifted with women's breasts (peaches) and male genitals. He recorded a song for the Okeh label in 1923 called "Peachtree Man Blues" singing about his "predicament":

My home aint here, it's down in Peach Tree land.
Everyone down home calls me that Brownskin Peach Tree man.

Openly gay bluesman George Hannah performed mostly in Harlem, but it was in Chicago that he recorded his songs, including "Freakish Man Blues," for Paramount in October 1930, with Chicago-born pianist Meade "Lux" Lewis.

She call me a freakish man, what more was there to do?
Just 'cause she said I was strange, that did not make it true.

I sent her to the mill to have her coffee ground.
'Cause my wheel was broke and my grinder could not be found.

There was a time when I was alone, my freakish ways to treat.
But they're so common now, you get one every day of the week.

A year later he recorded "The Boy in the Boat," his homage to blossoming lesbian love while the men were away fighting for Uncle Sam in World War I:

When you see two women walkin' hand-in-hand,
Just look 'em over and try to understand.
They all go to these parties, have the lights down low.
Only those parties where women can go.
You think I'm lying just ask Tacky Ann.
They took many a broad from many a man.

Although blues never disappeared in Chicago, much of it was siphoned off, bleached whiter than white, then watered down and handed over to the likes of Bing Crosby and Frank Sinatra, but the insipid ditties of the Rat Pack crooners were no substitute for the outspoken songs of Ma Rainey, Bessie Smith, George Hannah, and all the other lesbian and gay blues singers.

## Tony Jackson

It's a myth that jazz came to Chicago in 1917 when an influx of unemployed musicians arrived from New Orleans after the closure of Storyville, the city's notorious vice district. The truth is that jazz was played in Chicago long before that. While Storyville was still open, jazz and ragtime flourished in Chicago's gritty night spots like the Pekin Theater, De Luxe, and Elite clubs on the city's South Side, and by the end of World War I more elegant clubs like Royal Gardens, the Sunset Café, and the Dreamland Ballroom opened, catering to white "slummers" and "good-timers" visiting from the North Side.

In New Orleans, aside from sexual adventures, Storyville offered the best in jazz. Black musicians, unable to find regular work in other parts of the city, performed in the saloons and brothels. Although jazz was played in pre-Storyville New Orleans, and considered respectable, it was in the sexually charged "anything goes" atmosphere of open vice that the music took shape and grew. The greatest "professor" in Storyville was pianist and composer Tony Jackson, whom Jelly Roll Morton, not given to taking a back seat, credited with being the only piano player better than him. In Al Rose's book *Storyville, New Orleans* (1979), Morton describes Jackson as "real dark and not a bit good-looking, but he had a beautiful disposition. He was the outstanding favorite of New Orleans. . . . He had a beautiful voice and a marvelous range. His voice on an opera song was exactly as an opera singer. His range on a blues would be just exactly like a blues singer. . . . Tony happened to be one of those gentlemen that a lot of people call a lady or sissy . . . that was the cause of him going to Chicago. . . . He liked the freedom there."

Clarence Williams, another Storyville pianist, lauded Jackson's virtuosity, portraying him as an effeminate man whose style everyone copied. Jackson was born into a poor family in New Orleans on June 5, 1876. At age three he was the only male in the household, as his father and twin brother had died. His overly protective mother and four sisters shielded him from rough elements in the neighborhood, and he spent most of his time alone. At the age of five he showed a talent for music, and at ten he built a crude harpsichord from scrap, on which he entertained his family with hymns he heard in church. After New Orleans bandleader Adam Olivier heard Jackson play, he arranged for him to hone his skills in a saloon before it opened for business. At age fifteen, Jackson was considered the greatest musician in New Orleans and could play and sing anything from opera to ragtime.

Although Jackson's voice was never recorded, several of his songs appear on disc sung by others, often credited to a white composer. Jackson penned his most famous song, "Pretty Baby," for his male lover. However, when it was picked up for Fanny Brice to sing in Schubert's Passing Show, the lyrics were rewritten by Gus Kahn to fit Brice's wholesome image. Co-credited with writing the music was Egbert Van Alstyne, who had nothing to do with it, as Jackson was singing the song years before at Frank Early's My Place in New Orleans. In the *Chicago Defender* of February 3, 1917, composer Eddie Gray sends "An Epistle" from Havana, Cuba: "Here is a word of warning to all the Race's music and song writers: Beware of Jerome, Remmick & Co., in submitting manuscripts, I saw Tony Jackson's 'Pretty Baby' over here and the dance arrangement of it and Tony's name was entirely missing from the copy, no one's name but Van Alstyne & Mose

Gomery. I make this statement without fear of contradiction; the only firm I know that will give us a fair chance is the McKinley Company and possibly Will Rossiter."

In 1952 the song featured in the musical biopic *I'll See You in My Dreams*, starring Doris Day as Grace LeBoy Kahn, wife of Gus Kahn, who was played by Danny Thomas. "Pretty Baby" entered the repertoire of many singers over the years, including Dean Martin and Frank Sinatra. In the late 1930s Jelly Roll Morton recorded two other Jackson songs, "Michigan Water Blues" and "The Naked Dance." It wasn't only Jackson's music that influenced other musicians, but also his clothes, as he started the craze among ragtime pianists of wearing a gray derby, checkered vest, ascot tie, diamond stick pin, and garters on his arms to keep his sleeves up.

Jackson left New Orleans in 1904 and toured with the Whitman Sisters, including gigs in Chicago. The four sisters, billed as the "Royalty of Negro Vaudeville," were Mabel, the business brains behind the company; Essie, a comic singer; Alberta or "Bert," a male impersonator; and the youngest sister, Alice, was a tap dancer. The Whitman Sisters entertained for forty years, until in the late 1930s when they retired to Chicago as wealthy women. Bert Whitman, who married at least twice, also wore men's clothes off stage. Onstage she sang the male parts in duets with her sister Essie. Bert spent her final years living with her sister Alice at 425 East 48th Street in Chicago and died at age seventy-four in June 1964 at Cook County Hospital. Her body was taken to Atlanta and buried in the family plot.

In 1912 Tony Jackson settled in Chicago, working at a South Side bordello in the Levee District called Dago Frank's with a new singer in town, a sixteen-year-old Alberta Hunter, who only knew two songs, "All Night Long" and "When the River Shannon Flows." In *Hear Me Talkin' To Ya: The Story of Jazz as Told by the Men Who Made It* (1966), edited by Nat Shapiro and Nat Hentoff, Hunter remembers Jackson:

> Everybody would go hear Tony Jackson after hours. Tony was just marvelous—a fine musician, spectacular, but still soft. He could write a song in two minutes, and was one of the greatest accompanists I've ever listened to. . . . He had mixed hair and always had a drink on the piano—always! . . . Yes, Tony Jackson was a prince of a fellow, and he would always pack them in. There would be so many people around the piano trying to learn his style

that sometimes he could hardly move his hands—and he never played any song the same way twice.

After the vice squad closed Dago Frank Lewis's place, Jackson played at the Elite Café, the Grand, and the Pekin Inn through 1914. On February 17, 1921, William Bottom's Dreamland Café held a benefit for Jackson, who was seriously ill, with cabaret and vaudeville stars taking part, as well as famous boxers and wrestlers, with the proceeds going to care for "Tony." It was thought to be syphilis, incurable at the time. Tony Jackson died on April 21, 1921, at age forty-four. His funeral was held in the chapel of the Jackson Undertaking Parlor, 29th and State Streets, and was conducted by the Reverend H. E. Stewart, pastor of Quinn Chapel Church, with Miss Lizzie Hart Dorsey singing the Rosary. Among those attending were piano player Clarence Williams, Lovey Joe, Lilly Smith, Teenan Jones, Tom Lemonier, and members of the New Orleans Jazz Orchestra. Jackson was interred in Oakwood Cemetery.

## Alberta Hunter

Alberta Hunter was born in Memphis in 1895, the daughter of a brothel maid on Beale Street. At age twelve she either ran away to Chicago or came with her teacher, Florida Cummings-Elgerton, depending on which story you believe. After singing in low dives she became a star at the Elite, Panama, and De Luxe clubs, before hitting the big time at the Dreamland Ballroom, billed as the "Sweetheart of Dreamland." Hunter married young, but it ended quickly. Soon afterward, she met Lottie Tyler, and they became lovers. Later, Hunter and Tyler were Harlem socialites and treated as a couple in the weekly *Chicago Defender* New York Society column. On May 12, 1923, they appeared together at the tenth annual fashion show of the Utopia Neighborhood Club at Madison Square Garden, where Hunter was singled out for her stunning headgear made of henna horsehair net, trimmed with currants. On July 7, 1923, it was reported: "Miss Alberta Hunter and Miss Lottie Tyler, 225 W. 129th Street spent the weekend at Long Beach as the guests of Mrs. Bert Williams at her summer home." Then in November 1929 Hunter and Tyler, with gay writers Carl Van Vechten and Langston Hughes, attended a recital by Paul Robeson at the Carnegie Music Hall.

In 1921, Hunter left Chicago for New York, signing her first record contract with Paramount in July 1922. New York fell in love with Hunter's gutsy voice, and she was soon on Broadway, then London's Drury Lane where she played opposite Paul Robeson in *Show Boat*, and then to the Folies Bergère in Paris. She was a songwriter too. Bessie Smith recorded Hunter's "Down Hearted Blues."

Early in the 1950s Hunter quit singing to care for her ailing mother until she died in 1956, after which the erstwhile "Sweetheart of Dreamland" became a nurse at New York's Goldwater Memorial Hospital on Welfare Island until she retired at age eighty-one in 1977. That was the year she returned to the stage at the Cookery in Greenwich Village. The first song she sang on her opening night was "Down Hearted Blues," and she continued singing her raunchy blues and ballads until she died on October 17, 1984, at age eighty-eight.

## Ethel Waters

Another singer who honed her skills in Chicago's South Side clubs was Ethel Waters, a regular at the Monogram Theatre at 3435–40 South State Street. Waters was the first "real" woman to sing "St. Louis Blues," possibly the most famous blues song ever written. The song was published in 1914 and first sung by a female impersonator named Charles Anderson, famous for his yodels and mammy routine. In her autobiography *His Eye Is on the Sparrow* (1951) Waters writes that after hearing the song she got permission to use it: "That was how I, a seventeen-year-old novice, became the first woman—and the second person—ever to sing professionally that song which is now a classic."

Waters was born on October 31, 1896, in Chester, Pennsylvania, the product of her mother's brutal rape at knifepoint at the age of twelve. At thirteen Waters married Merritt Purnsley, an abusive man, whom she divorced after two years. It was while working as a chambermaid in Philadelphia that Waters sang in public for the first time at her seventeenth-birthday Halloween party. In the crowd were Clarence Braxton and Arthur Nugent, two popular vaudevillians, who hired her to join their act at the Lincoln Theatre in Baltimore. On account of her slight figure, Waters was billed as "Sweet Mama Stringbean," singing songs with titles like "Come Right in and Stay a While," "There Aint Nobody Here but Me," and "I'm Gonna

Shake That Tree until the Nuts Come Down." In 1921 Waters signed a contract with a clause promising she wouldn't marry for one year and that she would devote her time solely to Black Swan Records. The no-marriage clause was no problem as Waters's sweetheart was dancer Ethel Williams.

Waters made her debut in Chicago with her Black Swan Troubadours at the Grand Theatre on January 16, 1922. Often described as a diva with a violent temper, the title of Waters's signature tune, "Stormy Weather," could describe her turbulent relationship with Ethel Williams, whom she openly fought with in public. Not only was she "out" about her female lover but would play it up onstage, asking band members, "Where's that partner of mine? Where's that Ethel Williams?" The June 3 *Chicago Defender* described Williams as "almost white, with the form of a Venus and the eyes of a devil." Her act, which involved a lot of "shimmies and shivers," debuted in Chicago at the National Theatre, Halsted and 63rd in March 1914 when she was touring with the Darktown Follies in a cast of sixty other "coloreds" in a show called *My Friend from Kentucky*.

After settling in New York, Waters contributed to the creative vitality of the Harlem Renaissance and its homosexual subculture; she was known to loan her gowns to drag queens who frequented Edmond's Cellar at 132nd Street and Fifth Avenue. In April 1933 Waters first sang "Stormy Weather" at the Cotton Club, leading to her acting and singing career "crossing over"; on Broadway and in movies she was the first black woman to receive equal billing with white performers, albeit it in mammy roles. In 1939 she made two experimental TV shows, *The Ethel Waters Show* and *Mamba's Daughters*; then from 1950 to 1952 she appeared in the successful sitcom *Beulah*. In the late 1960s and 1970s she fell on hard times, singing at evangelist Billy Graham's Crusades, the only work she could get. Ethel Waters died penniless on September 1, 1977, in Chatsworth, California, at the age of eighty.

# 11

# Powder Puffs

In the late 1920s and early 1930s the Pansy Craze was the latest fad; a Chicago newspaper caused the "Rudolph Valentino Powder Puff Scandal," while a host of characters inhabited Chicago's pansy parlors, like Diamond Lil's, and sang along to "They call me Del Monte because I'm the sweetest fruit in town" at the Ballyhoo Café.

On July 18, 1926, while touring to promote *The Son of the Sheik*, silent movie star Rudolph Valentino became enraged when he read an unflattering editorial in the *Chicago Tribune* headlined "Pink Powder Puffs":

> A new public ballroom was opened on the north side a few days ago, a truly handsome place and apparently well run. The pleasant impression lasts until one steps into the men's washroom and finds there on the wall a contraption of glass tubes and levers and a slot for the insertion of a coin. The glass tubes contain a fluffy pink solid, and beneath them one reads an amazing legend which runs something like this: "Insert coin. Hold personal puff beneath the tube. Then pull the lever." A powder vending machine! In a men's washroom! Homo Americanus! Why didn't someone quietly drown Rudolph Guglielmo, alias Valentino, years ago?
>
> And was the pink powder machine pulled from the wall or ignored? It was not. It was used. We personally saw two "men"—as young lady contributors to the Voice of the People are wont to

describe the breed—step up, insert coin, hold kerchief below the spout, pull the lever, then take the pretty pink stuff and pat it on their cheeks in front of the mirror.

Another member of this department, one of the most benevolent men on earth, burst raging into the office the other day because he had seen a young "man" combing his pomaded hair in the elevator. But we claim our pink powder story beats his all hollow.

It is time for a matriarchy if the male of the species allows such things to persist. Better a rule by masculine women than by effeminate men. Man began to slip, we are beginning to believe, when he discarded the straight razor for the safety pattern. We shall not be surprised when we hear that the safety razor has given way to the depilatory.

Who or what is to blame is what puzzles us. Is this degeneration into effeminacy a cognate reaction with pacifism to the virilities and realities of the war? Are pink powder and parlor pinks in any way related? How does one reconcile masculine cosmetics, sheiks, floppy pants, and slave bracelets with a disregard for law and an aptitude for crime more in keeping with the frontier of a half a century ago than a twentieth century metropolis?

Do women like the type of "man" who pats pink powder on his face in a public washroom and arranges his coiffure in a public elevator? Do women at heart belong to the Wilsonian era of "I Didn't Raise My Boy to Be a Soldier"? What has become of the old caveman line? It is a strange social phenomenon and one that is running its course not only here in America but in Europe as well. Chicago may have its powder puffs; London has its dancing men and Paris its gigolos. Down with Decatur; up with Elinor Glyn. Hollywood is the national school of masculinity. Rudy, the beautiful gardener's boy, is the prototype of the American male.

Hells bells. Oh, sugar.

The criticism didn't sit well with Valentino, who responded by challenging the author to a duel. Valentino's friends rallied to his defense, claiming the "Latin Lover" was "a real man." The following day, Rudy called the *Chicago Herald-Examiner* and made a public statement calling the anonymous writer of the *Chicago Tribune* a coward and challenged him to appear at a designated time and place to settle this insult man to man. Rudy never forgot nor forgave this insult.

Journalist, editor, and critic H. L. Mencken wrote of meeting Valentino in New York soon after the "Powder Puff" incident and advising him to ignore the pansy slur, but the furious actor wouldn't let it drop; some say the lady doth protest too much. This incident took place shortly before the "pansy craze," a brief period in the early 1930s when effeminate men were de rigueur. The *Chicago Tribune* writer's opinion was typical for the period; Valentino's dark passionate eroticism attracted women and gay men, but to the red-blooded all-American male the smoldering sexuality of the Italian actor's effeminate on-screen persona posed a threat.

Valentino was born Rodolfo Alfonzo Raffaele Pierre Philibert Guglielmi on May 6, 1895, in Castellaneta, Italy, and after attending the Royal School of Agriculture in Genoa, moved to Paris before immigrating to New York in 1917, where he supported himself as a landscape gardener, dishwasher, tango dancer, gigolo, and petty criminal. As a gigolo he sold himself to both men and women and is rumored to have sunk to the depths of using blackmail. The former gigolo didn't help his reputation as a hot-blooded Latin male by sharing his life and films with lesbians and female impersona-tors. In 1919 he married lesbian starlet Jean Acker, a marriage that lasted a few hours, and then in 1922 he married bisexual dancer and set designer Natacha Rambova in Mexico. It was Rambova who encouraged him to play effeminate dandies and fops. After their divorce Valentino returned to masculine roles for his last two movies, *The Eagle* (1925) and *Son of the Sheik* (1926), but it was too late: he was already a tainted "painted pansy."

In his early films Valentino played small parts as shifty-eyed Latin lovers, but his career took off in 1921 when he was cast as Julio in *The Four Horse-man of the Apocalypse*; look for the butch/femme lesbian couple in the audience in the Paris nightclub scene. Valentino caused a sensation in his next film, *The Sheik* (1921), which inspired a furniture and clothes fad for all things Arab. A cursory glance through the Chicago newspapers saw a glut of ads for cash-in films like *The Queen of Sheba* (1921), and *One Arabian Night* (1920) starring Pola Negri, another of the lavender satellites orbiting Planet Valentino.

In 1920 the female impersonator Julian Eltinge starred in the movie *The Adventuress*, with the unknown Valentino taking a minor role, but three years later the film was rereleased as *Isle of Love* to cash in on the success of *The Sheik*. A review in the *Chicago Tribune* of February 11, 1923, was dismissive of Valentino's role, saying he appears "only twice, or perhaps three times" and that honors went to the real star of the film, Julian Eltinge: "The acting is all pretty good," the paper writes. "Mr. Eltinge is a nice looking man and a beautiful woman." Another female impersonator Valentino worked with was Ray Bourbon in *Blood and Sand* (1922); in an early scene Bourbon dies in the arms of Valentino, who plays Spain's greatest matador. Bourbon's sad and bizarre life began in 1892 in Texarkana, Texas. His birth name was Hal Wadell, and he became stage struck while at school in London, or so the story he told goes. What is known is that between 1922 and 1924 he toured in a vaudeville act with Bert Sherry, who played the straight man to Bourbon's outrageous potty-mouthed drag queen. In the late 1920s he performed his camp drag act in Chicago at one of Capone's speakeasies; the name and location is unknown, but it was most likely the K-9 Club at 105 East Walton.

In the 1940s Bourbon appeared in hundreds of gay clubs, but in March 1945 he was back in Chicago at the Studebaker Theatre as Florian in Mae West's *Catherine Was Great* with West playing the lead; Claudia Cassidy, in the *Chicago Tribune* on March 13, described West's performance as that of "an opulent damsel with bunions, her illustrious orbs lurk beneath leering brows, and like Pooh Bah, she was born sneering." Of Bourbon's acting: "Ray Bourbon is there, of course, primed and painted for the 'modiste' who make effeminate a word women ought to be able to sue." The review by Claudia Cassidy was headlined: "Mae West as a Connoisseur, Pronounced Sewer, of Amour . . ."

Over the course of his career Bourbon recorded dozens of albums—risqué "blue" party records sold mostly at his performances. Like all openly gay performers in the mid-twentieth century, Bourbon was hit by the McCarthy witch hunts and clamp down on "homosexual haunts," drag shows in particular. In the 1950s his career took a nosedive as club owners buckled under the weight of "Reds under the Bed" Cold War hysteria.

In May 1956 Bourbon tried to revive his career by jumping on the Christine Jorgensen bandwagon and telling the *New York Journal American* and *Variety* that he had undergone a sex-change operation. He hadn't. This was a ruse to get around the draconian antidrag laws: if he was a "real woman," he couldn't be "impersonating" a woman and he wasn't in drag. In July 1956 he was booked into Chicago's Brass Rail, at Randolph and Dearborn Streets, as "Rae Bourbon 'That Different Person.'" After the faux sex and name change Bourbon recorded an album of gender-bending skits called *Take a Look at My Operation*, but the name "Rae" Bourbon and the novelty of sex change confused the club owners; one advertised him as "Rae Bourbon—NOT a female impersonator."

Bourbon's bizarre life ended on January 19, 1971, in Howard County prison in Texas. Four years earlier he was driving across country in a car pulling a trailer containing his seventy dogs. When the car broke down in Texas he left the dogs with local kennel owner A. D. Blount. When Bourbon returned for the dogs some months later, he found that Blount, having received no money for their upkeep, had sold the dogs to a research facility. Incensed, Bourbon hired two men, Bobby Eugene Chrisco and Randall Crane, to rough Blount up and teach him a lesson, but the men killed him instead. Chrisco, Crane, and Bourbon were convicted of murder; Bourbon received ninety-nine years. He died at age seventy-eight while his case was on appeal.

Diamond Lil named himself after the Mae West play of the same name that opened in New York in April 1928; a year later it ran for fourteen weeks at the Apollo in Chicago. Lil opened a gay establishment at 909 North Rush Street on Monday, October 15, 1928. The club offered "Real Southern Cooking" from 5:00 p.m. to 9:00 p.m. and same-sex dancing later in the evening.

While studying urban homosexuals at the University of Chicago's School of Sociology, Constance Weinberger and Saul Alinsky, students of the groundbreaking urban sociologist Ernest Burgess, visited the Rush Street club and wrote:

> Diamond Lil's is not properly a dance hall. It is only because of its peculiar interest and because of its possession of one feature of the true dance hall, that we have taken the liberty of including it. It is owned and managed by Roy Spencer Bartlett, known as "Diamond Lil," after Mae West's play of that name now running in New York unless it has been closed by the police. This place is going into its third month of existence, and seems to be making a huge success. On Saturday nights by two o'clock they are filled up and people are turned away. Lil says his plan is to lease the entire building (he now has only the first floor) and to have dancing upstairs. He is, he asserts confidently, keeping strictly within the law. He serves no ginger ale, in fact nothing but coffee and sandwiches, in spite of the somewhat ambiguous menu. What liquor is consumed there is brought in and the management disclaims responsibility. The place is frequented by homosexuals. Not many women go there. Until very recently, there was a room at the back where

men danced together, but because Lil had no license for running a dance place, the police stopped this. When the place was enlarged, there will be dancing, Lil says; what kind he does not specify. Maxwell Bodenheim was there one night, and a man whose stage name is Crane Gilbert. The crowd is extremely Bohemian, although there are a lot of college men there.

The point this place has in common with the dance hall is that it is a place of meeting. Everyone turns to look at newcomers. Everyone stares quite boldly at everyone else, and if you want to talk to a person across the room or at the next table you simply walk over and begin talking. Many of these men appear to wear cosmetics. A lot of them wear slave bracelets, and other jewelry. Frequently they call each other by pet names. Lil wears a red tie with a huge imitation diamond stick pin. He makes no attempt to conceal what sort of a place it is, in fact, by the use of such a name, he advertises it. On the night Bodenheim was there, he was arguing about whether a woman would prefer for a lover a stupid man who was physically perfect or a genius who was deformed. He asked the women present what their preference would be. The place is faintly amusing, if you have that kind of a sense of humor.

In the 1920s and '30s the University of Chicago's Department of Sociology led the world in urban studies, with much of its research overseen by Ernest Burgess. Although Canadian by birth, Burgess grew up in the Midwest and was a graduate student in sociology at the University of Chicago from 1908 to 1912, receiving his PhD in 1913. After teaching at Toledo University in Ohio, he became assistant professor of sociology at Ohio State University. In 1916, at the age of thirty, he was appointed assistant professor of sociology of the University of Chicago, advancing to associate professor in 1921 and full professor in 1927, where he remained until he retired in 1952.

Burgess's expertise was crime and juvenile delinquency; in the late 1920s he sent his students out to study homosexuals. Weinberger and Alinsky's report on Diamond Lil's mentions seeing writer Max Bodenheim and actor/writer Crane Gilbert in the club; Gilbert was a "character" on the streets of Towertown; in today's parlance he was a media whore. The *Chicago Tribune* reported on May 13, 1928: "Police who picked up actor Crane Gilbert lying on a vacant lot manifested no sympathy at all, but held him, instead, for questioning." Gilbert claimed he was "kid-napped, drugged and slugged," but the cops decided it was a self-promoting publicity stunt; a threatening note pinned to Gilbert's coat was in the victim's own handwriting. Casting further doubt on the story was a similar occurrence five weeks earlier in San Francisco, when Gilbert vanished from his hotel leaving an overcoat and belongings. The San Francisco police launched a murder inquiry, but three days later, when the incident didn't produce the desired headlines, Gilbert turned up at the hotel to claim his coat. The police were not amused. Another staged crime in April 1931 was so transparently fake that the *Chicago Tribune* headline read: "Writer of Plays Casts Himself in Real Life Role"; the article begins: "If the next work from the pen of playwright Crane Gilbert . . . is a melodrama, Mr. Gilbert has available the episode of a lady gunman taken from real life." Gilbert spun this tale:

> I was walking home and at Elm street and Lake Shore Drive I met a young man who spoke pleasantly. We engaged in a brief conversation. When it was finished I started to walk on and a little way off I saw a woman who seemed to be in distress. As I walked over to her I took off my hat. I asked her what I could do to help her. She drew a pistol and said that it would help her if I gave her money. I gave it to her—$38.
>
> "Is that all she took?" asked a sympathetic sergeant.
>
> "No," said Mr. Gilbert," I forgot to tell you. She took my $1,200 diamond ring, too."

Aside from publicity stunts, Gilbert had other talents; in July 1928 he starred in his self-penned play *Driftwood*, staged by the Jack and Jill Theater in the French Room at the Drake Hotel. He was also a Chicago barometer of fashion, with his gaudy outfits written up in gossip columns. At the 1933 Century of Progress International Exposition, or World's Fair, he was seen sitting with Mary Pickford on a roller chair ride. Pickford was holding a notebook and was overheard telling Gilbert they ought to check the exhibits as they saw them. The "Front Views and Profiles" column by June Provines in the *Chicago Tribune* on July 9, 1934, reads: "Mr. Gilbert, crossing his legs to reveal checked socks that matched his shirt, tie and the handkerchief in the breast pocket of his navy blue linen suit, answered: 'I've checked and double-checked.'" Later, when a fan introduced himself to

Pickford calling her a shining light, the actress pointed to Gilbert and said, "I'm not a shining light, today I'm playing second fiddle to a wardrobe." Less than two weeks later Provines noted that Gilbert was again seen at the World's Fair, wearing "a suit of baby blue whipcord, with a pale white corded stripe, a baby blue shirt, tie, and handkerchief to match, and socks and shoes of baby blue. He had with him a baby blue camel's hair coat with pearl buttons."

On December 10, 1930, *Variety* published an article headlined "Pansy Parlors—Tough Chicago Has Epidemic of Male Butterflies":

World's toughest town, Chicago, is going pansy. And liking it.

Within the past six months some 35 new dim lit tea rooms, operated by boys who won't throw open the doors until at least two hours have been spent adjusting the drapes just so, have opened on the near North Side. The South Side of Chi, always reputed to be ready for battle any minute, also has had an increase of these sort of joints.

All have waitresses who are lads in girl's clothing. They are strong on the urge for single young men to sip tea in the little booths that line the walls of the spots.

Men with femme companions are welcome in these joints. Likewise all have duke readers. The readers pass for femmes in the dark.

Racketeers, who have made the near North Side their playground for some years, have gone strong for these boy joints in a big way. It's evidently something new for these gun-totin' lads and they are supporting them nobly for the laughs.

One pansy nightclub in the early 1930s was the Ballyhoo Café at 1942 North Halsted, managed by Marge and Mack, a lesbian and a gay man. Entertainment included Frankie and Johnnie, a gay couple. The late historian Gregory Sprague wrote in the *Advocate* on August 18, 1983:

They performed at the Ballyhoo as well as at other gay nightclubs and private parties. Their campy jokes and songs, usually in the gay slang of the period, were in great demand. The following lyrics are from a song sung by Frankie and Johnnie at a wild private party in the early 1930s.

Father Spanish, Mother Greek and I'm French.
They call me Del Monte because I'm the sweetest fruit in town.
Fairytown, fairytown, that's where all the boys go down.

Whoops! My dear.
Whoops! My dear, even the Chief of Police is queer.
When the sailors come to town—lots of brown, lots of brown.
Holy by Jesus
Everybody's got pareses in Fairy Town.

One of Burgess's students reported on a visit he made to the Ballyhoo September 24, 1933:

There were about 100 queer people in the café at the time I arrived—about 75 queer fellows and 25 queer girls. The hostess dressed in masculine style was queer as well as the male mc. Their names are Mack and Marge and are quite popular among the group. Mack, who is six foot three inches tall, often did female impersonations. His most popular number was "Alice in the Little Blue Gown." From appearance one could judge some of the fellows queer. The queer girls could be judged in a like fashion. A few of the queer fellows danced with the queer girls but for the most part the boys danced together—likewise the girls.

There was a good deal of laughter and singing in the place. Some of the boys sang out in what is known as "high c"—yelled at the top of their voices, rather effeminately.

Beer was served at 5 cents a glass—with no cover charge. The queer girls (mentes) who sat next to our table had a large bottle of gin which they drank throughout the whole evening, becoming partially intoxicated.

I asked one of the queer girls to dance with me and accepting she discussed some Jam people who were present at the cafe. She told me that queer people despise jam people.

On another visit, the student wrote:

As I passed through the entrance into the café, I noticed a rather good-looking woman dressed in an evening gown. As to her build, she was plump. I was much surprised when she called me by name and said, "Why, don't you know me?" I said, "No." Then he established his identity. It was Malliard whom I had met a few months previous. I congratulated him on his make-up, dress and his impersonation—the best I had seen.

In the middle of the floor, there was a homosexual dressed in a costume made entirely of paper. He sang in a deep voice, and his actions impersonated a woman. Slowly pulling off his paper dress, he showed his hips. Then he pulled up the upper part of his dress and showed in full view his back. The crowd, composed of many jam people, gave him a good hand.

Later, Mack, the master of ceremonies . . . gave his number. Dressed in female costume, he impersonated a woman and walked gracefully about the room making wisecracks. Someone in the crowd called out for him to give the "Alice in Her Little Blue Gown" number. As he sang the song he made gestures toward his lower extremities.

> Then in fashion it grew,
> and I did, do doodle do.

Etc.

The crowd laughed and gave him a hearty applause.

> I will wear it and adore it

Etc.

As he sang this, he placed one of his hands upon his anus. As an encore he sang the same song, only putting it in the present tense. After this number, he announced that the drag parade was about to start. There were six homosexuals in female costume, and three mentes in male attire. Each person presented himself to the crowd, walked around in a circle and then dismissed himself, the crowd expressing approval by hand claps. Each of the homosexuals, impersonated the role of a woman in accordance with his conception of the role. This conception was reflected in his impersonation . . . One in particular, who called himself "Perley" gave an interesting impersonation. As he walked around, he arched his back, tilted his head, and used his hands in an effeminate manner, gracefully. His role could be characterized as follows: A French demoiselle, aloof, smart, haughty, charming and graceful, head flung back. He had a very large hat which was tilted on his head, and which gave a smart effect. However, a fellow who they named Neomi (the fellow who met me at the door) was awarded a bottle of gin.

In the *Advocate* Sprague writes of the gay lexicon of the period:

By the 1930s the Chicago subculture had developed a complex, rich and specialized vocabulary. Some terms emphasized the difference between homosexuals and heterosexuals. Terms like gay, queer and temperamental were used by men from the subculture to differentiate themselves from heterosexuals, who were often called "jam." Labels like queen, belle, pansy and marge were applied to effeminate men. Auntie meant an older gay man who was interested in younger men. Bulldagger and mente meant lesbian. Dirt was a sex partner who would later blackmail or harm a gay individual. A tearoom was a public rest room where sexual contact was made. Words like butch (masculine characteristics) and swishy (effeminate gestures) labeled mannerisms. Plain sewing (masturbation), browning (anal intercourse), and Frenching (fellatio) were all slang words for sex acts. Coming out was defined by a gay man of the period as "you realize that there are other temperamentals like yourself."

A gay subculture existed in Chicago as early as 1889, when it first showed up on the radar of an inquisitive medical profession and the law. In April 1932 W. Beran Wolfe, MD, wrote an article for the *Modern Thinker*: "A few years ago the mention of the homosexual relationship was confined to textbooks of forensic medicine and the recondite volumes on sexual psychopathology, today every high school boy knows what a 'pansy' is; jokes about 'fairies' are to be heard on every vaudeville stage, and hardly a realistic novel is written in which a homosexual character, more or less thinly disguised, cannot be found. Before the War homosexuality was considered an exclusively foreign vice by the average American. Today homosexual 'drags,' homosexual plays, and homosexual clubs are known in every large American city."

Chicago was no exception.

# 12

# Gay Life in the 1930s

The K-9 Club, Chicago's drag speakeasy, was hopping until prohibition ended and it went legit; that's when Mayor Edward J. Kelly shut it down, as he later did with Lillian Hellman's play *The Children's Hour.* However, homosexual books began to be seen in libraries, and "temperamentals" still met at the bars, restaurants, bathhouses, beaches, and masquerade balls.

In the "Roaring Twenties" Chicago was hot for jazz, and smoky speakeasies, ballrooms, and dancehalls thrived in spite of prohibition, or in the case of speakeasies, because of it. The Volstead Act handed vice over to Al Capone and the profiteers; alcohol, gambling, and sex, including homosexuality, was controlled by the Mafia. It's rumored that one of Al Capone's cousins was homosexual and ran a mixed-race "buffet flat"—a brothel—on the South Side that hosted liquor and orgies. The late gay activist Jim Wickliff shared a story told to him: "I met one older guy and he really had a life, I suppose now we would call him a street person. He told me about a guy who owned a house maybe one block east of Lake Park in the 45th, 46th Street area, and he had a lot of Mafia friends, and he talked about going to parties there, and he said the whole house was fixed up like Arabian Nights, all kinds of brass things, hanging candles, and absolutely fantastic. And just about every night there was an orgy of some kind there. He would drop in and there were cops and Mafia guys."

Another story relates to an incident at a speakeasy, the K-9 Club at 105 East Walton. The female impersonators who worked there included Li-Kar, Billy Herrera, Johnny Mangum, Del LeRoy, Billy Russell, Art West, Billy Brennan, Billy Richards, and Earl Partello, with Sylvia Rose as the emcee. One night the club was raided by prohibition cops, and the "girls" fled the stage, out the back door, and down the fire escape. At the bottom a solitary cop waited to scoop them up, but Herrera whacked him over the head with a beer bottle, and they all lifted their skirts and escaped down an alley. When prohibition ended, the K-9 Club went legit as a drag bar/restaurant with Chinese cuisine and music by Bill Lyles and his orchestra. In June 1934 the K-9 advertised in the *Chicago American* as Chicago's "Oddest Nite Club" with a breakfast show every morning at 5:00 a.m. Five months later an ad read "PaLeeeze!! WHY SHOULD I BE MANNISH!" alongside a camp cartoon figure daintily waving a handkerchief. On December 8, 1934, Mayor Edward J. Kelly revoked the K-9's liquor, amusement, food, and cigarette licenses; the *Chicago Tribune* called the club an "eccentric night life rendezvous." Unable to find work, the performers scattered.

In the early part of the twentieth century, books on the subject of homosexuality were not available to the public, only to the medical profession. That changed in 1925 when the *Chicago Tribune* advertised *Homosexual Life* by William J. Fielding in the social hygiene section. You could only order the book through the mail from Haldeman-Julius Company in Girard, Kansas, purveyors of atheist and freethinker literature. By the late 1920s gay-themed books began to appear in Chicago's libraries and for sale in bookstores: *The Well of Loneliness* (1928) by Radclyffe Hall, *Strange Brother* by Blair Niles (1931), and *A Scarlet Pansy* by Robert Scully (1932). In 1930 Chicago's Eyncourt Press published the memoir *The Stone Wall* by Mary Casal. The book is a surprisingly frank account of a poor New England country girl and her life as a lesbian; on one of her partners she writes: "We decided that a union such as ours was to be made as holy and complete as the conventional marriages, if not more so." One intriguing mystery is why the book was published by Eyncourt Press in the first place, as their other books were on the history of printing.

Also available for purchase were under-the-counter French postcards. In his biography of Ben Reitman, *The Damndest Radical*, Roger A. Bruns writes that on August 5, 1937, Reitman, the syphilis doctor, took four public officials on a tour of sex spots: to Bughouse Square to lecture on VD, then to an illegal abortionist, and finally a pornographer called Hard-On-Slim. "'Are your pants buttoned,' Slim inquired of his guests as he darkened the room and rolled a movie showing two young men and a blond engaged in both heterosexual and homosexual sport."

Homosexual "haunts" in the 1930s included saloons, hotel bars, cafés, theaters, and restaurants. One venue where gay men met was the Casino Club in a basement at 4834 North Winthrop, which one visitor described as "a dingy place where they serve beer. The queens were groping each other and dancing together and acting very sissified." Cruising areas for men included public restrooms at train stations and the Public Library Building, State Street in the Loop, Michigan Avenue from Marshall Field's to the Drake Hotel, Bughouse Square, and Oak Street Beach. Sam, a "hoofer" in the last days of vaudeville, remembers cruising in the 1930s: "It was very strange, because you have to remember that this era was governed by a formidable paranoia. You were scared to death, and that's why it was hard to meet people. We met in parks after dark, and it was always dangerous . . . a lot of cruising on streets. You'd walk down Michigan Avenue, stop and look in a window, and somebody would come over and say something about a tie or jacket or something. There were two lines that always worked when cruising, and they were 'Have you got the time?' and the other was, 'Have you got a match?'"

To be obviously gay in the 1930s was to "drop your hairpins." Sam remembers living with the constant threat of violence: "Don't drop your hairpins, don't let it be known that you are looking, or that you're available in an active or a passive way. You could get beat up. You could be ridiculed, 'Hey, look at that queer over there.' Then everybody would start giving you a very, very bad time. It was very dangerous."

The late Charles B. remembers his first gay bar: "There was a bar on Rush Street for years, it was called Simon's and Ma and Pa Simon ran it, Ann and Sal. They had several bars in Chicago. I went in there once, I was about 17. . . . There used to be a lovely men's shop on Michigan Avenue called Gerard's, and my mother bought me a polo coat and a tie-over belt, and I wore it to Simon's all dressed up with a hat one night and they served me a beer and I got scared to death and I left. That was the first time."

Casual sexual encounters proved a portal into Chicago's gay underworld, a wider circle of friends and invitations to private parties. Though illegal, gay parties were popular, as men could dance together to the gay-themed songs of the period, like Beatrice Lillie's "There Are Fairies in the Bottom of My Garden." Lillie was a friend of Noël Coward, who once told her he would like to sing "There Are Fairies in the Bottom of My Garden," but he feared it would come out as "There Are Fairies in the Garden of My Bottom." Coward, incidentally, first appeared onstage in Chicago at the Selwyn Theatre in February 1926 in his own play *The Vortex*. Hannen Swaffer, a British writer, told the *Chicago Tribune* at the time that Coward's play made London's Mayfair district seem like it was inhabited solely by "adulterers, gigolos, dope-users and pansy-men."

One of Ernest Burgess's University of Chicago sociology students attended a gay party in the early 1930s and wrote:

When I arrived they introduced me to everybody by their first name. The party was sort of dead for about an hour. They talked about legitimate things. About three looked sissyfied. The rest were quite masculine, but I saw them necking one another. A fellow sat down near me and we started talking about swimming. Another fellow talked to me about school. He knew some girls up at my school. Then he started putting his hand on my leg. Then a girl came over and danced with me. She said that she could strip until perfectly nude and feel perfectly safe among these fellows. She said that she knew these fellows for a longtime. While the fellows were dancing, they started whooping it up and rubbed their penises together (socking it in. They still had on their clothes). They yelled: "Get hot. Get hot." There was three fellows dancing in costumes. One fellow had on a pair of tights. He's playing the leading role (dodger dance). The other fellow had on only a "g" string. The two did a regular dodger dance. One of the pair had on a shawl and was made up like a woman. They were announced as Mr. Fuck and Mr. Suck will do a number. Another fellow scantily clothe [*sic*] did a dance, shaking his fanny all around, like a rumba dance. He said it is tight but come and get it. I went out for a little walk. When I arrived back there were several new people at the party and the hostess (calling him so because they called him so being in drag) went around introducing me to new comers. There was another female impersonator at the party carrying on something mad, dressed in a long red taffeta dress full of ruffles with high neck low back and a very long train.

This fellow was very effeminate. In fact you could have really thought he was a woman. He had real long jewelry earrings, heavy make-up and a black wig done up in little curls at the back, just like the women are wearing today. This bitch went around trying to make and kiss everybody at the party, calling us dear and lovely, gorgou [sic] and what not. He went around passing nuts, saying, "These are the first nuts you have had in a long time." He was real good-looking, beautiful. You never knew he was a man. Well the party went on every body getting tighter and tighter and as for me I was even getting more sobber [sic]. At this time they were diving into couples, some of them were necking, some were dancing, and some had even left for the more private parties. This impersonator finally got his man and went off and partied. He also gave an interpretation of the rumba dance which he did very well, shooting his hands upward to and from his penis. His dress must have been very expensive, approximately costing $125.00. He is an entertainer at some club. There was a couple of jam people there who were greatly criticized.

## Turkish Bathhouses

Homosexual activity in the Roman Baths of the first century AD and in the hammans of Greece and Moorish Spain was an accepted fact; in the bathhouses of the puritanical United States not so much. On February 21, 1903, at New York City's Ariston Baths on West 55th Street, twenty-six men were arrested and seven received sentences of four to twenty years in jail. According to arrestees the cops knocked on cubicle doors and called "Come out here, Maude," and "Oh, there is the indignant lady" when the door opened.

In 1890s Chicago, the Lafayette Baths at 180 Wabash Avenue was notorious as a clandestine meeting place for homosexuals. In the early twentieth century, homosexual activity increased in Chicago's Turkish baths with the rise of indoor plumbing; men could bathe at home, and the necessity for public bathing tapered off, leaving the baths open for homosexual encounters. While some managers tried to curtail homosexual activity, others turned a blind eye; many got rich on the tips. Arthur Zwieback, operator of the Lincoln and Wacker Baths, lived a frugal existence, renting a $45-a-month room at the Lincoln Hotel at 1816 North Clark Street. Yet when he died in 1947, he left an estate of $110,860: $83,890 in $100, $50, and $20 bills in safety deposit boxes in the Cosmopolitan

National Bank and the First National Bank; $21,370 in savings and checking accounts; and $5,600 in war bonds. His attorney, Paul R. Goldman, had estimated Zwieback's estate at $15,000 and was surprised by his client's secret stash of money.

Whether Zwieback was gay or not is unknown, but his attorney Paul Goldman was known as the "fairy lawyer" throughout his fifty-six-year career. Goldman specialized in legal matters concerning gays. Though he was not gay himself, he was also a founding member of two gay groups: One of Chicago (1964) and Maturity (1975). Born in Chicago on February 2, 1907, Goldman was the son of a Jewish cobbler. In a 1979 *Chicago Tribune* interview, Goldman recalled focusing on gay issues after a much-loved college roommate committed suicide because of his homosexuality. After briefly working with a downtown law firm, Goldman opened his own offices at 100 North LaSalle Street with 90 percent of his clients gay; in criminal cases he preferred to reach plea agreements with prosecutors because gay clients were reluctant to appear in court, fearing their homosexuality would be made public. Reaching "plea agreements with prosecutors" was a nice way of saying that for $500 there's no way your client is getting off, for $750 there's a fairly good chance, but $1,000 will make it all go away. The client's money, of course, was divvied out to the police, the attorney, the judge, and sundry others.

In the 1930s several bathhouses in Chicago were popular meeting places for gay men: Jack's at Walton and Dearborn; the Lincoln Baths at 1812 North Clark Street closed down after multiple raids in the mid to late 1960s; the Wabash Baths at 28–32 East 8th Street was raided and closed January 23, 1976; and the Wacker Baths at 674 North Clark Street shut down in 1982. The Wacker Baths was also temporarily closed in March 1936, when Sergeant Frank O'Sullivan and his partner Thomas P. Lyons arrested three men for immoral practices after receiving complaints from customers. Judge Gibson E. Gorman imposed fines ranging from fifty to two hundred dollars, and Mayor Kelly revoked the premise's license.

## Masquerade Balls

Inspired by the harlot balls of Bathhouse John and Hinky Dink Kenna that ended in 1908, the city "tolerated" two drag balls a year, on Halloween and New Year's Eve; they continued until the mid-1970s. The South Side

Finnie's Ball started in 1935 and was run by a black committee, but the organizers of other masquerade balls in the 1930s remain a mystery; though the usual suspects—politicians, mob, and police—almost certainly had a hand in it.

Myles Vollmer, a divinity student at the University of Chicago and student of Ernest Burgess, attended "The New Year's Eve Drag" in the early 1930s and reported:

> Twice a year, with the knowledge and protection of Chicago's officialdom, do the homosexuals of the city gather in great numbers for their semi-annual costume ball, at which conventions and repressions are flung to the winds. New Year's Eve, and Halloween mark the occasions for the celebrations of the "shadow world."
>
> Picking our way carefully down South Wabash Avenue late New Year's Eve, through the "grey area" extending from Van Buren Street south, we arrived at the Coliseum Annex. The sidewalks and entrance to the hall were crowded with men hanging around, joking at the arrival of each newcomer in costume, overly eager to enter into conversation with you. Our guides told us that they were all "wise" and curious, some just looking on, others there for a possible pick up with some homosexual at the Drag, some there to prey on the less experienced boys who were inside cavorting to the music. We were soon to discover that where homosexuals congregate, there also are the racketeers, blackmailers, jackrollers, and all their ilk who prey on another's misfortune—made possible because a hypocritical society insists on calling homosexuality a "crime"—as though the poor unfortunates could help themselves!
>
> Entering the hall, one recognized at once the uniformed guards from the Chicago Stadium, very much in evidence, and also noted that they were selected for their size and by numerous uniformed policemen, and several plain-clothes men—for this was one occasion when official Chicago put its approval on the public appearance of its intermediate sex.
>
> Despite the rundown appearance of the Annex, it was an unusual and colorful sight—to see some five hundred persons dancing and standing about, swaying to the music of a colored jazz orchestra. It was a strange and unconventional sight, however, because

here we see two young men in street clothes dancing together, cheek to cheek, holding one another in close embrace, as any girl and boy would at any dance, save, perhaps, that the two youths were much more intense in their forbidden roles.

Here are two persons, both dressed in gorgeous evening gowns, one with a tiara, both in slim high French heeled satin slippers, and heavily jeweled, dancing together gracefully, without any suggestive movements. And both are men! Heavily powdered, with eye brows penciled and rouged lips and cheeks, their arms and hands making effeminate gestures, it is difficult to discern their true sex. One is clothed in what must have been a costly white evening satin gown, of the newest mode, form clinging at the hips, and falling in folds to the floor. The other is more colorful in a slim green gown with complementary accessories. One wears a titian colored wig, carefully arranged, to simulate his feminine role; the other is content to dance with only his gown and made up face. We learn that the "girl" in green is one of the theatrical world's best known female impersonators; but in the shadow world, "she" is just another "belle." The picture is repeated over and over—colorful evening gowns, satin slippers, French heels, silken hose, gracefully displayed, tiaras, feathered fans, flashing jewelry—all gliding about the hall. Gliding is the only name for it: no women could be more graceful. Trains are carefully held up by curled and manicured fingers. Couples dance together, swaying to every type of step, from the more restrained and dignified postures, to dancing of the most suggestive types. One sees two "girls" bowing courteously to one another, and a moment later, another couple—both young men, dancing cheek to cheek, bodies glued to one another in the most suggestive way. The "girls" (men homosexuals in female costume) move about swaying their shoulders, rolling their hips, and the only clue to their masculinity is their heavier skeletal frames, or occasionally a more masculine featured face.

Here is something else. Two young men, very slender, in sack suits well tailored, with ties and shirts well matched are dancing together. But they seem different from the other men in street clothes who are dancing together. This couple is too graceful for masculine movements. Then we see that they are two girls—both

127

lesbians, finely featured, with boyish bobbed haircuts, playing the role of young manhood. We begin to see many other similar couples together, lesbian girls with their lovers.

There are also the men in street clothes, lacking courage to come in drag, who are dancing with other men, occasionally embracing and kissing them in moments of abandon. Young effeminate lads, older men of more masculinity, and the old men, paunchy with bald heads and lustful expressions. These old men, we are told, are often businessmen with families, who have learned too late of their true sexual natures, and are now, rather pathetically, trying to make up for lost youth. Your information is true, for a moment later we see one of Chicago's well-known tradesman, a man of means, and a respected member of a north side church, dancing with a young pretty lad, and holding him in close embrace!

There are some pitiful creatures there: homosexuals who have been unable to make the adjustment to society's conventions, and are beaten. Lads who in bitterness and resentment have resorted to promiscuity, alcohol, and narcotics, as escape mechanisms. There is a slender youth, not more than seventeen, with what must have been at one time nice features, a clean cut boy who should have been home with his parents—now at the bottom of the ladder, sexually and socially. Woefully thin, due to excess, drinking heavily, his hair dyed a sickening peroxide yellow, and combed back in a mop, his eyebrows penciled black, his eyelids tinted blue, heavily rouged, and dancing in wild abandon with anyone who will dance with him. His shrill young voice ringing out wildly under the effects of the "weed."

Others too have lost their youth and are no longer attractive physically—and homosexuals demand physical attraction above all else—who wander about trying to "make" someone, or to strike up a friendship.

Around the edges of the hall are a fringe of on-lookers, like ourselves remaining in the semi-shadows. Some curious, others homosexual, but not daring to come out publicly and dance for fear of recognition; others occasionally slipping out for a dance when the urge became too strong; others who are waiting for their lovers; and finally those waiting for a pick up, to prey on the gullible homosexuals. All types are there, pimps, panderers, blackmailers, "trade," the oversexed lower classes with no high moral code, ready for a fling, be it man or woman; prize-fighters, the so-called "meat" for homosexuals—and athletes are strangely susceptible to the advances of an effeminate youth, who will make love to them passionately.

There are harlots there; not plying their trade, of course, for competition is too keen, but attending with their own parties. For there is a strange bond that links homosexuals and harlots together. Possibly it is because both are social pariahs.

Falsetto voices sound in our ears. We hear expressions such as "Maude"; "Dearie"; "Fannie"; there are shrill exclamations of glee and merriment as the men in women's clothing frequent the toilets marked plainly "Women." The men's toilets seem to be used only by those in masculine attire. It is not long before a real woman ventures into her proper restroom, and emerges to call a guard to dispossess the "girls" in there. A scuffle follows while a burly stadium guard attempts to expel the "girls" who shrilly protest that they belong in that particular restroom—the guard all the while trying to keep a serious face!

Physically, all types are there. Homosexuals thin and wasted, others slender and with womanish curves; others overfed and lustfully fat. Most of the younger homosexuals have pallid complexions with rather thin hair, due, perhaps to overindulgence. There is a preponderance of Jews and Latin nationalities, although homosexuality is no respecter of races. Many of the men are of Polish blood. Negros mingle freely with whites. There seemingly is no race distinction between them.

It is a garish affair, with a hollow, mocking, ring about it all. Many homosexuals of better class, who have succeeded in making some adjustment to society by bluffing the public, looked in, to leave at once in disgust. The group of onlookers are too dangerous to be seen with, blackmail is a common racket; and the homosexuals participating are going to the limit too freely in careless abandon. Discretion is flung to the winds, as they "let themselves go" on one of the two nights of the year when they can openly "be themselves," reveal their true natures, and be with others of their kind, without fear of arrest or public censure. All the pent up longings and desires of months are being given free rein on this rare occasion—and there is no question in our minds that the release will lead to excesses later.

## Mayor Edward J. Kelly's War on Vice

After the assassination of Chicago's mayor Anton Cermak, Edward J. Kelly took the reins of a city crushed by the Great Depression. The only ray of light was the 1933 Century of Progress World's Fair, which boosted Chicago's coffers and enhanced the city's reputation. Kelly's formidable Democratic political machine dominated Chicago politics from 1933 to 1947; his personal philosophy was to censor dissent and hope it went away. In 1934 he outlawed newsreels depicting riots and civil disobedience. This move was later overthrown in court.

Homosexuals fared badly under Kelly; the 1930s started out with the pansy craze and ended with gay men being "sex morons." Lesbians became a target too, with raids on the Roselle Inn at 1330 North Clark Street and the Twelve-Thirty Club (address unknown), frequented by "women who dress as men." Kelly didn't stop at taverns either, as the theater was also a popular target. Lillian Hellman's play *The Children's Hour*, about two teachers accused by a student of having a lesbian affair, opened in New York on November 20, 1934. The play was a critical and audience success, running for 691 performances. In 1936 the play was filmed as *These Three*, starring Miriam Hopkins, Merle Oberon, and Joel McCrea, with the lesbian content taken out. It was filmed again in 1961 as *The Children's Hour* with its original story line, starring Audrey Hepburn and Shirley MacLaine.

A headline in the *Chicago Daily News* on January 9, 1936, read: "Ban 'Children's Hour' by Direction of Mayor." The play was on the schedule of the 1935–36 season of the Theater Guild and the American Theater Society of Chicago. A copy of the script was sent to Chicago corporation counsel Barnet Hodes, a prerequisite for taking Mayor Kelly's indecency test. After reading the play Hodes and Kelly stamped it "INDECENT" and declared it would not be welcome in Chicago; the mayor pointed out he could not forbid the play from opening, but he could revoke the theater's license. The play was canceled to avoid a lawsuit. *The Children's Hour* wasn't staged in Chicago until May 1, 1942.

In March 1934, two years before Kelly's ban on *The Children's Hour*, another play set in a school, this one about a lesbian schoolgirl's infatuation with her headmistress, was performed in Chicago at the Blackstone Theatre to rave reviews. *Maedchen in Uniform* (*Girls in Uniform*) was adapted from Christa Winsloe's German novel of the same name. In November 1932 the film of the play, with an all-female cast and crew, starring Dorothea Wieck, Emilia Unda, and Hertha Thiele and produced by Leontine Sagan, was shown in Chicago with English subtitles at the Apollo Theatre on Clark and Randolph.

While on the subject of lesbian plays, almost a decade earlier, *Sin of Sins* by William Hurlbut, produced by A. H. Woods, was staged at the Adelphi Theater. It opened November 8, 1926, after a tryout in Atlantic City where it was called *Hymn to Venus*, the title of a poem by Sappho; *Sin of Sins* sounded more daring. The play starred British actress Isobel Elsom (who later appeared in dozens of films, including *My Fair Lady* playing Mrs. Eynsford-Hill) and film matinee idol Robert Warwick. In Atlantic City *Sin of Sins* was compared unfavorably to *The Captive*, another lesbian-themed play that had opened at New York's Empire Theatre on Broadway a month earlier. *The Captive*, adapted by Arthur Hornblow Jr. from *La Prisonnière* by the French dramatist Edouard Bourdet, was a huge success; there were 160 performances before it was shut down for indecency. If Hurlbut and Woods thought *Sin of Sins* would benefit from the success of *The Captive*, they were mistaken. After the play was trounced in Atlantic City it opened in Chicago to equally bad reviews. Theater critic Frederick Donaghey, in the November 14 *Chicago Tribune*, wrote:

> Three of four persons of proved judgment and controlled enthusiasms who have seen *The Captive* tell me that it is, regardless of its theme, a good play. *Sin of Sins* isn't . . .
>
> The big odor of the piece is supposed to be exuded in a scene of eccentric lovemaking by a female urning with an ingénue whose fiancé the former has murdered.

In his book *We Can Always Call Them Bulgarians: The Emergence of Lesbian and Gay Men on the American Stage* (1987) author Kaier Curtin notes that *Sin of Sins* was the first play with a lesbian character written in the English language. It was never published, making John Joseph's review in the *Chicago Herald-Examiner* important because it gives a plot outline. Headlined "*Sin of Sins* Brings Strange Fish into Adelphi Aquarium," Joseph begins: "The topic of *Sin of Sins* is one generally discussed in text books, though I believe it might have been mentioned in the Loeb-Leopold drama. In other words, perversion."

Joseph goes on to say that Lilith, the lesbian protagonist, has had three husbands, but her affections are for members of her own sex: "She has, poor soul, apparently kept her strangeness to herself, and she has selected a nice girl on whom to shower what everybody considers motherly affection." But when her love-interest falls for a man, the man ends up dead. Suicide? No. "[I]t's murder," continues Joseph, "and murder will out. Which it does in a breathless third act when the strange, female fish confesses her crime and the reason for it. She atones, too, but not, let it be said, by entering a convent."

The end is not revealed, but it's safe to assume that Lilith got her comeuppance in some way or another. We'll never know for sure.

Cover of early Chicago Mattachine Society newsletter, October 1954. Courtesy of Gerber/Hart Library and Archives.

Cover of *Tomorrow's Man*, July 1955. Author's collection.

Cover of *Night Life* magazine, November 13–20, 1964. Author's collection.

Cover of *Mars* magazine, 1968. Author's collection.

The Coliseum was the venue of Bathhouse John and Hinky Dink Kenna's outrageous First Ward Masquerade Balls. 1907 postcard. Author's collection.

In the early twentieth century, homosexuals in Chicago found one another by wearing red neckties on State Street. 1916 postcard. Author's collection.

Postcard from the pansy period, date unknown. Courtesy of Gerber/Hart Library and Archives.

Mystery photograph hanging on wall of Chicago's Gerber/Hart Library. Courtesy of Gerber/Hart Library and Archive.

The First Church of Deliverance
program, 1966. Author's collection.

The cover of the program to the
1967 Finnie's Club Masquerade Ball.
Author's collection.

Cover of Sloane Britain's book confiscated in Chicago, 1959.

Newspaper ad for the K-9 drag bar. *Chicago American*, 1934.

# Meet the Boy-ological Experts!

They Took
Show
Business
for
A Boy-Ride!

The first Jewel Box Revue was co-produced in 1939 by Danny Brown and Doc Benner. Recognizing that female impersonation is true art, and not the burlesque it had come to be, they decided to bring back the glories of a neglected field in entertainment. Since then, Danny and Doc have skyrocketed to the very tops in their producing profession. Combing the country for the very finest talent, they have staged some of the most lavish and spectacular reviews ever to be seen in show-wise metropolitan cities! They have discovered and sponsored innumerable young men who have achieved stardom through their critical encouragement and interest.

Danny Brown and Doc Benner started the *Jewel Box Revue* in 1939. *Jewel Box Revue* program, ca. 1958. Author's collection.

Gold Coast flyer, 1963. Author's collection.

Female impersonator Tony Midnite, 1950s. Signed photograph from author's collection.

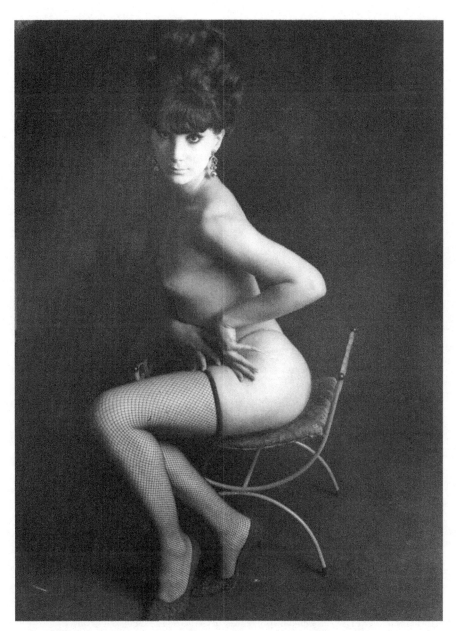

Unidentified Chicago female impersonator, ca. 1963. Author's collection.

Lesbian lawyer Pearl Hart, date unknown. Courtesy of Gerber/Hart Library and Archives.

# 13

# Bronzeville

The black pansy parlors on Chicago's South Side spawned
many stars in the world of female impersonation, including
"The Sepia Gloria Swanson" and Valda Gray. Many started
out in clubs like the Cabin Inn—"South Side's Oddest
Club"—and Joe's Deluxe. From the first Finnie's Ball in 1935,
the Queer Street Scandal in 1951, and trumpeter Ernestine
"Tiny" Davis's Gayspot Lounge, to the rise and rise of the
Reverend Clarence Cobb and the First Church of Deliverance,
the South Side was thriving.

On December 10, 1930, *Variety* reported on a new fad, "The Pansy Craze,"
and the growing number of pansy parlors in Chicago, but what the article
failed to note is that many of them were on the South Side in African
American neighborhoods. The most successful of these was James Pleasure's Pleasure Inn at 505½ East 31st Street. The popularity of the club was
due to the resident female impersonator who masqueraded under the name
"The Sepia Gloria Swanson" (real name Walter Winston); back then it was
common for female impersonators in the black community to adopt the
name of their white inspiration and prefix it with the word "Sepia." Chicago also boasted a Sepia Mae West.

Walter Winston was born in Atlanta, Georgia, on May 23, 1906, and
moved to Chicago with his family at an early age to escape the racism of

the segregated South. After attending Chicago's Forestville Elementary School and Wendell Phillips High School, he took to the stage, and by 1929 he was the doyen of Bronzeville's café society. His theme song was Fats Waller's "Squeeze Me," to which he added spicy lyrics. In February 1930 Gloria opened Gloria's Café, opposite the Sunset Café, at 315–17 East 35th Street. He was also in demand as an emcee, and on May 20, 1930, he was Mistress of Ceremonies at a banquet organized by James Pleasure at the Pleasure Inn, with celebrity guests like boxer "Young" Jack Thompson, and cabaret singer, dancer, and actress Caroline Snowden, who co-starred with Stepin Fetchit in *Old Kentucky*, reputedly the first movie depicting a black on black romance.

In early 1932 Gloria was in residence at the Monte Carlo, 6320 Cottage Grove Avenue, then spent the summer in New York, returning in October to the Radio Inn at 18th and Dearborn with his own show, the *Bronx Beauty Revue*, starring the cream of New York's nightclub entertainers, including dancers Ruth "Race Horse" Johnson and Henrietta Epps. Gloria's showstopper was Sophie Tucker's "Some of These Days." On December 1, 1932, he opened his *Bronx Beauty Revue* at the Pleasure Inn, but after a handful of shows the club was raided and closed down. In early 1933 Gloria traveled to Detroit to sing "Hot Nuts, Get 'Em from the Peanut Man!" at the opening of an extension to the Fisher Theatre, a multimillion-dollar movie and vaudeville house with an Aztec motif; the lobby was a jungle of banana trees, with a goldfish and turtle pond and colorful talking macaws clinging to perches to be fed grapes by audience members:

> Sellin' nuts, hot nuts, anybody here want to buy my nuts?
> Sellin' nuts, hot nuts, I've got nuts for sale.
> You tell me that man's nuts is mighty small,
> Best to have small nuts than have no nuts at all.
> Sellin' nuts, hot nuts, you buy 'em from the peanut man.

Early in 1934 Gloria was in New York sharing a stage at Harlem's Ubangi and Clam House clubs with the 250-pound "Bulldagger of the Blues" Gladys Bentley. In July Gloria returned for his final appearances in Chicago, accompanied by jazz clarinetist Jimmie Noone and his Apex Club Orchestra. They opened at a new Harlem-style basement club, the Midnight at 3140 Indiana Avenue, where the joint was hopping every night from 11 p.m. until dawn. It's likely Gloria's return to Chicago was prompted by Mayor Fiorella H. LaGuardia's purge of raunchy club acts in New York. It's not known if Gloria was one of those arrested, but male impersonator Gladys Bentley was taken in, as was her effeminate male chorus line at the King's Terrace at 240 West 42nd Street. Although Bentley's career was firmly rooted in New York, she sang in Chicago twice, most notably her April 1938 shows at the Swingland Café at 343 East 55th Street, where she belted out the blues and flirted with the women in the audience.

On May 1, 1940, in New York, Walter "Gloria Swanson" Winston died after a long, protracted battle with heart disease just shy of his thirty-fourth birthday. At his funeral, his mother, Sarah Meyers, and two hundred of his closest friends were at the Rodney Dade funeral parlor, 2332 Seventh Avenue and 137th Street, to hear the Reverend W. W. Monroe read the eulogy.

Gloria wasn't the only female impersonator in Chicago's black pansy scene; Gilda Gray was at Club Piccadilly, 2652 Indiana Avenue, in the early 1930s, and as late as November 1939 performed in *Dr. Rhythm Goes to Town*, in Centralia, Illinois, with impersonators Deanna Durban and Delores Del Rio. On May 13, 1931, Chicago's Ritz Café (address unknown) held a fashion show and masked drag ball hosted by Peggy Joyce, whose real name was Samuel Fouche. The *Chicago Defender* noted a drag queen wardrobe malfunction: "Everything was all right until 'Peg's' shoulder strap broke." A year later Peggy was at the Painted Doll at 4650 Vincennes Avenue, a small after-hours café. Later Peggy used the name "The Sepia Mae West" and moved to New York, where he appeared at Harlem's Small's Paradise club.

Women were also cross-dressing in Bronzeville; one act doing the rounds in 1930 was the "sister" team Billie de Bourbon and Tillie Keeble, the latter of whom performed as a man. Another cross-dressing woman was Bert Whitman of the Whitman Sisters, a family of entertainers on the Negro Vaudeville circuit. (Al)Bert(a) Whitman and Alice, her sister, did a "girl and 'boy'" singing and dancing double act. In August 1930 they were at the Grand Theater on 31st and State Streets in *Wake Up, Children* that included a dance scene called "Watermelon Moon." Other acts in the show included the singing midget Princess Wee Wee, and a grand finale of Bert Whitman in male attire singing "A Baby of Everyone."

## The Cabin Inn

Two clubs dominated Chicago's South Side pansy scene in the summer of 1934: the newly opened Annex Buffet at 2840 South State Street, and the Cabin Inn at 3119 Cottage Grove Avenue. The Cabin opened a year earlier with hostess Gilda Gray from Club Piccadilly. The Annex was the brainchild of Bennie Lustgarten and Arnold Meyer, who offered milk-fed fried chicken and unusual entertainment under the stars in an open-air garden. The star of the Annex show was Chicago-born Samuel "Sepia Mae West" Fouche, back from a successful run in Harlem's Small's Paradise. Other acts on the bill were risqué female singer Bertha "Chippie" Hill, William Holmes, and Ida Mae Maples's Merry Makers. On October 25, 1934, Lustgarten and Meyer opened the indoor Annex Buffet at 2300 South State Street, with Sepia Mae West launching his new revue, *The Gay Nineties*.

In the spring of 1935 Sepia Mae West moved on, to be replaced by another black Mae West, Dick Barrow, whose tenure at the Annex was short-lived. He soon moved to the Cozy Cabin Inn, the premier female impersonation club owned by Nathan "Big Ivy" Ivy and Jack Hardy. Hardy's background is a mystery, but "Big Ivy" was born in Marble Falls, Arkansas. He moved to Chicago in 1916 and became a successful entrepreneur, no doubt aided by his friendship with African American politicians like Alderman Louis B. Anderson and Ward Committeeman Dan Jackson.

In July 1934 the Cabin Inn featured female impersonator and blues singer Luzetta Hall and Blue and Jean, a two-man dance team who were known as the "Lady and Gentleman of the Carioca"—Jean was a boy in drag. With Dick "Mae West" Barrow at the helm the Cabin Inn flourished, adding more female impersonators to their roster, including Robert "Dixie Lee" Johnson and "Marlene Dietrich." The famous annual Finnie's Ball, organized by gambler and ne'er-do-well Alfred Finnie, that took place on the South Side of Chicago for forty years started in 1935 at the height of Cabin fever. In October 1935 the Cabin Inn hosted a double wedding: one the genuine article with the nuptials of midget dancer "Bullfrog Shorty" Burch to Muriel Borsack, and the other a same-sex wedding between female impersonator Jean Acker and Vernon Long, a man who was, according to the *Chicago Defender*, "a very handsome bridegroom." Mr. Luzetta Hall acted as Jean Acker's "bridesmaid." Guests came from as far away as Philadelphia, Madison, Detroit, and Indianapolis. As the cars pulled up outside the Cabin Inn, the guests alighted and entered the club on a street lit by "electric candles" and floodlights.

Police raided the "double wedding" and temporarily closed the club. Barrow skipped town to star in *The Brown Mae West* at the 808 Club and the Lincoln Theater in Los Angeles, where he was "lauded for his gorgeous gowns and graceful à la West curves." The *Chicago Defender* of December 21, 1935, reported that twelve employees were arrested and charged with obscenity in the Cabin raid: the owners Nat Ivy and Jack Hardy, bartenders Dewey Parker and Bob Henderson, floodlight operator Carroll Joseph, and seven female impersonators, three working at the Cabin and four guests at the wedding. In South State Street court, Judge Eugene McGarry dismissed all the charges, saying: "The testimony does not show any specific violations of ordinance. . . . It appears that these men were dressed in female clothes. The testimony shows it was a masquerade party. Female impersonators appear on stage every day. In the absence of any such testimony I have no choice but to find the defendants not guilty and that will be the order."

The Cabin Inn reopened with a new emcee, "Clem" Ruben Brown. Manhattan Pearl, a female impersonator from Harlem, was hired to star in the new show, *Varieties of 1935*. In 1937 female impersonator Valda Gray (born Harold Baker) was hired as the show's producer. Gray hired the best singing and dancing female impersonators in the business, including Jean LaRue, Nina Mae McKinney, Peaches Browning, and Petite Swanson. He also hired Herman Ferdinand, a wisecracking emcee whom the *Chicago Defender* on November 4, 1939, said "lays them in the aisle with his hokum." Gray, Ferdinand, and manager Eddie Woods were on hand in October 1938 when the Cabin Inn relocated to 3520 South State Street. At the grand opening Gray premiered his new show, *A Minute in Jazz*, starring female impersonators Doris White, Joan Crawford, Frances Dee, and Peaches Browning.

One Cabin impersonator who fell afoul of the law was George "Joan Crawford" Manus, who in July 1939 got into a scrape with police Sergeant Robert Harness. The *Chicago Defender* headline read: "Cocktails Get Female Impersonator in 'Dutch.'" A crapulous Manus, wearing slacks, high-heeled pumps, and a silk shirtwaist, threatened to slap Sergeant Harness across the face after being told to quit his rowdy behavior on the corner of 35th and State Street. The cop responded by grabbing Manus by the neck of his blouse and shaking him, to which the indignant "Miss Crawford" retorted, "Take your hands off my bosom!"

In court Manus, dressed in masculine attire with hair tied back into a braid, was cautioned and discharged by Judge Mason Sullivan, for "displaying conduct unbecoming a gentleman, let alone a lady." The *Chicago Defender* noted that Manus was sporting a black eye in court, earned not from the scuffle with the cop, but from "the handiwork of Manus's boy-friend."

On September 4, 1939, the Cabin Inn introduced clarinetist and bandleader Jimmie Noone to the lineup, and he and his twelve-piece band began a nightly live WBBM broadcast from the club. Sadly, in early 1940 Nat Ivy ran out of friends in high places, and after a run-in with the law over his entertainment license, "The South Side's Oddest Nite Club" closed down for good. Valda Gray opened a new show in the outdoor garden at James C. Martin's club, Martin's Corner at 1900 West Lake Street, that included song and dance man Joan Crawford. Next stop for the Cabin crew was Cyril Richards's Manchester Grill, 473 East 31st Street, through the winter of 1940–41. In May 1941, the show was picked up by Charles Christian, the manager of a new female impersonation club called Joe's Deluxe.

## Joe's Deluxe

In October 1939 Joseph "Joe" Hughes was voted the fifth mayor of Bronzeville; it was a largely honorary, though influential, title sponsored by the *Chicago Defender*. Hughes was a successful twenty-nine-year-old businessman, married to Velma Morris Hughes and the owner of two nightclubs, Joe's Deluxe, 6323 South Parkway, and the West Lake Inn, 2724 West Lake Street. Hughes had arrived in Chicago in 1919 from White Castle, Louisiana, with his parents, Alex and Edmonia.

Joe's Deluxe boasted a variety floorshow produced by Dick "Mae West" Barrow. On February 9, 1940, the Mayor of Bronzeville's inauguration ball was held at Joe's Deluxe with two celebrity guests, Bill "Bojangles" Robinson and Chicago mayor Edward J. Kelly; it is ironic that the mayor, who closed down gay bars six years earlier, should be in a club where the emcee was a Mae West impersonator. One crowd-pleaser was "Celebrity Night," where once a week the clientele dined on meals prepared by Chinese chef Mee Lum, enjoyed Valda Gray's show, and hobnobbed with the stars of the day, like Count Basie and his band, or light heavy-weight boxer Willie Joyce.

While World War II blazed in Europe and the Far East, Gray's shows at Joe's Deluxe continued uninterrupted throughout the war. In September 1943 while U.S. marines and allied forces landed on Italy's beaches, on the South Side of Chicago Valda Gray and six chorines staged a skit called *Six Girls Named Flo*. The *Chicago Defender* of October 3, 1943 wrote that the club's "sweetheart," Dixie Lee, started "stepping out with a line that pleases" and the "sinuous" Petite Swanson "tells the girls that it 'Aint Right,' and that they must love their sweeties with a feeling." Joe's Deluxe closed in 1954. Although none of Valda Gray's shows are known to have been recorded, one of its stars can be heard on two 78rpm records recorded in March 1947 by Alphonso "Petite Swanson" Horsley on Marl Young's Chicago Sunbeam record label. The songs are "Lawdy Miss Claudy" backed with "My Jockey Knows How to Ride," and "I'm Sorry" backed with "Did You Ever Feel Lucky."

## Queer Street Scandal

The Southside Workingmen's Club in the basement of 5228 South Parkway seems an unlikely venue for a lesbian and gay social club, but in 1951 the misleading title provided the perfect cover. Until, that is, a fourteen-year-old boy told his mother he engaged in sex acts at the club. The February 3 *Chicago Defender* headline read: "'Queer Street' Den Found by Police." The paper noted the club was "patronized by men wearing women's apparel and 'slack clad' women." The boy claimed that in order to be accepted into the "inner circle," he had to perform an unnatural act on another boy in front of the club's secretary. He later told the police that members of the inner circle were sent out on "calls" and that some members earned up to forty dollars a week.

The boy's mother contacted police, who raided the club on January 27, 1951, and arrested forty-eight-year-old Maude Mitchell, secretary of the club, the club's fifty-two-year-old president Hans Hampton, and twenty patrons. The club was interracial, male and female, and included both adults and juveniles. Some men carried cards with a male name on one side and a female alter ego on the other. The boy who made the original complaint was known as "Jeanie." Mitchell was charged with contributing to the delinquency of juveniles, Hampton with being the keeper of a disorderly house. The others, including six women, two wearing slacks, and two female impersonators, Alfred "Dorothy Lee" Gregory and Eugene "Skelly" Wright, were charged with being patrons of a disorderly house.

In court, all the charges were dropped after "Jeanie" refused to repeat his claims in front of a judge and jury.

## Jewel Box Revue

In the winter of 1957 Danny Brown and Doc Benner's drag extravaganza, the *Jewel Box Revue*, opened in Chicago at Herman Roberts's Roberts' Show Lounge at 6622 South Parkway. The show *25 Men and One Girl* was advertised as "The World's Most Unusual Show. You'll Have To See It To Believe It." The revue starred the popular white female impersonator Lynn Carter, best known for his take-off of lesbian cabaret singer Hildegarde, and also for his Pearl Bailey and Josephine Baker. Carter was a World War II veteran who saw combat at Iwo Jima.

The *Jewel Box Revue* was such a hit that it was extended for several months, taking a break in the fall and then returning to Roberts's the following year. The *Chicago Defender* described Toni Midnite's costumes as "an unbelievable wardrobe that you expect to see only in Hollywood or Las Vegas." *Jewel Box* performers were mostly white, except for Billy Daye, who impersonated Billie Holiday, and the emcee of the show and only "girl," the male impersonator Storme DeLarverie, sporting a tux and a crew cut. In the show she sang "St. Louis Blues" and Etta James's "I Want a Sunday Kind of Love."

DeLarverie was born on Christmas Eve 1920 in New Orleans and raised by foster parents. She began her singing career in 1940, touring the country with numerous bands, until 1955 when Brown and Benner of the *Jewel Box Revue* convinced her to become a male impersonator after hearing her deep baritone singing voice. DeLarverie's life is showcased in Michelle Parkerson's short film *Storme: The Lady of the Jewel Box* (1991).

In 1958 DeLarverie was the one "girl" in the *Jewel Box Revue*, along with "25 men," which included ballet dancer Jan Britton; Jene Korday, "The Boy with the Million Dollar Legs"; and Kim August, a beauty who later played Sadie in the movie *No Way to Treat a Lady* (1968). Another star of the *Jewel Box Revue* was James Tai, born James Tai Fujikawa in Hilo, Hawaii, on April 4, 1934. His mother was Hawaiian, his father Japanese. The *Chicago Defender* of April 2, 1960, referred to him as "oriental," and his act, "the highlight of the show." Tai did his own take on the "Bamboo Pole Dance," made popular by the Bayanihan Philippine Dance Company. In 1960 *Jewel Box* moved to the Balaban and Katz Tivoli Theater at 63rd and Cottage Grove. At the Tivoli *25 Men and One Girl* was performed between showings of the top movies of 1959 like *The Last Angry Man, The Purple Gang*, and *Suddenly Last Summer*. On September 20, 1960, there was a *Jewel Box Revue* cast party at McKie Fitzhugh's gay-friendly McKie's Club at 6325 Cottage Grove, where they held "Ladies' Fancy Pants Night" for masculine women. The resident singer at McKie's was gay celebrity Wilbur "Hi-Fi" White, who also sang at the Kitty Kat Klub.

In the mid-1960s White performed in clubs like the Bonanza at 7641 South Halsted, Peyton Place at 116 East Pershing Road, and Crazee Babee Lounge at 1240 East 47th Street. A personal friend of Chicago's Redd Foxx, White made a 1975 appearance on the TV sitcom *Sanford and Son*, where he played a flamboyant emcee at the Miss Watts Business Wife Pageant. White also appeared in the prison drama movie *Penitentiary* (1979), and his voice can be heard on two songs he recorded for Chicago's Bandera record label in August 1960: "Don't Look Now" backed with "In the Center of My Heart."

In May 1966 the *Jewel Box Revue* returned for a two-week engagement at the Regal Theater at 1645 East 79th Street, but its time had passed. The heyday of female impersonators singing live had been replaced by pretty drag queens in plastic Mary Quant miniskirts lip-synching three-minute pop songs. Times were changing. In 1961 Chicago's moral watchdogs, the Roman Catholic Church, PTAs, and other groups of concerned citizens, demanded the police deal with vice on the South Side. The *Chicago Defender* reported on March 2, 1961, that "three male sex deviates were arrested while standing on the corner of 64th Street and Woodlawn. They admitted their tendencies and said they had come to the street for immoral purposes. They were charged with 'loitering sex deviates.'" The next day the charges were dropped. In April 1966 police raided Lonnie Doyal's Lonnie's Sky-way Lounge, 135 West 75th Street, arresting Doyal and Gloria Smith, as co-keepers of a disorderly house, four waitresses, twenty-one patrons, and five female impersonators. The "girls" gave their names as Willie "Shirley" West; Alphonso Dixon, stage name "Alphonso Marlowe"; Charles

"Maggie" McNee; Harvey Williamson; and Raymond "Rae Del Rays" Navarro, the only white "girl."

All were later released without charge.

## Finnie's Balls

The first Finnie's Ball was held in 1935 and was most likely a spin-off of the "double wedding" at the Cabin Inn. Alfred Finnie, a street hustler and nightclub doorman who started the balls, is rumored to have died in a 1943 gambling dispute, long before his balls became the glittering Halloween masquerades of the 1950s, '60s, and '70s when upwards of three thousand people attended.

*Ebony* reviewed the 1951 ball in March 1952: "Ordinarily a man dressed in women's clothing and mincing down the street will be picked up by the police and tossed into the nearest lock-up, but once a year in big cities the cops will look the other way as the men who like to masquerade as women gather for annual public frolics." *Ebony* notes that it wasn't unusual to spend a thousand to three thousand dollars on a costume. The most common impersonation at the 1951 ball was Josephine Baker. A caption on the photograph of two Baker impersonators jokes: "Chicago 'Josephine Bakers' chat gaily before style show. Known as 'Miss Sweetcake' and 'Ginger' the two showed none of the feminine 'jealousy,' which usually results when two women appear at an affair with similar hairdos."

Ginger's talent was shake dancing, and she stripped down to "her" jeweled G-string and bra. Other contestants included "a tall, thin blonde in a blue mink cape [who] was announced as 'Bebe Daniels' . . . another dressed in a Gay Nineties hat and gown wearing a corsage of five white orchids [who] called himself 'Mae West.' Another dressed in a white, clinging outfit with a pattern of huge leaves on the skirt and wearing a single green glove was announced as 'Lena Horne.'"

*Ebony*'s favorite overheard quote of the evening came from a contestant who turned to "her" friend and said: "Alexis Smith won't be here tonight. She's been drafted into the Army." The winner of the 1951 ball was Billie St. Clair, who wore a white off-the-shoulder gown and blue mink stole. In 1955 the ball was held at the Parkway Ballroom at 4455 South Parkway, with Eddie Plique as emcee. Among the contestants were a Lena Horne, and for comic relief an "Expectant Mother."

Most years the *Chicago Defender* covered Finnie's Ball with good humor, but in 1960, the "Behind the Scenes" column by Robert Roy took a negative tone: "Twas disgusting indeed to hear one of those dress wearing men say just after putting his trousers on after the Finnie's Ball 'can't you see I WALK JUST LIKE A MAN?' The situation became even more alarming when observing his audience was composed of a number of young males—STILL WE PROFESS alarm over the fact that many of Chicago's youngsters are either members of gangs or leaning toward the questionable sex kick."

The 1967 Finnie's ball at the Coliseum Ballroom at Wabash and 14th Street was a glittering affair with the Rickey DePaul Dancers from Detroit warming up the crowd, followed by Clayton Whitehead and His Exotic Show Troupe, Macellus, and Heri Del Valle, Chicago's Judy Garland, all leading up to the Fashion Parade and the Crowning of the King and Queen. In 1972 Finnie's moved from the Trianon, Coliseum, and Pershing ballrooms on the South Side to the Grand Ballroom at the downtown Sherman Hotel, and in 1975 the fortieth was held in Uptown's Aragon Ballroom. However, the elegant days of decorating the Trianon as "The Streets of Paris" were long gone, and Finnie's Ball struggled on for another three years in small venues; the forty-third and last was held in 1978 at the Meat Packing House Center at 4849 South Wabash.

## Ernestine "Tiny" Davis

The Sweethearts of Rhythm all-girl swing band formed in 1937 after a newspaper ad requested girls interested in a career in music to contact "Jones" at Piney Woods Country Life School in Mississippi. The "Jones" referred to was actually two people: Rae Lee Jones, a director and teacher at the school, and Laurence C. Jones (no relation), the president and founder of Piney Woods, a school offering a high standard of education for rural black students. "Jones'" formed the Sweethearts, and they toured for two years until a gig at the Apollo Theatre in New York caught the attention of booking agents, and the Sweethearts were headed for stardom.

With success came resentment, as most of the band's earnings went to the school. The musicians were paid only eight dollars each a week. Also, some of the "girls" were now women. While touring, Rae Lee Jones, the Sweethearts' manager, secretly met with two wealthy booking agents, and a defection from Piney Woods school was planned. After finding members of the band who were agreeable, Jones "borrowed" the keys to the tour bus and drove to Memphis while students loyal to the school slept. From there the runaways caught a train to Washington, D.C., where they lived communally in a large house in Arlington, Virginia, that comprised booking offices and rooms for living, rehearsal, sleeping, dining, and recreation. The first thing they did was hire professional musicians, such as Boston saxophonist Roz Cron, trumpet player Jean Starr, and two lesbians, trumpet player Ernestine "Tiny" Davis and tenor saxophonist Vi Burnside. The Sweethearts also became "International" with members of all races, including blacks, Chinese, Native Americans, and Mexicans. They billed themselves as "The International Sweethearts of Rhythm. The World's Greatest All-Girl—All Nationality Band."

The Sweethearts were popular all over the country, but in October 1942 they broke box-office records in Chicago by selling out the Regal Theatre and the White City Ballroom. In April 1945 the Sweethearts were back in the city at the Rhumboogie, at 343 East 55th, a popular black-and-tan club (a club frequented by black, white, and all colors). The December 15 *Chicago Defender* singled out Davis and Burnside: "Tiny Davis, the 245 lb. 'girl with horn' whose trumpet renditions are a sensation. Miss Davis, aside from her horn tooting is a natural born entertainer. Attractive Vi Burnside, star sax technician, gives forth with that tantalizing tone you love to hear."

Davis left the Sweethearts in 1947, settled in Chicago, and played solo with a regular gig at the Blue Heaven Lounge, 742 East 63rd Street. In September 1949 Rae Lee Jones, the manager of the International Sweethearts of Rhythm, passed away and the band split up, with some members joining Tiny Davis's Hell Divers. One of the Hell Divers' early gigs was at Joe's Rendezvous Lounge at 2757 West Madison Street, but probably their most unusual was in a variety show at the "Coolest Spot in Town," the Crown Propeller Lounge at 868 East 63rd Street, where they were billed alongside the ventriloquist act Oscar and Stew and a bikini-clad Atlantis the Sea Nymph, a woman who danced a sensational aqua-tease ballet in five hundred gallons of brilliantly lit water.

On June 17, 1954, Davis and her lover, drummer, pianist, and bass player, Ruby Lucas (a.k.a. Renee Phelan), opened the new Out Door Dance Pavilion at their own jazz joint, Tiny and Ruby's Gayspot Lounge at 2711 South Wentworth. The opening night featured Tiny Davis and her Hell Divers, and from Kansas City, Tiny's daughter Dorothy Davis on bass, and Evelyn Twine on piano. The following month tenor saxophone player

Paul Bascomb played there, also lesbian Vi Burnside, but by October 1955 the club was sold. Davis returned to music, and in May 1956 the Hell Divers played at Velma's Jet Lounge at 6342 Cottage Grove and at other clubs in the 1960s. In 1965 they were at the Bowery at 1504 North Wells Street, warming up the audience for the Ink Spots.

Ernestine "Tiny" Davis died in Chicago on January 30, 1994. There are two documentaries featuring her life, both produced and directed by Greta Schiller and Andrea Weiss: *International Sweethearts of Rhythm* (1986) and *Hell Divin' Women* (1988).

## The Reverend Clarence Cobbs

The Metropolitan Spiritual Churches of Christ Inc. (MSCC) was founded on September 22, 1925, in a living room at 1903 East 9th Street, in Kansas City, Missouri, by Reverends William Frank Taylor and Leviticus Lee Boswell. From humble beginnings the church grew rapidly with its potent message: "Jesus Is the Light of the World." The MSCC's most renowned minister, the Reverend Clarence Henry Cobbs, known as "Preacher" to his congregations over five decades, rose rapidly from obscure pastor to leading light in Chicago's South Side community through his work at the First Church of Deliverance. Cobbs was born on February 29, 1908, to Luella and Frank Cobbs. The marriage didn't last. In an interview with the *Chicago Defender* in January 1965, Cobbs reminisced about his father turning up at his grade school graduation and presenting him with a gold watch: "That was the last time I saw (him) until I was grown and encountered him in Madison, Arkansas, where he lived with his wife until he died three years ago. His wife died two weeks later."

When the marriage to Frank Cobbs ended, Luella came to Chicago during World War I in search of work, leaving Clarence with her mother. In Chicago she remarried, to a man named Willie Williams, and she sent for her son and mother to join them. It was at 3363 South Indiana Avenue, in the home of Luella and Willie Williams, that Cobbs founded the First Church of Deliverance with the Reverend Mattie B. Thornton. The first service was on May 8, 1929, and by August they had affiliated with the Reverends Taylor and Boswell of MSCC in Kansas City.

The First Church of Deliverance gospel choir was formed on October 29, 1929, and in 1934 they sang on the first of Cobbs's radio broadcasts on WSBC. Nearly two decades later they were the first African American church to broadcast televised services. Many can recall Cobbs's opening remarks, always spoken softly: "You in the taverns tonight; you on the dance floor; you in the poolrooms and policy stations; you on your bed of affliction—Jesus loves you all, and Reverend Cobb is thinking about you, and loves every one of you. It doesn't matter what you think about me, but it matters a lot what I think about you. "

In May 1936, on the seventh anniversary of the church, MSCC co-founder and now Senior Bishop William F. Taylor was guest of honor at the celebrations. The congregation was growing rapidly. In July 1939 the *Chicago Defender* published "The Architect's Conception of Rev. Cobb's New $55,000 Church," a sketch of the new church under construction at 4315 South Wabash Avenue. Then four months later the paper broke a story, on November 18: "Rev. Cobb [*sic*] Denies Scandal; Defends Self against Rumors in Broadcast." David Orro in the December 2 *Chicago Defender* explained: "Rev. Clarence H. Cobbs was this week facing the possibility of questioning by state's attorney's police concerning wide-spread rumors of a scandalous nature. These rumors have become so general that the pastor has had to come to his own defense over the air on several of his Sunday night broadcasts. On one occasion, he said: 'I am full man, don't believe any gossip you hear circulated about me.'"

Although the paper doesn't repeat the rumor, it seems Cobbs had been outed after an "unsavory incident of serious proportions." As reported on November 25 and December 9, when the *Chicago Defender* confronted Cobbs, he asked, "Have you any public records of such a happening?" When the *Chicago Defender* said "no," he answered, "Well, then, there's nothing to discuss and, of course, I have nothing to say to you."

The Reverend Cobbs wasn't the only prominent figure implicated in the scandal, as the names of other "well known citizens, some of them prominent politicians and holders of high city offices" were also alluded to, though none were named in print. The *Chicago Defender* of November 25 hinted at a cover up. When asked to comment, County Commissioner Edward M. Sneed pleaded ignorance of the incident. The paper noted that Sneed was "a personal friend of the minister."

According to the December 2 *Chicago Defender*, Cobbs still broadcast his live Sunday night sermon, opening by saying: "I welcome you all, friends and enemies alike, and regardless of what you feel was the reason for your coming, I love you. I love you because I know God sent you here tonight. That is really why you're present!" As the broadcast went out, another minister, the Reverend William S. Bradden, pastor of Berean Baptist church at 52nd and Dearborn Streets, stood at his pulpit accusing Cobb of being "a travesty on the sacredness of the Christian church."

Things heated up further when Cobbs sued the Robert S. Abbott Publishing Company, publishers of the *Chicago Defender*, for libel: "Radio Pastor Sues *Defender* for $250,000; Says 'Virtue and Integrity Were Injured'" ran the December 9 headline.

Cobbs's "Virtue and Integrity" took another blow on February 12, 1940, when a second scandal broke after Senior Bishop William Frank Taylor and the Reverend Leviticus Lee Boswell were arrested in Kansas City for sodomy. Taylor was arrested in a parked car canoodling with a young male member of his church. The young man told police sexual relations between them had continued for years and that he was financially rewarded. Boswell was arrested later at Taylor's home after another youth admitted sexual relations with him. According to the *Chicago Defender* of February 24, 1940, while in custody, Boswell told police he and Taylor had "indulged in exchanges of affection" with each other for fifteen years. They both faced two years in jail. Whether they were ever incarcerated is unclear, but Boswell's ultimate fate has been scratched from the official church history and Taylor "went to be with the Lord" on March 17, 1942, at age fifty-five, in Los Angeles with Cobbs by his side.

On April 19, 1940, Cobb had his libel suit thrown out of court. In June, Cobbs's appeal was also thrown out, and Judge Peter Schwaba, head of the law division of the superior court, ordered him to pay one hundred dollars in court costs. That should have been the end of it, but the lawsuit pinballed around the courts until an unlikely gathering took place in February 1941, when four hundred "civic-minded" citizens attended a banquet in Bacon's Casino to honor Reverend Cobbs. The guest list was surprising, as it included County Commissioner Edward M. Sneed, whom the *Chicago Defender* hinted had orchestrated a cover-up of the scandal, and Mrs. Edna Denison Sengstacke Abbott, president of the *Chicago Defender*. The *Chicago Defender* on March 22, 1941, reported that the Appellate Court of Illinois decided in Cobb's favor. Vindicated, Cobb instructed Bernard A. Fried, his "white lawyer," to release the paper from any liability. "I am not interested in any money from the *Chicago Defender*. As is told us in Proverbs, chapter XXII. 'A good name is rather to be chosen than great riches.'"

That was the end of that.

Not everyone revered Cobbs. In *Black Metropolis: A Study of Negro Life in a Northern City* (1945), authors St. Clair Drake and Horace R. Clayton dismiss the preacher: "The Rev. Cobbs wears clothes of the latest cut, drives a flashy car, uses slang, and is considered a good sport," they say. "Such a preacher appeals to the younger lower-class people and to the 'sporting world'—he's 'regular.'"

They add: "Brother Cobbs symbolizes the New Gods of the Metropolis. He is the alter ego of the urban sophisticate who does not wish to make the break with religion, but desires a streamlined church which allows him to take his pleasures undisturbed."

After Taylor died, Cobbs took the reins as president of Metropolitan Spiritual Churches of Christ Inc. On May 8, 1942, at a ceremony in Chicago, Cobbs's induction service was presided over by assistant pastor Reverend Mattie Thornton, aided by the disgraced Reverend L. L. Boswell. Cobbs was nothing if not brazen.

In December 1945 the First Church of Deliverance was destroyed by fire. The church was rebuilt, even more elaborate than before. Another Cobbs-owned firetrap was a building at 4302–4 South Wabash. One gay African American man remembers living there with his mother from 1945 to 1950:

That building had been condemned every year. We had two rooms, the toilets you couldn't flush, you had to pour a bucket of water in it, and half the time there wasn't a seat on it. You couldn't take a bath because the water was backed up with sewage. And this was Rev. Cobb.

Most people there were gay. He'd fill the building with lesbians and gay people. Certain rooms in the building were broken up, like in five rooms they might have five different families . . . and everybody used the same bathroom. So what would have been apartments would have about 25 people in it. Half the time you couldn't take a bath because there was no hot water and the basement would flood, and Rev. Cobb and his cohorts lived like kings. I would go around there and complain, and tell him to get someone to fix it, and he would say, "That's a bunch of niggers around there and they should get out anyway" . . . that's the way they would talk to you, like you were dirt. He used to smoke a big cigar and he liked to gamble. You'd see him in his big limousine coming down the street and everybody knew who he was . . . a Black politician.

The reason he got popular was that churches back then didn't accept gay people, and the white gay folks were looking for a church. They wanted to be included in religion. So Rev. Cobb said he don't care what you is . . . blah blah blah . . . and that was one church, the First Church of Deliverance, where white people actually came to a Black church in a Black community.

And Mayor Kennelly was gay, undercover of course, and he came to Rev. Cobb's church, and he gave Rev. Cobbs a certain amount of political clout with that building.

In 1958, three years after Cobbs's guardian angel, Mayor Martin H. Kennelly, was ousted by Richard J. Daley, Fire Marshal Eugene Brennan of the Fire Prevention Bureau declared the gay-occupied building "very dangerous." There were 150 people living in 57 one-room units with corridors littered with furniture, fire exits blocked, and overloaded wiring. The *Chicago Defender* noted that Cobbs was unable to comment as he was away in California. At the time, Cobbs was living at 4801 South Woodlawn, a twenty-room Hyde Park mansion with a four-door garage that he bought in 1951.

Cobbs was a slumlord who fed the poor, campaigned for civil rights, welcomed lesbians and gay men into his fold, and enjoyed gambling and drinking. He could also draw huge crowds. In 1956 ten thousand people turned up for his Mothers' Day Tea at the First Church of Deliverance Nursery and Community Center; another three thousand came to the Thirty-First Annual Congress of the Metropolitan Spiritual Churches of Christ Inc., which included an address by Mayor Richard J. Daley.

Preacher died on June 28, 1979, at age seventy-one. Ironically, it was the tenth anniversary of Stonewall. The hearse bearing his coffin led 121 limos and several thousand mourners through the streets of Chicago to his final resting place at Burr Oak Cemetery.

# 14

# World War II and the 1940s

---

---

Chicago goes to war with Rosie the Riveter cross-dressing factory girls, and gay bars like Benny the Bums and the vice joints on South State Street are out of bounds to military personnel. Homosexual cruising centers on hotel bars, where piano players like Jacqui O'Shea kept the gay boys in check. Less salubrious were dives like the Primrose Path and its "risqué songs," and the Windup Lounge, the latter raided in 1949 in a crackdown on vice.

World War II had a dramatic affect on the lives of Chicagoans, a story documented in the book *We've Got a Job to Do: Chicagoans and World War II* (1992) by Perry Duis and Scott La France. Because Chicago is a railway hub the city would always profit from wars, and World War II brought an economic boom that benefited rich and poor alike. New factories sprang up, and skilled and unskilled workers arrived from all over the country. The upheaval of the war also muddied the tranquil waters of "traditional marriage"; the preordained path of a husband working to feed his family and a wife keeping house was disrupted. As Duis and La France sum it up in their book: "There was a violation of the family model." After Pearl Harbor, Chicago witnessed an increase in marriages as men were drafted and sent off to war, leaving an unsettling pall over a generation of women left behind. Wives were left to fend for themselves. In 1943, 43 percent of

Chicago women were working, many taking jobs in factories to support the war; no doubt many were inspired by Norman Rockwell's Rosie the Riveter poster, which later became a lesbian icon.

Although women were required to "cross-dress" in overalls and "practical clothing," men-in-government were mindful of blurring the gender line and zealously protected femininity; in 1943 the government restricted the manufacture of luxury goods, except for lipstick—it was important for factory women to remain feminine and sexually attractive to men. In Chicago, working women embraced the newfound freedom and independence, earning their own money and interacting with women from all walks of life. Amid the workplace camaraderie in the all-female factories it's hardly surprising latent homosexual desires were sometimes laid bare.

With the prospect of the draft and the unpredictability of war marriages, young Chicagoans adopted a philosophy of "eat, drink and be merry, for tomorrow we may die." A sharp rise in VD cases resulted in the federal government opening the Chicago Venereal Disease Hospital in 1942, the nation's first facility of its kind. Chicago was chosen to spearhead the anti-VD effort to safeguard the health of recruits in the surrounding military training centers: Fort Sheridan processed 417,000 recruits during the war, Great Lakes Naval Training Center housed between 50,000 and 70,000 men at one time, and at the Curtiss-Wright Airport 1,000 cadets were trained every three months.

Young men and women from small towns poured into Chicago, and far from the scrutiny of family, neighbors, and church ministers, they discovered a city where vice was carved into the political and social landscape. In *Coming Out under Fire: The History of Gay Men and Women in World War Two* (1990) Allan Bérubé notes upwards of fifty thousand soldiers and sailors converged on Chicago's Loop area every weekend. The city was "wide open"; the mob controlled vice, including the lucrative gay bars, and the payoffs to corrupt police and politicians guaranteed business as usual throughout the war.

Although the military blacklisted gay bars, some enterprising Chicago tavern owners posted "Off Limits" signs above the door to inform gay military personnel where to go. On South State Street in the Loop, among the seedy brothels and burlesque and peep shows, locker clubs sprang up where military personnel left their uniforms and rented civvies to escape detection from MPs patrolling the gay bars. One popular bar was Benny the Bums at 549 North Clark Street. It was always crowded on weekends and held up to 450 people. It was owned and managed by a Jewish couple, Si and Mollie Ginsberg; Si's brother, Sol, worked at the bar and was the business brains behind the enterprise. Chicagoan LeRoi remembers Benny the Bums: "It was dirty, raunchy and you felt like a bum if you went in, and you never wore good clothes."

Charles B. recalls drag shows: "On Sunday afternoon they had a drag contest, amateur drag. And you had to move your drinks because the queens would parade on the bar." The bar closed down in June 1949, and the *Chicago Tribune* column "Tower Ticker" noted: "Benny the Bum's place on North Clark Street, has become the Gayety Café. Vags [*sic*] can now get the bum's rush with a merry laugh."

In the 1940s, hotel bars were meeting places for homosexuals, because they were thought to be safer than gay bars. In Chicago two hotel bars were known for picking up soldiers and sailors: the Town and Country at the Palmer House and the Dome at the Sherman. The Town and Country opened after the war in August 1946; the two cocktail bars had a garden motif, with an abundance of indoor plants, and a garden area outside. In 1949 the *Chicago Tribune* noted: "Nobody seems to enjoy serving you more than the grinning Filipino boys at the Palmer House's Town and Country club." Though it opened after the war, the Town and Country was popular with Navy personnel from Great Lakes Naval Base for the next two decades. The Dome at the Sherman, known affectionately as the "Do-Me Room," was a piano bar that boasted a gay clientele from the 1930s to the 1960s. The Sherman bordered Randolph, Clark, and LaSalle Streets, with two entrances to the Dome bar, one from the street and another from the lobby. On each door stood a "house officer" to control the crowds and keep out the riffraff. The hotel was demolished in 1980. In the 1950s it was famous for its female piano players: in 1951 Virginia Torcom alternated nights with Barbara Sims, a retired college professor who taught music theory at the University of Indiana; the following year it was Patti Goodman and Avis Kent; and then in 1953 it was Peggy Gay and Jacqui O'Shea.

O'Shea recalls the gay crowd: "I always say that at the Dome I wasn't a pianist, I was a social secretary. One would come in and say, 'If Joe comes in tell him to meet me at Kitty Sheon's but if Jim comes in tell him you haven't seen me tonight.'" The owners of the Dome knew the bar was gay, but O'Shea didn't:

I remember when I started there, I thought, "Oh my goodness, this is Utopia, maybe I'll get a husband." And one of the girls said, "Forget it kid, they're all gay." And I said, "Well, I don't understand what that means." I was really stupid, you know.

The guys used to give me jewelry for birthdays and Christmas, and then on Halloween they would borrow it all back. All my evening bags went out on Halloween, but they always brought me pictures of themselves in drag, and it was wonderful.

Homosexuals were not allowed to touch one another back then; some bars insisted customers keep their hands on top the bar at all times. House officers patrolled the Dome looking for indiscretions. "I used to laugh," said O'Shea, "because the piano bar was set up so there was four inches between the piano and the bar and you could see through there, and you would see a little bit of hand-holding now and again, and I'd go, 'Uh uh uh. Watch it.'"

Piano bars were popular with gay men in the 1940s, and each of these smoky cabarets had a "star entertainer" in residence, often a straight middle-aged woman who sang and acted as mother hen to her clutch of gay kids. Frank W. remembers gay bars in the 1940s: "It was the entire social life for gay men at that time. There were no gay churches, bowling leagues, baseball teams, etc."

At the Primrose Path, 1159 North Clark Street, the star performer was Minnesota-born comedian Joy Page, who played piano, sang "dirty ditties," and told risqué jokes to a gay audience. Another popular chanteuse in the 1940s was Lucrezia at the Carousel on Oak and Dearborn; the bar was gay downstairs and mixed upstairs, all managed by a Jewish couple, Ann and Sol, who ran several other gay bars in the city. The Carousel was a "swanky joint." Not all the nightlife in the 1940s was as sophisticated as the Carousel; the Near North Side was a cornucopia of vice, and amid the strip clubs, drug dealers, gambling dens, and burlesque and peep shows were a dozen or so gay bars. Prostitutes, both male and female, offered love for sale on street corners, in doorways, and in the lobbies of cheap hotels that rented rooms by the hour. The book *Chicago: Confidential!* (1950), by New York newspapermen Jack Lait and Lee Mortimer, is a scurrilous exposé of Chicago's "thoroughfares and its alleys, its beauty-spots and its sordid muck." In the book the authors tell of visiting a strip joint on Rush Street recommended by a cab driver:

It was rather like the run of such establishments, except that the girls were juveniles, two no more than 15 years old. There were other men there but the talent seemed to attract many lesbians. The stripping was complete and the tricks were obscene, but circumscribed by lack of imagination. The prices were high and the cabby told us he got $5 for every party he delivered. We had to be okayed by him, as it is in a remodeled private house. There is no sign and the doors are not open to strays. The inevitable B-girl was at the bar and she, too, was a juvenile who should have been asleep after doing her homework. Instead, she was surrounded by obvious lady-lovers who were pawing her and buying her drinks.

## The Raid at the Windup Lounge

The windup of the Windup, State Street, sin den where boy met boy before Police Capt. Harrison raided it, proves that the lower the lights, the greater the scandal power.

"Tower Ticker," *Chicago Tribune*, January 14, 1949

Mayor Edward Kelly held office until 1947 and was succeeded by Martin H. Kennelly. Kennelly was an odd fish in Chicago politics: a self-made businessman and millionaire, he had avoided any sordid entanglement with the city's corruption. Kennelly was a "confirmed bachelor." Although his sexuality is unknown, old-timers insist he was "in the life." Kennelly presided over a postwar economic boom, but he inherited a city deeply entrenched in corruption. In 1949 a scandal in the East Chicago Avenue Police District simmered, boiling over in 1950 with the Kefauver Commission. Back in 1945, Representative Carey Estes Kefauver, chair of the House Judiciary Subcommittee, exposed links between organized crime and certain U.S. federal judges. As a senator he formed the Kefauver Commission and set out on a nationwide tour to investigate gangster infiltration into politics and the police force; he opened his Chicago hearings on October 17, 1950.

The Kefauver Commission issued subpoenas to six prominent police captains, one to Captain Thomas Harrison of the East Chicago Avenue Police District, who oversaw the mob-controlled vice area on the Near North Side with its 348 saloons. When Harrison testified, he was asked how a police captain earning $5,200 a year had assets of $100,000. Harrison's explanation didn't satisfy Colonel George H. White, the Kefauver Commission committee investigator.

Before the Kefauver hearings, Harrison tried to purify his image and clean up his district. A *Chicago Tribune* headline on January 17, 1949, read: "Capt. Harrison Jails 24 in War on Degenerates." Assisted by six detectives and a paddy wagon, Harrison arrested fifteen men and nine women in gay bars on the west side of North Clark Street, along the strip between Chicago Avenue and the Chicago River. "Harrison questioned hundreds of patrons in taverns, sent degenerates to the police station for investigation, and broke up couples who had newly met," the paper gloats. "After being processed thru the police bureau of identification, all 29 were charged with disorderly conduct. Most were freed on bond. The women will appear in Women's court today, and the men will appear in E. Chicago Avenue police court."

Harrison told the *Chicago Tribune* there were "at least 18,000 sexually maladjusted men" in Chicago, "all potentially dangerous." He added that many homosexuals "maintain luxurious apartments where they entertain young, unsuspecting 'recruits' with food, music, liquor, and obscene literature." Harrison also claimed that most of Chicago's degenerates were members of a national organization run by a man named Brown living in or near Miami. Doctor Harry R. Hoffman, the Illinois state alienist, told the *Chicago Tribune* that homosexuals should be incarcerated in institutions "for the protection of society."

The largest haul of "degenerates" was made a week earlier, when Harrison raided the Windup Lounge at 669 North State Street, a popular gay bar. As early as 1944 the Windup had shown up on the police radar when James De Angelo, one of the owners, was found dead, his body stuffed into the trunk of a car in front of 1526 North LaSalle Street; his skull was crushed, several ribs were broken, and he was trussed up with fifty feet of clothes line. Then again, the Windup was listed in a *Chicago Tribune* article on November 14, 1948, headlined: "Dive Keepers on N. Clark St. Get Warnings." Captain John J. Walsh, then head of the East Chicago Avenue police district, warned saloonkeepers "to quit violating the law or quit business." He ordered Venetian blinds in tavern windows be removed and assigned detectives to patrol the district nightly and scrutinize moral behavior through the window. A special focus of Walsh's was saloons that "cater to degenerates." The *Chicago Tribune* continues: "many men who infest the saloons which thrive on the business they bring are morally depraved. They make no effort to conceal their depravity. In fact, they proudly display the earmarks of their trade, the waved hair, the mincing walk and feminine make-up. And since their activities are illegal, the dives in which they congregate wink at the law."

The warning to gay bars was in response to an earlier incident. Two men caught canoodling in Lincoln Park fled in their car at eighty miles per hour, chased by a squad car with guns blazing; the chase ended when the men's car knocked a streetcar off its tracks. The two men admitted meeting at the Windup Lounge. Other gay bars threatened included the Shanty Inn at 716 North Clark Street, a shoddy saloon licensed to Syd Rosenthal and Jerry Abraham; the Green Lantern Club at 714 North Clark Street, licensed to Helen Benedict; the Sewer at 620 North State Street; and Abby's Jungle Club, owned by Abby Davis, at 5 West Erie Street.

On January 9, 1949, Captain Thomas Harrison and six vice cops raided the Windup. Frank W. remembers that night: "Captain Harrison came a little after midnight and went around talking to a few people. I was running the '26' dice table and he came over and asked me to write my name on a slip of paper, saying he wanted 'to be sure he had it.' I did so, and then I signaled one of the floor men over to ask what was going on. He pointed out that we had been under arrest for over an hour and that plain-clothed officers on the door were letting people in, but not letting anyone leave. We were taken to the station in 'Black Marias' and it was a very messy night for all. The newspapers had photographers covering the front door as we were led out one by one to the wagons, it was terrifying."

Dozens of men were arrested and taken to the East Chicago Avenue police station, fingerprinted, and herded into the drunk tank downstairs, where there were no toilet facilities. Frank W., who was twenty-one at the time, was among them: "I had a lover named Vincent, who was a bartender at the White Spider. When I was taken to the police station, I was the only person who had someone who cared enough and had the courage to stand outside the jail all night long and into the next day, sending messages into me to ask what he could do and what did I want him to do."

Frank W's parents turned up with a lawyer and "bought" the arrest records. Frank W. was released. The morning after the raid the *Chicago Tribune* front page read: "File Charges against 87 in Vice Net."

"When the police burst in many of the panicky inmates threw powder puffs and cosmetic cases on the bar in an effort to dispose of incriminating evidence," embellished the paper.

An article on the raid written by Captain Tom Connelly and Lieutenant Bill Drury in the *Chicago Herald-American* began:

> Not satisfied with running gambling and ordinary vice dens, members of the Guzik-Ricca-Capone mob are helping run some of the most notorious dives catering to degenerates. . . .
>
> Although the license for the Windup was in the name of a Paul Medor, the real owner is James Allegretti, who also has an interest in several other questionable places on the Near North Side.
>
> Allegretti is a close associate of Guzik-Ricca-Capone mob's "Three Terrible Doms"—Dominic (Libby) Nuccio, Dominic Brancato and Dominic De Bello—who control syndicate gambling on the North Side.

Jimmy "The Monk" Allegretti was well known to the cops as the mob's vice lord and fixer on the Near North Side; his résumé showed a long career in narcotics, counterfeiting, bootlegging, bribery, bombing, and murder. Another gangster who had a stake in the Windup was Russian-born Jake "Greasy Thumb" Guzik, Al Capone's bookkeeper, who remained the financial manager for the Chicago mob long after Capone's death in 1947. Allegretti ran the Windup with the help of his wife, Florence Ramsay Allegretti, and his brother Tony (a.k.a. Anthony Policheri).

Allegretti and Kaplan were charged with running a disorderly house, and seventy-two customers were charged as inmates. The court appearance lasted four hours: twenty-three men were discharged, two were fined, six requested a jury trial, and forty-one were ordered examined at the court's psychiatric unit. The twenty-three men who were discharged contributed a total of two hundred dollars to the March of Dimes fund at the suggestion of the judge, and the Windup lost its liquor license and was closed down.

Captain Thomas Harrison continued to purge the Near North Side of "degenerates." On February 28, 1949, Hakon Simonson was sentenced to ninety days in jail, and fined one hundred dollars and costs by Judge Mason S. Sullivan in East Chicago Avenue court. Simonson was arrested with nine others in a raid on the Old Huron Bath, a Turkish bathhouse at 679 North Clark Street. A cop testified that Simonson approached him in the bathhouse and made an indecent proposal. Whether the cop's story was true or not is open to question, as they fabricated evidence on a regular basis—take the case of the raid on the Hollywood Bowl, 1300 North Clark

Street, on July 20, 1949. That night police officers Leo Stanko and Edward Szpajer raided the popular gay lounge after observing acts of perversion committed by two men sitting at the bar. The license, in the name of Anna Lauda, was revoked and Captain Michael Ahern of the Hudson Avenue station described the Hollywood Bowl as "a hangout for perverts, homosexuals and degenerates." On September 16, when Lauda took her case to the city's liquor appeal commission, Stanko and Szpajer changed their story, admitting no act of sexual perversion had taken place. The two officers were suspended.

# 15

# The Cold War

The local ramifications of a national tragedy, the McCarthy witch hunts of "reds and pinks" caused FBI director J. Edgar Hoover to pursue Illinois governor Adlai Stevenson for his alleged homosexuality. Did a Chicago lesbian kill the "Black Dahlia"? Why was homophobic Senator Everett M. Dirksen visiting a gay bar? The "outing" of Senator Joseph McCarthy, Cold War hysteria, and Bruce Scott versus the Civil Service Commission all happened in Chicago.

Wisconsin Republican senator Joseph McCarthy is often credited with instigating the 1950s witch hunt of homosexuals working in federal government, but he was only exploiting a purge that dated back to an incident a decade earlier. In September 1940, Under Secretary of State Sumner Welles, a lifelong friend of President Franklin D. Roosevelt, became embroiled in a sex scandal; while traveling on the presidential train Welles attempted to proposition several black Pullman porters. When FBI director J. Edgar Hoover called for the firing of Welles, Roosevelt refused, claiming his friend was drunk at the time. The incident proved a potent weapon in the arsenal of Republicans in 1940, and the scandal simmered until Ralph O. Brewster (R-Maine), a close ally of McCarthy, threatened to launch a Senate probe into the incident. Welles resigned, divorced his wife, and spent his twilight years in a disastrous relationship with Gustave, his bisexual butler. He died in 1961, at age sixty-eight, in Bernardsville, New Jersey.

Republicans discovered that "outing" homosexuals equaled power. Before World War II sexual improprieties in government circles were largely ignored, but the upheaval of war brought homosexuality out of the shadows and into the spotlight of partisan politics and Cold War paranoia. The late 1940s also saw a rash of horrendous sex crimes. FBI director Hoover stirred the pot with a magazine article called "How Safe Is Your Daughter?" He wrote: "The most rapidly increasing type of crime is that perpetrated by degenerate sex offenders. . . . [S]hould wild beasts break out of circus cages, a whole city would be mobilized instantly. But depraved human beings, more savage than beasts, are permitted to rove America almost at will."

Three Chicago doctors disagreed with Hoover. In November 1949, Doctor Clarence A. Neymann, professor of psychiatry at Northwestern University, told the *Chicago Tribune*: "Sex criminals were as numerous proportionally in the Elizabethan era as they are today." Doctor Edward J. Kelleher, chief of the municipal court psychiatric institute, agreed and disputed Hoover's assertion that sex offenses were up 50 percent. "The total number arrested in this field has been virtually the same in the last few years," said Kelleher. "According to the police commissioner's office the total arrested in 1948 was 2,001 and in 1949 was 1,970."

The witch hunt for reds and pinks under the bed reached absurd proportions, with homosexuals blamed for all the nation's ills. The *Chicago Tribune* on March 5, 1947, reported on a new twist in the murder case of Elizabeth Short, "The Black Dahlia," found hacked to death on January 15 in a Los Angeles suburb. A Mrs. Marie Grieme, a former resident of Chicago, told LA police that a Chicago woman called Billy—a former WAC and judo expert—confided that she killed Short "in a fit of jealousy during a lover's quarrel." Chicago police picked up thirty-eight-year-old Mildred "Billy" Kolian for questioning, but she had an alibi, had never been a WAC, and knew nothing about judo. The article ends: "Police also were questioning four other women, some of them members of a homosexual ring, in connection with the case."

In the 1950s homosexuals were depicted as sexually rapacious, loose-lipped, and untrustworthy, making them easy blackmail targets for Russia to recruit as spies. Gay men and lesbians as a whole were viewed as a sinister Soviet "Trojan Horse," fifth columnists infiltrating the U.S. government. In his book *Lavender Scare: The Cold War Persecution of Gays and Lesbians in the Federal Government* (2004), David K. Johnson documents the rise of McCarthyism. Johnson writes that although McCarthy railed against Communists and queers, he excused himself from hearings of homosexuals, leaving the purging of gay men and lesbians to Senators Styles Bridges, Kenneth Wherry, and Clyde Hoey. McCarthy's witch hunt began on February 9, 1950, with a speech in Wheeling, West Virginia, when he waved a piece of paper at the cameras claiming it contained the names of 205 Communists employed by the State Department. Deputy Undersecretary John Peurifoy, testifying before a congressional committee, denied the charges, but admitted that ninety-one homosexuals, including two women, had been fired as security risks in the previous three years. McCarthy leapt on this statement and for the next four years pursued his Salem-style witch hunt; "Let's Clean up the State Department" emerged as the GOP's mantra.

McCarthy's speechwriter was *Chicago Tribune* reporter Willard Edwards. On March 26, 1950, the paper published a report by Edwards headlined "Assert Truman 'Gag' Is Hiding Moral Laxities." It begins: "Informed investigators said today that the Truman gag of FBI reports on federal employees prevented the disclosure of a large group of men of unnatural tendencies on the government payroll." Edwards goes on: "History discloses that the rise to power of such men has frequently been a problem disturbing rulers. They are often ambitious men of intellectual attainments, attracting others of their like, forming an influential clique which strives to shape policy to its own ends. Such men have a fatal weakness when occupying positions of trust with access to confidential records. They are subject to blackmail thru exposure of their sordid practices and thus may be induced to furnish foreign agents with their country's secrets."

Three days later Edwards reported that Lieutenant Roy Blick, head of the District of Columbia police vice squad, had handed a Senate appropriations subcommittee a history of depravity in government bureaucracy. This time a new threat was revealed: "Blick added a new chapter to the revolting record of sex perversion among government payrollers," wrote Edwards. "He displayed police statistics showing the presence of a large group of lesbians—the feminine counterpart of homosexuals—in the State and other departments."

While free speech advocates defended the rights of Communists, nobody came to the defense of homosexuals, least of all the American Civil Liberties Union (ACLU). In 1951 a dishonorably discharged lesbian WAF requested help from the civil rights group and was told to drop her complaint and seek medical treatment to control her desires. The ACLU supported the American Psychiatric Association's diagnosis of homosexuality as an illness. The only course of action for homosexuals in government was to resign, enter a faux marriage, or curtail their social lives.

Soon after McCarthy's revelations about Communists, Senator Clyde Hoey, a Democrat from North Carolina, was appointed to lead the investigating committee into homosexuals in federal government. One statistic used by the committee was attributed to Doctor R. H. Felix, director of the National Institute of Mental Health, who stated that 4 percent of white adult males in the United States were "confirmed homosexuals." Chicago psychiatrists disagreed. In the *Chicago Tribune* of April 9, 1950, Doctor Paul Hletko, Illinois state alienist, said: "Dr. Felix's figure is shooting at the moon. We don't find anything like that among patients in our mental hospital system. I doubt if more than one half of one percent of the white adult males in and out of hospitals are confirmed homosexuals." Doctor V. G. Urse, medical director of the Cook County psychopathic hospital, agreed: "I'd like to know what Dr. Felix means by 'confirmed' homosexuals. He must be including those who exhibit effeminate traits, but are not otherwise classifiable as homosexuals, and also may be referring to latent homosexuals, to arrive at such a high figure." Doctor Harry R. Hoffman, director of the Chicago health department's division of mental hygiene, questioned whether reliable statistics were even possible: "It's difficult to get admissions from homosexually inclined individuals. We find them out only when they get into conflict with society. On such a basis, Dr. Felix's figure is extremely high."

Senator Hoey's investigating committee report *Employment of Homosexuals and Other Sex Perverts in Government* confirmed that homosexuals were a threat to government. He wrote: "The lack of emotional stability which is found in most sex perverts and the weakness of their moral fiber, makes them susceptible to the blandishments of the foreign espionage agent. It is the experience of intelligence experts that perverts are vulnerable to interrogation by a skilled questioner and they seldom refuse to talk about themselves."

In 1952, when Republican Dwight D. Eisenhower was elected president, he signed an executive order denying employment to homosexuals, a law that remained in place until 1975. The 1952 election was particularly contentious. FBI director Hoover, an Eisenhower supporter, maintained that the Democratic presidential candidate, Illinois governor Adlai

Stevenson, was once arrested in New York for a homosexual offense. The rumor was borne out by the candidate's ex-wife, Ellen Borden Stevenson, who spoke openly of her ex-husband's homosexuality at dinner parties, though her story is suspect as she allegedly suffered from a mental disorder.

Though highly respected as a thinker and politician, Stevenson's belief in democracy was easily trampled by the political thugs of the time. His mild-mannered demeanor led to his enemies suggesting he was "fruity." In 1947 he vetoed the Broyles bill, which would require public employees to take an oath of loyalty: "The whole notion of loyalty inquisitions is a national characteristic of the police state, not of democracy. . . . The history of Soviet Russia is a modern example of this ancient practice. . . . I must, in good conscience, protest against any unnecessary suppression of our rights as free men." He was an easy target for Hoover's muckraking. Stevenson first crossed swords with Hoover in 1949, when the Illinois governor was a character witness for suspected Communist Alger Hiss and denounced the witch hunt. When Stevenson ran for president in 1952, Republican vice-presidential candidate Richard Nixon led the attack, aided by a rabid Senator McCarthy; Hoover's contribution to the assault was a smear campaign based on nineteen pages of trumped-up charges. Stevenson lost the election.

In 2005 the personal files of J. Edgar Hoover were released, including a record of his thirty-five-year campaign against Stevenson, whom he nicknamed "Adeline." Hoover claimed Stevenson was one of the "best known homosexuals in Illinois." In a November 2005 interview with WLS Channel 7, Chicago's ABC television affiliate, former FBI agent M. Wesley Swearingen detailed how he and another agent were assigned to dig up dirt on Stevenson's alleged homosexuality in the early 1950s. "The other agent and I went into different gay bars around North Avenue," Swearingen told Channel 7, "and I think the best we could find out he went to the gay bars, but he wasn't gay. We talked to about 100 different gay people, and they said 'Yeah, he came in here for a drink. So what?'"

Swearingen was an FBI Special Agent for twenty-five years, assigned to Chicago from 1952 to 1962. His memoir, *FBI Secrets: An Agent's Exposé* (1994) blows the whistle on FBI integrity or the lack of it. Swearingen admits to being active in Hoover's dirty tricks department, in which he conducted hundreds of "black bag" jobs (illegal burglaries) on suspected Communists and other groups and individuals in Chicago.

Stevenson wasn't the only Illinois politician visiting gay bars, as Republican Senator Everett M. Dirksen was a regular at the Shoreline 7, a syndicate-owned bar located at 7 East Division Street. A bartender confirms that Dirksen often shared a liquid lunch in the backroom with police officials and mobsters. The *Hollywood Citizen-News* of September 23, 1954, reported that Dirksen gave a speech to the National Federation of Republican Women in Los Angeles, in which he berated Democrats, including Franklin D. Roosevelt, Harry S. Truman, and Adlai Stevenson, saying: "Never were the destroyers and traitors in government so busy as during the 20 years of Democratic rule." He went on to say it was no easy task ridding the government of "the wreckers and destroyers, the security risks and homosexuals, the blabbermouths and drunks, the traitors and saboteurs."

After losing the presidential election, Adlai Stevenson stepped up his criticism of McCarthy, but Eisenhower was reluctant to silence the Wisconsin senator who had helped him to power. In 1952 McCarthy hired Roy Cohn, a New York district attorney, as chief counsel to the Government Committee on Operations of the Senate. Cohn's anti-Communist credentials were impeccable; he had assisted in the 1951 prosecution of Soviet spies Julius and Ethel Rosenberg. Cohn was also a homosexual and one of the most vicious, rabidly homophobic individuals to enter the political arena. He is said to have threatened Senator Lester Hunt (D-Wyo.), a critic of McCarthy, with making public his son's arrest for lewdness. As a result, Hunt declined to run for reelection and on June 19, 1954, committed suicide in his Senate office.

Cohn's first move was to hire his lover, G. David Schine, as his chief consultant. Schine was heir to the Schine Hotel Corporation millions. The dramatic meltdown of the McCarthy, Cohn, and Schine triumvirate began in October 1953, when McCarthy opened an investigation into Communist infiltration of the military. Not welcoming the intrusion into their private affairs, the army retaliated by leaking tidbits of gossip to anti-McCarthy reporters, including Evanston, Illinois–born *Washington Post* columnist Drew Pearson. On December 15, 1953, Pearson accused McCarthy and Cohn of abusing their position by trying to exempt Schine from the draft.

It was in this toxic milieu that from April 22 to June 17, 1954, the Army–McCarthy hearings were televised. The hearings were convened to investigate charges against the army by McCarthy, and vice versa. According to the army, when Schine was drafted in 1953, Cohn pressured military officials to grant him special privileges. When the army presented a detailed chronology of Cohn's intrusions, McCarthy hit back by accusing them of holding Schine hostage to deter his committee from exposing Communists within military ranks. The nation was hooked on the hearings, and for the first time the public saw McCarthy's ill-mannered outbursts and Cohn's arrogant posturing. The two fared badly when compared to the calm and thoughtful Joseph N. Welch, the army's special counsel. The climax came when McCarthy suggested Fred Fisher, a lawyer working for the same firm as Welch, harbored Communist sympathies. Welch responded by saying: "Until this moment, Senator, I think I never gauged your cruelty or recklessness. . . . [H]ave you no sense of decency, sir, at long last? Have you left no sense of decency?" The gallery erupted into applause as McCarthy was slapped down in front of millions.

Cohn resigned after the hearings and remained a closeted homosexual until his death from AIDS on August 2, 1986. G. David Schine completed his military service, and in 1957 married Hellivi Rombin, a former Miss Sweden and Miss Universe; they had six children. In the 1960s Schine acted in TV's *Batman* and produced the movies *The French Connection* (1971) and *That's Action* (1977). On June 20, 1996, Schine, his wife, and son Berndt were killed when their single-engine plane crashed in Southern California.

McCarthy's final disgrace came on December 2, 1954, when by a vote of 67 to 22 he was censured by the U.S. Senate. Rumors of McCarthy's homosexuality circulated for years. His political rivals referred to him as a "pixie." As early as January 14, 1952, Drew Pearson noted the rumor in his diary. The rumor surfaced in print when the *Las Vegas Sun* published an article on October 25, 1952, by Hank Greenspun: "Joe McCarthy is a bachelor of 43 years. He seldom dates girls and if he does he laughingly describes it as window dressing. . . . It is common talk among homosexuals in Milwaukee who rendezvous in the White Horse Inn that Senator Joe McCarthy has often engaged in homosexual activities."

In another article, Greenspun claims McCarthy had once been the guest of honor at a Young Republican convention in Wausau, Wisconsin, spent the night in a hotel with a former official of the Milwaukee Young Republicans, and engaged in illicit acts. Instead of suing the paper, McCarthy married Jeannie Kerr, his secretary, on September 29, 1953, in Washington, D.C. The *Chicago Tribune* noted that "the 43-year-old McCarthy, a confessed jittery individual, fumbled with the platinum wedding ring as he slipped it on his 29-year-old bride's finger. He forgot to kiss the bride at the allotted moment."

Whether McCarthy ever kissed his bride is not known, but in January 1957 the couple adopted a baby girl, Tierney Elizabeth, from the New York Foundling Home.

Senator Joseph McCarthy died on May 2, 1957, at age forty-eight, from cirrhosis of the liver.

## Bruce Scott

One federal employee who did fight back against the gay witch hunt was longtime Chicago resident Bruce Chardon Scott, who took the Civil Service Commission (CSC) to court in 1963, as documented in materials at the Gregory Sprague Collection at the Chicago Historical Museum. Scott was born on March 7, 1912, in Portland, Oregon. At age ten, after his parents divorced, he moved to Chicago with his mother, where he graduated from Tilden Technical High School and then earned a BA in Political Science at the University of Chicago in 1933. Scott worked as a research associate in the Office of the Corporation Counsel in Chicago, until the passage of the Labor Standards Act in 1938, when he became a wage and hour inspector in the Department of Labor. After serving in the army for eighteen months during World War II, he relocated to Washington, D.C., where he resumed his career at the Department of Labor until 1956, when he was forced to resign when it came to light he had been arrested twice, and charged once with loitering.

The first arrest was in 1947 in Lafayette Park, a well-known meeting place for homosexuals in Washington, D.C. In 1962, when he reapplied for federal employment, he gave the following account of the arrest during an interview with the Civil Service Commission:

> At Lafayette Square men's room I was picked up by a police officer. After asking questions I would not answer, he charged me with loitering. There was a man in the men's room who was behaving in an odd manner. I found I was unable to urinate and stepped outside to wait for him to come out. I went back in about ten minutes later and found this fellow was still in the men's room in the same odd position (leaning over a urinal with his hands propped against the wall). The police officer followed me in and when I was leaving he said he wanted to talk to me. The police officer drove up in a

Park police cruiser when I was outside the men's room waiting for the other fellow to come out. He watched me for five minutes before I walked back in.

There were no charges in the second arrest, but the police officer at the time made this statement:

> About 12:15 a.m. October 3, 1951, this man was observed standing over a white soldier in a door way on the 12th Street side of the Greyhound bus station. What first drew our attention was the above man would look up and down the street to see if anyone was coming, then he would run his hands around the soldier's pockets, at one time this man was in the doorway sitting with this soldier. The soldier was too drunk to be questioned at this time so he was turned over to the A.S.P.D. until he was sober enough to be questioned.

The arrests caught up with him in 1956, and when questioned Scott resigned, neither admitting nor denying he was gay. After that, he found it impossible to find work he was qualified for, so he took lesser jobs, like in a bank as a clerk and in an employment agency. Both positions were terminated when his past caught up with him, as being discharged by a federal agency for sex perversion led to blacklisting by private employers. In June 1959 Scott was hired by Fairfax County, Virginia, but again, he was dismissed eighteen months later when his arrests came to light. In 1962, when Scott reapplied for federal employment, James D. Keys, the Budget Research Director at the Personnel Department in Fairfax County, gave a report to the CSC. Keys described Scott as an "oddball." Highlights of the report read:

> He does not have any stand-out characteristics that would be considered as effeminate, but his thinking runs along lines which are not common in a man . . .
>
> Later I confronted him directly with the question as to whether he was a homosexual and he said it was true. He then told me that he was perverted since he was a young boy. He also mentioned that he lived in Alexandria, Virginia, with an employee of the Government who he considered as his lover.

After reading a news report in late March 1961 about the case of *Franklin Edward Kameny v. Wilbur M. Brucker, secretary of the Army, et al.*, the first challenge to the government's antigay employment policies to reach the Supreme Court—albeit with the justices denying the petition—Scott contacted Kameny for advice. Kameny, an astronomer fired from the U.S. Army Map Division, steered Scott in the direction of David Carliner, an ACLU lawyer who eventually took the case to court. Carliner, a civil rights lawyer, had a long resume of challenging state and federal laws on segregation, mixed-race marriages, and the rights of illegal immigrants.

Later, along with Kameny, author Jack Nichols, and others, Bruce Scott founded Mattachine Society Washington in November 1961, serving as secretary and vice president. Scott tried again for federal employment on October 3, 1961, and yet again on November 13 with no success. On March 20, 1962, he applied to the government again, this time sitting and passing the Civil Service Commission tests for personnel officer and management analyst positions. At a hearing on April 27 an official informed Scott that the commission "has information indicating you are a homosexual. Do you wish to comment on this matter?" Scott answered, "No, I do not believe the question is pertinent insofar as my job performance is concerned." Turned down again, he appealed the decision. The CSC wrote to him on June 7 in a letter signed by Kimbell Johnson, Director of the Bureau of Personnel Investigations:

> This is in reference to your appeal from the decision of the Division of Adjudication of May 16, 1962, in rating ineligible the application filed under the Federal Administrative and Management Examination, U-167. You were also barred from employment in the competitive Federal service for a period of three years; any pending applications were rated ineligible; and all eligibilities existing on Civil Service registers were cancelled.
>
> Careful consideration has been given to your appeal and the entire record in your case. The evidence clearly substantiates the facts on which the previous decision was based, and you have furnished no new or additional information on appeal which would justify a reversal of that action.
>
> It is the decision of this office that the previous action taken was warranted by the facts and required under established standards of suitability for the competitive Federal service. Accordingly, that action is affirmed.

This decision may be appealed further to the Commission's Board of Appeals and review.

Scott appealed again, and the final CSC decision was dated October 25, 1962, and signed by Nicholas J. Oganovic, Acting Executive Director:

The Civil Service Commissioners have given careful consideration to your request, and found that error has not been demonstrated in the decisions of the Commission's Bureau of Personnel Investigations and Board of Appeals and review, rating you ineligible on suitability grounds . . .

[T]he decision issued in your case by the Board of Appeals and Review on August 3, 1962, will remain as the final decision of the Commission, thereby exhausting your administrative remedies.

In April 1963, with ACLU counsel David Carliner, Scott filed suit against the CSC, claiming the denial of federal employment to homosexuals was "arbitrary and discriminatory." The lawsuit was widely reported in the national and local press. In the first round, in January 1964, the ACLU argued homosexuality was a private affair and the government should have no interest in it unless it affected job performance. Judge George L. Hart of the U.S. District Court disagreed and ruled against Scott, saying CSC laws and regulations were constitutionally reasonable, determining that "homosexuality is immoral under the present mores of society and is abhorrent to the great majority of Americans."

"Maybe it shouldn't be," he added, "but it is."

Scott, unable to find suitable employment, returned to Chicago. *Scott v. Macy* came up before the very liberal U.S. Court of Appeals for the D.C. Circuit on June 16, 1965. The court ruled in a 2–1 opinion that the government had improperly denied employment to Scott. Chief Judge David L. Bazelon ruled the CSC had treated Scott unfairly because they never revealed exactly what the alleged offenses were: "The Commission must at least specify the conduct it finds 'immoral,'" Bazelon wrote, "and state why that conduct related to occupational competence or fitness." Bazelon went on to say that Scott had the right to be free from "government defamation" and the government must justify imposing the "stigma of disqualification for immoral conduct."

Victory was short and sweet. The CSC reformulated the charges, and *Scott v. Macy II* headed back to the courts to follow the same path as before.

In January 1967 U.S. District Court Judge George L. Hart again decided in favor of the Civil Service Commission, only to have the case overturned a second time in the appeals court. In 1968 the CSC gave up fighting the case, though it took many more court challenges before the government ban on hiring homosexuals was lifted on July 3, 1975. In the new guidelines, as reported by the July 4 *Chicago Tribune*, the U.S. Civil Service Commission concludes: "While a person may not be found unsuitable based on unsubstantiated conclusions concerning possible embarrassment for the federal service, a person may be dismissed or found unsuitable . . . where the evidence exists that (his or her) sexual conduct affects job fitness."

And: "As the courts have ordered, there must be some rational connection between the individual's conduct and the efficiency of the service."

After winning his case Scott remained in Chicago working for the Illinois State Labor Department until he retired in 1985. In 1993 he was inducted into the City of Chicago Gay and Lesbian Hall of Fame. Bruce Chardon Scott died on December 26, 2001, at age eighty-nine.

# 16

# Masculinity and
# the Physique Culture

Bodybuilder Eugen Sandow brought physique culture to Chicago in 1893. Chicago physique magazines like *Tomorrow's Man* thrived in the 1950s, but in the early '60s husband-and-wife team Jack and Nirvana Ward Zuideveld, editors of *Vim* and *Gym*, fought the law and lost. But it was the 1960s that saw the rise of businessman Charles "Chuck" Renslow, through *Mars* magazine, Kris Studios, the art and choreography of Domingo "Etienne" Orejudos, and his connections with author and tattoo artist Samuel Steward.

The birth of the modern physical culture movement in the United States was at the Chicago World's Columbian Exposition of 1893, when "Sandow the Magnificent" posed motionless as a Greek marble statue for the crowds. Eugen Sandow was the prodigy of Chicagoan Florenz Ziegfeld, who used the Prussian bodybuilder's amazing feats of strength to draw the crowds and revive the flagging fortunes of his Trocadero Theatre. Chicagoans had been introduced to Sandow four years earlier when a headline on the front page of the October 30, 1889, *Chicago Tribune* read: "Stronger than Samson: A London Audience Amazed at an 'Unknown's' Feats of Strength." During a show at the Royal Aquarium in London, Samson, then considered the strongest man in the world, was introducing his pupil, Cyclops, who, by all accounts, was a brute of a man. Samson challenged anyone in the audience to come forward and equal the feats of Cyclops for a cash prize. A muscular "unknown" stepped forward, and after lifting dumbbells and weights of between fifty and four hundred pounds, the interloper won the prize. The upstart's name was Eugen Sandow.

Sandow moved to New York and performed at the Casino Theatre in a musical farce called *Adonis*, whence Ziegfeld poached him for his own show in Chicago. The Trocadero Vaudevilles included acts like the Flying Jordans, Amann the great character impersonator, the Lucifers, Tom Brown the double-note whistler of the Gaiety Theater London, and Miss Scottie, a Scottish collie dog "who is possessed of human intelligence." The show opened at Chicago's Trocadero Theatre on August 1, 1893, with music by Dutch pianist and composer Martinus Sieveking, Sandow's lover. The show was a hit. Sandow also used his physique for the benefit of medical science. On August 21, 1893, Sandow entertained members of the Chicago Medical Society at Orpheus Hall, Schiller Building, where the 250-pound Charles Earl, president of the society, stood on the Prussian's hands and was lifted onto a table.

At the time the idea of health and bodybuilding for the average man was unheard of: the unhealthy eating habits of the poor and the gluttony of the rich precluded the notion. Yet Sandow, with his rugged looks, dark curly hair, waxed mustache, and rippling muscles, inspired men to consider their physical appearance for the first time since the Greeks and Romans.

Eugen Sandow was born Friedrich Wilhelm Mueller on April 2, 1867, in Königsberg, Germany, where he lived until the family moved to Rome, where he was expected to join the priesthood. In Rome he visited art galleries and studied the male physique. His bodybuilding career began after seeing a performance by Professor Louis Attila (real name Ludwig Durlacher) and becoming the strongman's pupil. They toured Europe together between 1887 and 1889. After Ziegfeld made Sandow famous, Attila cashed in on his former pupil's notoriety by opening gyms in London, New York, and, in 1908, Chicago. Attila was a revolutionary for his time, as he viewed women as equals and encouraged them to learn self-defense. In Attila's gyms women were taught to lift weights, box with a punching bag, and even compete against men in the ring. His most successful prodigy in Chicago was Caroline Baumann, an Austrian immigrant, who after ten months training at his gym lost 25 pounds and could lift 400-pound weights off the floor and 140 pounds over her head. Another strongman, who came to Chicago "in search of new fields to conquer," was the Spartan-born and Spartan-trained Nikolas Props. The *Chicago Tribune* wrote on March 13, 1898: "There are strong men yet in Greece—strong as those who battled in the Olympian Games." While visiting Chicago, Props took a crowd to the freight yards on the lakefront, put his shoulder to a freight car filled with 48,000 pounds of grain, and pushed until it began to roll.

After touring the United States with the Trocadero Vaudevilles, Eugen Sandow returned to London and married Blanche Brookes. Though the marriage produced two daughters, Helen and Lorraine, it was far from idyllic, as Sandow's constant touring and sexual adventures made his wife jealous. Particularly galling was his love affair with fellow bodybuilder and concert pianist Martinus Sieveking, with whom he lived in New York. Sieveking's first piano recital in Chicago was October 23, 1893, in the Banquet Hall at the Lexington Hotel. The *Chicago Tribune* review said he opened with Schumann's *Études en forme de variations* and that "there was a tendency to pound. On the other hand, a group of original compositions were given with captivating delicacy and musical appreciation." It was better than his review when he played New York's Carnegie Hall on November 15, 1896: "He is a muscular player, and the vigor of his attack suggests the athlete who consciously exploits his strength. The quality of his playing is unpleasantly monotonous."

Sieveking, who also had a wife and a son in London, wrote the music for Sandow's shows, traveled with him on tour, and was also his bodybuilding pupil. Sieveking had an impressive physique himself. In 1898 Sandow edited a journal called *The Magazine of Physical Culture* and opened his Physical Culture Studio in London, the first of its kind to focus on all aspects of health, including diet. On September 14, 1901, he held the world's first bodybuilding contest to focus on musculature and not just weightlifting, selling out the Royal Albert Hall.

Sandow died in London on October 14, 1925, at age fifty-eight. He was buried in Putney Vale Cemetery in an unmarked grave. In 2008 Chris Davies, Sandow's great-great-grandson, added a gravestone, a half-ton pink sandstone monolith inscribed "SANDOW."

## Gay Muscle Mags

The successful magazine *Chicago Bodybuilder*, published by Norbert Grueber and Abe Marmel, lasted from July 1946 to September 1950.

Although straight, it had a large gay readership, though physique magazines denied any gay connection. In the June 1957 issue of *Strength and
Health*, an editorial, written by Harry B. Paschall, is headlined: "Let Me
Tell You a Fairy Tale" and begins: "The menace of homosexual magazines
is more serious than ever before, and the cause of clean physical culture is
threatened by peddlers of pornography." He goes on to list *Vim, Body
Beautiful, Male Figure*, and *Adonis* as publications aimed at the "swish"
trade, and notes that "they have infiltrated the bodybuilding field in recent
years, contributing to juvenile delinquency and debauchery." He continues:
"These dirty little books are aimed directly at a very profitable market, the
homosexual or 'fairy' trade. They are on the stands for one reason only—to
make a profit. Circulation figures show they do just that, because they out-
sell the regular physical culture journals."

The heyday of "Beefcake" magazines spanned the 1950s and '60s. One
early gay muscle mag was *Physique Pictorial*, first published by photographer
and filmmaker Bob Mizer in 1950. In 1945 Mizer founded the Athletic
Model Guild in Los Angeles, an agency for finding modeling work for unemployed actors. Mizer soon discovered selling photographs of naked
young men was far more lucrative than finding them work, so he sold his
photosets by placing ads in wrestling and other men's publications. In 1950
he launched *Physique Pictorial* using the endless stream of Hollywood
hopefuls flooding into the city as models. Two years later, Irvin Johnson, a
gay man in Chicago, launched *Tomorrow's Man*, a health and fitness
magazine that became the largest-selling publication of its type in the
1950s. The seeds of it were sown in 1947 when Johnson, a dietician and
health expert, opened Johnson's Health Club at 22 East Van Buren Street.
G. F. H., who worked for the magazine, tells the story: "Irv lived at the
YMCA on Wabash. At that time, Wabash Avenue was derelict, and although
there were shops on the street level, there were vacant apartments above
many of the buildings. Irv stored his weights in one of these lofts where he
would work out. He got friendly with the boys at the 'Y' and they wanted
to work out so he charged them 25c to use his weights, and from there it
just grew until he was able to rent a place and set himself up."

The first issue of *Tomorrow's Man* was published in 1952. "It was
monthly," said G. F. H. "To promote Irv's line of health foods. He would
take really awful looking people and put them on these diets, and it was
fantastic. He called them 'Before and After' cases." In the March 1957 issue

of *Vim* magazine, an ad for Johnson's health system appears under a photograph of a "Before and After" case. It reads: "Here you see a pupil of Irv Johnson who put on 26 pounds of muscle in just 35 days. He supplemented his diet with Irv Johnson's concentrated nourishment. One of the main products he used was Johnson's Protein 60 . . . developed and marketed exclusively by Johnson Laboratories."

Johnson took most of the photographs published in *Tomorrow's Man*, though he never took full-frontal nudes. "It was dangerous," recalls G. F. H. "I don't think people realized the power of the Postmaster; if they suspected you of sending obscenity through the mails, they could put a padlock on the door of your business. After the magazine got started, we received photographs from young bodybuilders from all over the United States. Quite a few of them were totally nude. When Bill Bunton [the associate editor] got these things through the mail, he had a pot of India ink and a brush on his desk, and he had to brush a jockstrap over exposed males. You never knew, a postal inspector might walk in the office and see them."

One of Johnson's early models was Chicagoan Glen Bishop, whom he first photographed at the age of sixteen after watching him train at the gym with his friend Richard Alan. Both appeared in early issues of *Tomorrow's Man*. Bishop, who later married—though he allegedly had a rich male "sponsor"—appears full frontal nude in the January 1954 issue, albeit with his genitals inked out. Another Chicago lensman who photographed Bishop was Cliff Oettinger, who, along with Irv Johnson and Charles Renslow at Kris Studios, completed the triumvirate of local physique photographers. Oettinger, who shot many remarkable images in his short career, seems to have faded into obscurity. G. F. H. stayed on the payroll at Johnson's Health Club until January 3, 1955. In July of that year *Tomorrow's Man* announced it was moving to New York. Although Johnson sold the magazine, he held on to the gym. His interest was waning, however, as he focused more on promoting his health products. G. F. H. recalled:

> Across from the gym there were three buildings together called the Lorraine Hotel. Irv took four rooms there, knocked out the walls and made one big beautiful studio out of it, with mirrors and white carpeting. He wanted it to be a spaceship: the windows were blocked, the temperature controlled, as was the humidity. He

wanted a positive atmosphere. He was a visionary in a way. People would come up and he would feed them his protein ice cream. He would also take his famous protein drink up to the Chez Paree and feed it to the visiting stars. That's how I met Liberace.

Johnson's visits to the Chez Paree nightclub opened celebrity doors that led to him relocating to California, where he changed his name to Rheo H. Blair—on the advice of a numerologist—and reinvented himself as "The Nutritionist to the Stars." He was the personal trainer of popular TV and movie actor Robert Cummings, among others. The fey health nut with a penchant for puffy sleeved yellow silk shirts went from the Chicago YMCA to feeding protein supplements to stars like Charlton Heston, Raquel Welch, Liberace, Bruce Lee, Lawrence Welk, and Regis Philbin. Whatever the ingredients were in his milk and egg protein supplements, it worked, as Jim Park, whom he trained in his Chicago gym, became Mr. America 1952 and Mr. Universe 1954.

In the 1970s the popularity of Johnson/Blair's products waned as the health conscious turned their backs on gyms and fatty supplements and took up jogging. It was also a time when bodybuilders discovered steroids. Irv Johnson died in mysterious circumstances in 1983 at age sixty-three. A friend at the time described his death as "untimely." Before moving to California, Johnson sold Irvin Johnson Health Club, Inc. to Chicago gay businessman Charles "Chuck" Renslow, who renamed it the Triumph Gym. Renslow's interest in photographing male nudes came in 1952 when he met his lover, the artist and dance choreographer Dom Orejudos (Etienne). "One of his drawings was published in *Tomorrow's Man*," explained Renslow, "Dom knew Irv Johnson because he worked out at the gym, and so he submitted work to Irv and he published it. He submitted it under the name Domingo, which was his real name. Afterwards, I said 'You should have used a pseudonym, you shouldn't have used your own name.' Dom said, 'That's right.' So he went to Irv and said, 'Can I change it?' And Irv said, 'No, it's already in press, but we can change it as long as it's the exact same number of letters.' So Dom translated his middle name into French, Stephen became Etienne, and he painted under that name for the next 40 years."

Renslow also trained at Johnson's Health Club, and in 1959, a year after purchasing the gym, he won a bronze medal in weightlifting at the Pan-American Games in Chicago. He and Orejudos also started Kris

Studios at 1953 North Larrabee Street, for physique photography. "My main reason for buying the gym was to get models," explained Renslow. "In those days models were hard to find, not like they are today, where people are clamoring. So what we did was give some of the bodybuilders . . . the Mr. Chicagos and Mr. Illinoises . . . free gym membership in exchange for photographing them in a 'G' string, and also I would take a whole series of photos of them with trunks on, for themselves. The gym gave me access to a tremendous number of models."

Photographs from Kris Studios were published in magazines worldwide, including *Young Physique, Adonis*, and the Swiss gay magazine *Der Kreis*. In July 1961 Renslow published one issue of *Triumph* magazine to publicize his Triumph gym. "It had articles about weightlifting and working out," said Renslow. "*Tomorrow's Man* used weightlifting to get beefcake photos out, but *Triumph* was a true weightlifting magazine like *Strength and Health*." Johnson prodigy Jim Park flexed his muscles on the cover of *Triumph*, and the magazine's themes were listed as "muscular development, physical symmetry and health and vitality." The one issue also boasted a "Ladies Department," which was to be a regular feature had the magazine continued.

Renslow's photographic career started in the late 1940s: "A photographic magazine was having a contest. I knew this girl and I took some pictures of her in the nude. I sent them in and I won first place. So then I started Century Studio downtown and I sold pictures of her and several of her girlfriends, and I sold them through the mail. I advertised in *Popular Photography* and *U.S. Photography*, and those types of magazines. You could show tits and butts but no pubic hair. As long as it was artistic they didn't bother with photographs of women at all."

The next publication from Kris Studios was in May 1963 with *Mars*, a bimonthly magazine. Gone was any pretense of bodybuilding and health, as *Mars* was a homoerotic celebration of the male physique. Renslow's photographs broke away from the traditional Greek "discus throwing" poses to include models in more casual situations: in the locker room with friends, astride a motorcycle, reclining on a sofa, or couples in a potentially sexual situation. The photographs were complemented by Etienne's artwork—muscular males with oversized genitals in larger than life situations. *Mars* was printed, distributed, and sold by Herman L. Womack in Washington, D.C., the publisher of *Grecian Guild* and several other physique magazines. Renslow describes him as "a 290-pound albino." The profits were to be split 60/40, but Kris Studios never saw a penny from *Mars*. "He never lived up to his agreements," said Renslow, "but it didn't make any difference because that was an advertising medium for us. Our ads were in the back and our main business was mail order photographs, so it was very lucrative for us."

*Mars* specialized in images of leather-jacketed bikers, street hustlers, and tattooed sailors that hinted at sadomasochistic and dangerous encounters in dark alleys. With *Mars*, Renslow and Kris Studios tapped the murky underworld of "rough trade," with each issue increasingly more daring: bare butts in issue 2, leather and motorcycles by issue 4, and in issue 18 physical contact between two nude men in the guise of wrestling. The last issue of *Mars* was dated April 1968. Kris Studios had one clash with the law in May 1966 when they were raided, and Renslow, Orejudos, Patrick Finnegan, and Karrol Efthernis were arrested and promptly released after a judge ruled the search warrant was improperly obtained.

Things improved when the law against mailing photographs of male nudes was struck down by the U.S. Supreme Court on June 25, 1962. In the case *Herman L. Womack and Manual Enterprises v. Day*, the court decided three of his publications, *MANual*, *Trim*, and *Grecian Guild*, were "unpleasant, uncouth and tawdry" but lacked "patent offensiveness." The era of the posing pouch was over. In September 1968 Kris Studios published the short-lived *Rawhide*. The first issue depicted a full-frontal nude on the cover. Inside, no articles, just photographs of naked men, some with erections and captions like: "Young sailor Skip Mahoney strikes a cocky pose for Kris."

*Rawhide* lasted five issues. Renslow's interest in the leather and S&M image extended beyond photography and magazines, as in 1958 he became manager of the Gold Coast bar at 1130 North Clark Street, turning it into a gay leather/Levi bar. The local gay leather scene consisted of five or six men hanging out at another bar, Omar's at 10 North Clark Street, where they were kicked out because they scared the customers. They moved to the Gold Coast, where after a few months the owner died and his son asked Renslow if he wanted to manage the bar. He did and bought it on March 16, 1960. The Gold Coast flourished for nearly thirty years as Chicago's premier leather bar: in 1962 it moved to 1110 North Clark Street, then to 2165 North Lincoln Avenue in 1965, then to 501 North Clark Street in 1967, and finally to 5025 North Clark Street in 1984. In 1985 the bar was sold to Frank Kellas but closed on February 10, 1988.

After Stonewall, Renslow opened other bars and businesses, including Sparrow's at 5224 North Sheridan Road, Zolar's at 936 West Diversey, Center Stage at 3730 North Clark Street, and the Chicago Eagle/Man's Country Bathhouse at 5015 North Clark Street, and he was publisher of Chicago's *Gay Life* newspaper for several years. In 1979 Renslow also co-founded the International Mr. Leather contest with Etienne Orejudos, still one of Chicago's most prestigious annual events. After Etienne's death in 1991, Renslow inherited his artwork and, along with Tony DeBlase, the publisher of *Drummer* magazine, made plans for the Leather Archives and Museum, which would house the collection. It opened its doors to the public in 1996 at 5015 North Clark Street. The museum is currently located at 6418 North Greenview Avenue.

In 1991 Charles "Chuck" Renslow was inducted into the City of Chicago Gay and Lesbian Hall of Fame.

## Domingo "Etienne" Orejudos

Domingo Orejudos was born in Chicago on July 1, 1933, of Puerto Rican parents. He graduated from McKinley High School in 1950. At age sixteen his career as a dancer began. On May 19, 1957, the Ballet Guild of Chicago presented Loyd Tygett's *Petites Histoires* with music by Rameau, Rossini, and Schubert with a pas de deux by Dom Orejudos. The following year Orejudos joined the Illinois Ballet Company, formed by Richard Ellis and his wife, Christine Du Boulay, two dancers from Britain's Sadler's Wells Company. Orejudos stayed with the company for fifteen years, as principal dancer, costume designer, and then nine years as choreographer. The company made their debut on April 10–12, 1959, at the Saint Alphonsus Athenaeum, where among the pieces performed were Orejudos's own *Thais* and *LA la Foire*. He received three grants from the National Endowment for the Arts and choreographed over a dozen pieces for PBS, earning three Emmys along the way.

Orejudos's first major break came in January 1963 when he performed in, choreographed, and designed the costumes for the psycho-ballet *Metamorphosis of the Owls*, an experimental piece written by University of Chicago student Daniel Jordan. Orejudos danced the role of the nightingale. He also wrote and danced in his own piece, *The Charioteer*, broadcast on Christmas Day 1968 on Chicago's public television station, WTTW

Channel 11. Other pieces he wrote included *Songs of the Wayfarer, This Persistent Image, The Stone Medusa, Spanish Suite . . . And Short!* and *Mementos*, commissioned by the Washington Ballet Company.

However, in the gay community, Orejudos is better known as Etienne, the artist who created images of hypermuscular, well-endowed, leathermen, truckers, sailors, bikers, and cowboys as the modern-day Greek Adonis. His artwork spans forty years, from the physique magazines of the 1950s through the series of Meatman books in the 1980s. Over the years Etienne designed newspaper ads for Circus Vargas, illustrations for *Drummer* magazine, and posters for the International Mr. Leather contest, and he painted murals for the Gold Coast bar. Etienne was known as the Court Jester of Erotica, his humor permeating his artwork, as in one image depicting a scene of punishment and degradation in *Star Trick*, a comedic slant on *Star Trek*. He had many influential friends and admirers, and in 1979 a joint exhibition of Etienne and Tom of Finland paintings in Stompers gallery in New York's Greenwich Village boasted Andy Warhol and Robert Mapplethorpe attending the opening night.

In 1981 Orejudos and his lover Robert Yhunke left Chicago to live in the shadows of the Rocky Mountains in Boulder, Colorado, where the Court Jester focused on his painting. His first battle as a result of AIDS was in 1987, when he was struck with pneumonia while traveling to China and Tibet. The disease caught up with him on September 24, 1991. He was fifty-eight.

## *Vim* and *Gym* Magazines

The draconian U.S. obscenity laws in the 1950s and early '60s resulted in court cases becoming farcical affairs with lawyers and judges locked in scholarly debate on the subject of "excessive genital delineation" in a model's posing strap. Although Charles Renslow and others had their run-ins with the law, it was *Vim* and *Gym* magazines, based in Oak Park, Illinois, that were dragged over the coals by the press.

In 1959, prior to the *Vim* and *Gym* raids, the U.S. Supreme Court ruled in favor of seventy-five-year-old Eleazer Smith, a Los Angeles bookstore owner who was appealing a thirty-day jail sentence for possessing an "obscene" lesbian-themed book, *Sweeter than Life* by Mark Tryon. Smith testified he was unaware of the book's subject matter. On October 20,

1959, before the U.S. Supreme Court, Smith's lawyers argued that a book-seller couldn't be expected to read every book in the store. The court decided in Smith's favor, ruling the Los Angeles obscenity ordinance unconstitutional, effectively neutering similar statutes around the country, including Chicago.

The *Chicago Tribune* on March 3, 1960, reported that two police officers had been placed on full-time detail to hunt down pornography. The clamp-down came after two vendors were charged with selling obscene literature. Chicago's antismut campaign in 1959–60 netted over a hundred businesses. The public whipped themselves up into a frenzy and antismut groups formed, cheered on by religious groups and women's organizations. One group called Delegates for Decency, run by Mrs. Donald Krahn and Joseph Heidecker, turned their ire toward "Brigitte Bardot–type movies."

On March 4 police padlocked the Apollo School of Photography at 3541 Chicago Avenue after police arrested the owner and ten others as they were photographing a seminude woman. On March 10 Judge Grover C. Niemeyer dismissed a suit against Capitol News Agency, 2429 Wabash Avenue, after police confiscated ninety-nine publications on November 27, 1959. One of them was *Playboy*. The judge declared Chicago's obscenity law unconstitutional, citing the U.S. Supreme Court decision in the Eleazer Smith case.

On April 14, 1960, a new Chicago obscenity ordinance was enacted. It held that "a publication is obscene when its calculated purpose or dominant effect is to substantially arouse sexual desires, and if the probability of this effect is so great as to outweigh whatever artistic or other merits it may possess." The ordinance was tested on October 8 when another fifty news-stand operators were hauled into court, where the ordinance was upheld and fifteen vendors found guilty, one, Newsstand Library, Inc., for selling three lesbian novels: *First Person, 3rd Sex* by Sloane Britain, and *Veil of Torment* and *Fear of Incest* by March Hastings.

A headline in the *Chicago Tribune* on January 17, 1961, read: "U.S. Indicts 53 in Breakup of 'Smut' Club." What the paper describes as "an international club" for the "exchange of pornography" was, in fact, a gay pen-pal group called the Adonis Male Club, run by husband and wife Jack and Nirvana Ward Zuideveld of Oak Park, Illinois. Membership was five dollars, and for that you were listed in a members-only yearbook along with your photograph and personal information, including city, state, nation, occupation, hobbies, and other special interests. The Zuidevelds were charged with conspiring to send obscene literature through the mail. Jack Zuideveld was the editor of *Vim* and *Gym*, two physique magazines he used to promote the Adonis Male Club. The ads in *Vim* and *Gym* read: "The Adonis Male Club, world's largest, completely different pen-pal club for males who like the unusual" and "build close personal relationships with fascinating males from all walks of life."

Whereas the pen-pal ads may have been subtle, a two-page article in the April 1960 issue of *Gym* was not. While other physique magazines condemned homosexuality, Jack Zuideveld wrote a sympathetic article called "Homosexuality . . . on the Increase" that most likely contributed to his problems with the law. He compares the new liberal attitude toward homosexuality in Britain, that "tight little isle," to a similar phenomenon in the United States. "The city of Chicago is a good case in point," he writes. "More than a dozen cocktail lounges on the near north side of the Windy City are almost exclusively patronized by homosexual and bi-sexual males. Large sums are paid to the police to keep these establishments open and only continued and heavy traffic would make such an operation profitable. One grizzled veteran of the Gold Coast area remarked that ten years ago there would not have been enough business to keep a single such bar in operation but that today it is the most profitable type of saloon business in the city."

The article ends: "As homosexual activity increases, the need for a more adequate and honest sex education program is needed in our schools and churches. Though the basic purpose of a Divine Being in making man and woman for the purpose of procreation must be emphasized, it must also not be ignored that some males will remain, by choice, celibates and others will find other avenues of emotional outlet."

Chicago postal inspectors spent six months gathering evidence on the Adonis pen-pal club, which led to the arrest of fifty-two men and Nirvana Zuideveld on January 16, 1961. The Zuidevelds were charged with conspiring to send obscene matter through the mails. The *Chicago Tribune* listed the names and addresses of the arrestees, including a teacher, who was later dismissed. Another man indicted was seriously injured after he ran into the path of a car on a one-way-street. He survived. One other died before appearing in court. A later *Chicago Tribune* article on July 28, 1965, claimed several of the men arrested in the Adonis Male Club case committed suicide.

In Washington, D.C., Postmaster General Arthur E. Summerfield described the Chicago smut ring as "one of the most vicious, filthy, and widespread operations postal inspectors have ever investigated." The Zuidevelds were sentenced to one year and one day in jail, followed by two years' probation. They took their case to the United States Court of Appeals Seventh Circuit on May 1, 1963, where the Zuidevelds' lawyers argued there was no evidence they sent obscene material through the mail or that they conspired to do so; the only mailed obscenity had taken place between members of the club. The court noted that while *Vim* and *Gym* magazines claimed to reach an audience of men interested in physical culture and sports, the photographs revealed "homosexual double entendre intent." The court also noted the magazines were not on trial.

The court upheld the lower court's guilty verdict. Court documents reveal that prior to editing *Vim* and *Gym*, Jack Zuideveld was a radio announcer and writer, and Nirvana was a commercial artist. In the spring of 1959 Jack began working for the Victory Printing and Publishing Company in Chicago, owners of both physique magazines. In August he obtained the publishing rights, and with his wife he started Nirvack Publishing. The idea for the Adonis Male Club was Nirvana's, and the first ad appeared in *Vim* and *Gym* in early 1959. Applicants were asked to fill out a questionnaire and mail it to International Body Culture Association at the Zuidevelds' home in Oak Park, Illinois. The questions included personal information, and also what type of man the applicant would like to correspond with; there were sixteen types, ranging from male models to truck drivers.

The club's business was overseen by Nirvana, who signed herself "Ed Nolan," as it seemed more fitting to use a male name. Within a year there were 650 members; at five dollars for an annual membership and twenty dollars for the yearbook, the Zuidevelds earned a hefty income. In the March 1960 issue of *Gym*, Nirvana advertised an Adonis Male Club members-only sketchbook showing "action sketches." Other ideas included a monthly newsletter for club members and a summer camp organized by her husband, two projects nipped in the bud when the police closed the club down. On September 16, 1960, Nirvana was ordered to turn over club records and correspondence to the federal grand jury in Chicago. This she did. The *Chicago Tribune* of January 17, 1961, reported that during the subsequent trial the government produced letters written by forty-five club members to one another, many innocuous, while others contained what the court described as "language and pictures, which can only be described as obscenity of a most vile and shocking character."

The defense argued that the Zuidevelds were not responsible for the content of correspondence among the members. In answer to the question of whether the Zuidevelds had any reason to know what might and did happen, prosecutors cited the club application form on which many of the men answered the question "Measurement?" by giving the size of their genital organs. Nirvana answered that she thought they were just being "smart aleck" and didn't think it reason enough to bar them from joining the club. Other members' letters sent directly to the club included one from a man who expressed an interest in photographs of nude males not in the bodybuilding style, another from an applicant who desired a man to come and live with him "who cares not for women," and a third who thanked the club for putting him in touch with "hot uninhibited studs like myself."

Although *Vim* and *Gym* magazines weren't on trial per se, both publications collapsed. An editorial in *Strength and Health* (May 1961) read: "A while ago I reported that there must have been a dozen or so of those dirty little queer magazines for homosexuals cluttering up the nation's news racks. Court action eradicated several of them . . . but does that mean the plague is lessened? Not sos' you could see—the other day in New York City I counted 20 different titles of this type displayed on a tiny corner newsstand! Apparently, like Hydra, every time one of these rags gets chopped down, two spring up to take its place."

## Samuel Steward and Alfred Kinsey

Males do not represent two discrete populations, heterosexual and homosexual. The world is not to be divided into sheep and goats. Not all things are black nor all things white.

Alfred Kinsey

In 1948 Doctor Alfred Charles Kinsey's study *Sexual Behavior in the Human Male* laid bare the truth about men's sexuality. Kinsey's findings contrasted starkly with the country's accepted view of family life, laws, and religious beliefs. The book exposed high rates of masturbation, adultery, and pre-marital sex among the eighteen thousand men interviewed. Kinsey also noted that 37 percent of men had engaged in at least one homosexual act to orgasm since puberty, that 4 percent were homosexual throughout their whole lives, and that 10 percent of males had been exclusively homosexual for the last three years.

Kinsey's book was a bestseller, garnering praise and condemnation in equal measure. The chorus of disapproval was not surprising, as the book was published at a time of heightened sexual conservatism: masturbation was said to sap manhood; oral sex, even between husband and wife, was illegal in many states; and homosexuality was viewed as a "disease" affecting a small minority. In the 1950s the American male had two dueling identities: Traditional Family Values Man v. Rebel without a Cause. One side promoted a template for an idyllic world reflected in the "honey, I'm home" sitcoms—white nuclear families with mother as nurturing home-maker, father atop the familial pyramid, and teens whose only problem was arranging two dates on the same night. Problems were deftly solved by a man-to-man talk with Dad, who was always "firm but fair." The flipside of the identity coin were the "sensitive, tortured" males appearing in Hollywood movies, and white teens embracing the sexually liberated atti-tudes of the black community and culture, the Beat poets with jazz and bebop, and the hip-shaking hose-down-the-pants sexuality of Elvis Presley reworking Big Mama Thornton's "Hound Dog."

Kinsey's studies into male sexuality began in Chicago when he inter-viewed homosexuals living in a rooming house on Rush Street. One Chicago resident who aided Kinsey with his research into homosexual sadomasochism was the writer Samuel M. Steward. In his book *Chapters from an Autobiography* (1981) Steward recalls the first time he met Kinsey, describing him as "a solidly built man in his fifties wearing a rumpled grey suit." Steward writes that Kinsey was "a landmark of rebellion in the gay movement" and ranks him alongside Sigmund Freud and Havelock Ellis. After that meeting in 1949, Kinsey invited Steward to be an "unofficial collaborator" at his Institute for Sex Research, which he founded in 1947 at Indiana University. Kinsey filmed Steward in sadomasochistic "scenes" with Mike Miksche, a sadist from New York. Miksche was a freelance artist who designed fashion layouts for Saks and other Fifth Avenue stores. Also, under the name Steve Masters, he produced homoerotic ink drawings for the growing leather and S&M market in physique magazines of the 1960s.

In his autobiography, Steward wrote: "Mike was quite a ham actor, every time he heard Bill Dellenback's camera start to turn, he renewed his vigor and youth like the green bay tree; and at the end of the second afternoon I was exhausted, marked and marred, all muscles weakened."

Samuel M. Steward was born on July 23, 1909, in the village of Woodsfield, Ohio. His family later moved to Richmond, Virginia. The defining moment in Steward's life was meeting Gertrude Stein and her lover, Alice B. Toklas. While studying at Ohio State University in Columbus, Steward took courses with Clarence Andrews, the gay author of *Innocents of Paris* (1928), later made into a movie starring Maurice Chevalier. While in Europe, Andrews attended Stein's salons. Upon Andrews's death in 1932, Steward wrote to inform Stein, and thereby initiated a correspondence that lasted years. Steward published the letters as *Dear Sammy: Letters from Gertrude Stein and Alice B. Toklas* (1977). In 1937 Steward first met Stein and Toklas in person. He later fictionalized the lives of the lesbian couple in his detective novels *Murder Is Murder Is Murder* (1985) and *The Caravaggio Shawl* (1989).

A literary groupie, Steward befriended other writers, such as Thomas Mann and André Gide, had a sexual encounter with Oscar Wilde's muse Lord Alfred Douglas, and was briefly the lover of Thornton Wilder; Steward described himself as Wilder's "Chicago piece." Wilder, a part-time lecturer in comparative literature at the University of Chicago between 1930 and 1937, failed to accept his own homosexuality. Steward explained: "There was a double-lock on the door of the closet in which he lived. . . . Thornton went about sex as if he were looking the other way, doing something else. . . . [A]fter ninety seconds and a dozen strokes against my belly he ejaculated."

In 1936 Steward was teaching at the State College of Washington at Pullman, a job abruptly terminated when it came to light he had published a racy novel called *Angels on the Bough* (1936) that included a streetwalker. Steward was saved by a job offer from Loyola University in Chicago. "I sent a copy of my novel to the dean there, explaining all," wrote Steward in his autobiography. "He found it innocuous, and I was hired to teach in an English department." This was surprising for a college founded by Jesuits. Steward's first impressions of Chicago were unfavorable: "When I first arrived in Chicago," he wrote,

> I hated its filth, the squalor of the South Side tenements, the mud
> of the backyards, the dirt of its gutters—all in contrast with the

gleaming lakefront and the bright shops of Michigan Avenue. The paradox of State Street astounded me—beginning in nothingness at the river, running a few blocks down through the proud stores . . . into what? You crossed Van Buren and were in a skidrow of tattoo joints, burlesque houses, prostitutes, winos and flophouses.

Gradually, however, I came to think of Chicago as a man-city, healthy, sweaty, and sensual. It was Gargantua of the lakefront— his head in Evanston, his feet in Gary; and he lay relaxed and smoldering along the water. The trees of Lincoln Park were the curling man-hair of his chest, the trees of Jackson Park the foliage on his legs, the tall buildings of the Loop his sturdy upstanding phallus—the whole anatomy of the city his outstretched body.

After twenty years Steward gave up on academia and, using the name Phil Sparrow, set up shop as a tattoo artist on Chicago's skid row, before moving to Oakland, California, where he became the official tattooist for the Hell's Angels. In his autobiography, Steward writes: "After about 1956 there was a noticeable change in the number of homosexuals getting tattooed. When the 'leather movement' began, their numbers rapidly increased. Most of the tattoos on the S&M crowd were masculine symbols—tigers, panthers, daggers entwined with snakes." Steward relates the story of Ed, a sailor stationed at Great Lakes Naval Training Station: "He disappeared for four years during his Navy hitch. When he returned just before his discharge he had a great many tattoos. He came in the last time with a buddy of his, and in a double scroll under a flower he asked for the names Ed and Chuck. They had successfully been lovers in the navy for four years without having been discovered."

The *Chicago Tribune* published a letter on September 14, 1959, from Sparrow with another tattoo tale:

> I thought you should know about the sailor, on whose forearm I put a picture of his girl, made from his wallet photograph. That was on a Thursday. On Friday morning the poor lad got a "Dear John." Saturday he was back in the shop, wanting to have the face covered up. I explained that it was too fresh: it would have to be completely healed before it was covered, etc. etc. So he said, "Well, can't you at least put a mustache on her?" And now, wandering around some place out at Great Lakes is a sad swabbie with a gal's

picture on his forearm, wearing a big handlebar mustache on her face.

Throughout his life Steward published novels, nonfiction, and hundreds of short stories, but his greatest gifts to the gay community were the erotic books he wrote under the name Phil Andros. (In Greek *philos* is "to love," and *andros* means "Man.") The genesis of "Phil Andros" came after Kinsey introduced Steward to the Swiss gay magazine *Der Kreis*, edited by Rolf Rheiner. In *The Ideal Gay Man: The Story of Der Kreis* (1999) Hubert Kennedy writes that the magazine was first published January 1932 as *Freundschafts-Banner* and was the joint project of two Zurich-based organizations: the lesbian group Amicitia and the gay men's Excentric-Club Zurich. In 1958 Rudolf Jung (a.k.a. Burkhardt), one of the editors of *Der Kreis*, visited Chicago to meet Charles Renslow at Kris Studios, as Renslow had contributed photographs to *Der Kreis*. While in the city, Jung also visited Steward's tattoo shop. Steward describes Jung as a "roly poly bilingual German . . . an expert in the spreading of honey. Flattery is a potent weapon, and he knew how to handle it perfectly. The result was that he teased me into composing 'at least an essay, if you don't feel like writing fiction' for his magazine."

Steward wrote and contributed artwork to *Der Kreis* under such pseudonyms as Donald Bishop, Ward Stames, John McAndrews, and Thomas Cave. The name Phil Andros came later when he published *$tud* (1969), a collection of eighteen stories woven into a novel. Samuel Steward continued writing under the name Phil Andros for the rest of his life, while working as a tattoo artist in Oakland. He died on New Year's Eve 1993, at age eighty-four.

# 17

# Lesbian Pulp Paperbacks and Literature

The 1950s saw the emergence of trashy dime store lesbian novels, with Chicago's Newsstand Library Books publisher leading the pack, until a judge ordered their books "obscene and nonmailable." One local author of lesbian pulp fiction was Valerie Taylor. Another local author, Jeannette Howard Foster, who compiled *Sex Variant Women in Literature*, accused one pulp fiction writer of "diarrhea of the pen."

Gore Vidal's *The City and the Pillar* (1948) was savaged by critics but most likely benefited from the negative publicity, as by 1950 it had sold over two million copies. Two other influential gay books from 1950 were *Quatrefoil* by James Barr, published by Greenberg Press, and Tereska Torres's *Women's Barracks* by Fawcett's Gold Medal Books. Barr's book, a gay romance, was inspired by his service in the U.S. Navy, during which he attended officers training at Great Lakes Naval Base in Chicago. Torres's *Women's Barracks*, thought to be the first lesbian pulp novel, was sold as "the frank autobiography of a French girl soldier"; the story is set in a London barracks for women of the Free French Forces. *Women's Barracks* sold two million copies. Lesbian pulp fiction was hot! Publishing houses sprang up everywhere, often run by shady businessmen who knew a cash cow when they saw one. For the next two decades a slew of lesbian pulp novels hit the newsstands, with titles like *Lavender Love Rumble*, *Bitter Love*, and *Lesbo Lodge*. These trashy dime-store novels were treasured by lesbian readers, as they depicted the lives of regular people like themselves, even though the stories all had the obligatory tragic ending: suicide, murder, or some other payback for sin.

In 1950, Fawcett Publications launched Gold Medal Books. Among their lesbian titles were *Spring Fire* (1952) by Vin Packer and *We Walk Alone through Lesbos' Lonely Groves* (1955) by Ann Aldrich, both pseudonyms of Marijane Meaker. Although popular with readers, Packer's books were vilified by lesbian group the Daughters of Bilitis. A review of one of Packer's books, *The Evil Friendship* (1958), in the Daughters' publication *The Ladder* in January 1959 read: "It is a sad state of affairs when an admitted lesbian must continuously and vituperatively denounce lesbianism. This well-documented true story of two teenage girls suffering from paranoia coupled with delusions of grandeur hardly represents a picture of typical lesbian relationships. These pitiful children plan and execute the murder of one of their mothers." Chicago lesbian Jeanette H. Foster, author of the 1956 classic *Sex Variant Women in Literature*, described, in the August 1960 *Ladder*, Aldrich/Packer's writing as "diarrhea of the pen."

In 1959 Chicago's Newsstand Library Books published *First Person, 3rd Sex* (1959) by Sloane Britain (real name Elaine Williams), about a schoolteacher coming to terms with her lesbianism. Britain's early novels were popular, but her later books became increasingly cynical, and in 1964 she committed suicide over her lesbianism. After publishing *First Person*, Newsstand Books was busted; in 1960 the post office claimed nineteen of their titles were "nonmailable." *First Person, 3rd Sex* was listed, as were two other lesbian-themed books, *Veil of Torment* (1959) and *Fear of Incest* (1959) by March Hastings (real name Sally Singer). On October 4, 1960, in Washington, D.C., Hearing Examiner Jesse B. Messitte heard the case against Newsstand Books. Saul J. Mindel spoke on behalf of the Post Office testifying the books were "obscene, lewd, lascivious and indecent." After reading the books, Messitte denounced eighteen as obscene and nonmailable, including those by Sloane Britain and March Hastings.

The *Chicago Tribune* on August 28, 1966, noted that Chicago's smut publishers were closing up shop: "Down in South State street pornography shops the whole atmosphere has changed. Gone are stares of furtive passion, the wheezes of heavy breathing, replaced by frowns of disappointment and sighs of despair. Suddenly the most daring publication in the house is *Playboy*—no whips, no chains, no black leather lingerie, not a fetish in a carload. And consider the plight of the Chicago author, Sylvia Sharon, who specialized in tales of lesbian love for Lancer's defunct Domino series. 'You can't find my books anywhere now,' complains Sylvia in that distinctive bass-baritone voice. Like most (maybe all) lady pornographers, Sylvia is a man. The theory behind the phony name is that it takes a woman to write convincingly on the subject, and the theory works because your average smut hound knows even less about lesbianism than Sylvia does. That is to say, it used to work. The market having dried up, Sylvia is going back into the advertising business from whence he came."

## Valerie Taylor

According to one obituary, Valerie Taylor once described herself in a poem as "an inevitable revolutionary" because in this society she was an "'eight-time loser': I am a woman, a lesbian, a creative spirit, a laborer, a handicapped person, a peace worker, an Indian (Potawatomi), and over sixty." Taylor was born Velma Nacella Young in Aurora, Illinois, on September 7, 1913. In 1935 she received a scholarship to Blackburn College in Carlinville, Illinois, a small independent liberal arts college, where she befriended labor activists Ada and Clarence Henry (Hank) Mayer. In her freshman year Taylor joined the American Socialist Party and began a lifelong career in grassroots activism, not that surprising as her father's two grandmothers were both suffragettes. In the late 1930s she worked on the staff of the *Illinois Miner*, an influential union paper whose contributors included Agnes Burns Wieck, the coalminer's daughter who later became president of the Women's Auxiliary of the Progressive Miners of America.

As Taylor explained to her biographer, Tee A. Corinne, about the beginnings of her writing career in 1935: "My first published work made me very angry," said Taylor. "I had an older friend who was a very bustling, officious, managing woman . . . the kind of person who regards one as a protégée and I'm nobody's protégée then or ever. I gave her some poems to read and to my dismay she subsequently showed up with a copy of a little magazine. . . . [S]he had sent some of my work to it and it had published one. I was quite angry." After college Taylor taught in several Illinois schools, and in 1939 she married William Jerry Tate; they had three sons, Marshall in 1940 and twins Jerry and Jim in 1942. In the mid-1940s Taylor began publishing her poems in magazines, about two hundred in all, under the name Nacella Young. Her first novel, *Hired Girl*, was published in

1953, and its royalties paid for her divorce that same year; by all accounts the marriage was abusive. In an interview with Studs Terkel, included in his book *Coming of Age: The Story of Our Century by Those Who've Lived It* (1995), Taylor says her husband was an alcoholic, as was her son Jerry, who died from the disease in 1990.

After the divorce, Taylor lived at 7251 South Shore Drive, an artists' colony, with her three sons. The colony of eighteen cottages, surrounded by trees and thick brush, dated back to the Columbian Exposition of 1893. Ronald Kotulak of the *Chicago Tribune* interviewed residents for an article of August 16, 1959, including Taylor: "Tenants range from nuclear scientists to what some people might call 'beatniks,'" she said. "Because of the perpetual summer camp atmosphere where the people clop around barefooted, the colony attracts people with intelligence and character who want to be free from strain." While living in the colony Taylor supported her family by writing for Bernarr MacFadden's *True Stories*, and as an assistant editor at Henry Regnery & Sons, a right-wing publishing house; during Taylor's tenure they published books by conservative commentator William F. Buckley Jr. In the 1990s Regnery published two disinformation volumes about AIDS: *The Myth of Heterosexual AIDS* (1990) by Michael Fumento, which reinforces the erroneous theory that homosexuals are more likely to develop AIDS than heterosexuals; and *Inventing the AIDS Virus* (1996) by Peter Duesberg, in which the author claims AIDS is not caused by the HIV virus. More recently they've published books by Newt Gingrich and Ann Coulter.

Taylor left the company in 1961. Her first lesbian novel was *Whisper Their Love* (1957), under the name Valerie Taylor and published by Fawcett Gold Medal Books. The back cover reads: "Theirs was the kind of love they dared not show the world. . . . Desire and torment swept through Joyce's trembling young body at the gentle touch of Edith's cool hand upon her face. She had never felt like this before. It frightened her . . . and filled her with a terrible excitement! Joyce was eighteen, a freshman at a fashionable school for girls. Suddenly all that mattered to her was a woman twice her age. A haunting and shocking story of how a young girl's hunger for love made her prey to tormented and forbidden passions." The book sold two million copies and is considered a historic milestone for its realistic interpretation of lesbian lives. Other lesbian-themed novels followed, including a series of four set in Chicago: *Stranger on Lesbos* (1960), *A World without Men* (1963), *Return to Lesbos* (1963), and *Journey to Fulfillment* (1964).

Taylor's most financially successful book was *The Girls in 3-B* (1959). The story documents the lives of Annice, Pat, and Barby, three friends from Iowa, who move to Chicago to find independence and love in the big city, where all three break the rules of 1950s convention, with Annice entering the drug world of beatniks, Pat torn between her wealthy married boss and a regular guy, and Barby finding true love in the arms of an older woman. The only downside to the novel—that is, politically incorrect—is that Barby's lesbianism is the result of rape. It's often stated in Taylor's online biographies that a sanitized version of *The Girls in 3-B* became a nationally syndicated newspaper comic strip; not true. The confusion stems from *Apartment 3-G*, a strip created in 1961 by psychiatrist Nicholas P. Dallis with the similar theme of three young women moving to a big city.

The lesbian pulp novels of the 1950s could only hint at sex, as with Eileen seducing Barby in *The Girls in 3-B*: "'I'm a very direct person,' Eileen said, 'I don't finagle around and try to put over a deal, not where my personal life is concerned.' She looked at Barby, the long straight look that had melted her heart the first day, as if she could see through her eyes and into her mind. 'You're very young . . . You don't have to commit yourself to anything, I want you to think it over. But will you stay with me here tonight?'"

Barby touched Eileen's hand: "'Yes, I've been waiting for you to ask me that.' Much later when they stood together at the bedroom window, watching the soft flakes of snow drive against the glass and shatter, she said, 'It's what I've wanted all my life. How could anybody want a man when there's this?'"

In 1961 Taylor sojourned in Tenerife, the Spanish island off the coast of Africa, returning a year later to Chicago, where she rekindled her writing career, including poetry and a short story for the lesbian publication *The Ladder*. In 1967 Ace published *The Secret of the Bayou*, a gothic romance that Taylor wrote as Francine Davenport. The cover, typical for the genre, depicts a distraught woman fleeing a creepy old house in the background. The cover reads: "The sinister whispers of the time-haunted house terrified the young governess of Fairlawn."

In July 1965 Robert Sloane Basker, Pearl Hart, and Ira Jones formed the gay rights group Mattachine Midwest, and Taylor joined to become the editor of their newsletter. As a spokesperson for the gay community, she was interviewed on Studs Terkel's WFMT radio show, along with local gay activists Jim Bradford and Henry Weimhoff. Taylor campaigned

tirelessly for gay rights. On June 28, 1973, she spoke for the Gay Grandmothers of America at a rally and kiss-in at the Civic Center Plaza (renamed the Richard J. Daley Center in 1976). Between 1974 and 1978, along
with writer, activist, and historian Marie Kuda and others, Taylor organized
the annual Lesbian Writers' Conferences. At the first event, held at the
Unitarian Church in Hyde Park, Taylor addressed 130 women on the
subject of the history of lesbian writers. Her keynote speech, titled "For
My Granddaughters," was published by Womanpress and sold at the
following year's conference for fifty cents.

On March 22, 1975, Taylor's life changed when her close friend Pearl
Hart died of pancreatic cancer, and the pulp fiction author retired to
Margaretville on the border of the Catskill State Park in Upstate New York
in October 1975. Earlier that year Taylor received the Paul Goldman
Award, presented by ONE of Chicago at the Como Inn for her work as a
peace and gay activist, and she accepted the prize on behalf of "all women."
Two weeks before leaving the city she attended the second Lesbian Writers'
Conference, a weekend of events in honor of author and scholar Jeanette
H. Foster, who at the time was ailing in a nursing home. Taylor, along
with writers Tee A. Corinne, Lee Lynch, and others, initiated the "Sister-
hood Fund" to raise money for Foster's medical fees. In 1976 Womanpress published *Two Women: The Poetry of Jeannette Foster and Valerie
Taylor*.

Taylor's involvement in the Lesbian Writers' Conferences brought
renewed interest in her work, and in 1977 Naiad Press published *Love
Image*. The following year Taylor moved to Tucson, Arizona, where she
became the much-loved "Grandmother" of the lesbian community, and
continued writing novels: *Prism* (1981), *Ripening* (1988), and *Rice and Beans*
(1989). In 1992 she was inducted into the Chicago Gay and Lesbian Hall of
Fame, though she was too frail to attend the event. She died at age
eighty-four on October 22, 1997, in a Tucson hospice, and is survived by
two sons and five grandchildren. Her papers, including poetry and two
unpublished novels, were donated to Cornell University Library's Human
Sexuality Collection.

## Jeannette Howard Foster

In 1918 Jeannette H. Foster, author of the groundbreaking book *Sex Variant
Women in Literature* (1956), attended Rockford College in Rockford,

Illinois, following in the footsteps of another lesbian, Jane Addams, who began her studies there in 1877. Foster went on to receive MA and PhD degrees at the University of Chicago, and a BA in library science from Emory University in Atlanta. She was a library science professor, librarian, teacher, and writer for the rest of her life.

In the foreword to *Sex Variant Women in Literature*, Foster recalls being on the student council at the all-female Rockford College, and attending a meeting to discuss what action should be taken against two girls who spent too much time together. The exact nature of the girls' transgression was never explained, and Foster, unaware of lesbianism, failed to grasp why two friends locking themselves in a room together could provoke such close scrutiny. After the two girls received probation for their "indiscretions," Foster sought out more information on the subject, beginning with *Studies in the Psychology of Sex* by Havelock Ellis.

Foster's ignorance of lesbianism is understandable given the subject was never discussed openly and could only be found under "nature's anomalies" in medical books or "crimes against nature" in the police files. It was into this myopic world that Jeannette Howard Foster was born on November 3, 1895, in Oak Park, Illinois. After the incident with the student council, Foster began to study and collect lesbian writings, which became the basis for *Sex Variant Women in Literature*, a book that documents 2,600 years of overt and covert lesbian writings from Sappho to Virginia Woolf and Djuna Barnes.

In 1948 Foster was the first librarian to work at the Kinsey Institute for Sex Research, where she catalogued ten thousand books, which proved to be a goldmine for her research. When Foster completed her book, she was unable to find a publisher and eventually self-published with Vantage Books in 1956. This was a mistake, as without Foster's permission, the rights were sold to the British publisher Frederick Muller Ltd., who re-published it in 1958.

The book disappeared without a trace, but Foster continued writing for library journals and articles and fiction for *The Ladder*. The mid-1970s found a renewed interest in Foster's work. In 1974 she was presented the Third Annual Gay Book Award for *Sex Variant Women in Literature*, and in 1975, the book was republished by Diana Press (later by Naiad Press). This belated success came as Foster's health was failing. She had retired to Pocahontas, Arkansas, where she lived with Hazel Toliver, a professor in Latin and Greek, and Dorothy Ross, a former physical education teacher at Lindenwood College. She died at age eighty-six on July 26, 1981.

# 18

# Negro Arts and Literature

In 1934 Gertrude Stein visited Chicago to attend the opening of *Four Saints in Three Acts*, an opera she wrote to Virgil Thompson's music with an all-black cast. Chicago was also the birthplace of Lorraine Hansberry, who wrote the play *Raisin in the Sun*; the adventurous hobo Willard Motley, whose novel *Knock on Any Door* became a Hollywood film; and in the *Chicago Defender*, "Simple," the creation of Langston Hughes.

In the first half of the twentieth century, African American theater groups staged plays intended for a black audience, while Caucasian groups strived for a white audience. One production that broke down that barrier by showing an all-black cast to a white audience was the opera *Four Saints in Three Acts*, with a libretto by Gertrude Stein and music by Virgil Thompson, both gay Americans living in Paris. In fact, *Four Saints* broke all the rules of theater; for example, when the opera opened at New York's Wadsworth Athenaeum, the audience was brought to tears, a remarkable feat given the opera made no sense whatsoever. Even the title is misleading—*Four Saints in Three Acts*—the piece has four acts and features many, many saints.

Nobody was surprised that an incomprehensible opera with a puzzling "plot" could stream from Stein's pen, as she believed the sound of a word was more important than its meaning. She did with words what Picasso did with paint. Stein's book *The Autobiography of Alice B. Toklas* (1933) was published six months before the opening of *Four Saints*, and made her a bona fide star. *Four Saints* fell into the category of modernism, in which the artist intentionally discards traditional thought and seeks new ways to express ideas. Steven Watson, in his book *Prepare for Saints: Gertrude Stein, Virgil Thomson, and the Mainstreaming of American Modernism* (1998), suggests that *Four Saints* was "developed hand in hand with the largely homosexual constellation of Harvard-trained art professionals who would define modernist taste in America."

After its successful run on Broadway, *Four Saints* opened in Chicago at the Auditorium Theatre on November 7, 1934. Stein and her entourage—her lover Alice B. Toklas, and the author and photographer Carl Van Vechten—flew into town from New York; it was Stein and Toklas's first flight in an airplane. A solitary policeman was sent to the airport to guard Stein from "mobs of pursuers." According to that day's *Chicago American*, Stein's press agent was heard to remark: "Oh, my dear, did you ever see so many persons so naively excited?" One reporter asked Stein about her book *Tender Buttons*. "Just when are buttons tender?" asked the reporter. "I don't know," answered Stein. "You'll have to ask the buttons."

Although *Four Saints* had an all-black cast, the African American paper the *Chicago Defender* didn't seem interested in the opera; its existence was noted, but beyond that nothing. The opening night was a major society event, with the *Chicago American* of November 8, 1934, reporting that Stein wore "a rich well-made dress of prune colored faille, she wore a single diamond brooch at her throat, a spray of orchids pinned where it seemed easiest to pin them, brown woolen hose, low-heeled walking slippers and—to and from the theater—the same smug and shapeless velvet cap she was wearing when she arrived at the airport earlier in the day."

The paper also noted the confusion of the audience: "It was with mixed emotions that society witnessed the premiere of Gertrude Stein's opera *Four Saints in Three Acts*, last night at the Auditorium. Whether to laugh it off or admit that it 'had something' . . . or give up and retire to the bar and forget about it—the veteran opera-goers couldn't quite decide."

Another critic in the same paper wrote:

The notoriety of this opera is due largely to the reputation of the librettist, but such value as the work possesses is due entirely to the composer. . . . A sillier and more meaningless book of words can scarcely be imagined. . . .

Mr. Thompson has created a trickle of music, much of it rather charming, and spread it thin through the arid wastes of Miss Stein's nonsense.

He finishes with: "We shall not see 'Four Saints' again and we trust we shall not be called upon to review anything like it for a long time to come, but those who are interested in the notorious things of the moment will not be altogether disappointed in their expectations."

## Lorraine Hansberry

Lorraine Vivian Hansberry was born in Chicago on May 19, 1930, to middle-class college-educated parents. Her father, Carl Augustus Hansberry, was a realtor, civic leader, and businessman who fought against restrictive clauses in real estate. Her mother, Nannie Louise née Perry, the daughter of an African Methodist Episcopal preacher, was a schoolteacher and activist against Jim Crow laws. Lorraine had three siblings: Carl Augustus Jr., Perry Holloway, and Mamie.

In October 1936 Hansberry's family moved to a Chicago neighborhood with a restrictive covenant prohibiting the occupancy of colored people. After white neighbors objected, the Hansberrys went to court but lost the case, which forced the family to move out. Next, they purchased a property at 6140 Rhodes Avenue, in another restricted neighborhood. This time, despite repeated vandalism and violence from neighbors, Carl Hansberry fought the case all the way to the U.S. Supreme Court and won. It was against this backdrop of racism, injustice, and litigation that Lorraine Hansberry shaped her views and applied them to her short life, using her own story to inspire her award-winning play *A Raisin in the Sun*.

Hansberry graduated from Englewood High School and went to the University of Wisconsin in Madison, where she joined the Young Progressive League and worked on Henry Wallace's presidential campaign in 1948. After college Hansberry moved to New York to work on the Harlem-based publication *Freedom*, a progressive newspaper founded by activist, scholar, and singer Paul Robeson. Hansberry became associate editor of the paper, honing her writing skills on news stories, while also producing short stories and poetry. Hansberry married Robert Barron Nemiroff, a Jewish writer, on June 20, 1953, but they separated in 1957 and divorced in 1964. In 1956

Hansberry began work on a play called *The Crystal Stair*, after a line in the poem "Mother to Son" by Langston Hughes: "Well, son, I'll tell you: Life for me ain't been no crystal stair."

The play was later renamed *A Raisin in the Sun*, after another line in a different poem by Langston Hughes, called "Harlem (What Happens to a Dream Deferred)":

> What happens to a dream deferred?
> Does it dry up
> like a raisin in the sun?

The play *A Raisin in the Sun* made two stops before its arrival at the Blackstone Theatre in Chicago on February 10, 1959, for a four-week run. It received rave reviews in New Haven, Connecticut, and at the Walnut Street Theatre in Philadelphia. The play starred Sidney Poitier, Claudia McNeil, Louis Gossett, John Fiedler, Diana Sands, Ivan Dixon, and Ruby Dee. It was directed by Lloyd Richards and produced by Philip Rose and David J. Cogan. After Chicago, it opened on March 11, 1959, at New York's Ethel Barrymore Theatre on Broadway to more rave reviews from critics. Brooks Atkinson of the *New York Times* wrote: "The play is honest. . . . Since the performance is also honest and since Sidney Poitier is a candid actor, *A Raisin in the Sun* has vigor as well as veracity and is likely to destroy the complacency of anyone who sees it." John Chapman of the *New York Daily News* found it "a beautiful, loveable play . . . affectionately human, funny and touching, and it is acted by a company of actors who really are a company and not just a set of players."

*A Raisin in the Sun* was the first Broadway production penned by a black woman, and in April 1959 Hansberry received the New York Drama Critic's Circle's Best Play award. The *Chicago Defender* took an acute interest in the filming of *A Raisin in the Sun*. "Chicago's Northside was one of the principal locations for shots of the movie," the paper wrote on July 11, 1960. "In true Chicago fashion, the white residents were aghast and for the most part against the idea." The paper was referring to scenes filmed at 4930 West Hirsch Street, the home of Mr. and Mrs. Anthony Casaccio, a middle-class Italian family with two young sons. Like the movie plot, Casaccio's neighbors objected to the filming of a "'Black' movie on their street." Two scenes were shot in the Kitty Kat Club, a gay bar at 611 East 63rd Street. After filming, the Kitty Kat cashed in on their newfound fame with ads in the *Chicago Defender* reading: "Hollywood's Choice, Make It Yours" and "Where Scenes from 'A Raisin in the Sun' Were Filmed."

Hansberry's second play, *The Sign in Sidney Brustein's Window*, opened on October 15, 1964, at New York's Longacre Theatre, but it didn't live up to the promise of *A Raisin in the Sun*. When it opened at Chicago's Studebaker Theatre, the *Chicago Defender* of March 27, 1965, wrote: "It not only is not a good play, it is quite desperately dull."

In 1963 Hansberry was diagnosed with pancreatic cancer. In 1964 she divorced her husband, Robert Nemiroff; their marriage, in the traditional sense, was over years before, though they remained friends and shared a professional working relationship. Clues of Hansberry's lesbianism came in the form of a letter to the editor of *The Ladder* (May 1957), signed LHN (Lorraine Hansberry Nemiroff): "I'm glad as heck you exist," she writes. "You are obviously serious people and I feel that women, without wishing to foster any *separatist* notions, homo or hetero, indeed have a need for their own publications and organizations. Our problems, our experiences as women are profoundly unique as compared to the other half of the human race." Hansberry's letter spoke to the issues of lesbian dress codes, discretion, and making oneself acceptable to the "dominant social group," something she knew about being an African American in a white society. "What ought to be clear is that one is oppressed or discriminated against because one is different," she writes, "not 'wrong' or 'bad' somehow. This is perhaps the bitterest of the entire pill."

On January 12, 1965, at thirty-four years of age, Hansberry lost her battle with cancer. After her death, Nemiroff took the reins of her legacy, editing and publishing her finished and unfinished plays. He produced *Le Blancs*, a play about a revolution in Africa, and edited *Les Blancs: The Collected Last Plays of Lorraine Hansberry*. In 1969 he adapted more of her work for the stage production *Young, Gifted and Black*, the longest-running off-Broadway show in the 1968–69 season. On October 2, 1971, the show opened in Chicago at the Auditorium Theatre as a benefit for the American Civil Liberties Union's Ghetto Project.

At Lorraine Hansberry's funeral, Paul Robeson gave the eulogy: "Sometimes I feel like a mourning dove; sometimes I feel like a mourning dove, like a mourning dove. Sometimes I feel like an eagle in the air; sometimes I feel like an eagle in the air, like an eagle in the air. At this farewell, Lorraine Hansberry bids us keep on to our strength and power soar like an eagle in the air."

## Willard Motley

Willard Francis Motley was born on July 14, 1909, into a fairly affluent Catholic family in Chicago's Englewood neighborhood. His family life was complicated: his uncle was the artist Archibald Motley, though they were raised as brothers; Archibald Motley Sr. and Mary "Mae" Motley, his "parents," were really his grandparents; and his "sister," Florence, who lived in New York, was his mother. At age thirteen Motley was hired as a columnist for the *Chicago Defender*. The column "Bud Says" appeared in the paper's "Junior" section and was written under the pseudonym Bud Billiken. It's a common misconception that Motley created the Bud Billiken persona, but that honor goes to a youngster named Robert Watkins, whose first Bud Billiken column was published on April 2, 1921. Motley took it over on December 2, 1922, and next to his photograph as a studious young man with large spectacles, a cap, and collar and tie, he writes: "Do you know who I am? Well, if you don't, I want you to know that I am Willard Motley." In the column he wrote short fiction and tackled subjects of interest, both serious and superficial. Motley was later ousted from the paper when he angered Robert S. Abbott, the publisher, by printing his own school newspaper, called *Motley's E Weakly*. It didn't last; his diary entry for February 23, 1926, reads: "Then the bolt into the blue— the faculty won't allow us to publish the paper anymore!"

Motley's plans to attend the University of Wisconsin were thwarted by the ravages of the Great Depression. After graduating from Englewood High School, Motley hit the hobo trail, bicycling from Chicago to New York. He set out on July 3, 1930, on his "Knight Errant of Englewood," and after breaking a pedal spent his first night of vagrancy in a jail in Michigan City, Indiana. Motley arrived in New York fifteen days later. During the following nine years on the hobo trail, he worked odd jobs like football coach, coal hiker, baker's helper, waiter, janitor, chauffeur, and handyman, all the while writing for newspapers and magazines. In December 1936 Motley headed west in an old 1928 Buick sedan with his friend John. Leaving Chicago, the two adventurers had only $5.84 in cash, fifteen gallons in the tank, and another fifteen in cans. By the time they reached North Platte, Nebraska, they were broke and siphoning gas from other cars. In Pine Bluffs, Wyoming, they were caught and arrested; Motley was sentenced to sixty days in the county jail in Cheyenne and John thirty. Motley took to prison life with enthusiasm, all good experience for a budding crime author.

Throughout his travels Motley met individuals who inspired the characters for his later novels, not least a Mexican teenage ne'er-do-well called Joe "Nino," whom he met in a Denver detention home. Motley became infatuated with the handsome Nino, who inspired the character of Nick Romano, the clean-cut Italian boy destined to be a death row prisoner in his first novel, *Knock on Any Door* (1947).

Motley returned to Chicago in 1939 and took up residence near the city's legendary Maxwell Street. It was on skid row that Motley contributed to Jane Addams's *Hull House* magazine. In the November 1939 issue a short story titled "Hull House Neighborhood" describes bustling South Halsted Street: "People come out on the street. A formless, rabble rank of shapeless bodies, hunched shoulders, hard faces. A scare-crow parade of battered felts, baggy pants, ragged coats. Through the hush of half-light they find their way, these abstract shapes, specters in the city fog of smoke and grit, of lifting dark and spreading dawn." It was on Maxwell Street, among the blues singers, street vendors, hobos, and deadbeats, that Motley found his voice as a writer. In 1940 he signed up for the Federal Writers' Project (FWP), a New Deal arts program created by the U.S. government to support writers through the Depression.

Motley's greatest success came with the publication of *Knock on Any Door*, a gritty tale, with a homosexual subtext, of Nick Romano, an Italian American altar boy turned street punk who, driven by poverty, takes the road of petty crime that leads to murder and the electric chair. The book sold 47,000 copies in the first three weeks. In Chicago the story touched a nerve, because the city had long struggled with the problem of juvenile delinquency. On May 19, 1947, the author spoke to a large gathering at the Eleventh Street Theatre, at 62 East 11th Street, an event sponsored by the city's social service agencies. The subject was juvenile delinquency and *Knock on Any Door*.

In October 1947 David O. Selznik bought the rights to the novel, and the movie was to be produced by Mark Hellinger and to star Jennifer Jones, Humphrey Bogart, and a little-known actor called Marlon Brando. But when Hellinger died on December 21, 1947, Bogart bought the rights and produced the film with John Derek playing bad boy Nick Romano. The film cut out the homosexual subtext, and without that essential ingredient the movie failed. When *Knock on Any Door* opened in New York, Lillian Scott, the *Chicago Defender* theater critic, headlined her review "Acting is Great, Pix Mediocre."

Motley's second novel, *We Fished All Night* (1951), was less well-received. The story deals with three Chicago men—Chet Kosinski, a Polish immigrant; Aaron Levin, of Russian Jewish heritage; and Jim Norris, an all-American boy—and how World War II changes each of them for the worse. Most critics agree Motley was covering too may topics at once, leaving the reader confused. His third novel, *Let No Man Write My Epitaph* (1958), was more successful and is a sequel to *Knock on Any Door*, with Nick Romano's illegitimate son, Nick Romano Jr., turning to alcohol and drug abuse in another slice of gritty urban realism. However, not everyone was impressed; author Nelson Algren slammed it in the *Chicago Tribune*: "It is a sequel to the same author's *Knock On Any Door*, the best seller of some years back. The quality of pity, however, which distinguished the earlier novel has turned, in this one, to a syrup that pours too slowly. . . . Its reading is impeded by the author's habit of building flashback behind flashback; as well as by a habit of setting the reader up with the warning—'Catch!'—and then ducking behind the backstop to look for the ball. Mr. Motley spends most of this one looking for the ball." In 1960 *Let No Man Write My Epitaph* was made into a movie, starring Burl Ives, Shelley Winters, and teen idol James Darren. Also appearing was Ella Fitzgerald, who later recorded an album called *Ella Fitzgerald Sings Songs from "Let No Man Write My Epitaph."*

After the failure of *We Fished All Night*, Motley moved to Mexico, where he adopted Sergio Mendez, a Mexican street urchin, whom he lived with until his death in the Sanatorio De La Torre from massive intestinal gangrene in a neglected cyst on March 4, 1965. He was fifty-five. According to Mendez in the *Chicago Defender* of March 25: "Willard always prided himself on not ever being sick. He let this illness go too long before getting proper medical treatment." Willard Motley is buried in Cuernavaca, "the city of eternal springs," fifty-three miles south of Mexico City. His last novel, *Let Noon Be Fair*, which he finished two weeks before he died, was published posthumously in 1966 and is about the U.S. exploitation of Mexico, how capitalism and greed turns a small fishing village into a tourist town with brothels and major hotels. His town of Las Casa was based on Puerto Vallarta.

One of Motley's last writing projects was to edit and "tighten the sentences" of an autobiography by jazz singer and piano player Lillian Hardin Armstrong, ex-wife of "Satchmo." "But," she bluntly tells the *Chicago Defender* in an interview, "he ups and dies."

## Langston Hughes

> Chicago is still a savage and dangerous city. It's kind of an
> American Shanghai. And almost everybody seems to have been
> held up and robbed at least once.
>
> Langston Hughes in a 1936 letter to his friend Noel Sullivan

James Mercer Langston Hughes was born in Joplin, Missouri, on February 1, 1902, the second son of James Nathaniel Hughes and Carrie Mercer Langston Hughes; their eldest son had died in infancy two years earlier. Like many descendents of slaves Hughes was an ethnic mix, in his case of African, European, Jewish, and Native American. Soon after his birth his parents divorced. His father moved to Cuba and then Mexico to escape racism and better his career, and his mother traveled the Midwest in search of work; Langston grew up mostly with his grandmother in Lawrence, Kansas. While Hughes was at high school in Cleveland, Ohio, his mother remarried, to a chef called Homer Clark, and was living in Chicago. Hughes's introduction to the Windy City was visiting her in the summer of 1917. She lived on Wabash Avenue south of the Loop, a bustling area of city workers by day, pimps and prostitutes by night. It was while attending high school that Hughes discovered the Chicago school of poets like Vachel Lindsay and Carl Sandburg, and became radicalized by the Russian revolution. He began writing for the high school paper, and also penned poems, short stories, and plays. He wrote his first jazz poem, "When Sue Wears Red," in high school.

At Columbia University in New York, Hughes immersed himself in the swirling thrill of Harlem. He had long since been aware of his sexual attraction to black men and it was in Harlem's literary circles that he acquainted himself with other homosexual African American writers like Alain Locke and Countee Cullen. To support his poetry Hughes took a job as mess boy on the ship SS *Malone*, which took him to Africa. He left the ship in Europe and took up residence in Paris, where he made contact with other African American ex-pats. For a while he was a doorman at the Chez Bricktop nightclub. He returned to New York in 1924. On his first night back he met author, photographer, and one-time reporter for the *Chicago American* Carl Van Vechten, who would become an influential figure in Hughes's career. Hughes had already sold poems to *The Crisis* and other publications, but his short stories were first published in *The Messenger* and *Harlem* magazines, both edited by Wallace Thurman, another gay black writer who once lived in Chicago.

Hughes also started publishing his poems in *The New Negro*, the leading voice of the New Negro Renaissance in Literature literary movement. It was edited by Alain Locke, who later in life described himself as a "philosophical midwife" to aspiring black writers in the 1920s. But it was through Van Vechten that Hughes got his first collection of poetry published. In 1926 Alfred A. Knopf published *The Weary Blues*, and the following year a second volume, *Fine Clothes to the Jew*.

Not everyone appreciated the jazz poems in *The Weary Blues*, particularly black critics; even his friend Countee Cullen wrote of the "jazz poems as interlopers in the company of the truly beautiful poems in other sections of the book." While some old-school African American writers whitewashed their work, Hughes celebrated his African roots and the black cultural rhythms of jazz.

In January 1936 Hughes was back in Chicago to collaborate with black poet Arna Bontemps on the ill-fated play *When the Jack Hollers*. It premiered at Karamu House in Cleveland, staged by the Gilpin Players, but the comedy about black sharecroppers in the South was not a success. To raise much-needed funds, Hughes gave a lecture titled "Asiatic Peoples under the Soviets" for the Chicago branch of the Friends of the Soviet Union. Hughes had embraced left-wing politics years before. In 1932 he went to Russia with twenty-two other black writers and intellectuals. Hughes extended his Russian trip, continuing on alone to China and Japan. In July 1933 a headline in the *Chicago Defender* read: "Langston Hughes Driven out of Japan." After meeting with left-wing radicals in Tokyo, Hughes was questioned at length by Japanese officials and then ordered out of the country.

While in Chicago in 1936 Hughes met and collaborated with pianist and composer Margaret Bonds, who wrote music for several of his poems, including "The Negro Speaks of Rivers"; the same poem was also set to music by classical composer Howard Swanson, and Marian Anderson sang it at Carnegie Hall. Four years later Hughes was back in Chicago taking a break from a lecture tour, and while there he completed two projects with Arna Bontemps, "Boy of the Border," a children's book that remains unpublished, and "Jubilee: A Cavalcade of the Negro Theatre," a musical commissioned by the American Negro Exposition in Chicago and canceled at the last minute due to lack of funds.

Hughes is most remembered in Chicago for his column in the *Chicago Defender*, which first appeared on November 21, 1942, with the title "Here to Yonder": "Things that happen a way off yonder affect us here. The bombs that fall on some far-off Second Front in Asia rattle your dishes on your table in Chicago or New Orleans, cut down on your sugar, coffee, meat ration, and take the tires off your car." On February 13, 1943, Hughes wrote a column titled "Conversation after Midnight," in which he introduced the most enduring character in African American literature, the outspoken and intransigent Jesse B. Semple, or "Simple." Simple, a resident of Harlem, hung out in bars talking with Boyd, a dull but educated narrator, on the issues of the day. Hughes claimed the character was inspired by a fellow he met in Harlem's Patsy's Bar and Grill, who when asked his occupation, answered that he made cranks in a defense factory. When Hughes asked him what kind of cranks, the man replied that the white folks had never told him and that "I don't crank with those cranks, I just make 'em." His girlfriend, who was sitting with him, accused the man of being "simple." The column ran for over twenty years and spawned five books, *Simple Speaks His Mind* (1950), *Simple Takes a Wife* (1953), *Simple Stakes a Claim* (1957), *The Best of Simple* (1961), and *Simple's Uncle Sam* (1965). A sixth volume, *The Return of Simple* (1994), edited by Donna Akiba Sullivan Harper, was published posthumously.

The column raised Hughes's profile in Chicago, and on September 26, 1948, the life of the "Shakespeare of Harlem" was dramatized on radio in *Destination Freedom*, broadcast over NBC's Chicago outlet WMAQ, with Fred Pinkard playing the author. After that, Hughes spent three months in 1949 as poet in residence at the University of Chicago Laboratory Schools. Throughout the 1950s and '60s Simple voiced the frustrations and anger of African Americans suffering in a racist society. One spin-off from the column was the musical *Simply Heavenly*, written by Hughes with music by David Martin; it opened in New York in May 1957 off Broadway at the 85th Street Playhouse, presented by Stella Holt, directed by Joshua Shelley, and starring Melvin Stewart as "Simple." A review of Stewart's performance in the *Chicago Defender* of June 1, 1957, read: "You feel that he is never too mad because really Simple loves everybody. His love for the 'enemy' (as he would probably call white people—except Mrs. Roosevelt) is not of the

Martin Luther King variety—but it smacks of a ready willingness to forgive and forget if his paler brothers will only be a little less simple." The play opened on Broadway in August, and in October 1957 NBC Radio's *Monitor* show took a backstage look at *Simply Heavenly*, interviewing the cast and Hughes himself.

James Mercer Langston Hughes died on May 22, 1967, at age sixty-five, from complications of prostate cancer. His ashes are interred under the floor of the Arthur Schomburg Center for Research in Black Culture in Harlem.

# 19

# The Night Life

From the mid-1940s until the mid-1960s, Dearborn and Division Streets were "Queerborn and Perversion," a gay nightclub area controlled by mobsters. It was in these "homosexual haunts," and others around the city, that skirmishes took place between the Mafia and the Chicago police force, including the raid on Cyrano's Tavern after the murder of Richard Miller in a South Side park; the bizarre cast of characters at the Shoreline 7; the wheeling and dealing of Nathan Zuckerman at the Front Page; the raid on Louis Gager's Fun Lounge; and why Chicago's premier "fag hag" Kitty Sheon was immune from prosecution. And then there were the lesbian bars.

The *Chicago Sun-Times* on July 8, 1951, noted that in spite of the new Near North Side police captain John T. Warren, the area was still a "cesspool of wickedness." This "cesspool" included a gay neighborhood of bars and low-rent rooming houses around North Dearborn and West Division Streets, or "Queerborn and Perversion" as it was known. On December 31, 1951, police raided Cyrano's Tavern, 8 East Division Street, "a reputed hangout for homosexuals," Captain Redmond Gibbons of the Hudson Avenue station told the *Chicago Tribune*. Fifty-eight people were arrested for being inmates of a disorderly house, and the owner, Howard Blencoe, and two bartenders with serving liquor to intoxicated persons. The raid was part of an ongoing investigation into the murder of twenty-nine-year-old Richard Miller, a man fatally shot on the South Side of Chicago.

On April 13, 1951, at 5:00 a.m. the police found Richard Miller's body in Jackson Park at Stony Island and 63rd Street, shot in the stomach. The park was a notorious homosexual cruising area. Miller, who was a navy veteran and choir singer at Paul Union church, worked at the National Fire Insurance Company, where his colleagues described him as a quiet man who lived with his mother and kept to himself. Police questioned Rosario Eccesso, a male friend of Miller's who owned the Artistic Beauty Shop at 1613 East 67th Street. He told police that after the two dined at a restaurant that night, they stopped for a nightcap at Cyrano's Tavern, then returned to the beauty shop, where they parted ways. An hour later Miller was dead. Looking for the killer, the cops began arresting and questioning homosexuals in Jackson Park. On August 10 Rodovan Lazarevias, a thirty-three-year-old steel-mill worker, was shot and wounded in the park after propositioning an undercover cop and then making a run for it. The outcome of the Miller murder case is unknown to the author, though Miller was included in an October 1951 list of unsolved murders.

One popular gay bar from the mid-1940s to the mid-1960s was the Shoreline 7 at 7 West Division Street. The liquor license was in the name of Johnny Campbell, a tiny ex-boxer. Ralph Marco, the manager, is rumored to have once owned a bar in Chicago for dwarves; in 1946, there was a midget bar in Chicago at 355 East 79th Street, owned and staffed by little people. One feature of the Shoreline 7 was Smiley, Marco's Harlequin Great Dane, and in 1950 the *Chicago Tribune* reported this den of iniquity had two goldfish bowls behind the bar. Blondina, a bartender, remembers Marco as "a big hammy man. He had bluish eyes and was chunky, muscular and big. We always called him father, and everyone who worked there he called his daughters. He was a loving man."

The Shoreline 7 was "syndicate-owned." A back room at the bar was used for card playing and meetings among police captains, mobsters, and politicians. Although gay bars never advertised as "gay" back then, ads for the Shoreline 7 appeared in *Night Life in Chicago*, a sleazy publication focusing on stripper bars, restaurants, and drag shows. One ad for the Shoreline 7 read: "An interesting spot in the heart of the Gold Coast, with unusual entertainment nightly. A 'must' stopover for visitors."

Among the characters at the Shoreline 7 was Fran Wilson, who worked the "26" dice table, exploiting a loophole in the gambling laws. Wilson was famous for having a mouth like a trucker and selling Benzedrine out of her bra. Drag queen Dee LoBue recalls Fran Wilson as having "flaming red hair, a heavy build, great personality and the biggest eyes because she was always on uppers. She was just a joy to be around. Loved gay kids." Another "26" girl at the Shoreline 7 was a dwarf named Opal. She was 36 inches tall, glamorous, and wore a blonde wig, gowns, and furs. It's rumored she worked undercover for the syndicate, keeping an eye on light-fingered bar staff. She vanished from the Chicago gay scene in the late 1960s.

The Shoreline 7 specialized in comic drag. Blondina recalls one performer: "Terri Jackson was straight, he had long curly hair and he went with a woman. He worked for the telephone company during the day, and at night he came in and did drag. He got a big bucket and filled it with water and sat in that damn bucket and did 'Splish, Splash, I'm Taking a Bath' . . . everybody was soaked, the bartenders were soaked, the audience were soaked, and it was just amazing."

Dee LoBue remembers the seedy side of the Shoreline 7: "One day I was there, and Papa [Ralph Marco] says, 'Dee, I want you to tend bar a couple of nights.' I said, 'Sure.' Then he said, 'Let me show you something.' And he took me behind the bar and strapped in six different places was a gun. He said, 'Here are guns, and they're all loaded. Now, in case something happens, and someone comes in, I want you to take the gun and shoot the person if they try to attack you. Then I want you to put a knife in their hand and say, "He came after me with a knife."' These were things you did in those days. I remember one time the police were chasing a robber and they came in the front door and out the back door and they shot the guy in the alley."

Raids on gay bars were commonplace. On July 5, 1962, the Shoreline 7 was raided by vice cop Frank Guerra of the East Chicago Avenue district. Five were arrested, including two female impersonators.

Another popular bar was the Front Page at 530 North Rush Street. John Coleman was the manager. The "owner," a title applied loosely to Chicago gay bars, was Nathan Zuckerman. The Front Page comprised two bars, the upstairs Headline Room, a straight pick-up joint, and the downstairs gay bar. Zuckerman was arrested at least twenty-eight times. His first bust was in 1923, for being a handbook operator and "fence." In 1954 he was arrested in connection with an armed robbery of a jewelry store, along with a former police magistrate-gone-bad Robert R. Lee and Walter Lasczynski. In 1962, at the age of sixty-one, he was sent to jail for possession of stolen U.S. Savings Bonds worth seven thousand dollars.

The Front Page had several spats with the law. In the *Chicago Tribune* on March 27, 1962, a headline read in part: "Witness Two Men Kissing and Move In." The article read: "Thirty-nine men and a woman were arrested last night in a police raid at the Front Page lounge. . . . Detectives Arthur Tyrrell and Edward Kalaich said they found two men kissing each other at the bar and saw several other men dancing with each other. They then announced the raid. Six squadrols were called to take forty to the East Chicago Avenue station." Earlier that same day another twenty men were arrested in a raid on the Art Deco–fronted Patio Theater, 6008 Irving Park Road, described by police as "a meeting place for homosexuals." The *Chicago Tribune* published the names, addresses, and occupations of those arrested. Most, if not all, would have lost their jobs.

## Kitty Sheon

Chicago's most prominent "fag hag" was Kitty Sheon (real name Kathleen Schert), a stout, homely woman who, according to patrons of her bars, resembled Mayor Richard J. Daley in drag. Sheon's first bar was Cullen's Green Parrot, 3478 North Broadway; it's not known if it catered to a gay clientele. Her second bar, Kitty Sheon's Little Club, 3916 North Sheridan, which opened in the summer of 1944, was gay. Mame, one of her piano players, described Sheon as "a bleached blonde, a sort of Sophie Tucker type. Rough on the outside, but with a heart of gold on the inside, is what she wanted everybody to think. She perpetuated her own legend in that respect. If being a tough old broad would make her money, then she'd be the toughest old broad on the block, and if she had to be the sweet grand-motherly type to make money, she'd do that too."

Another of Kitty's piano players was Eleanor, who worked there between 1955 and 1957, singing parodies of songs, adding gay/vulgar meanings, songs with titles like "Wait 'til Your Son Turns Nelly" instead of "Wait 'til the Sun Shines, Nellie." In 1958 Sheon opened Kitty Sheon's Key Club at 745 North Rush Street. Sheon's bars were noted for their elegance, pink lighting, strict tie and jacket dress code, and "no touching" rule. One reason Kitty Sheon's was popular with gay men is that it was never raided. A regular explains, "Kitty ran a good place, and she and George [her hus-band] kept the customers out of trouble. They kept the cops away. George was formerly a policeman during the days of Big Bill Thompson back in the 1920s. He knew how it worked."

George L. Schert joined the police force in 1925 and retired in 1960 when he was hired as a security guard at the *Chicago Tribune*. George Schert died at age seventy-one on December 13, 1969, in his home at 40 East Oak Street. Kitty passed away on October 22, 1977, at age seventy-four. They're buried together in the mausoleum at Rosehill Cemetery.

## Lesbian Bars

In the 1950s, lesbian bars included the Midget Inn at Kedzie and Lawrence. Downstairs was a straight bar for railroad men working on the El, and upstairs it was blue-collar bulldykes and femmes. Another popular lesbian bar was the Volli-Bal at 2124 North Clark Street, initially fronted by drag performer Volli Charles. Dancer and choreographer Bic Carrol remembers Charles: "He was a tall, thin blond who came to Chicago from Florida. He worked pantomime in men's clothes with a lot of props: hats, wigs, shawls, etc. While most of his work was comedy, he also did serious impersonations of singers Frances Faye and Judy Garland."

Before it featured the Volli-Bal, the location witnessed one of Chicago's most famous events: it was next door to the S-M-C Cartage garage, scene of the Saint Valentine's Day Massacre. In the 1950s, when the Volli-Bal was in business, the bar owner's father often took customers into the back of the old S-M-C Cartage garage to view the crime scene. Bic Carroll remembers putting his fingers in the bullet holes. "He was an old timer," explains Carroll, "who told us wonderful stories about the old days of the Mob."

The Volli-Bal had an oval bar at the front, a dance floor (though same-sex dancing was illegal), and a small stage where Volli Charles did his one-man show. Charles lasted a year, then left abruptly after crossing a gangster. That's when the Volli-Bal went lesbian. This was at a time when lesbian bars were raided and women arrested for cross-dressing. Tessie remembers: "You would go into a bar and the police would harass you. Women couldn't cross-dress, couldn't wear pants with zippers in the front; you had to have pants with buttons on the side. You couldn't wear men's shirts. The buttons had to be, women on the right, men on the left, or they would arrest you, put you in a paddy wagon, and you'd go to jail for cross-dressing."

In the *Chicago Tribune* on November 8, 1964, a headline read: "Nab Women in Raid": "Fifteen women, who police said were male impersonators, were arrested early yesterday in a vice raid on the Chat-Chat Lounge, 4526 Sheridan Rd." Owners of lesbian bars were careful to enforce the legal dress code. One popular bar was Lost & Found, at 2959 West Irving Park (it later moved to 3058 West Irving Park), opened by Shirley Christensen in 1965, and later co-owned with her lover Ava Allen. In the 1960s Cab Driver Joey remembers being turned away at the door: "I couldn't even get in because I dressed in all men's clothes. I walked in and Shirley picked up my shirt and said you can't get in here, you've got a fly front."

Another popular lesbian bar was Big Lou's at 731 North Avenue, run by three-hundred-pound lesbian Lou Kane (real name Lucille Kinovsky). One regular described her as "a big dyke who appeared tough but was really a sweetheart." Another said that she was "a big blousy white-trash type woman." The bar offered music by two African American piano players, Theresa Whitehead and Theury Dry. On February 16, 1952, the bar was raided and closed down, with thirty-six women and twenty-eight men arrested. The *Chicago Tribune* on February 17 read: "Police charged the place is a hangout for perverts. They said the women generally were attired in men's clothing and were dancing together. The men, police said, were consorting with one another." On February 24 Big Lou lost her license, as did two other nearby gay bars, the Hollywood Bowl, 1300 North Clark Street, and an unnamed tavern at 1942 North Sedgwick, operated by Mary Anderson. Two years later, in the same neighborhood, Annabelle's, 1801 North Avenue, a lesbian tavern run by Ruth Gemende, was also closed down.

A few doors away from Big Lou's, another gay bar, called the Palm Gardens, was run by Henry Bevier. On September 25, 1960, it was raided and closed down. Bevier was arrested for keeping a disorderly house; fourteen customers, eight men and six women, were charged with soliciting for prostitution and resisting arrest. Then on November 14, 1962, three people were shot in the bar. The incident started when a woman named Edith Shields was stabbed in the alley behind the bar. The suspect was another woman. Nancy Davis, the bar owner's daughter, carried the twenty-five-year-old Shields into the bar and tended her wounds. That's when Robert Wilson walked in and opened fire, shooting Davis, Barbara Kramer, and Robert Miller, the bartender. What the incident was about is unclear, but the Palm Gardens lost its license again. It reopened on February 13, 1964, with a new licensee named Marvin Mykytyn. This didn't fool Commander

John McDermott of the Chicago Avenue police, who criticized city officials for renewing the bar's license, saying Mykytyn was penniless and "may not be" the owner. The Palm Gardens closed soon afterward.

Another lesbian bar was Club Evergreen at 1322 North Clybourn Avenue, a black jazz club with female exotic dancers. The proprietor of the club was Corwin "Pokie Dott" Marbly, with Minnie Drewitt as manager. In August 1952, entertainment at Club Evergreen included blues singer Lil "Upstairs" Mason, the Jack Cooley Band, and the exotic dancer Eleanor King. Other dancers were Big "House Rockin'" Bertha, Modernistic Shake Dancer Verda Gibson, Little "Miss Korea," Laverne Satis, and Sheila Collazo. From October through December 1952 Buster "Leap Frog" Bennett played the club; his bass player was William Lee, father of filmmaker Spike Lee. In March 1953 Club Evergreen held its first "Parade of the Lilies Bathing Beauty Contest." The winner was crowned "Miss Evergreen of 1953." The club stayed open until the end of 1960, and one of the last shows was a Jazz Jamboree starring King Kolax and Danny Overbea with Foxie the stripper and Allen Young the ventriloquist.

## The Raids on the Lincoln Baths and Goethe Street Party

The most notorious of Chicago's bathhouses was the Lincoln Baths in the basement of the Lincoln Hotel at 1812 North Clark Street. On June 13, 1964, the baths were raided after a detective reported seeing four men engaged in sex acts in the steam room. In all, thirty-three men were arrested. The manager, William J. Anderson, was charged with being the keeper of a house of ill fame, and the rest with being inmates. On June 30 in the South State Street Court, seven members of staff were fined, as was the manager. The others were released.

On March 5, 1966, the police raided the Lincoln Baths again, this time netting thirty-two men. The *Chicago Tribune* printed all their names, addresses, and occupations. Vicki St. John tells of one man who fought back: "I had a dentist who had offices at 102 E. Chestnut. His name was Jerry C. When they raided the Lincoln Baths, the first name in the paper the next day was his." Jerry C. is said to have sued the *Chicago Tribune* for publishing his name before the trial and won.

It wasn't only gay bars and bathhouses that were raided in the 1960s. On May 3, 1964, police broke up a private house party at 20 East Goethe

Street. The next day the *Chicago Tribune* headline read: "Sex Party — 58 Are Seized, Including Two Juveniles." Among those arrested was an activist for gay Catholic rights, the late Ron Helizon (The Polish Princess):

> I was to graduate from Holy Name Cathedral High School in three weeks. I went to the party . . . these two guys were getting together and having a wedding. All of a sudden the place got raided. There must have been 20 paddy wagons in front of the building and we were all taken off to jail. We got out the next day and our names and addresses were printed in the *Tribune*.
>
> There were people who were ruined. I called the high school and they told me I couldn't come back. It was three weeks before graduation, and I couldn't come back. They said I couldn't even get back on the property. There was a Father George Malone, who was at the Cathedral in those days and he tried to get me my diploma, but they wouldn't give it to me, so I never graduated from Cathedral High School. I was fortunate because I was able to go to night school and get my diploma, and go on with my life.

Vicki St. John was also at the party:

> This was billed as the social event of the season. There was a restaurant on Diversey, east of Clark Street. Everybody hung out there, and so did the cops in plain clothes. So everyone was talking about this party at 20 E. Goethe Street.
>
> About two days before, word went around that the cops were going to raid it. Of course, I didn't believe them, so I went. There must have been 100–150 people in that apartment. All of a sudden we hear there's a raid. A friend of mine, a little Jewish American Princess, ran into the bedroom, got out on the fire escape, and ran down. Just as he was letting it go, a cop came around the corner and said to him, "Where the hell are you coming from?" He said, "Did you see my little poodle, it got away from me, it ran down the alley, and I'm trying to find it, did you see it?" The cop said, "Get the hell out of here." Then the cop pulled the fire escape down and climbed up . . . anybody else who came out got pushed back in.
>
> During all this time I looked out the windows of the apartment and the Pump Room had emptied out into the street; they had

paddy wagons backed up to the building with floodlights. It was like an opening on Broadway, with women from the Pump Room in mink coats and guys wearing tuxedos and suits. The whole street was full of squad cars, people and paddy wagons; you would have thought this was the biggest thing to happen ever. The news media was there. It was awful.

When they raided the guys who threw the party were in an apartment across the hall getting dressed for an impromptu drag show. The owner of the apartment was a tad bit of a jackass, and when he came out the cops grabbed him and he started mouthing off. They hauled his ass down in the elevator and outside he did a Marilyn Monroe routine. The media were there with cameras rolling, the floodlights were turned on, and this guy comes out doing a Marilyn Monroe swish and blowing kisses to the crowd, before he gets shoved into the paddy wagon.

A lot of the kids arrested were straight.

## The Raid on Louis Gager's "Fun Lounge"

In the mid-1940s Louis Gager opened his first Fun Lounge at 2320 North Mannheim Road in a notorious strip of syndicate-owned cheap motels and seedy nightclubs known as "Glitter Gulch." Although the Fun Lounge was the only gay bar in the area, there were other clubs that hosted drag shows, including the Miami Moon at 4500 Washington Boulevard, a roadhouse saloon with a troubled history. On November 1, 1949, five shotgun blasts came through a window, narrowly missing the owner, James Scallon, and several customers. In 1950 Scallon sold the bar to ne'er-do-well James J. Cleary and his wife, Marie, for $55,000. Four years later Cleary was charged with murder in Reno, Nevada, after stabbing a Western Union clerk in the neck. This was typical of the unsavory characters that ran some of the gay bars in Chicago.

The original Fun Lounge was a shack on the side of the road with six stools, an upright piano, and a dirt floor. Gager's legal problems started on August 26, 1948, when he was fined a hundred dollars for possession of a slot machine. Then in October 1949 complaints from local residents led to another raid on the Fun Lounge. No morals or liquor violations were found, suggesting the bar was tipped off, as it was usually filled with gangsters, drug dealers, homosexuals, prostitutes, artists, burlesque stars, strippers, showgirls, and anyone else who counted themselves a part of Chicago's nefarious underworld. Later in the 1950s the Fun Lounge relocated to 2340 Mannheim Road, where it remained until January 29, 1960, when it was destroyed by two explosions and a fire. The body of a twenty-seven-year-old bartender, Robert Niewinski, was found in the rubble. Two other buildings were damaged, a barbershop and a vacant restaurant. The cause was reportedly a gas leak. The Fun Lounge was rebuilt with a tile facade, no front windows, no sign, and a thick steel door. The structure was later extended until it took up four lots, with the tavern operating from the south half of the building, and Gager living in the north half, though some say he resided in another suburb with his mother.

Gager weighed an estimated 270 pounds. A Chicago-area native born on July 13, 1910, his organized crime credentials were no secret to the police. The myth was that as the bar lay between two townships it was immune from the law. Not so, though Gager did have a guardian angel, Tony "Big Tuna" Accardo, crime boss of the Chicago outfit until he handed over the reins to Sam Giancana in 1956. The Fun Lounge was packed on weekends, with carloads traveling out from the city to hear Georgia White, a black piano player famous for her "dirty ditties." Her signature tune was a reworking of *Bye Bye Blackbird*: "Back your ass against the wall, here I come balls and all, bye bye cherry." One Fun Lounge regular described her as "a Black Belle Barth."

Old Marlene, who knew White, described her as "a thin woman who often forgot to wear underwear. She'd pull up her dress and show everything that God gave her." When the Fun Lounge closed in 1964 White moved to the Blue Pub at 3059 West Irving Park Road, where she led sing-alongs until her death from a heart attack brought on by cirrhosis of the liver, not surprising given she could, and did, drink any man under the table. Louis Gager's downfall came when he made a powerful enemy during the tax evasion trial of mob leader Tony Accardo in 1960. Richard B. Ogilvie, a government prosecutor with political aspirations (he was later governor of Illinois, 1969–73), headed a campaign against Accardo, who boasted an unsavory résumé; as Al Capone's bodyguard he was a suspect in the Saint Valentine's Day Massacre. Ogilvie finally nailed Accardo for tax evasion. The mob leader was charged with falsifying his 1956–58 income tax returns by deducting expenses for using his sports car on his job as a beer salesman.

On October 25, 1960, two tavern owners appeared in Federal District Court to testify in Accardo's defense. One of them was Louis Gager, who claimed Accardo drove up to his tavern in a red Mercedes sports car in July 1956 and took an order for twenty-five cases of beer. Gager added that Accardo and Jackie Cerrone—Accardo's chauffeur—dropped into the Fun Lounge frequently after that. Two weeks later Accardo was found guilty, a decision overturned by the United States Circuit Court of Appeals on January 6, 1962.

Soon afterward, Ogilvie was elected Cook County Sheriff. Still after Accardo, he railed against Louis Gager's Fun Lounge in his campaign speeches. In the *Chicago Tribune* of October 8, 1962, he described the tavern as "too revolting to describe in detail in public. . . . Gager advertises special parties which start at 5 a.m. Under-age drinkers, including high school students, mingle with degenerates to watch indecent shows." Sheriff Ogilvie waged war on vice. High on his list was Louis Gager. He took his revenge on February 25, 1964, by sending chief investigator Richard S. Cain and his officers to raid the Fun Lounge. The following day the press was brutal, listing the names, addresses, and occupations of the 109 arrested. The *Chicago Sun-Times* headline on April 26, 1964, read: "Area Teachers among 109 Seized in Raid on Vice Den": "A massive sheriff's narcotics raid on a notorious suburban vice den owned by an avowed friend of crime syndicate mobster Anthony J. Accardo sent public officials scurrying Saturday to check the list of 108 arrested with the owner of the den."

Over the next few days the newspapers tore into the arrested, paying special attention to a suburban junior high school principal, eight teachers, six minors, a retired judge, and several government employees. The police said they confiscated marijuana and barbiturate pills sold over the bar. Cain described the Fun Lounge as a speakeasy-type establishment and "a notorious hangout for sex deviates of both sexes." He added that many of the men arrested carried powder puffs and lipsticks and wore wigs.

The process of booking 109 arrestees at the Criminal Courts Building at 26th and California took six hours, and all, including six women, were released on a bond of twenty-five dollars. Also, two bartenders paid two hundred dollars in bond for serving liquor to a minor. On May 15, 1964, in Oak Park, Circuit Court Judge Wayne Olson dismissed charges against ninety-nine of those arrested, saying there was no evidence of wrongdoing, a ruling that came too late for those who had lost their jobs, families, and homes.

Only one man came to the defense of those arrested at the Fun Lounge and the party at Goethe Street. An article in the May 11, 1964, *Chicago Daily News* was headlined: "Professor Assails Wholesale Vice Arrests." Professor Claude R. Sowle, a criminologist and law professor at Northwestern University, criticized police for releasing the names of those arrested. He noted, in both the cases of the Fun Lounge and Goethe Street, the respective judges had criticized police for their lack of evidence. Police countered by saying the defendants were arrested for being in a place where a crime was taking place. But Sowle pointed out that police were on "shaky ground" in arresting "observers" of obscene acts who weren't participating themselves. He reminded police that it wasn't illegal for homosexuals to engage in sex acts in private. "Just being there, by and large, is not a crime," Sowle said. "While it is not a question of condoning (deviate behavior) it appears that the vast majority (in both cases) were not guilty of criminal offenses under the law." Sowle suggested the raids were just harassment, pure and simple. Or, he added, "It is good politics."

# 20

# Trouble with the Law

The Chicago police force gets its comeuppance when gays fight back for the first time. Dean T. Kolberg and Ralf L. Johnston, owners of the Trip bar, take the city to court after being raided and closed in Mayor Richard J. Daley's clean-up-vice campaign before the 1968 Democratic National Convention. In 1973 Captain Clarence Braasch and twenty-one other police officers are arrested for shaking down gay bars, and John J. Pyne, an ex–Chicago police officer, is jailed for running a blackmail ring.

In early 1968 Mayor Richard J. Daley set about cleansing the city of vice in preparation for the Democratic National Convention in August. At the time, the Democrats were in disarray over the Vietnam War, and add to this the assassinations of Martin Luther King Jr. in April, Robert F. Kennedy in June, and the expected mass protests by Yippies and peaceniks, and the month of August was expected to be hotter than usual in Chicago. It was. The running street battles between antiwar demonstrators and Mayor Daley's hard-line Chicago police force underscored the gulf between old-style politics and a radical counterculture that embraced women's and gay rights. While the police turned their nightsticks on Yippies, the protestors chanted "The Whole World Is Watching." Now the whole world could see what the city's lesbians and gay men had known for years: that the Chicago police force was out of control.

On September 8, 1967, Dean T. Kolberg and Ralf L. Johnston opened the elegant Trip restaurant and bar at 27 East Ohio Street. The Trip was raided twice, first on January 28, 1968, when police arrested fourteen men, eight of whom were charged with public indecency, the rest with being employees of a disorderly house. Ralla Klepak, who defended hundreds of cases involving gay men, was attorney for the defense. On March 29 in jury court, the charges were dismissed because the police entered the bar illegally, by impersonating members of the club after illegally obtaining cards. Two months later the bar was raided again, and plainclothes officers arrested an employee and a patron. This time the owners appealed to the City Liquor Board, and the Trip's license was "temporarily" suspended between May 13 and May 20. In 1968 when a Chicago tavern was raided it was required to stay closed until the case came to court, up to two years, effectively putting the bar out of business. Kolberg and Johnston fought back, and on March 27, 1969, the Illinois Supreme Court decided in their favor, ruling the law allowing Chicago to close taverns until revocations were appealed was unconstitutional. The Trip grand reopening was on June 18, 1969, and the bar thrived until it closed down in November 1976. On June 29, 1986, Johnston died at age fifty-seven. His partner, Kolberg, a World War II veteran, ran the Book Store in Geneseo, Illinois, until his retirement in 1995. He died at home on October 15, 1997.

## The Arrest of Captain Clarence Braasch

It was common knowledge the mob had a stake in Chicago's gay bars, and that police were shaking them down. But it wasn't until 1973 that U.S. Attorney James R. Thompson (later governor of Illinois, 1977–91) investigated the problem. In June 1973 the *Chicago Gay Crusader* reported forty-seven policemen from three districts had been indicted by a federal grand jury for extortion in shaking down taverns, many of them gay-owned or with a gay clientele.

The trial of Captain Clarence Braasch and twenty-two other police officers from the East Chicago Avenue Police District began in August 1973. Braasch, charged with extortion and perjury, denied any knowledge of the shakedowns. After Thompson granted four officers immunity in return for giving evidence, the web of corruption began to unravel. One told the court that payoffs were referred to as the "vice package" and tavern owners "members of the vice club." This is how it worked: After a bar was targeted for shakedown, police visited several times in one evening, brandishing shotguns, checking the liquor license, and lining the customers up against a wall to check IDs. Later the owner was invited to join the "vice club" with a promise that harassment would end and police would "slant" reports of any trouble on the premises. Each bar paid upward of a hundred dollars a month, the money shared between vice cops, Captain Braasch, and others at police headquarters. Although not mentioned in court, it was implied that a percentage of the payoffs went to Police Super-intendent Conlisk himself. Beat cops were raking in $250 a month, and Braasch's share was estimated at $3,710 a month.

To counteract police retaliation, State's Attorney Bernard Carey said in the September 15, 1973, *Chicago Tribune*: "I am pledging full protection to any witness who will come forward to testify about illegal activities by police. I can and will see that such a witness need fear no retaliation from the crooked police or from their political pals. I urge the citizens of Chicago to cast aside fear and come forward to join us in this effort."

Nearly every gay bar on the Near North Side from 1966 to 1970 was named as a victim, including the popular King's Ransom, 20 East Chicago Avenue, and New Jamie's, 1110 North Clark Street. Reporter Robert Davis in the *Chicago Tribune* on August 17, 1973, updated the growing list of gay taverns lined up to testify, including the Hayride and Ifs, Ands or Burt's—amusingly misspelled "Ifs, Ands and Butts" by the paper. A bartender at both bars told the court of payoffs of $100 a month at the Hayride and between $150 and $300 at Ifs, Ands and Burt's.

Salvatore Strazzante, a former assistant state's attorney who resigned his post when called to testify in the Braasch trial, said he paid a hundred dollars a month over a three-year period on behalf of his father, the owner of the Kings Ransom. Then Myron Minuskin, a former Chicago assistant corporation counsel, admitted he acted as lawyer and payoff conduit for Claudia Murphy, owner of the Inner Circle. He also admitted charging Murphy fees for making the shakedown payments and failing to report the money on his tax returns. Other bar owners who stepped up to the plate were Charles "Chuck" Renslow of the Gold Coast; Julius and Walter Fleishman, brothers who operated Sam's and the Normandy; Nick Argiris, former assistant manager of Bently's; and representatives from Alfie's, the Baton, the Haig, Togetherness, Croydon Circle Lounge, and the Baron

Lounge, 629 North Clark Street. One owner told the court, according to the August 17 *Chicago Tribune*: "The way the laws are in Illinois, they can close you up any time they want to. They call it a setup." He explained that he paid up because he didn't want police harassing his homosexual clientele: "If any police officer would walk in, everybody would walk out."

As the trial of Captain Braasch and his vice officers continued, the extent of Chicago police corruption became clear, and U.S. state's attorney Thompson expanded his investigations into other police districts: Austin, Town Hall, Englewood, and Foster Avenue. On October 5, 1973, after a litany of damning evidence, Braasch was found guilty of extortion and perjury along with eighteen of his former vice squad officers. Two months later Braasch was sentenced to six years in prison.

## Blackmail Rings

A *Chicago Tribune* headline on June 8, 1949, read: "Captures 'Cop'; Tells Story of Extortion Plot." John G. Boyd and Theodore Self were charged with extorting $2,500 from Walter H. Lambert. Boyd was also charged with impersonating a police officer. Lambert told police he met Self at Oak Street beach and went to a hotel bar. They visited the restroom together, and while they were there, Boyd walked in, said he was a police vice officer, and claimed he caught them in an immoral act. Lambert was "arrested" then released. Boyd contacted Lambert later in the day telling him he could "fix a case" for $2,500. Lambert handed over the money, but became suspicious when he saw Boyd on the street later. He contacted the police and both Boyd and Self were arrested.

This case is only exceptional in that the victim went to the police. Blackmail was an ever-present threat for homosexuals. In March 1963 another blackmail ring was uncovered, this one operating at Chicago's Greyhound Bus terminal. After a sixteen-year-old was arrested for loitering, he told police he picked up homosexuals and steered them to four co-conspirators for a "shakedown." The four charged were Virgil Lamb, the bus terminal manager; Herman Westerhoff, a captain for the Inter-State Detective Agency; Henry Meyer, an Inter-State patrolman; and Ronald Monaco, whom police described as "a pander [*sic*]." Helped by the sixteen-year-old, the thugs were trapped in a sting operation when the youth "picked-up" an undercover cop and handed him over to the gang. After "arresting" the cop, they punched him in the face and took eighty dollars from his wallet. The four were arrested.

The largest and most vicious blackmail ring was a nationwide operation based in Chicago. The *New York Times* on August 17, 1966, reported that John Fellebaum, a twenty-seven-year-old former weightlifter from Monroeville, Pennsylvania, was found guilty of "conspiring to use interstate communications to shake down homosexuals." He received the maximum sentence of five years in prison and a ten-thousand-dollar fine. Fellebaum's role was to pick up gay men in bars, take them to a hotel, then steal their credit cards and other forms of identification. Later, other members of the gang, posing as detectives, approached the victim at home to tell him he was required to appear in court as a witness against Fellenbaum. The "detectives" then suggested a bribe.

According to the December 9 *New York Times*, in sentencing the judge told Fellebaum: "It has been a long time since I have come upon a case that was so revolting as your case. I think you are so steeped in filth that as I read the report I cringed, and my flesh crept as I read the depth of iniquity to which you have allowed yourself to sink." Fellebaum's sentence was three years in jail.

The leader of the ring was fifty-one-year-old John J. Pyne, a former Chicago police officer. His role in the scam was to supply police badges, other IDs, arrest forms, and extradition warrants, all the paraphernalia needed for a con man to pass himself off as a police officer. Pyne was arrested on June 24, 1966.

Pyne and his gang lured hundreds of businessmen, movie actors, television performers, government officials, and others into sex traps, then demanded money. Victims were intimidated by threats of arrest from phony cops, and from threats of exposure by a "reporter" in Chicago who phoned their homes; the reporter was never arrested, but most likely it was Pyne. On May 17, 1967, an unnamed thirty-seven-year-old Utah contractor told the court how he had been shaken down for ten thousand dollars. He was the key witness in the trial of Pyne and Robert Schwartz of Bellmawr, New Jersey. The Utah man testified that in 1964, while attending a convention in Chicago, Schwartz approached him in the Loop, calling out to him by name. Schwartz urged the contractor back to the hotel to talk business. While in the contractor's room, Schwartz made an indecent proposal, and when the Utah man became angry, Schwartz flashed a badge and identified himself as a policeman. Then he left. When the contractor returned to Utah, Pyne turned up with a Chicago warrant for his arrest. The contractor paid a bribe, but also recorded his conversations with Pyne and promptly turned the tapes over to the FBI. Pyne and Schwartz each went to jail for five years, while John Fellebaum, Sherman Chadwick Kaminsky, Elwood Lee Hammock, and Edmund Pazewicz each got four years for conspiring to use interstate facilities to rob and extort.

# 21

# Trans-Forming Drag

In the 1950s George/Christine Jorgensen brought her one-gal show to the Black Orchid during sex-change mania, when Chicago resident Carl Rollins Hammond, once a side-show "freak," became Hedy Jo Star. It was a time when Tony Midnite, costume designer and female impersonator, brought the *Jewel Box Revue* to the South Side, which heralded the 1960s Chicago drag boom.

On December 1, 1952, a front-page headline in the *New York Daily News* read "Ex-GI Becomes Blonde Beauty; Operations Transform Bronx Youth" and George/Christine Jorgensen was outed as the first person in the world to change sex. This, of course, was not true, as in 1931 Danish artist Einar Wegener had a sex change to become Lili Elbe, though the process was not successful, as she died from complications after a fifth operation attempted to implant a uterus.

Jorgensen went on to make a career out of her "sex change" notoriety. On July 3, 1956, she opened in Chicago at the Black Orchid nightclub at Rush and Ontario. She described her act to Robert Wiedrich of the *Chicago Tribune* in an article published the next day: "It's a philosophical comedy number which shows life is full of changes. It's brilliant. If you're going to be what people consider a star, you've got to live the part. The idea of trying to be the girl next door is silly." After trying her hand at acting, singing, and photography, Jorgensen took up writing and published *Christine*

*Jorgensen: A Personal Autobiography* (1967). She also spoke of her life and experiences on university campuses around the country. On January 9, 1969, she appeared on *Chicago*, a TV talk and guest show, along with several local female impersonators, including the Cuban legend Heri del Valle (real name David de Alba), at the time Chicago's most famous Judy Garland impersonator.

In 1952, after Jorgensen's sex change story broke, interest in transsexual affairs spawned an underground cult, with filmmaker Ed Wood making *Glen or Glenda?* (1953) and the publication of a slew of paperbacks with titles like *Man into Woman* by Neils Hoyer (1953) and *The Lady Was a Man* by Mark Shane (1958). *Half* (1953) by Jordan Park, a pseudonym for Chicago science-fiction writer Cyril M. Kornbluth, is a fictionalized account of a Polish American man living on the South Side of Chicago struggling with his sexuality and gender. "You've heard about 'men' like Steven Bankow," the cover reads. "You've read about them in your daily newspapers. But here—for the first time—a novelist tackles the problem of a man who tries to change his sex."

In the autobiography *I Changed My Sex* (1965) by Hedy Jo Star, the first recipient of a sex change in an American hospital, she writes: "In the instant that I awoke from the anesthetic, I realized that I had finally become a woman." In 1920 Star was born Carl Rollins Hammond in Prague, Oklahoma. In his late teens he became a Half-Man/Half-Woman side-show freak in a circus. In the 1930s and '40s most circuses, carnivals, and traveling freak shows included a tent with a banner emblazoned "Sex Paradox" or "Sex Enigma" and the "freak's" name underneath: Anna–John, or Roberta–Ray, or Leo–Leola the Double Sex Wonder, and Joseph–Josephine the Polish Austrian hermaphrodite supposedly split down the middle, one side male one side female. Star stayed with the circus until the outbreak of World War II, when he was drafted into the army, where he escaped detection and carved a niche for himself entertaining the troops in touring shows like Irving Berlin's *This Is the Army*.

After breast implants in New York's Park East Hospital, Star completed his surgery in the Methodist Hospital in Memphis, Tennessee, and on July 31, 1962, Carl Rollins Hammond became Hedy Jo Starr. At the time Star was operating a theatrical costume company in Chicago's Loop, making clothes for female impersonators, strippers, burlesque stars, and circus folk. Star also worked in nightclubs as a hypnotist. In September 1966 she was at the Swing, 48 East Walton, doing magic and hypnosis, in a variety show of "mental telepathy, dance interpretations and an all star revue with Asmara, Bambi, and Linda Gibson." Later, Star wrote an advice column called "Both Sides of Love" for the *National Insider*. Little is known about Star's later life, but it's said she married a doctor. Hedy Jo Star died in 1999.

## Tony Midnite

In 1949 Captain Thomas Harrison of the East Avenue Police District began purging the Near North Side of gay bars and vice dens. So when Tony Midnite arrived in Chicago with his hatboxes two years later, he found no work for female impersonators. But this didn't deter him. He had come a long way from his Texas roots growing up in a Depression-era farming family. "My father was from a family of nine sons, no daughters, very macho ranching and what have you," said Midnite, in an interview with the author published in *Windy City Times*. "I was the youngest of six children, but I showed artistic tendencies. I used to steal paper out of my sister's notebooks and I'd go off somewhere and be sketching designs from the Sears Roebuck catalog. Anytime my father caught me, he'd snatch it away and tear it up, because he didn't want me doing unmanly things like that. But I found a way to get away from him."

At fifteen, Tony left home and headed for San Francisco, using a fake ID to get a job at Finocchio's drag club, where he was fascinated by the female impersonators. After the war he returned to Texas and got his first job in a drag show at the Granada Club in the red-light district of Galveston. "I was about 17 years old and I'd put together a few drags and a few songs I'd learned off the Hit Parade. The club was owned by a Madame, who had a whole string of cat houses. The first show I ever did was for the prostitutes who worked for her. Straight up!" That gig lasted until election year, when the friendly police chief was replaced by a zealous moral campaigner, and the Granada and the brothels on Post Office Street were raided and closed down. "I'll never forget that night, because they took us down in drag," remembered Midnite. "I had on this long cape, and a Texas Ranger was standing there at the door and I said, 'Well, open the door for a lady.' And he opened the door for me." After Midnite's brush with the law, he toured the West Coast drag circuit for twelve weeks before heading east to Pittsburgh, where he joined the *Jewel Box Revue*, the premier female impersonation show run by lovers Danny Brown and Doc Benner. Midnite became the protégé of Stanley Rogers, their costume designer, eventually taking over his job when he retired.

In 1951 Midnite took a brief hiatus from *Jewel Box* and moved to Chicago, a city starved of drag shows. That changed when shows opened at the Miami Show Lounge at 2822 55th Street, and Sid and Millie Schwartz's Argyle Show Lounge near the Argyle El stop, where his piano player was William Friedkin, who later directed such movies as *The Boys in the Band* (1970), *The French Connection* (1971), and *The Exorcist* (1973). Midnite's stage career suffered a setback in the mid-1950s when he developed throat problems, so he set himself up as a costume designer, catering to transsexuals, female impersonators, and all manner of exotic stage performers. "There were about fifty strip clubs in Chicago, Calumet City and Cicero, and as I went for flash and had a sequin machine, the strippers loved my wardrobe," he explained. Business was booming at Midnite's workshop and studio in the basement of the Lorraine Hotel at 411 South Wabash Avenue. In 1957 he rejoined the *Jewel Box Revue* for a season of shows at Roberts's Show Lounge at 6622 South Parkway, owned by Herman Roberts, whom Midnite describes as "a handsome African American man." The show ran for eight months and proved a huge financial success; Midnite was given unlimited funds to produce the gowns. But despite packed houses and rave reviews, Brown and Benner decided to take the Revue to Monticello in the Catskills in Upper New York State and return to Chicago the following year with a bigger show. After touring the East Coast, the show ended up in Times Square's Loew's State Theater under a marquee that read: "A 2 Hour Musical Extravaganza! Jewel Box Revue the World's Greatest Femme Impersonators."

The working conditions at Loew's were abysmal, because with three shows a day, and with a movie shown between each one, the cast in full make-up couldn't leave the building for sixteen hours a day without fear of arrest. With tempers frayed, the *Jewel Box* moved to Ben Massick's Town and Country club in Brooklyn, but Tony Midnite tired of the show and accepted an offer from Mathew Jacobson, owner of Club 82 at 82 East 4th Street. Midnite worked there for four years, with an annual clothing budget of forty thousand dollars. In the late 1950s–early '60s, Club 82 was the hottest drag club in New York City, frequented by celebrities like Judy Garland, Bob Hope, Milton Berle, Kirk Douglas, Elizabeth Taylor, the Gabors, and the Kennedys. "Marlene Dietrich would come in and kid around with the lesbians," said Midnite. "We had all lesbian waiters there, and we called them 'Tailor Girls.' They were all in tuxedos. Greta Garbo would come in and sit up on the balcony wearing a big floppy hat, thinking nobody knew who she was."

More throat problems brought Midnite back to Chicago, where he returned to making costumes for strippers and female impersonators. Midnite's last stage appearances were in a show called *The Fantasy Revue*, starring female impersonator Timmie Starr, with Mark Vickers handling the choreography. Midnite "pantomimed," that is, lip-synched, a few numbers and emceed the show, which opened at the Granada Lounge, 525 Arlington Place, then relocated to the Blue Dahlia, 5640 North Avenue. Midnite later handed over the show to transsexual Gayle Sherman.

In 1996 Tony Midnite was inducted into the Chicago Gay and Lesbian Hall of Fame for his talents as a costume designer and his gay activism. He died in Las Vegas on August 31, 2009.

## The 1960s Drag Boom

In 1964 Chicago experienced a drag boom, with over a dozen bars and clubs featuring female impersonation shows. Before the 1960s, performers sang with their own voices, but the 1960s queens pantomimed to 45rpm records. Lip-synching opened the floodgates to pretty boys who could carry off a female impersonation but couldn't carry a tune.

Another reason for the boom is that drag queens were popular with the mob. Some gangsters dated female impersonators, many paying for their "girl's" sex change, and it's rumored that a couple of elderly widows tossing herbs into the Timbale di Riso in Cicero once taped their genitals between their legs and pantomimed to Doris Day songs. The syndicate bosses were also aware of the crossover appeal of female impersonators, and many 1960s drag bars drew busloads of straight tourists, like the Nite Life, Blue Dahlia, Granada Lounge, Chat-Chat Lounge, and the Time in Vodvil Lounge.

The Nite Life was the longest-running drag bar in Chicago's history, opening in the early 1940s, closing briefly in 1973 after a fire, and then closing down for good in April 1981. The bar was often raided. On April 28, 1964, it was busted after a female impersonator allegedly solicited a detective for lewd purposes and six men were arrested in what the *Chicago*

*Sun-Times* called "a lounge that features exotic dancing by men dressed as women." In the 1960s the big star at the Nite Life was pre-op transsexual Gayle Sherman (given name Gary Paradis). Sherman was the prodigy of Tony Midnite. What Sherman lacked in singing talent he made up for in looks, as he was a twin for Sophia Loren. In a four-part interview in the October 1963 issue of *National Insider* headlined "I Want to Be a Woman," Sherman refers to himself as a "sexual cripple" born into the wrong gender.

Chicago's sleazy *Night Life* magazine of July 1963 had a cover photo of Mr. Gayle Sherman, "Beauty in Motion," advertising his show at the Nite Life with Vicki Marlene "Mr. Emotion," Kay Leslie "Face, Figure, Person-ality," Roby Landers "Comedian Extraordinaire," and Chris Cross "Man of Many Faces." These were the crème de la crème of Chicago's femme de la femme at that time. Vicki Marlene had previously starred in Bookie and Morrey's Diplomat Revue at the Diplomat Cocktail Lounge along with Fat Jack, Toni Albright, Edie Lloyd, Jerri Daye, Bobbi Johns, and Win Wells. In Detroit, Marlene was known as "Mr. Peel." At the Nite Life, Marlene's signature piece was to jump on the bar and cancan the length of it in spiked heels. But even this couldn't compete with Gayle Sherman, who drew gasps of horror and delight from the audience when he dressed as a witchdoctor and roasted a baby over a fire while lip-synching an Yma Sumac song.

Sherman dated women and, presumably, was a lesbian after the sex change. Female impersonator Vicki St. John, a contemporary of Sherman's, recalls her living quarters: "Gayle had a bedroom that looked like a whore-house. The carpet was fire engine red, she had red velvet drapes on all the walls. In the middle of the room was a crystal chandelier hanging over a king-size bed with a red velvet bedspread and red and white velvet toss pillows. Then on the floor at the foot of the bed were more pillows and a little white teddy bear." Female impersonation was a lucrative means to an end for Sherman, as it paid for her hormones and surgery. After transi-tioning, Sherman had to quit female impersonation, and so she changed her name to Brandy Alexander and with her new forty-eight-inch bust embarked on a second career as a stripper. Using the stage name "Alexandra 'The Great 48,'" she peeled off in adult movie theaters between porn films, starting at the Town Theater, Armitage and Clark Streets; then in Sep-tember 1966 she starred at the 1st Annual Fanny Hill Festival at the Plaza Art Theater, 308 West North Avenue. Two months later she was at Kim Art, 6217 South Halsted Street. When Mayor Daley pulled the licenses of

all Strand Art Theaters in 1967, Gayle Sherman/Brandy Alexander is
rumored to have gone into hairdressing.

## The Chesterfield and the Annex

In the mid-1960s the epicenter of Chicago's gay nightlife was at Clark
Street and Diversey Avenue and revolved around several bars, including
the gay/straight Orange Cockatoo at 2850 North Clark Street, the Century
at 2810 North Clark Street, and Ruthie's at 2833 North Clark Street, but
the most visible were two gay drag bars, the Club Chesterfield at 2831
North Clark Street and the Annex at 2863 North Clark; Club Chesterfield
and the Annex were both operated by Nick Dallesandro and his wife,
Shirley, and profits were shared between the cops and Nick's "silent partners," the syndicate who protected him.

In the summer of 1965 Dallesandro hired Skip Arnold, a drag comedian
who had recently relocated from Kansas City, where he worked in a straight
drag club. Arnold caused a stir in Chicago with his hilarious songs and
comedy routines. "Good evening, ladies and gentlemen, my name is Skip
Arnold" was an intro guaranteed to bring the house down at the Annex,
Chesterfield, Trip, and later at the Alameda Club, 5210 North Sheridan
Road, where on December 4, 1973, Arnold celebrated his fifty-first birthday. Off-stage, Arnold was a quiet, thoughtful man who advocated equal
rights for gays and lesbians; in August 1965, he spoke with eloquence at
a meeting of Mattachine Midwest at the Midland Hotel in Chicago.
Onstage he was a riot. Arnold was a central figure in the book *Mother
Camp: Female Impersonators in America* (1972) by Esther Newton. In 1965
Newton, an anthropologist, studied and wrote about gay life in New York,
Kansas City, San Francisco, and Chicago, where her focus was on two gay
bars she calls the Shed and the Marlboro, in reality the Annex and the
Chesterfield. In the book, Newton transcribes one of Skip Arnold's rou-
tines, which is amusing, though time-specific and riddled with in-jokes.
You had to be there. One other testament to Skip Arnold's time in Chicago
is a vinyl 45rpm EP recorded at the Annex with a pianist, bassist, and
drummer. Listening now to Arnold's fey, campy voice reveals a very different time, just four years before the Stonewall Rebellion and the birth of
Gay Liberation:

### Side A: Welcome to Fairyland

[*drum roll*] Thank you very much and welcome to the Annex, Chicago's liveliest show. I'm very excited about seeing you . . . in fact I'm so excited I'm just all over come. [*to bartender*] Darlin' would you bring mother something to suck on while I sit up here and talk dirty to the neighbors. Oh isn't that marvelous. Oh you have brung it to me . . . Snort! . . . [la de las song from "Carmen"] . . . damn, I hope I didn't shrink anything. Well howdy and welcome to Fairyland. We want you to sit back, relax, and have a ball, or whatever you brought with you, because we think you're going to enjoy this evening, at least we hope so. Remember, I was telling you about my momma? How you would love her, but it would cost you. Well, not a hell of a lot. Momma was one of those old Southern ladies, she could wail on a saxophone "When the Saints Come Marchin' Home" just like a pro . . . which was a word we were never allowed to use around Momma's house.

Well, you know Momma always wanted a house, but the government wouldn't let her open it. But she got one . . . Oh, she was so unhappy: she'd gone down town to the department store and bought brand new sheets but she hated them—she said she got screwed on all of them.

I'll never forget that raid. They come up there, you know, and they grabbed a hold of Momma and took the girls away. It was terrible. And there was Momma . . . she put a big sign out front, "Gone to jail, beat it!"

That's when I found out you can put on women's clothes and make money. I grabbed the first thing that was there, and it was my mother's smock, her high heels, and her switch, and I was a sensation overnight. [*to woman entering the bar*] Oh, there's a woman. You are a woman, aren't you, honey? Well, you'll meet a few other ladies in here too. Honey, when you say ladies and gentlemen in this place we make them sort themselves out. At least . . . we've got everything around here tonight. [*piano introduces "Road to Mandalay"*]. [*wailing*] Ahhahahaha! I just prayed for rain, I hope it drowns you. I bet this is the first time you've ever seen a Jewish Indian. [*sings*] *By the old Moulmein Pagoda, looking eastward to the sea* . . . oh the sun shines east, the sun shines west, but I know where you can get it best . . . I just threw that in, I wish I'd have thrown it up . . . *there's a Burma gal awaitin' and I know she waits for me*—silly, any girl who waits for anybody as nelly as I am is out of her fruit mind, let her wait . . . *Oh the wind is up your* . . . where the hell is the wind? Oh, don't move me we'll find out . . . *Come ye back ye gritty soldier* . . . I haven't known any gritty soldiers. I knew an Australian soldier once; oh my, did that Australian crawl . . . *Come ye back to Mandalay, come ye back to Mandalay. Ohhhh!* . . . Damn! Did you hear that note? Oh, that was so gorgeous. [Opera diva and silent movie star] Geraldine Ferrar would have given her left tit for a note like that . . . *On the road to Mandalay, where the old flotilla lay* . . . a flotilla by the way is a group of ships, and a group of ships have a group of sailors, and lay they will. Hell, I know . . . we used to play the damndest games, like Drop the Soap . . . we played it my way, Ivory Flakes . . . well, all you need is a sticky finger, and you should have seen them officers snapping at the bubbles . . . *Can't you hear those paddles chonkin' from Rangoon to Mandalay. Ohhhh!* . . . sometimes I get so good it just scares the what do you call it out of me . . . *the road to Mandalay, where the flying fishes play* . . . flying fishes are airline hostesses . . . *and the dawn comes up like thunder out of China-a-a-a* . . . kind of sissy, ain't it? Sixty dead men on a dead man's chest . . . you know, that's not bad if you're a queer ghost . . . *across the bay. Olay!*

### Side B: Snow White vs. the Watch Queen

Fairy tale time! Once upon a time in a far-off kingdom there was a wicked old drag queen. She lived high in a castle on a hill and she had a magic mirror. And she used to say, "Mirror, mirror on the wall, who's the fairiest of us all?" and the mirror used to say, "You are, girl." It always made her feel so good. Of course, she also had a little charge named Snow White that she used to make do the damndest things, like wash out the trick . . . wash out the towels and the cobblestones. One day, Snow White was out there washing off the cobblestones and here comes Prince Charming just romping across the pampas. Now, when he sees Snow White he wants her, so he gets off his horse and he says, "Snow White, ride away with me." So she mounts his horse . . . well, he soon rectified all that. She said, 'I'd love to ride away with you, but if that Queen sees you, she'll want you too, you better go.' As he rides away she sings one of those English madrigals "Someday My Prince Will Come."

All this time the Queen is up there looking in that mirror. She looks in that mirror because she's a watch queen. She said, "Mirror, mirror on the wall, who's the fairiest of us all?" And the mirror said, "I've got news for you, girl, Snow White has grown up and she's gorgeous." She said, "I've got to get rid of her." She said, "I know what I'll do, I'll call the man with the big gun" . . . nobody we know. She called the man with the big gun, and he came up there and she said, "I've got something I'd like for you to do," and he said, "Love to." She said, "This is no time for romance, I want you to shoot Snow White." He went down there where Snow White was, and he tapped her on the shoulder and said, "Pardon me darling, but wouldn't you like to go where the fairies are dancin'?" She said, "Isn't this against the law?" He said, "Not unless you're wearing Scarlet Ribbons." [This is a reference to another gay bar, called the Scarlet Ribbon.] He took her where the fairies were dancing and she had a hell of a time. She doesn't know whether she's followin', leadin', or parking a truck. She looked up and there was the man with the big gun. She said, "What are you going to do?" He said, "I'm going to blow you to hell." She said, "Don't talk, work." He said, "I can't shoot you, you're too pretty, I want you to run, run, run, which means go, girl, go." She took off, she ran down the highways through the woods, through the forest, through the canyon, finally at last she was all-fagged out . . . if you'll excuse that expression. And she went to sleep in the arms of Morpheus and she woke up in the arms of Mother Nature. If that don't make her bisex . . . if that doesn't confuse her nothing will. She woke up and there was all of the beautiful day around her . . . flora and fauna and a couple of nice lesbians she knew, so she waved. Over here are a bunch of fairies making a daisy chain so she joined them. They're playing a new game called Knit One Drop One Purl

Two Drop a Daisy . . . Oops! Then they were down at the bus station where they sing that wonderful old song "How Can You Whistle While You Work?"

All this time that Queen is up there looking in that mirror. She looks in that mirror 'cause she's a never-say-die Queen. The most never-say-die Queen I've seen in my whole and entire. She said, "Mirror, mirror on the wall, who's the fairiest of them all?" And the mirror said, "I told you, girl, Snow White, she ain't dead she's living with seven dwarves." She said, "Seven dwarves, how long can a girl go?" She said, "I know what I'll do, I'll become a wicked old witch, I'll make a poisoned apple, I'll rub it with KY and Campho-Phenique and if that don't kill her nothing will." Isn't that ridiculous? It wouldn't harm a soul. She went down there and knocked on the door, and Snow White said, "Who is it?" She said, "Let me in, Sweetie . . ." She said, "What do you want me to do?" She said, "I want you to take a bite out of this fruit." So, naturally, Snow White bit her. She said, "Out of the apple, you damn fool." She took a bite out of the apple and she dropped over dead. When the seven dwarves came home, they were all flaked out there and they didn't know what the hell to do with her, because she's a girl. So they picked her up and they put her in a glass coffin and they took her down by the river and they all knelt around her . . . crazy picture.

About this time here comes Prince Charming just romping across the pampas. Now, when he sees Snow White he wants her, so he gets off his horse and the seven dwarves see him and they want him. So they start an Indian raffle for him. This causes such a commotion the glass coffin breaks, Snow White rolls out into the river, a great big fish comes by and kisses her and she and the fish live happily ever after. [sings] *So fairy tales can come true, whatever happens to you, just stay young at heart . . .*

Ralph "Skip" Arnold died on March 2, 2005, in Margate, Florida, and was survived by his longtime companion, Lee "Bunny Legs" Lackey, whom he met while they were both serving in the navy.

The Chesterfield closed circa 1967, almost certainly due to a raid after someone "forgot" to pay off the cops. The Annex lasted longer, but it was not without legal problems. In 1968 the bar was raided for allowing sexual deviate acts on the premises and serving alcohol to a minor, charges trumped up by a corrupt police force. According to court documents, Detective Eugene Sullivan testified that he entered the Annex at approximately 1:50 a.m. and observed seventy male patrons in the bar. After buying a drink he observed two pairs of men fondling each other, though on cross-examination Sullivan admitted the couples had their backs to him and customers stood between him and them. The men were not arrested, but Dwight Menard and David Towell, the bartenders, were charged with sexual deviate behavior. Sullivan testified he saw Menard stand behind Towell, place his hands on his shoulders, and whisper in his ear for fifteen to thirty seconds. Sullivan was then asked, "Did you see any parts of their bodies touch any time while they were talking to each other?" Sullivan answered, "The area of the penis against the buttocks."

Menard denied touching the other bartender, saying the area behind the bar was small and on busy nights they would often bump into each other. He also said bartenders sometimes whisper to each other about customers who have had too much to drink. On March 27, 1974, after years of legal wrangling, the Appellate Court of Illinois decided there was no evidence of deviate sexual acts. The Annex stayed open for a couple more years, and even added a small dance floor, but with gay liberation in the air, this straight-owned bar couldn't compete with the post-Stonewall discos and gay-run clubs opening all around.

# 22

# The Sodomy Laws

In 1809 the punishment for sodomy in Illinois was up to five years in prison, a hundred- to five-hundred-dollar fine, and a flogging of a hundred to five hundred lashes. The laws changed over the years; *Honselman v. People* in 1897 decided fellatio was a crime against nature, while *Smith v. People* in 1913 decided cunnilingus wasn't. And why did Illinois forget to recriminalize homosexuality in 1961?

When the Pilgrims founded Plymouth Colony in 1620 the devout religionists brought with them the harsh penalty for sodomy that existed under British law, which was death. In 1636, under the leadership of William Bradford, the Plymouth Colony adopted a draconian legal system, with five crimes meriting the death penalty: murder, arson, sodomy, adultery, and selling one's soul to the devil. On February 3, 1809, the U.S. Congress approved an act separating Illinois from the Indiana territory, and the penalty for sodomy changed from death to up to five years in prison, a hundred- to five-hundred-dollar fine, and a flogging of a hundred to five hundred lashes. In 1845 the flogging and fines were dropped, but the jail sentence increased to one year to life, and in 1874 a new code was adopted that capped the maximum jail sentence at ten years.

The state of Illinois has a history of legal firsts with its sodomy laws: in 1827 it was the first state to bar a convicted sodomite from voting or sitting on a jury; in 1897 it was the first state to convict an individual under the sodomy law for an act of fellatio; in 1913 the Illinois Supreme Court was the first to rule that cunnilingus was not an act of sodomy; and in 1961 Illinois was the first state to decriminalize homosexual acts between consenting adults.

In the 1890s a spate of arrests for crimes against nature took place in Logan County, Illinois, but it wasn't until the case of *Honselman v. People* in 1897 that an arrestee appealed his conviction. Police officer Charles Honselman was tried for performing oral sex on Lloyd Kesler, who was sixteen years old at the time of the trial, though the incident had happened one and a half years earlier. A jury found Honselman guilty and sentenced him to a jail for committing "a crime against nature." Prior to the trial a motion to quash the count was overruled. The defense argued the charge against Honselman was unclear. The problem lay in the vagueness of the law: though section 47 of the criminal code read "the infamous crime against nature, either with man or beast," the statute gave no definition of what the crime consisted of. The defense argued that as Honselman "made use of his mouth" no act of sodomy had taken place, assuming the Illinois statute covered sodomy, or buggery, as denominated in the English statute.

The judges disagreed. Justice James Cartwright wrote:

> While the "crime against nature" and "sodomy" have often been used as synonymous terms, paragraph 279 of our Criminal Code, defining infamous crimes, plainly shows that the legislature included in the crime against nature other forms of the offense than sodomy or buggery. It is there enacted: "Every person convicted of the crime of sodomy or other crime against nature shall be deemed infamous." The method employed in this case is as much against nature, in the sense of being unnatural and against the order of nature, as sodomy or any bestial or unnatural copulation that can be conceived. It is within the statute.

Explaining the vagueness of the law, Cartwright wrote:

> The statute gives no definition of the crime, which the law, with due regard to the sentiments of decent humanity, has always treated as not fit to be named. It was never the practice to describe the particular manner or the details of the commission of the act, but the offense was treated in the indictment as the abominable

crime not fit to be named by Christians. The existence of such an offense is a disgrace to human nature. The legislature has not seen fit to define it further than by the general term, and the records of the courts need not be defiled with the details of different acts which may go to constitute it. A statement of the offense in the language of the statute, or so plainly that its nature may be easily understood by the jury, is all that is required.

The defense also questioned Lloyd Kesler's motives and why his evidence was sufficient to convict Honselman when he was an accomplice to the crime; no third party had witnessed the act. It was suggested there was bad blood between the two, since Honselman, acting as a police officer, evicted Kesler from a fairground after the youth had entered without a ticket. The defense claimed that Kesler accused Honselman as an act of revenge. Kesler denied this. The Supreme Court judges decided it was unlikely Kesler would fabricate the story, as he would gain nothing from it but shame and disgrace for himself. Judge Cartwright wrote: "The jury and the trial judge believed Kesler, and, with much better means of judging of the credibility of the witnesses than we have, were convinced of the defendant's guilt. We cannot say that they were wrong in their conclusion."

The November 1, 1897, decision in the Honselman case, to define oral sex as a crime against nature, was challenged in 1901 in *Kelly v. People*, which, not surprisingly, failed, as the case involved C. V. Kelly, an adult male, and a prepubescent boy. Another unsuccessful challenge was made in 1931 with *Fitzgibbons v. People*, which also involved two young boys. In 1913 the Illinois Supreme Court made history again when presented with the country's first challenge to the crime against nature law in respect to an act of cunnilingus, in the case of *Smith v. People*. In a 6–1 decision, the court overruled a lower court ruling by saying cunnilingus did not violate the law, as sodomy had to involve a male sex organ. Judge Frank Dunn wrote that Horace L. Smith had not broken the law with

the insertion of his tongue in the private parts of the little girl, who was 11 years old. It is insisted that this proof did not establish the offense charged, and that the unnatural use of the male sexual organ is an essential element of the crime. . . . In all the cases in which convictions have been sustained of which we have knowledge, the male sex organ was involved. . . . Acts, such as that testified to, do not constitute the offense for which defendant was sentenced, but the law has provided for their punishment by the act to define and punish crimes against children.

On July 28, 1961, Illinois became the first state to adopt the American Law Institute's Model Penal Code (MPC), designed to assist legislators in updating and standardizing U.S. penal law. In Illinois the MPC, enacted by the Seventy-Second General Assembly as House Bill No. 342, took effect January 1, 1962. In the revamped Illinois Criminal Code, sex crimes fell under the heading "Deviate Sexual Conduct," because the committee decided that "due to its historically limited and expanded meaning, the term 'crime against nature' is not accurate, and much confusion still arises regarding the specific acts included within the term." The first thing the committee decided was to limit the law to "unnatural acts of sexual gratification between humans" and to remove bestiality from the list. This decision was due, in part, to Alfred Kinsey's assertion that sexual acts with animals are brief, youthful "experiments" rather than "patterns of conduct that either contributes to or constitutes a significant degeneration of the individual involved." It was therefore decided that it would serve no purpose to make public an incidence of a person having sex with an animal, as it "may seriously impair the development of the accused to a normal life."

Morris J. Wexler, the secretary of the Joint Committee of the Illinois State and Chicago Bar Associations to revise the Criminal Code, published a paper "Sex Offenses under the New Criminal Code" in the *Illinois Bar Journal* of October 1962. He wrote: "Art. II (Sex Offenses) seeks to rationalize the underlying principles amongst the various sex offenses by means of four policy considerations: 1) The protection of the individual from forcible sexual attacks; 2) The protection of the young and immature from sexual advances of older and more mature individuals; 3) The protection of the institution of marriage and normal family relationships from sexual conduct which tends to destroy them; 4) The protection of the public from open and notorious conduct which disturbs the peace, or openly flouts accepted standards of morality in the community."

Only the fourth point applies to homosexuals. Wexler wrote that one of the offenses in article 11-9 is performing a sexual act, either intercourse, deviate sexual conduct, lewd exposure, lewd fondling, or caressing the body of another person of the same sex in public. There was no mention of same-sex intimacy in private. On April 11, 1962, the Reverend Charles

Sheedy, C.S.C., addressed the Chicago Bar Association on the subject of law and morals. Sheedy said:

> I wish to make some points about law and morality, the difference between them, and their overlap; and to illustrate these points by reference to some practices which are now covered in the public law, and covered by reason of a moral code once common in Anglo-American culture, but not now so commonly held . . .
>
> One of the requirements of a good moral-legal law is that it closes the door to practices which, in fact, might lead to a grave breakdown of the external order and public peace. Homosexuality is an example. Nearly all the states have laws in the Criminal Code on the "detestable and abominable sin against nature." Moral writers from St. Paul through the medieval to modern writers have shown a special hatred for this. It should be noted that the medieval Catholic writers did not lay on such vigorous external penalties, but exhorted the delinquent to repent. But the modern Anglo-American laws have vigorous penalties which tend to become more lenient, but which still exist. It could be suggested that homosexual practices between consenting adult males might very well be removed from the criminal code. This excludes the solicitation of children below the age of knowledgeable consent, and also excludes women. Also excluded would be any civil recognition, such as homosexual marriage, for inheritance purposes or joint property. But the legal crime of homosexual practices between adult consenting males probably does not belong in the criminal law because these practices are not destructive of the general moral fabric.

The Illinois Criminal Code of 1961 arrived with little fanfare and was ignored by the local press, with the exception of the *Chicago Sun-Times*. On December 21, 1961, a headline buried in the paper on page 43 read: "New Criminal Code in Effect Jan. 1." "The code, signed by Gov. Kerner July 28 after passage by the General Assembly, reflects new outlook on philosophy and morality," wrote the paper. The *Chicago Sun-Times* noted that it took six years of a joint committee of the Illinois and Chicago Bar Associations to draft the new code so it would "conform more closely to current attitudes on crime and punishment." Claude R. Sowle, a criminal law expert and assistant professor at Northwestern University, wrote a one-hundred-page explanation of the code published as a booklet. The

*Police Officer's Guide to Criminal Code 1961* was distributed to members of the Chicago Police Department. Sowle commented to the *Chicago Sun-Times* at the time:

> I think that the state has taken a vast step forward with the enactment of the code. It reflects a more mature attitude toward immoral conduct.
>
> Though most people and the community consider certain offenses morally wrong, a number of them do not constitute a danger to society. The law should not be cluttered with matters of morality so long as they do not endanger the community. Morality should be left to the church, community and the individual's conscience.

The *Chicago Sun-Times* article then reads: "Under the new code it will not be a criminal offense for homosexuals to engage in sexual relations in private as long as the participants are adults, neither of whom has been pressured into the acts."

That was it: no outcry from the police, no condemnation from religious groups, and no snide remarks from the press. Most gay Illinoisans seemed oblivious to the historical importance of the new code. Illinois had become the first state in the United States to legalize homosexuality. After 350 years of discrimination under the law, the Illinois Criminal Code of 1961 was the first crack in the armor of the nation's institutionalized homophobia. The San Francisco–based *Mattachine Review* wrote in October 1962: "The Illinois Revised Criminal Code . . . has apparently by omission, silence and implication, repealed the sodomy law." The lesbian magazine *The Ladder* wrote in March 1962: "While the homophile movement has long expounded the need to change our sex laws to this effect, now that it has happened I can't help wondering if there will be any appreciable difference in attitude of law enforcement regarding the homosexual. The legality of homosexual practices in private will not bring social approval; nor will there be an abatement by law enforcement officers in their drive against gay bars or apparent homosexual activity in public."

The article included a response by Chicago lawyer and lesbian activist Pearl M. Hart:

> It is true, of course, that the new legislation is not likely to be accompanied by social approval; nor will it abate the over-activity

of certain police officers whose own feeling of guilt, perhaps, results in violence towards others; nor will it discourage to any appreciable degree the attempts of professional blackmailers.

"A protracted educational process," is necessary to effect far reaching results. But the homosexual himself can make a contribution, if he will conduct himself in such a manner as not to draw special attention to himself, and if he will act as any other responsible person expects to act publicly and in public places. It is not necessary for the homosexual to exercise any restraint other than that which is obligatory upon all other persons constituting our society.

On the other hand, he should not expect special treatment.

# 23

# The Gay Pioneers

After World War II, women were expected to return to the kitchen throughout the country, blacks to segregation in the South, and gays to a life of invisibility and fear. The postwar emergence of gay groups laid the foundations on which was built the rebellious spirit shown at the Stonewall Rebellion. Craig Rodwell contributed with a "sip in" and the opening of New York's Oscar Wilde Bookshop, while in Chicago, lesbian attorney Pearl Hart, Young Democrat Ira Jones, and left-wing activist Bob Basker founded Mattachine Midwest.

After World War II the antigay frenzy intensified: On April 1, 1950, the Civil Service Commission took a "no prisoners" approach in its persecution of lesbians and gay men in government positions; two years later, the American Psychiatric Association published its first list of mental disorders diagnosing homosexuality as a "sociopathic personality disturbance," leading to the United States barring homosexuals from immigration; and in April 1953, President Dwight D. Eisenhower issued an executive order barring gay men and lesbians from federal jobs, a ruling adopted by many state and local governments in their own hiring practices. One positive contribution to the public debate on homosexuality was the publication of *The Homosexual in America* (1951) by Donald Webster Cory (a pseudonym for Edward Sagarin), the first comprehensive study of the lives of homosexuals in American written by a gay man; at times, it reads like a gay manifesto. One man inspired by the book's radical agenda was Craig Rodwell, who opened the Oscar Wilde Memorial Bookshop in Greenwich Village, New York, in November 1967; it was the first bookstore in the world to focus on gay literature and authors. Rodwell was born in Chicago on October 31, 1940, and attended the Chicago Junior School, an all-boys Christian Science boarding school in Elgin, Illinois. In an interview in *Gay Crusaders* (1972) by Kay Tobin and Randy Wicker, Rodwell recalls gay life at the school: "In the 7th and 8th grades, we were going steady, although we didn't call it that. We used to hold hands, had one best friend, and had sex too, usually out in the woods or in the dorm after the housemother went to bed. When she saw us holding hands, the housemother used to make us stop, and we couldn't understand why."

Rodwell writes of his entrée into Chicago's gay subculture at age thirteen, when he was arrested:

> I had had sex with a guy who was thirty. I had picked him up. And we were walking down the street afterwards and were stopped by the police, who grilled me and threatened to call my parents. So I spilled the beans. I just told the truth. And there was a big court trial. The guy was charged with a crime against nature because of my age. And the D.A. took me into the hallway and wanted me to testify that the guy had given me money. I guess they could have put him away for a longer period of time if I'd said that. But I told the truth. I guess they couldn't believe I picked *him* up. So the guy went to prison for three or four years.

Rodwell was put on probation and ordered to visit a psychiatrist, who, far from trying to cure him, was reassuring and told him stories about ancient Greece. A few years later, Rodwell became aware of the Chicago Mattachine Society, but he was too young to join. So at the age of seventeen he took gay activism into his own hands by printing up a hundred copies of a flier exhorting "Homosexuals Unite! Tear off Your Masks!" and then dropping them into mailboxes in his neighborhood. Years later, he heard his naïve act led to the eviction of two hairdressers—presumably the only "obvious" homosexuals in the area—as local residents assumed they were responsible. By then Rodwell had left Chicago and was studying ballet in Boston on a scholarship to the American Ballet School. In 1958 he moved to New York and volunteered at the offices of the Mattachine Society, but

Rodwell found them too staid, so he joined the more radical Homosexual League of New York, run by Randolfe Wicker; Wicker was one of the first people to come out as a homosexual on national television when he appeared on *The Les Crane Show* in January 1964.

In 1965, New York Mattachine took a more radical stance, due, in part, to Rodwell bringing younger members to the group with his slogan "Let's get Mattachine moving!" He organized the first chartered buses to carry New York gays to picket the White House in Washington, D.C., and in Philadelphia. In *Gay Crusaders* he said: "At the time, a total of 50 or 60 gay people wore suits and ties, the women wore dresses. Except for our 'Equality for Homosexuals' buttons, we looked like a church group."

On April 21, 1966, Rodwell, along with John Timmins and Dick Leitsch, staged a "Sip In," reported in the *New York Times*, the *New York Post*, and the *Village Voice*; the three Mattachine members took along four reporters and a photographer. They were protesting a State Liquor Authority (SLA) regulation that allowed bar owners to refuse service to homosexuals. The protest was sparked by a sign reading "If You're Gay, Stay Away" in a restaurant in East Greenwich Village. The protestors found the restaurant closed. Lucy Komisar in the *Village Voice* on May 5, 1966, wrote: "The advance guard of reporters peered through the windows of the somewhat tatty place . . . torn red plastic covered the barstools." She said they could see the handwritten antigay sign, next to others reading "No Credit," "No Dancing," and "No Spitting on the Floor."

In an article headlined "3 Deviates Invite Exclusion by Bars" the *New York Times* noted the protest moved to the Howard Johnson restaurant at Avenue of the Americas and Eighth Street, where Leitsch read a statement to the manager: "We, the undersigned, are homosexuals. We believe that a place of public accommodation has an obligation to serve an orderly person, and that we are entitled to service as long as we are orderly. We therefore ask to be served on your premises. Should you refuse to serve us, we will be obligated to file a complaint against you with the State Liquor Authority."

According to the *New York Times*, the manager, Emile Varela, "doubled with laughter." The *Village Voice* said Varela asked: "How do I know you are homosexuals?" After laughing, he added, "Why shouldn't they be served a drink? They look like perfect gentlemen to me. I drink. Who knows if I'm a homosexual or not? . . . It's pretty ridiculous that anybody should determine what anybody's sex life is. I think there's plenty of lawmakers whose sex life I could challenge—and they drink too. I don't think the government has any right to question any man's sex life. If the government does, I think there ought to be a few marches."

Varela turned to the waiter and said, "Bring the boys a drink."

They were also served at the Waikiki, a Polynesian-themed bar, a block away, where the manager told the *Village Voice*: "Certainly, I serve anybody as long as he doesn't annoy anybody."

Finally they tried Julius's at Waverley Place and 10th Street, well known as a closeted gay bar. The manager refused to serve them. The Mattachine Society filed a formal complaint with the City Commission on Human Rights, and the State Liquor Authority promptly backed down and dropped the discriminatory regulation.

On May 18, 1966, Rodwell returned to Chicago to speak to Mattachine Midwest about the New York bar "Sip In"; he returned again in October. While this was going on, Rodwell worked, saved his money, and on a budget of a thousand dollars opened the Oscar Wilde Bookshop at 291 Mercer Street (the store moved to 15 Christopher Street in 1973) on Thanksgiving weekend 1967; his mother flew in from Chicago to stock ten shelves with twenty-five titles, three copies of each—titles like James Barr's *Quatrefoil* (1950) and Richard Amory's *Song of the Loon* (1966). The Oscar Wilde Bookshop was a porn-free zone; Rodwell wanted no seedy shades-down or Adults Only signs.

Three days after the Stonewall Rebellion, Rodwell and a group of friends made plans to celebrate the uprising every year to honor it as the birth of gay liberation. The resolution passed at the Eastern Regional Conference of Homophile Organizations, and Rodwell became a founding member of the coordinating committee of the first annual Christopher Street Liberation Day (Gay Pride March) in 1970.

Craig Rodwell died from stomach cancer on June 18, 1993, at age fifty-two. The Oscar Wilde Bookshop closed on March 8, 2009.


## Pearl M. Hart

Pearl Hart was born in Traverse City, Michigan, on April 7, 1890, the fifth daughter and only American-born child of David and Rebecca Harchovsky. The Harchovskys came from Novoradok in Polish Russia. In 1895 the family moved to 190 Newberry Avenue in Chicago. Hart's father was a rabbi and kosher butcher in the stockyards, and Pearl lived with her parents until they died. By 1923 she had her own home at 211 East Chestnut. After graduating from high school, Hart worked first as a stenographer, then as a law clerk at Ferguson and Goodnow, 69 West Washington Street. Here she learned family law, which stood her in good stead when she defended two women in high-profile divorce cases in 1934 and '36. While working as a law clerk, Hart took evening classes at the John Marshall Law School, where she later taught for twenty years. In 1914 she changed her name from Harchovsky to Hart and was admitted to the bar, and from 1915 to 1916 she served as president of the Women's Law League. It was the beginning of a long and distinguished career defending the civil rights of minorities. Later, Hart was a founding member of the Chicago Committee to Defend the Bill of Rights, the National Lawyer's Guild, and the Committee to Defend the Foreign Born.

On July 18, 1931, Hart was appointed public defender in the morals branch of the municipal court by Chief Justice John Sonsteby. It was a good year for Hart, as the December 1931 issue of *American Hebrew* lists Pearl Hart in a "Who's Who among American Jews," alongside other Chicagoans like Julius Rosenwald, part owner and leader of Sears, Roebuck Company; Salmon Oliver Levinson, lawyer and peace activist; and philanthropist Benjamin F. Lindheimer.

Hart was also in demand as an orator. Throughout the 1930s she was guest speaker at dozens of women's groups, including the Cook County Federation of Women's Clubs, the Southwest League of Women Voters, Morgan Park Women's Club, and the Flossmoor League. In January 1937 she joined Mayor Kelly's committee to eradicate venereal disease, in March she was on WCFL Radio on a panel discussing "Divorce," and later that year Hart cosponsored the League of Women Shoppers, a group investigating goods, prices, and labor conditions under which goods are produced. Hart's energy showed no sign of dissipating in the next decade. In 1942 she was guest chair at an Office of Civilian Defense (OCD) morale-boosting meeting at the Chicago Historical Society on the subject "Women Fight on Every Front," and in 1943 she cofounded the George and Anna Portes Cancer Prevention Center, a clinic for the early detection of cancer in women.

In 1948 Pearl Hart backed Henry A. Wallace, the presidential candidate for the Progressive Party, because of his radical platform of ending segregation, ensuring full voting rights for blacks, and establishing universal government health coverage. Hart focused her energy on Wallace's campaign, and on April 17, 1948, she became the party's candidate for chief justice of the municipal court. The Chicago Bar Association's committee on candidates declined to endorse her, however, possibly because of her links to communists. On October 26, 1947, *Chicago Sun-Times* columnist Milburn P. Akers gave her the thumbs-up, however: "Miss Hart would make, in the opinion of this writer, an eminently fair and impartial judge; one who would use her high office for the benefit of the people, especially the little people; and not for the benefit of the political gangs and hangers-on."

After World War II Hart worked with the American Committee for the Protection of the Foreign Born (ACPFB), a group founded in 1933 for the purpose of protecting the rights of aliens. In the 1950s the ACPFB focused their attention on members of the Communist Party facing deportation. According to the Pearl Hart Collection at the Chicago Historical Museum, at her sixtieth birthday celebration in 1950 Hart said: "I defend the foreign born against the present deportation hysteria because of a consciousness that it was the foreign born and their children who built this nation of ours and who have been its most loyal partisans."

In Chicago three of the aliens threatened with deportation were Vincent Andrulis (former columnist for *Vilnis*, a Lithuanian newspaper; he had been in the United States since 1911), Moses Resnikoff (business manager of the Yiddish-language *Jewish Daily Morning Freiheit*; he had been in the United States since 1903), and James Albert Keller (a.k.a. Carl Sklar). Hart was one of three lawyers to represent the accused, the others being Irving G. Steinberg and Max Naiman. Andrulis was allegedly a Communist Party member, Resnikoff, a member of the International Workers Order, and Keller a party organizer and active in the United Packinghouse Workers Union. Keller, under his birth name Carl Sklar, was on the wanted list after he escaped police when they raided Chicago's Communist Party headquarters at 2021 Division Street on February 27, 1930. Police caught up with Keller in Brawley, California, and after serving three years of hard labor in either Folsom or San Quentin, he was deported to the Soviet Union. He later slipped back into the United States under the name James Albert Keller. In June 1954 the court ordered Resnikoff be deported, but the Soviet Union refused to take him. Andrulis remained in Chicago, became the editor and publisher of *Vilnis*, and died on December 14, 1972; the ultimate fate of Resnikoff and Keller/Sklar is unknown to the author.

Hart's increasing reputation for defending "Reds" resulted in accusations she may have Communist sympathies. On January 3, 1971, the *Chicago Tribune* published an interview with Hart by Patricia Schofler with this exchange:

> **Schofler:** "From your choices of clients and causes, there have been implications that you are connected to the Communist Party and causes. Are you aware of this?"
>
> **Hart:** "Yes, if you represent a certain kind of client in a particular era, you must also be a Communist, they say. But after all, under our Constitution, the Communist also has a right to be defended just as well as anyone else. That's my position. The implications are strong merely because I have always advocated the right of civil liberties, however much I disagree with someone. You know it is awful easy to charge someone with being a member of the Communist Party. The moment that you disagree or take the part of the individual who had two strikes against him, you are tarred with the same feathers. I try my cases as a lawyer and no other way. I have a sound respect for the Constitution of the United States. It is a wonderful document, if we just stick to it."

On January 8, 1953, Hart spoke at a meeting in Walsh's Hall, 1012 Noble Street, sponsored by the committee to obtain clemency for Jewish American Communists Julius and Ethel Rosenberg, who at the time were on death row after being convicted of spying for Russia. A petition to President Elect Dwight D. Eisenhower was passed around the four hundred supporters in attendance. The *Chicago Tribune* of January 9, 1953 reported that Hart told the meeting: "It was the atmosphere, and not the facts, that resulted in the Rosenberg conviction." The Rosenbergs went to the electric chair on June 19, 1953. On December 31, 1960, Hart found herself again associated with "Reds," as she braved anticommunist pickets outside a dingy building at 4818 North Kedzie, where she was speaking before delegates of a national youth conference that FBI director J. Edgar Hoover labeled communist-inspired. The pickets shouted "traitors" and "dirty communists." Hart told the *Chicago Tribune*: "There are some people who think there is a spy under every bed and they're not necessarily there." She spoke to the press at the youth committee's information center in the basement of the Three Links hotel at 4750 North Western. The January 1, 1961, *Chicago Tribune* noted the center shared a space with "a Turkish bath and massage parlor." In 1941 the Three Links Baths were advertised in the *Chicago Tribune* as a "health spa," though the depiction of a slender woman wrapped in a bath towel hinted at other delights. In 1974 the *Chicago Tribune* noted that the Three Links Baths had reinvented itself as a "mind, body and spirit" oriented establishment with "separate steam, sauna, massage and exercise facilities for men and women." In 1977 the baths were sold, then reopened as Man's World, a notorious gay bathhouse.

Pearl Hart never came out as a lesbian, believing her sexual orientation was nobody's business but her own. The love of Hart's life was Jessamine Blossom Churan, an actress and singer she met in the early 1920s. Hart worked in the offices of Blossom's father, the acclaimed Chicago lawyer Charles A. Churan. Blossom was born in 1897, and her childhood was one of moneyed privilege, though it was not happy. Blossom's parents, Charles and Jessie, were regulars in Chicago's society pages. The Society page in the *Chicago Tribune* of August 20, 1895, reads: "Mr. and Mrs. Charles A. Churan will be at home this afternoon and evening at 1831 Arlington Place. Mrs. S. Wright Golding, Mrs. Charles E. Latimer, Miss Grace Golding, and Miss Florence Latimer will assist in receiving." Then in the April 19, 1903, issue: "Mrs. Charles Adelbert Churan and Miss Blossom Churan have returned from California." And on August 27, 1910: "Mrs. Charles A. Churan, 2818 Sheridan Road, Miss Blossom Churan and Chauncey Churan have returned from abroad. They spent the summer in Italy, Switzerland, and England and were in Lucerne at the time of the flood there."

A run of bad luck hit the Churan family in 1911. On February 22, Jessie and Blossom were involved in a car crash when Philo Graves, their chauffeur, drove into a streetcar. Mother and daughter suffered lacerations from flying glass. Jessie had eight cuts to her scalp and face and a fractured wrist, and Blossom seven deep wounds on her face, a sprained left arm, and a lacerated left leg. Graves received a four-inch cut to his left leg down to the bone. Another disaster that year was Charles and Jessie's scandalous divorce. In July the *Chicago Tribune* reported Charles had sued for divorce, citing his wife's "uncomfortable and ungovernable temper," and her frequent bouts of intoxication. He also mentioned her "cigaret smoking, sleeping powders and seven men." Jessie countered by naming Marie Whitney as her husband's "other woman." Jessie also charged that her husband kicked

Blossom until she was bruised. A few days later, the couple made up and were back together for the sake of the children. The marriage lasted until May 13, 1913, when Jessie left and took the children to London. Charles filed for divorce in August 1915 and remarried in 1918.

On Pearl Hart's only trip overseas in 1922 it seems likely she was visiting Blossom. Later in the 1920s Blossom returned to Chicago and reinvented herself as actress Patricia O'Bryan. In 1931 she was a member of the radio troupe W-G-N Players. The radio station WGN first broadcast in 1922 and was operated by the *Chicago Tribune* out of the Wrigley Building, then in the early 1930s out of the Drake Hotel. The W-G-N Players presented *Under Arizona Skies*, described in the *Chicago Tribune* of June 21, 1931, as "the old melodrama of the Mexican border with its story of the love of two kinds of women. The half-breed played by Patricia O'Bryan, the society girl by Alice Munson." Blossom appeared in many radio plays after that, and also *Easy Aces*, a comedy show set around a card table. Blossom's acting career after the 1930s is unclear; it's possible it began and ended in the 1930s with the W-G-N Players.

In the 1940s Blossom fell into the arms of Doctor Bertha Isaacs, a professor at Northwestern University medical school. Not wanting to lose the love of her life, Hart proposed the three of them live together, so in 1947 she and Isaacs bought a property at 2821 North Pine Grove, where the three resided for thirty years. In 1954 Hart began offering legal counsel to early incarnations of Chicago Mattachine. All were short lived, but in the spring of 1965 she met with Bob Basker, Ira Jones, and others to form Mattachine Midwest. Hart spoke at the first public meeting at the Midland Hotel, 172 West Adams Street, on July 27, 1965.

"Retirement" wasn't an option for Pearl Hart and at the age of eighty-one she was still working six days a week, although slowing down with arthritis and heart problems. In May 1971, she opened the Women's Law Center at 54 West Randolph Street with attorneys Renee C. Hanover and Gabrielle Pieper, both of whom had been students of Hart's at the John Marshall Law School. Carol Kleiman profiled the center in the *Chicago Tribune* on February 6, 1972. "They are not the only women attorneys who share offices and practices in Chicago," she wrote, "but they are different because of their commitment to women and women's legal problems."

Pearl M. Hart died on March 22, 1975, at Northwestern Memorial Hospital at the age of eighty-four, ending a career spanning sixty-one years.

On April 13 a memorial was held at the Midland Hotel, where Hart's close friend, author and radio personality Studs Terkel, said: "Her mission was to defend the underdog—in a sense recognizing the illness of the overdog as well. Pearl Hart is certainly dead. She is dead because she first lived."

In 1992 Hart was posthumously inducted into the Chicago Gay and Lesbian Hall of Fame.

The love of Hart's life, Jessamine Blossom Churan, died in October 1973 after a protracted illness; the fate of Bertha Isaacs is unknown to the author.

## Ira Jones

Ira Henry Hillyard Jones was born on February 28, 1925, in the small town of Chehallis, Washington, though his family later moved to Portland, Oregon. From an early age he dedicated his life to political activism, serving as president of the Oregon Young Democrats and executive secretary of the Oregon Democratic Party; in 1948 he was an alternate delegate for Multnomah County, Oregon, at the Democratic National Convention in Philadelphia, where incumbent Harry S. Truman was nominated for president; one of Jones's earliest memories in politics was arranging a program at which Truman spoke while on the campaign trail.

Jones arrived in Chicago on January 1, 1954. In a June 17, 1981, taped interview with the late historian Gregory Sprague, Jones explained: "I stayed in my hometown until 1952. I finally left home for the sole reason that I wanted to pursue my gay lifestyle, and I didn't want to embarrass my family, and conditions with the family in my town were such that it would be embarrassing." After moving to San Francisco, Jones took a job with a detective agency, and after a brief stint sleuthing in New York, he ended up in Chicago working for the railroad. There he made contact with the first incarnation of the Chicago Mattachine Society. In his interview with Sprague, Jones describes the group as "strictly social and extremely closeted and underground." Jones had a friend called Sam, who wrote him a letter:

He couldn't telephone me . . . he had no way of telephoning with reasonable security, so he wrote me a letter, and put me in touch with the law clerk, that was one of the leaders of the organiza-tion . . . and we met in a restaurant, and talked about it, and another month or so later after I was checked out, I was invited out to a home in [unintelligible] and we had a social meeting there, with maybe two dozen people, and we couldn't bring any guests. It was really a cloak-and-dagger situation, it's almost humorous now to think about it.

The "law clerk" was Bob Meyer, who founded the first Chicago Mattachine, though nothing is known about him, except his name. In fact, apart from Jones, no members of this society have ever been found. The membership of the group was estimated at over forty, with everyone using pseudonyms. "The mailing list was extremely closeted, it was very carefully guarded," Jones told Sprague. "If you knew a person's real name it would be a very unusual situation. In the whole group, I can't recall knowing three people's real identity, and I only knew where one worked."

Only one name was public. In July 1954 the newsletter thanked Frank Beauchamp, who "generously offered to relinquish his privilege of anonymity" in order to file the chapter's papers. The early 1950s were a dangerous time to be gay, as it was thought that homosexuals infiltrated "normal" society and destroyed it from within. In February 1954 *Jet*, the Chicago-based African American news magazine, described lesbian trickery: "If she so much as gets one foot into a good woman's home with the intention of seducing her, she will leave no stone unturned . . . and eventually destroy her life for good."

Chicago Mattachine was purely a social group. "There wasn't any real effort to have officers," Jones said. "It was just someone to contact people, and a home to meet in, and someone to prepare refreshments." The group was short lived. In July 1965 Jones cofounded the more influential Mattachine Midwest with Pearl M. Hart and Robert Basker. Jones remained actively involved in the group until his death from heart failure on July 30, 1986; six months later, Mattachine Midwest dissolved.

In the late 1960s Jones operated Finochio's Lounge, a drag bar on Broadway near Diversey. He then opened the Machine Shop at 504 North Clark Street, at the time the only adult bookstore in Chicago with an exclusively gay movie arcade, and later Ira's Male Box at 53 West Hubbard. Jones was also a regular contributor to *GayLife* and actively involved in several groups, including the Gay and Lesbian Coalition of Metropolitan Chicago, Integrity/Chicago, the Metropolitan Business Association, the Prairie State Democratic Club, and Black and White Men Together (later renamed Men of All Colors Together). A large man himself, Jones was also president of Chicago's Girth and Mirth, a social group for big gay guys, and he was the national president of the Affiliated Big Men's Clubs of America.

A religious man, Jones helped to found Integrity/Chicago, the gay Episcopal support group. He was also a member of the Church of the Ascension and the American Church Union, and he sat in the congregation of the First Church of Deliverance, the Reverend Clarence Cobb's gay friendly church on the South Side. When Cobb died, a protégé of his, the Reverend Lucius Hall, formed the First Church of Love and Faith, for which Jones served as a trustee.

Ira Jones is buried in the family plot in Rose City Cemetery in Portland, Oregon.

## Robert Sloane Basker

Solomon Sloane Basker was born in East Harlem, New York, on September 30, 1918, the youngest of five sons born to Polish Orthodox Jewish immigrants who operated a grocery store. He attended Hebrew school but later claimed his real education came from the men he met in the subway station bathrooms at 100th and Lexington. These casual acquaintances provided an entrée into the world of the arts, giving him an appreciation of classical music, ballet, and opera. In World War II, Basker joined the army and fought in Europe. He received an honorable discharge in 1944 and became a sales manager for Encyclopedia Britannica, where in 1952 he was promoted and transferred to Chicago. There he married Greta, had three children, and though they later divorced, the two remained friends for life.

Basker and Greta worked tirelessly for left-wing causes, including supporting families who were victims of the Smith Act, a 1940 federal statute making it a crime to "knowingly or willfully advocate, abet, advise or teach the duty, necessity, desirability or propriety of overthrowing the Government of the United States." This statute led to a witch-hunt of left-leaning political figures.

In the late 1950s and early '60s, a renamed "Robert" and Greta Basker became active in the civil rights movement as members of the NAACP. After assisting a black family moving into their all-white Skokie, Illinois, neighborhood, the Baskers were subjected to death threats, obscene phone calls, and a firebomb. The stress led to the couple's divorce. Robert Basker was an inveterate letter writer. In the *Chicago Tribune* on May 28, 1964, he wrote: "The following is part of a letter I've written to Sen. Dirksen: 'Let's get in step with history. Have the courage to extend equal rights to all Americans. Let's become a first class country by eliminating second class citizenship.'" And in the *Chicago Tribune* on February 13, 1965: "I have today sent the following telegram to President Lyndon B. Johnson: 'Thought Goldwater's defeat saved us from trigger-happy government. Urge immediate cessation of our barbaric retaliations in Viet Nam.'"

On October 25, 1964, state legislature candidates from all political parties were invited to give their views on "the role of law to achieve equal housing opportunities for all citizens" at one of three rallies organized by the United Citizens' Committee for Freedom of Residence in Illinois. The meetings were held on the North Side, West Side, and South Side of Chicago; Robert Basker was the South Side speaker at the Beth Am-The People's synagogue, 7133 South Coles.

In 1965, a single man, Basker reinvented himself as gay activist Bob Sloane, who along with Pearl M. Hart and Ira Jones founded Mattachine Midwest. Basker was the founding president. In an interview in the June 25, 1982, issue of *GayLife*, Basker spoke of those early days of Mattachine: "Before we actually organized, we had organizational meetings. We had committees set up. We had a religious concerns committee; we had a social concerns committee; we had a telephone answering setup. We had a good structure. . . . We developed panels of names of doctors, lawyers, psychiatrists and ministers who might be of service to the gay community. Sometimes people just needed someone to talk to before they jumped out of a window."

Two months after the group was founded, Basker resigned and left Chicago for Miami, then to Cuba, where his ex-wife and children were living. There he taught English as a second language at the John Reed School of Languages. He returned to the States in 1971 and to gay activism; he helped found the Miami Gay Activist Alliance, started a shelter for runaway gay kids, and joined the Dade County Coalition for Human Rights (DCCHR) campaign against antigay beauty queen and the face of Florida orange juice, Anita Bryant.

In 1978 Basker moved again, this time to San Francisco, where in 1983 he cofounded the Alexander Hamilton Post #448 of the American Legion, the only post with LGBT members, all honorably discharged veterans who had served their country in times of war. Robert Basker died on April 6, 2001, of heart failure, at age eighty-two.

# 24

# Mattachine Midwest and the Struggle toward a Greater Visibility

Early 1950s incarnations of the Mattachine Society in Chicago were covert operations working in secrecy, but by the late 1960s, some members were speaking out openly on TV and radio. In 1965 Mattachine Midwest formed and, along with the Daughters of Bilitis and One of Chicago, forged links with groups in other cities and helped create a national movement. This was in spite of Chicago police officer John Manley cruising public restrooms and entrapping gay men by the hundreds.

The Mattachine Society first met in Los Angeles on November 11, 1950, with founding members Harry Hay, Rudi Gerneich, Dale Jennings, Bob Hull, and Chuck Rowland. The word Mattachine comes from Société Mattachine, a secret society of unmarried male troubadours who performed dramas in medieval France. The group wore masks in public, danced, and performed magic rituals in the woods and countryside on the Feast of Fools. By May 1953 there were two thousand members.

The first Mattachine chapter outside of California was in Chicago. Little is known about that first group—only that it was founded by a law clerk named Bob Meyer, that forty people attended the first public meeting on May 31, 1954, and that the first issue of a newsletter was published in July. There are only sketchy reports of the group's activities. The national *Mattachine Review* of March/April 1955 listed three chapters in Chicago working under the banner of the Chicago Area Council of the Mattachine

Society. An editorial in the April 1955 Chicago Mattachine *Newsletter* reads: "This is NOT an organization attempting to create a 'homosexual society' but rather an organization seeking the integration of the homosexual as a responsible and acceptable citizen in the community. The Society will not tolerate use of itself or its name for any subversive political or reprehensible conduct."

*The Ladder* in August 1957 reported a booklet titled "Your Legal Rights," based on the Illinois Criminal Code, had been prepared by the Legal Department of the Chicago Area Council of the Mattachine Society and written by lesbian lawyer Pearl M. Hart. That same month the *Mattachine Review* reported the Chicago chapter was still hosting events, but with less frequency. Membership dropped over the winter, and in July 1958 Chicago Mattachine was listed as "inactive." On the occasion of Mattachine Midwest's fifteenth anniversary, author Valerie Taylor wrote in the April/May 1980 issue of *Mattachine Midwest Newsletter*: "Mattachine of Chicago, the forerunner of Mattachine Midwest carried on bravely for a time with a small membership and no budget. I was asked to speak before this group in the winter of 1960; the officers decided to open the meeting to the public and to run a small ad in the *Chicago Sun-Times*. This newspaper refused the ad on the grounds that homosexuality was a taboo subject."

Chicago Mattachine lasted until 1962.

In 1965 Mattachine Midwest was founded by Robert Sloane Basker, Ira Jones, and Pearl Hart. In early 1965 there were only two gay groups in Chicago, the conservative One of Chicago and a chapter of the San Francisco-based lesbian group the Daughters of Bilitis (DOB), the latter founded in 1961–62 by Del Shearer, who resigned in 1965 over her objection to picketing. Barb McLean took over and ran it until 1969, when she moved to California and became president of DOB Los Angeles. In Chicago, the DOB Dances, held at clandestine locations, were popular, with 100–150 women attending; other events included Gab and Java meetings, picnics, potlucks, hiking, biking, and camping trips. On February 11, 1966, Mclean took the negative in a "Lesbians Are Sick" debate at Chicago's College of Complexes, a debating group dating back to the lavender-tinged Seven Arts Club and Dil Pickle Club of the 1920s and '30s; she spoke there again on May 14.

Many of those involved in starting Mattachine Midwest used pseudonyms, for fear of being outed and losing their jobs. At a June 22, 1965, meeting Bob Basker was named president under the name Robert Sloane, and Jim Bradford (real name Jim Osgood) vice president, to serve until the November election. On July 4 some members of Mattachine Midwest were among the thirty-nine individuals, men wearing jackets and ties and women in dresses, who picketed Independence Hall in Philadelphia at the first "Annual Reminder" with signs reading "HOMOSEXUAL BILL OF RIGHTS" and "15 MILLION HOMOSEXUAL AMERICANS ASK FOR EQUALITY, OPPORTUNITY, DIGNITY."

The first *Mattachine Midwest Newsletter* was published in July 1965, a single sheet, advertising a soon-to-be-in-operation twenty-four-hour hotline and the first public meeting in the Grand Ballroom of the Midland Hotel at 172 West Adams. That first meeting was a huge success. Speakers included lawyers Pearl M. Hart and Ralla Klepak. A spokeswoman from Chicago DOB also addressed the crowd, and Bob Basker made his introductory address, tracing the history of minorities overcoming oppression, comparing the gay rights movement to the abolitionists, and women suffragists campaigning for the right of women to vote.

The following month 140 people attended the open meeting, which had two guest speakers: drag performer Skip Arnold, and Doctor Carl J. Cohen of the Chicago Board of Health VD program, who presented a slide show and talk. Over the next couple of months, speakers tackled topics like religion in "The Churches' Attitudes" and medical matters in "Recent Ideas on Homosexuality." In September Ralla Klepak moderated a panel of five speakers from the Jewish, Catholic, and Protestant faiths in a heated debate. Also that month Bob Basker resigned as president and moved to Miami, to be replaced by vice president Jim Bradford, who with his lover Ed del Vayo (real name Edward Louzao) helped with the formation of the group.

On September 24–26, 1965, Mattachine Midwest members Bob Basker, Terry Grand, Mark Howard (real name Ira Jones), and Bill Kelley attended the East Coast Homophiles Organization (ECHO) third annual conference. ECHO was formed in 1963 by homophile groups in New York City, Philadelphia, and Washington, D.C., to more closely coordinate national group activities. As a result of networking at the ECHO conference, Mattachine Midwest hosted a media event on November 13–16, 1965, that included four national homophile leaders: Doctor Frank Kameny, founder of the Mattachine Society of Washington, D.C.; Randolfe Wicker, secretary of the Mattachine Society of New York; Clark Polak, president of the Janus Society of Philadelphia; and Larry Littlejohn, president of the Society for

Individual Rights, San Francisco. The weekend kicked off with an appearance on Irv Kupcinet's TV program *Kups Show* on WBKB-TV, Channel 7, with the topic "The Homophile Movement in America." The following night the same guests appeared on John Calloway's *Night Line* program on WBBM Radio.

Mattachine Midwest's first social event was a Christmas party on December 21, 1965, for which members were encouraged to donate canned foods to Mayor Daley's "Christmas Basket for the Poor" campaign. The party provided a chance for members to meet the newly elected board: Jim Bradford, president; Gene Grove, vice president; William Kelley, secretary; and Ira Jones, treasurer. On February 18–20, 1966, several members of Mattachine Midwest and one from Chicago DOB attended the National Planning Conference of Homophile Organizations (NPCHO) at the State Hotel in Kansas City, Missouri. Fourteen homophile organizations were represented from across the United States and Canada. Foster Gunnison Jr., one of the organizers, insisted at the conference that a national homophile organization was needed to save the movement from being taken over by "fringe elements, beatniks, and other professional non-conformists." The conference was contentious. A vote to form a national homophile organization failed, with Dick Leitsch of Mattachine New York and Phyllis Lyon and Del Martin of DOB the main dissenters. Concerns were the loss of autonomy, with DOB refusing to hand over the reins of a lesbian group to a male-dominated organization.

Out of the NPCHO another meeting was called for August 25–27, 1966, in San Francisco, where the umbrella group North American Conference of Homophile Organizations (NACHO) was formed. Guest speakers at the conference were California state assemblyman Willie Brown Jr., later mayor of San Francisco, and psychologist Evelyn Hooker. Chicagoans who attended were Mattachine Midwest's Roland Keith and William Kelley, and Richard H. Shane of One of Chicago.

Between August 11 and 18, 1968, NACHO was hosted by Mattachine Midwest, only days before Chicago's violent clashes between antiwar protestors and police at the 1968 Democratic National convention. While Mayor Richard J. Daley's cops geared up for the influx of "peaceniks," few noticed the seventy-five delegates representing forty groups gathering at the Trip. Among them was the Reverend Robert Warren Cromey, vicar of Saint Aidan's Episcopal church in San Francisco. A heterosexual, married with three daughters, Cromey was integral to the formation of the Council on Religion and the Homosexual (CRH), formed in 1964, after clergymen hosted a retreat to discuss the problems of homosexuals on the streets of San Francisco's Tenderloin district.

Mattachine Midwest's William Kelley was secretary at NACHO in 1968. Among other NACHO attendees were Chicago-born Shirley Willer, a past president of the Daughters of Bilitis; Larry Littlejohn, president of the Society for Individual Rights; Barbara Gittings of New York DOB; and Frank Kameny of Washington, D.C., Mattachine. The conference, conducted mostly in private, was as contentious as ever. In fact, the DOB pulled out of NACHO altogether after the Chicago gathering. However, the event is remembered for adopting Frank Kameny's slogan "Gay is Good," a twist on "Black is Beautiful." The *New York Times* on August 19, 1968, reported that NACHO delegates recommended sending questionnaires to those seeking political office, forcing them to take a public stand on homosexuality. In the *New Republic* on September 7, 1968, a sidebar on the NACHO conference was added to a major article on the antiwar protests and street battles at the DNC convention. It read:

> It had been rumored that the Yippies would hold a "Homosexuals for Humphrey" rally in Chicago. The "homophiles" claim to be fifteen million strong, and argue that no politician can turn up his nose at that many votes.
>
> Unlike other minority groups, the homosexuals have few defenders. One college professor recently traced the nation's ills to an undercurrent of "hippies, homos and hooligans." While medicine and psychiatry continue trying to unravel the complexities behind homosexuals' inverted lives, they are stalked and caged by vice cops who perch on toilet seats to peer through peepholes.

There were two more NACHO gatherings, 1969 and 1970, but the Stonewall Riots in June 1969 shifted the emphasis from the old guard's softly-softly approach to the young radical in-your-face confrontational zaps of the Gay Liberation Front. Things came to a head at the 1970 conference in San Francisco, when Gay Lib hijacked the event and passed resolutions supporting the Black Panthers, Women's Liberation, and the withdrawal of troops from Vietnam. *Gay Sunshine* in October 1970 called this "the battle that ended the homophile movement."

After Jim Bradford became president in November 1965, Mattachine Midwest took a more activist turn, primarily targeting an out-of-control Chicago police force. Three times the police refused Mattachine's invitation to discuss "The Police and the Homosexual," their excuse being they "had inadequate knowledge of the topic." The April 1966 issue of the *Mattachine Midwest Newsletter* reported: "Chicago's homosexual community once again faces the dangers of a jittery police department and politicians as election time draws near. . . . [A]lleged syndicate interests in gay bars produced a series of raids that shook responsible homosexuals to the core." Robert Wiedrich of the *Chicago Tribune* reported on March 15, 1966, that the mob had "muscled" into "14 floundering taverns" on the Near North Side and turned them into "lucrative hangouts for homosexuals . . . putting at least one million dollars a year into crime syndicate coffers." The next day police raided New New Jamie's, 1116 North Clark Street, arresting eleven people and "dispersing" another thirty-five. Wiedrich reported in the *Chicago Tribune* on March 17 that police found ledgers indicating four hundred dollars in weekly payments to "Joe." This was thought to be mob boss Joseph "Big Joe" Arnold. New New Jamie's was owned by brothers Dominic and John Gattuso; John, formerly a Cook County deputy sheriff, was married to mobster Jimmy (The Monk) Allegretti's niece. Aside from gay bars, John Gattuso ran strip joints and was a hit man for the mob. On July 14, 1983, he was found dead in the trunk of a car in Naperville.

Evidence of the increasing visibility of lesbians and gay men came on June 20–23, 1966, when the *Chicago Daily News* ran a four-part series on the city's homosexual community. The articles, written by Pulitzer Prize-winning reporter Lois Wille, read like an anthropological study of a strange breed of "Fifth Columnists" who wormed their way into "normal" society by nefarious means. One subheading reads "Experts Doubt They're Dangerous." Wille writes that reporters spent weeks "unearthing the secrets of this tormented twilight world, listening to whispered confidences and frank confessions." The first article, "Chicago's Twilight World—The Homosexuals—A Growing Problem" begins: "The problem of homosexuality in Chicago has long been one of the city's most sensitive open secrets. Now, with the increasing openness of its manifestations, it has become the subject of growing concern by psychiatric, legal and religious leaders as well as law enforcement officers." Wille estimated twenty to fifty thousand homosexuals lived in the city. She writes that homosexuality is legal in

Illinois: "Yet despite the new law, the homosexual's greatest dread continues to be exposure and ruin. . . . They are harried by police raids and arrests for disorderly conduct or indecent behavior. They are officially barred from military and government service." Wille goes on to differentiate between the "flagrant effeminates" and those hiding behind a mask for fear of losing their jobs: "The great unknown mass, most of them not 'sissyish' at all. . . . But nearly all live a strange life of their own—a scorned but defiant minority with its secret codes, status cliques, network of hangouts, desperate fears and struggles for acceptance."

Wille poses the question: "Can and should deviates be contained to keep them from spreading further? . . . Or are these disturbed, misunderstood men needing help and the freedom to live their own way? . . . Society soon may have to decide by facing both the mystery and new visibility of homosexual life."

At the time of the *Chicago Daily News* articles, the epicenter of gay life was at Clark and Diversey Streets. "This area is the prowling ground for the dregs of the invert world: aging male prostitutes, painted, grossly effeminate 'queens,' and those who prey on them," wrote Wille, adding that the area's coffee shops were "infested" with underage gays. Another hangout for "young punk showoffs" with "lavender shirts and tight white pants, their hair poufed and tinted" was on the steps of the Chicago Public Library.

Mattachine Midwest wrote to the editor of the *Chicago Daily News*, thanking the paper for the "fair and accurate treatment of our organization," but expressing concern about the sensational and prejudicial language: "Stereotyped and biased phrases such as 'deviates' and 'bizarre double-life' shed no new light on the subject," wrote the *Mattachine Midwest Newsletter* in July 1966. In August 1966 the new pocket-sized newsletter gave dire warnings of renewed police activity in bars, bathhouses, restrooms, and on the street. In his President's Corner column, Jim Bradford pointed to "unmanly traps" in restrooms, a thinly veiled reference to Officer John Manley, a notorious cop who entrapped gay men in bathrooms. In the September 1969 newsletter, David Stienecker, the editor, wrote an amusing piece about Manley, hinting the blue-eyed blond cop might be gay himself and "getting off" on the arrests.

On February 7, 1970, Manley arrested Stienecker at his home—the charge, "criminal defamation." At Foster Avenue police station Stienecker spent four hours being processed before being released on twenty-five dollars bond. Manley was surprised Stienecker contested the charges. On May 6, 1970, after three Kafkaesque court appearances the case was dismissed.

In November 1966 Bradford was voted out of office, and the Reverend Tom Maurer, under the name Norman Benson, took over as president of Mattachine Midwest. The closeted Maurer was pastor of Community Church in suburban Park Ridge. In 1971, at the age of fifty-three, Maurer did finally "come out" while he was a United Church of Christ minister in California. However, in 1966, Maurer was the new conservative, patriotic face of Mattachine Midwest. In the April 1967 newsletter, his "President's Corner" was illustrated with an American bald eagle and the cover read "PRINTED IN THE U.S.A." The newsletter was entirely printed in upper case and read like Maurer was pontificating from the pulpit.

The anonymous cover story of the April 1966 issue begins: "FREEDOM LIBERTY. LOVELY WORDS AREN'T THEY?" The sermon goes on to talk about behaving responsibly: "THE FACT IS TOO OFTEN FORGOTTEN BY ALL PEOPLES, AND WE BRING IT UP NOW BECAUSE HOMOSEXUALS ALSO FORGET THE FACT THAT OUR FREEDOM ENDS WHEN WE INFRINGE ON THE FREEDOMS OF OTHERS. WE CANNOT HAVE A TOTAL ABSENCE OF RESTRAINT. UNFORTUNATELY THE HOMOSEXUAL DOES HAVE THE FEELING OF BEING HAMPERED. WE DO NOT HAVE THE RIGHT TO SAY OR DO ANYTHING WE WISH. WE MUST ASSUME OUR RESPONSIBILITIES. WE HAVE NO SPECIAL PRIVILEGES BECAUSE WE ARE HOMOSEXUAL. OUR PUBLIC BEHAVIOR CANNOT BE OFFENSIVE TO OTHERS IF WE ARE TO *EARN* ACCEPTANCE."

Another article in the same issue is titled: "A FRUITY FRUIT WORLD." The author takes the line that gays provoke police harassment by giving the impression they want the whole world to be gay. Police are under the impression that "IT IS THE AVOWED GOAL OF ALL MALE HOMOSEXUALS TO ESTABLISH A 'FRUIT WORLD.' THE STRANGE LOGIC UNDERLYING SUCH A CHARGE WOULD BE CONSIDERED ALMOST HILARIOUS IF THERE WEREN'T A SEMBLANCE OF TRUTH IN IT." The article goes on to say that homosexuals who believe in establishing "A FRUIT WORLD" were "DISTURBED." The writer suggests effeminacy and camp talk is to blame. Saying things like "HECK HE'S STRAIGHT, HE'S FRUITIER THAN YOU & I, DARLING," or "I THINK HE'S JUST A CLOSET QUEEN," and referring to other males as "SHE" gives the impression that there is no such thing as a completely heterosexual male. Self-deprecating articles like "A FRUITY FRUIT WORLD" bothered activist members like William Kelley, Ira Jones, and Jim Bradford, who began holding meetings in secret; Bradford called it a "board in exile." Maurer was president for sixteen months, and during his tenure all activism ceased.

On March 7, 1967, CBS aired *The Homosexuals* as part of a series of award-winning *CBS Reports* documentaries; this was the first network program on the subject of homosexuality. The program, anchored by Mike Wallace, featured interviews with gay men, psychiatrists, and legal experts, and it included footage of a gay bar, hustlers on the street, and a police sting. Most of the gay men interviewed were either hidden in the shadows or sitting behind a potted palm.

Predictably, the Mattachine Midwest newsletter railed against the "radicals" in the TV show: "AUTHOR GORE VIDAL'S COMMENTS WERE, IN MANY INSTANCES, RIDICULOUS. THIS REPORTER HAS LITTLE PATIENCE WITH IDIOCY OR EXTREMISM BEING FOISTED ON THE AMERICAN PUBLIC AS RATIONAL COMMENTS."

In May 1967 the attacks on radicals and feminine men continued. In a column titled "MOLLIE SPEAKS," Anon writes: "IT WOULD SEEM TO ME THAT ANYONE WHO WAS IN A MINORITY GROUP WOULD TRY TWICE AS HARD TO SET A METICULOUS BEHAVOR PATTERN SO THAT NARY AN UN-FAVORABLE COMMENT COULD BE HEARD. SO, ACTUALLY I AM SPEAKING OF THE LESS MASCULINE MEMBERS OF OUR GROUP WHO SEEM TO PRIDE THEMSELVES IN PUBLIC DISPLAYS OF PSEUDO-FEMININITY. I'VE DIS-CUSSED THIS SUBJECT WITH MANY 'STRAIGHT' PEOPLE, YOUNG AND OLD, AND THEIR OPINION SEEMS TO BE: 'GAY PEOPLE ARE NOT SO BAD TO BE WITH, EXCEPT FOR THE "FEMMES."'"

After the July newsletter, the next issue appeared in October, and then it ceased publication until May 1968, after Jim Bradford was voted back in as president. With the newsletter's return came the new listing of board members: Jim Bradford, president; William B. Kelley, vice president; Paul Baker, treasurer; Ron Ellison, secretary; and directors Ed del Vayo, Joe Brunner, and Don Schultz. The editor of the newsletter was now Valerie Taylor.

The *Chicago American* on June 8, 1967, and the *Chicago Sun-Times* on June 9, 1967, reported that the Illinois Senate passed a bill creating a com-mission to study "the problem of homosexuality in the state." The measure was offered by Senator G. William Horsley (R-Springfield) and passed 30–8. Horsley claimed schoolchildren were becoming "hooked" on homosexual practices, and that "the time has arrived to come up with some medical answers to this problem of homosexuality. . . . [It] is contaminating youth in Illinois and is a serious problem. We can't ignore it."

Senator Alan Dixon (D-Bellville), Senate minority whip, advised caution: "The bill gives the commission subpoena power. Apparently many leading business and professional men in public life have a homosexual problem. I hope you would not want to embarrass any of them. . . . [T]hey shouldn't be asked to appear before a commission with TV cameras and reporters."

Senator Hudson C. Sours (R-Peoria) agreed: "This is one thing we should not delve into. The dangerous factor is exposure of homosexuals, because you can wreck their lives." He goes on to say homosexuality is "one of those insoluble problems which should be treated from a medical standpoint. Homosexuals clearly are misfits."

Senator James P. Loukas (D-Chicago) warned: "Homosexuals are organized and are a cancer on our society." He then added his theory that "the dissolution of the glory that was once Greece was caused basically by homosexualism." Senator Joseph Krasowski (R-Chicago) agreed the bill had merit: "Homosexuals do bother people. It is embarrassing. I have been approached myself on the streets of Chicago. My big concern is teenagers being contaminated by this way of life."

Nothing came of the commission.

In March 1968 Jim Bradford was again voted president of Mattachine Midwest, at a time when U.S. opinion was torn on the Vietnam War, and the assassinations of Martin Luther King Jr. and Robert Kennedy were just over the horizon. Bradford's condemnation of police harassment put Mattachine Midwest in step with the other radical movements of the 1960s. In May 1968 Bradford was in a fighting mood: "I intend to comment regularly on events in the news as they tie in with the homophile movement. This will no doubt irritate some people, because there are, unfortunately, a number of homosexuals who have not profited from their own painful brushes with the law."

Before the 1968 Democratic Convention, Mayor Richard J. Daley and the city's police set about cleaning up vice, first by raiding gay bars, starting with Maxine's lesbian bar at Jeffrey and 71 Streets, then others around the city. In August the NACHO conference at the Trip was ignored by Chicago's mainstream press, only the underground paper *Kaleidoscope* wrote it up. They reported that the twenty-six homosexual-rights groups attending approved a "Bill of Rights," pinpointing ten areas of concern: (1) Police and other government agents shall cease the practice of enticement and entrapment of homosexuals; (2) Police shall desist from notifying the employers of those arrested for homosexual offenses; (3) Neither the police department nor any other government agency shall keep files solely for the purpose of identifying homosexuals; (4) The practice of harassing bars and other establishments and of revoking their licenses because they cater to homosexuals shall cease; (5) The practice of reviewing less-than-honorable military discharges, granted for homosexual orientation or practice, shall be established, with the goal of upgrading such discharges into fully honorable; (6) The registration of sex offenders shall not be required; (7) City ordinances involving sexual matters shall be rescinded and these matters left to state legislatures; (8) Conviction for homosexual offenses shall not be the basis for prohibiting issuance of professional or any other license nor for the revocation of these licenses; (9) No questions regarding sexual orientation or practice shall appear on application forms, personal data sheets, or in personal interviews; and (10) No government agency shall use the classification of homosexuality as an alleged illness to limit the freedom, rights, or privileges of any homosexual.

After the tear gas cleared from the Democratic Convention, James Ridgeway of the *New Republic* wrote in an article titled "The Cops & the Kids": "The clashes between police and demonstrators began as calculated maneuvers by the National Mobilization Committee to End the War in Vietnam (MOB), and the Youth International Party (YIP). The strategy was to confront the Chicago police, and thereby demonstrate that America was a police state." On the subject of the riots, the *Mattachine Midwest Newsletter* of September 1968 read: "[T]he whole world saw the hatred and violence of which Chicago police are capable, whether one's sympathies are with the demonstrators or not, the police tactics during the week of the convention . . . belong in a history of Nazi Germany."

Judith Crist, film critic for the *New York Times*, named 1968 "The Year of the Third-Sex." On June 28, 1968, one year to the day before the Stonewall Riots, *Time* magazine published "Trends: Where the Boys Are," which begins by quoting a transvestite in Federico Fellini's *La Dolce Vita* (1960) who says: "By 1970 the entire world will be homosexual." The *Time* article reads: "Looking at some recent American films, the moviegoer might be inclined to believe that the prognosis is already coming true.

Hollywood has suddenly discovered homosexuality, and the 'third sex' is making a determined bid for first place at the box office."

None of the 1968 lavender-tinged movies painted a rosy picture of homosexuals, but the characters were a long way from the dandified sissies of the silent era. In *The Detective*, starring Frank Sinatra, Lee Remick, and Jaqueline Bisset, Sinatra plays New York cop Joe Leland, who investigates the murder of the gay son of a department store magnate. The movie gives a glimpse into the twilight world of gay bars, gay hotels, and bodybuilding clubs. *Chicago Daily News* film critic Sam Lesner is said to have described *The Detective* as a "spreading malaise" with "fags" as practitioners.

Among other gay movies that year were *The Fox*, about a lesbian couple whose relationship falls apart over a man; *The Queen*, a documentary of a New York City female impersonation beauty pageant; *The Sergeant*, with Rod Steiger playing a lovesick and jealous homosexual U.S. Army officer; and the British lesbian classic *The Killing of Sister George*, an adaptation of the 1964 play by Frank Marcus. *Time* magazine called the movie "an autopsy of a homosexual affair." On March 12, 1968, the Marcus play opened in Chicago at the Studebaker Theatre, with Claire Trevor as Sister George; her sweet babydoll love-interest Alice "Childie" McNaught was played by Patricia Sinnott; and Natalie Schafer was Mercy Croft. In a *Chicago Tribune* review headlined "Good Taste, Humor Help as Taboo Theme Comes to Stage," William Leonard writes that Sister George, a character in a British soap opera, is a "tough, hard drinking, cigar-smoking old bat who dominates her weakling roommate sadistically. . . . It is not, despite its characters, a play about lesbianism. It is, rather, a hilarious attack on the idiocy of network broadcasting—the world of the soap opera, which has ensnared more square, unsuspecting housewives than marijuana has entrapped beatniks."

Two other gay-themed plays of 1968 later adapted for films were Charles Dyer's *Staircase* and Mart Crowley's *The Boys in the Band*—both plays opened in Chicago the following year. *Staircase*, starring Murray Matheson and Kenneth Haigh, opened at the Ivanhoe Theatre on May 1, 1969, and William Leonard's *Chicago Tribune* review describes the play as "a close-up view of the painful world of the homosexual who is disdainful of the world, yet frightened to death." The play was later adapted into a movie starring Rex Harrison and Richard Burton. When *The Boys in the Band* opened at the Studebaker Theatre on December 2, 1969, Leonard described it as "a smash": "There are horse laughs all thru Act 1 at the lavender dialog and the four-letter words of the lads, a tight little circle of faggots, who have gathered to throw a silly birthday party for one of their number, Ho, ho, ho! Look at those queers! But the laughs fade as the evening progresses."

In the February 23, 1969, issue of the *New York Times*, Ronald Forsythe wrote "Why Can't 'We' Live Happily Ever After, Too?," a plea for more positive images of homosexuals in the arts:

> Much like the American Negro of 20–30 years ago who saw himself on stage and screen—and read about himself in novels—as Black Joe or Prissy or Shoe Shine Boy, the American homosexual has a complaint: He does not believe his life must end in tragedy and would like to see a change in his image reflected in the entertainment he pays to see and the books he buys to read. Like any minority group, he, too, would like his "Place in the Sun." He has been striving for it in life by seeking the revocation of laws that harass him unjustly; he would like also to achieve it in the creative worlds of the novel, plays, films, music, art, and television.

It was against this backdrop of negative pop-culture images that homophile groups attempted to educate the public and campaign for equal rights. In September 1968, the *Mattachine Midwest Newsletter* published "Your Rights if Arrested." On December 10, 1968, Jim Bradford, William Kelley, and Bill Brackett, an ACLU-liaison attorney, met with Director John R. Neurauter, head of Chicago's Vice Control Division, a meeting that led to "some degree of understanding." The following month Jim Bradford's "President's Corner" read: "Neurauter apparently is hip in our area. He realizes that the usual stereotyped views of homosexuals are not true."

The harassment of homosexuals continued unabated, however. In February 1969 the newsletter warned of two cops: "Mark Davilo, tall with a plaid checked jacket and a goatee, is enticing homosexuals at the Monroe Theater and the Palmer House. Anthony LoBue (Tony the Bull) has been given the Prudential Building for his assignment . . . but he works the first-floor men's room by Stouffer's."

LoBue was still working men's restrooms seven years later. In the *Chicago Tribune* of July 25, 1976, he was interviewed for an article headlined:

"'Vice Versa' Squad Fights Male Hookers." A new report estimated 5–10 percent of Chicago's prostitution arrests were male, and Officer Anthony LoBue, wearing "a T-shirt and pants, both tight fitting," was the bait. He and his partner had just raided the Monroe Theater, where LoBue had "observed homosexual sex acts." LoBue told the paper: "A man tried to solicit me to perform a sexual act for $15. . . . While my partner detained several men in the washroom, I went to the ticket taker and complained, as a citizen, about what was going on. He shrugged and said, 'So?'" LoBue then arrested the ticket taker.

Lieutenant George Bicek, head of vice control, told the *Chicago Tribune*: "[H]omosexual prostitution has been present here for a long time. Homosexuals have come out of the closet these days, and male prostitutes are more visible. But I still believe most male prostitutes we arrest are female impersonators." LoBue added: "I've arrested thousands of guys for indecency or prostitution charges, and 90 percent of them are married men with families."

In the early hours of June 28, 1969, a riot broke out after a police raid on the Stonewall Inn in Greenwich Village in New York City. In Chicago's bars that night, gay men were enjoying Arthur Blake at the Trip doing impersonations of Phyllis Diller, Mae West, Carol Channing, Bette Davis, Carmen Miranda, and political figures like Eleanor Roosevelt and Senator Everett Dirksen. Woodrow "Woody" I. Moser's El Salon de Crystal at the 21 Club served potent cocktails and candlelight dinners. Bartending on roller skates, Jim Flint (a.k.a. Felicia) had just opened the Normandy House, and piano bars like Mr. T's and the Blue Pub were packed. On the downside, security police at the Lawson YMCA were purging each floor of so-called "illegal sexual activity," and Chicago police were loitering in Margate Park on the North Side and East End Park on the South Side entrapping gay men.

In Chicago the Stonewall rebellion received no coverage from either the mainstream or the underground press, though it did merit a cursory mention in the July 1969 issue of the *Mattachine Midwest Newsletter*. On October 3, 1969, Henry Weimhoff, a former student at the University of Chicago, placed a classified ad in the "Roommates Wanted" section of *Maroon*, the student paper, that read: "2 Gay Students Wanted to Share 5 Rm Unfrn. Apt (53rd & Harper) $52 & Utils. 955-7433. (Keep Trying)." The handful of students who answered the ad placed another ad in the

*Maroon* of October 24, 1969: "GAY POWER IN 69–70 Anyone interested in joining the Hyde Park Homophile League formed last qt at UC write Box 69, c/o Maroon. Replies kept confidential."

In December the group changed its name to the Chicago Gay Liberation Front.

But that's another story.

# Bibliography

## Chapter 1. The Explorers

Ellis, Havelock. *Studies in the Psychology of Sex.* Vol. 2, *Sexual Inversion.* London, 1897. Reprint, New York: Arno Press, 1975.

Katz, Jonathan Ned. *Gay American History: Lesbians and Gay Men in the U.S.A.* New York, 1976. Reprint, New York: Meridian, 1992.

Roscoe, Will. *The Zuni Man-Woman.* Albuquerque: University of New Mexico Press, 1991.

## Chapter 2. The Chicago Doctors

"20,000,000 Gay People Cured!" *Chicago Gay Crusader,* Jan. 1974.

"Close Mails to Vice Report." *Chicago Tribune,* 27 Sep. 1911, 3.

"Doctors Vote Paper by Denslow Lewis Unfitted to Publish." *Chicago Tribune,* 9 June 1900, 9.

Hollender, Marc. "A Rejected Landmark Paper on Sexuality." *Journal of the American Medical Association* 250 (8 July 1933): 228–29.

Kiernan, James G. "Forensic Medicine: A Case of Probable Contrare [*sic*] Sexualempfindung." *Medicine* 5, no. 6 (June 1899): 526–28.

———. "Sexual Inversion, Jealousy and Homicide." *Alienist and Neurologist* 20 (October 1899): 669–71.

Lewis, Denslow. "The Gynecological Consideration of the Sexual Act." *Journal of the American Medical Association* 250 (8 July 1983): 222–27.

Lydston, G. Frank. *Addresses and Essays.* Louisville, Ky.: Renz and Henry, 1892.

Van, Jon. "Nation/World: 'Too Frank' Article on Sex Education Finally Finds Print—84 Years Later." *Chicago Tribune,* 8 July 1983, 8.

## Chapter 3. Chicago's Cesspools of Infamy

"Among the Lowly: Abodes of Wretchedness in Chicago." *Chicago Tribune*, 23 July 1871, 3.

Andrews, Shang. *Chicago Street Gazette*, 15 Sep. 1877, n.p.

"Big Dance Is a 'Sizzler.'" *Chicago Tribune*, 7 Jan. 1903, 3.

"Coughlin Yields; Orgy Called Off." *Chicago Tribune*, 10 Dec. 1909, 3.

"Craig 'Belle' of Ball." *Chicago Tribune*, 23 Dec. 1903, 3.

"Dean Takes Hope to Levee." *Chicago Tribune*, 25 Dec. 1907, 1.

Decency. "Look under the Bridges, Officers." The Voice of the People. *Chicago Tribune*, 18 May 1879, 6.

"Democracy Again in Society." *Chicago Tribune*, 8 Feb. 1909, 11.

Ellis, Havelock. *Studies in the Psychology of Sex*. Vol. 2, *Sexual Inversion*. London, 1897. Reprint, New York: Arno Press, 1975.

"First Ward in Annual Orgy." *Chicago Tribune*, 10 Dec. 1907, 5.

"Ill Health of Dean Sumner Delays Chicago Vice Report." *Chicago Tribune*, 17 Mar. 1911, 3.

"John the Bath and the First Ward Ball." *Chicago Tribune*, 15 Dec. 1940, 12.

Johnson, Curt, with R. Craig Sautter. *Wicked City—Chicago: From Kenna to Capone*. Highland Park, Ill.: December Press, 1994.

"Levee's Hordes Storm Coliseum." *Chicago Tribune*, 15 Dec. 1908, 1.

Longstreet, Stephen. *Chicago, 1860–1919*. New York: McKay, 1973.

Mayne, Xavier [Edwin Irenaenus Stevenson]. *The Intersexes: A History of Similisexualism as a Problem in Social Life*. Naples, Italy, 1908.

"Police Court." *Chicago Tribune*, 3 May 1864, 4.

"The Police Investigation: Roger Plant Refuses to Testify." *Chicago Tribune*, 10 Jan. 1868, 4.

"Police Matters." *Chicago Tribune*, 24 Oct. 1866, 4.

"Puts Vice Report up to Uncle Sam." *Chicago Tribune*, 24 Sep. 1911, 1.

"Roger Plant in Difficulty." *Chicago Tribune*, 19 Oct. 1866, 4.

"Scarlet Sisters Everleigh." *Chicago Tribune*, 2 Feb. 1936, D7.

"Sees Pagan Rome in 1st Ward Ball." *Chicago Tribune*, 6 Oct. 1908, 7.

Stead, William T. *If Christ Came to Chicago*. Chicago: Laird & Lee, 1894. Reprint, Chicago: Chicago Historical Bookworks, 1978.

"Threaten Bomb for Orgy: Chief Censors Costumes; Patrol Wagons to Await Offenders." *Chicago Tribune*, 4 Dec. 1909, 1.

Vice Commission of Chicago. *The Social Evil in Chicago*. Chicago, 1911.

"Vice Faces Fight by Business Men." *Chicago Tribune*, 16 Nov. 1910, 1.

Washburn, Charles. *Come into My Parlor: A Biography of the Notorious Everleigh Sisters of Chicago*. New York: National Library Press, 1936; reprint, New York: Bridgehead, 1954.

Wendt, Lloyd. "John the Bath and the First Ward Ball." *Chicago Tribune*, 15 Dec. 1940, J2.

Wendt, Lloyd, and Herman Kogan. *The Lords of the Levee: The Story of Bathhouse John and Hinky Dink*. New York: Bobbs-Merrill, 1943.

"Where Is Money for Vice Enquiry?" *Chicago Tribune*, 7 Mar. 1910, 3.

Wilson, Samuel Paynter. *Chicago and Its Cesspools of Infamy*. Chicago: Samuel Paynter Wilson, n.d.

Wilson, Samuel Paynter. *Chicago by Gaslight*. Chicago: Samuel Paynter Wilson, 1910.

## Chapter 4.  Mannish Women

"Baron Sued for Damages." *Chicago Tribune*, 11 July 1908, 8.

Blanton, Deanne, and Lauren M. Cook. *They Fought Like Demons: Women Soldiers in the Civil War*. New York: Vintage, 2002.

"Death Bares Dual Life." *Chicago Tribune*, 20 Dec. 1906, 3.

"De Raylan Inquest Is Begun." *Chicago Tribune*, 21 Dec. 1906, 2.

"'Fags and 'Nips' Don't Give Girls Beards; No, Sir!" *Chicago Tribune*, 23 Aug. 1921, 17.

"A Line of Type or Two: Old Veteran." *Chicago Tribune*, 14 Sep. 1966, 10.

"Little Trick That Did Wonders." *Chicago Tribune*, 29 Apr. 1915, 14.

Luciano, Phil. "Civil War Veteran Kept Identity Secret." *Peoria Journal Star*, 10 Dec. 1995, A1.

"The Mannish Woman." *Chicago Tribune*, 26 May 1888, 16.

"Masculine Corsets." *Chicago Times*, 13 Apr. 1889, 8

"Mme. De Raylan to Phoenix?" *Chicago Tribune*, 22 Dec. 1906, 4.

"'Mrs. De Raylan' Sells Lot." *Chicago Tribune*, 18 June 1907, 11.

"Must Learn Decedent's Sex." *Chicago Tribune*, 26 May 1907, 5.

"New Story of De Raylan and His Chicago Wife." *Chicago Tribune*, 30 Dec. 1906, 2.

"One's in Fun and One's in Ibsen." *Chicago Tribune*, 2 May 1926, 13.

*Pike County Republican* (Pittsfield, Ill.), 14 May 1916, n.p.

"Reliving a Civil War Battle That—for One Soldier—Also Was a Masquerade." *Chicago Tribune*, 20 May 1984, K25.

"Sex of Russian Diplomat of Chicago Bared by Death?" *Chicago Tribune*, 19 Dec. 1906, 3.

"Should Women Wear Bloomers?" *Daily Inter Ocean*, 9 June 1895, 13.

"Solving a Mystery of Sex." *Chicago Tribune*, 24 May 1907, 9.

"Some Joans of Arc." *Chicago Tribune*, 7 Feb. 1909, P10.

"A Tandem of Female Impersonators." *Chicago Tribune*, 25 May 1896, 3.

"Women Warriors." *Chicago Tribune*, 24 July 1898, 35.

## Chapter 5. The *Little Review*

"300 Brave Men Hear Mrs. Ellis." *Chicago Tribune*, 5 Feb. 1915, 1.

Anderson, Margaret. "Mrs. Ellis' Failure." *Little Review*, Mar. 1915.

———. *My Thirty Years' War*. New York: Horizon, 1930.

"Art or Blank Pages for 'Little Review.'" *Chicago Tribune*, 28 Aug. 1916, 14.

Baggett, Holly A. *Dear Tiny Heart: The Letters of Jane Heap and Florence Reynolds*. New York: New York University Press, 2000.

Butcher, Fanny. "Autobiografy [*sic*] Flames Only Occasionally." *Chicago Tribune*, 4 Nov. 1951, B15.

"Honestly, Ain't This Just the Swellestpome?" *Chicago Tribune*, 2 Sep. 1915, 13.

Margaret Anderson Papers. Newberry Library, Chicago.

"Ours Is the Life, Others Are Odd: Miss Anderson." *Chicago Tribune*, 9 Aug. 1915, 13.

Peattie, Elia W. "Books and the People Who Write Them." *Chicago Tribune*, 9 Jan. 1915, 8.

Smith, Alson J. *Chicago's Left Bank*. Chicago: Henry Regnery, 1953.

"Society and Entertainments: Mrs. Ellis Speaks at Woman's Athletic." *Chicago Tribune*, 3 Feb. 1915, 11.

"Society and Entertainment: Mrs. Havelock Ellis Guest of Mrs. Armour." *Chicago Tribune*, 12 Feb. 1915, 15.

Webster, Ronald. "The Harmless Sexuality of Syncopated Music." *Chicago Tribune*, 7 Feb. 1915, E1.

## Chapter 6. Kings and Queens of Burlesque

"Actresses Win Fame Wearing Male Attire." *Chicago Tribune*, 6 Jan. 1907, J3.

"Americans at Paris Fair." *Chicago Tribune*, 8 July 1900, 9.

"Arlington, Kelly, Leon and Donniker." *Chicago Tribune*, 28 Sep. 1863, 4.

Carpenter, John Ava. "Boston Gets Loie Fuller." *Chicago Tribune*, 4 Oct. 1908, H9.

"Chicago Dancer Dead in Paris." *Chicago Tribune*, 3 Jan. 1928, 1.

"Chicago Man Satisfied on a Roof: Home of Leon, Once Famous Female Impersonator." *Chicago Tribune*, 22 June 1902, 51.

"The Courts." *Chicago Tribune*, 2 Mar. 1877, 2.

"Developments Extraordinary!—A Woman in Male Disguise Marrying." *Chicago Tribune*, 1 May 1856, 1.

Duncan, Isadora. *My Life*. New York: Boni and Liveright, 1927.

"Ella Wesner's Voice." *Chicago Tribune*, 17 May 1885, 14.

Forbes Herrick, Genevieve. "Seek Harmony in Flutter Over the Queen Here." *Chicago Tribune*, 9 Nov. 1926, 1.

Fyles, Franklin. "August Shows in New York." *Chicago Tribune*, 9 Aug. 1908, F1.

Globe Theatre ad. *Chicago Tribune*, 10 Nov. 1872, 9.

"Hooley's." *Chicago Tribune*, 24 June 1879, 5.

"How to Dress Well." *Chicago Tribune*, 5 Jun. 1895, 16.

Hubbard, W. L. "News, of the Theaters." *Chicago Tribune*, 5 Oct. 1903, 4.

"Kenosha." *Chicago Tribune*, 16 July 1876, 12.

"'La Loie' Arrives in New York." *Chicago Tribune*, 23 Feb. 1896, 1.

"La Loie in Perihelion." *Chicago Tribune*, 12 Apr. 1896, 1.

"Loie Fuller and Her 'Salome.'" *Chicago Tribune*, 17 Mar. 1895, 36.

"Loie Fuller Appears Again." *Chicago Tribune*, 9 Sep. 1900, 9.

"Loie Fuller Art for Boston." *Chicago Tribune*, 14 Feb. 1909, A1.

"Loie Fuller May Go Blind." *Chicago Tribune*, 2 Apr. 1899, A1.

"Loie Fuller Patents a Dance." *Chicago Tribune*, 5 Sep. 1896, 4.

"Loie Fuller's Ballet Will Tour Country with Queen Marie." *Chicago Tribune*, 23 Oct. 1926, 2.

"Loie Fuller's New Quarrel." *Chicago Tribune*, 15 July 1900, 9.

"Loie Fuller's Parisian Success." *Chicago Tribune*, 26 Feb. 1893, 38.

"The Minstrel Tragedy." *Chicago Tribune*, 17 Dec. 1867, 4.

"More Concerning an Unusual American." *Chicago Tribune*, 12 Feb. 1928, G3.

"Music and Drama." *Chicago Tribune*, 20 Sep. 1900, 7.

"Music and Drama." *Chicago Tribune*, 17 Oct. 1900, 7.

"New York." *Chicago Tribune*, 18 Oct. 1872, 1.

"Relief for Soldiers' Families." *Chicago Tribune*, 31 Jan. 1864, 4.

"Review of Amusements." *Chicago Tribune*, 15 Nov. 1874, 7.

"Rumania: Royalty Rumbles." *Time*, 1 Nov. 1926, n.p.

"Sada Yacco." *New York Dramatic Mirror*, 17 Feb. 1906, 11.

"A Shocking Homicide." *Chicago Tribune*, 15 Dec. 1867, 1.

"Student of Psychology Studies Serpentine Dance." *Chicago Tribune*, 14 Mar. 1903, 7.

"They Like to Don Masculine Garb." *Chicago Tribune*, 20 Oct. 1907, G8.

"Titled Star Put in Asylum." *Chicago Tribune*, 21 Mar. 1930, 5.

Toll, Robert C. *Blacking Up: The Minstrel Show in Nineteenth-Century America*. New York: Oxford University Press, 1974.

"Vaudeville." *Chicago Tribune*, 1 Dec. 1907, A8.

"Vesta off the Stage." *Chicago Tribune*, 9 Jun. 1895, 13.

"Vesta Tilley, Who Sang in Chicago in 1903, Dies at 88." *Chicago Tribune*, 17 Sep. 1952, C10.

"A Wedded Puzzle." *Chicago Tribune*, 18 July 1892, 2.

"Wood's Minstrels." *Chicago Tribune*, 20 July 1860, o_1.

## Chapter 7. Towertown

"16 Women and Men Taken in Green Mask Raid." *Chicago Tribune*, 5 Sep. 1922, 3.

"35 'Bohemians' Seized in Raid on 'Green Mask.'" *Chicago Tribune*, 11 Jan. 1923, 1.

"At the Wind Blew Inn." *Chicago Tribune*, 13 Feb. 1922, 3.

"Author of Stage Play." *Chicago Tribune*, 18 July 1928, 29.

Beck, Frank O. *Hobohemia*. Ringe, N.H.: Richard R. Smith, 1956.

Butler, Sheppard. "Fate Helps Out a Bit at the Palace." *Chicago Tribune*, 1 Feb. 1922, 21.

Bruns, Roger A. *The Damndest Radical: The Life and World of Ben Reitman, Chicago's Celebrated Social Reformer, Hobo King, and Whorehouse Physician.* Urbana: University of Illinois Press, 1987.

"Can't Enforce 1 O'clock Order, Ettelson Holds." *Chicago Tribune*, 5 Mar. 1922, 3.

"Club on Study Tour Freed in Morals Court." *Chicago Tribune*, 18 Nov. 1930, 5.

Collin, Dorothy. "Can Bughouse Square Revive?" *Chicago Tribune*, 23 June 1980, C1.

"Cops Blew Inn at the Wind Blew Inn; It's Closed." *Chicago Tribune*, 24 Feb. 1922, 1.

"Cops Blow In the Wind Blew Inn; Blow Out with 40." *Chicago Tribune*, 12 Feb. 1922, 1.

"Friends Recall and Honor the Memory of Henry B. Fuller." *Chicago Tribune*, 18 Jan. 1930, 9.

Gregory Sprague Collection. Chicago Historical Museum, Chicago.

Hirschfeld, Magnus. "Sexual Reform on a Scientific Basis." *Earth*, March 1931.

"Hobohemia's Temple Burns." *Chicago Tribune*, 23 Apr. 1922, 10.

Hyde, Henry M. "Anarchist Book Shop in Chicago Radical's Mecca." *Chicago Tribune*, 11 May 1915, 13.

Leonard, William. "Chicago's New 'Left Bank.'" *Chicago Tribune*, 23 Nov. 1958, F27.

"Night Life Gets Tryout by Mr. Williamson." *Chicago Tribune*, 8 Mar. 1922, 1.

"'Petting Parties' in Wind Blew Inn?" *Chicago Tribune*, 15 Feb. 1922, 17.

Provines, June. "Front Views and Profiles." *Chicago Tribune*, 12 Oct. 1940, 17.

Reitman, Ben. "The Dill Pickle Club." *Chicago Times*, 22 Aug. 1937, n.p.

Rexroth, Kenneth. *An Autobiographical Novel*. New York: New Directions, 1964.

Rohm, Harland. "Breezes from the Lake." *Chicago Tribune*, 6 Feb. 1927, F2.

Rosemont, Franklin, ed. *The Rise and Fall of the Dil Pickle: Jazz-Age Chicago's Wildest and Most Outrageously Creative Hobohemian Nightspot.* Chicago: Charles H. Kerr, 2004.

"Seek to Make Cities Conscious of 'Little Paris.'" *Chicago Tribune*, 6 Mar. 1932, F3.

Twombly, Robert. *Louis Sullivan: His Life and Work*. Chicago: University of Chicago Press, 1986.

"U.S. Seizes WO Teuton Papers and 'Red Store.'" *Chicago Tribune*, 7 Sep. 1917, 1.

"Vaudeville Wit." *Chicago Tribune*, 6 Aug. 1916, G4.

"Wind Blew Inn Is Now Green Mask; Fight? Yep!" *Chicago Tribune*, 22 July 1922, 11.

Zorbaugh, Harvey W. *The Gold Coast and the Slum*. Chicago: University of Chicago Press, 1929.

## Chapter 8. Henry Gerber and the German Sex Reformers

Barbedette, Gilles, and Michel Carassou. *Paris Gay 1925*. Paris: Presses de la Renaissance, 1981.

Cornebise, Alfred E. *The Amaroc News: The Daily Newspaper of the American Forces in Germany, 1919–1923*. Carbondale: Southern Illinois University Press, 1981.

Gerber, Henry. "The Society for Human Rights—1925." *ONE* magazine 10, no. 9 (September 1962): 5–10. http://www.glapn.org/sodomylaws/usa/illinois/ilnews02.htm.

———. "Voice of the People: Are Indecent Shows Realistic?" *Chicago Tribune*, 2 Mar. 1925, 8.

"Germany: Bibliocaust." *Time*, 22 May 1933, n.p.

"Girl Reveals Strange Cult Run by Dad." *Chicago American*, 13 July 1925, 1.

Gregory Sprague Collection. Chicago History Museum, Chicago. Source of letters/ notes to/from/about Henry Gerber unless otherwise indicated.

Hirschfeld, Magnus. "Marriage Will Continue to Decrease." *Chicago Tribune*, 6 Jan. 1901, A37.

Lauritsen, John, and David Thorstad. *The Early Homosexual Rights Movement (1864–1935)*. New York: Times Change, 1974.

Schultz, Sigrid. "Berlin Youth, 22, Wins Right to Dress as a Girl; Herbert Is Now Hertha and Student Nurse." *Chicago Tribune*, 30 Mar. 1930, 22.

Schultz, Sigrid. "Girl Slayer of Two Babes Stirs German Science." *Chicago Tribune*, 31 Jan. 1927, 20.

## Chapter 9. Some in the Arts

"Among the New Books." *Chicago Tribune*, 1 Dec. 1901, 9.

Anonymous. Review of *Bertram Cope's Year*. *Outlook* magazine, 21 Jan. 1920.

Arrow Shirts newspaper ad. *Chicago Tribune*, 27 May 1929, 4.

"Art." *Chicago Tribune*, 26 December 1897, 42.

"Fashions in Books." *Chicago Tribune*, 23 Oct. 1892, 33.

"Friends Recall and Honor the Memory of Henry B. Fuller." *Chicago Tribune*, 18 Jan. 1930, 9.

Fuller, Henry Blake. *Bertram Cope's Year*. Chicago, 1919. Reprint, New York: Turtle Point, 1998; New York: Broadview, 2010.

Gilder, Jeannette L. "Extraordinary Cases." *Chicago Tribune*, 10 May 1896, 48.

"Given the Name 'High Bohemia.'" *Chicago Tribune*, 16 Feb. 1896, 12.

Hayes, Donald Jeffrey. "Young Poet Makes Plea for Freedom in Literature." *Chicago Defender*, 21 Apr. 1928, A1.

"Henry B. Fuller, Famous Chicago Novelist, Dies." *Chicago Tribune*, 29 July 1929, 27.

Henry Blake Fuller Papers. Newberry Library, Chicago.

"In and Out of the Women's Clubs." *Chicago Tribune*, 17 May 1897, 9.

Rascoe, Burton. "Saturday Page of Book News and Reviews." *Chicago Tribune*, 8 Nov. 1919, 13.

Senelick, Laurence. *Lovesick: Modernist Plays of Same-Sex Love, 1894–1925; At Saint Judas's* [Henry Blake Fuller]. London: Routledge, 1999.

"A Star That Will Brighten." *Chicago Tribune*, 5 Aug. 1929, 14.

"Tyros in Symbolic Role." *Chicago Tribune*, 19 May 1897, 5.

"Van Vechten, Novelist and Critic, Dies." *Chicago Tribune*, 22 Dec. 1964, B18.

## Chapter 10. The Blues and All That Jazz

"Big Benefit." *Chicago Defender*, 26 Feb. 1921, 4.

"Black Swan Jazz Babies are Great." *Chicago Defender*, 3 June 1922, 7.

"The Darktown Follies." *Chicago Defender*, 7 Mar. 1914, 6.

"Ethel Must Not Marry." *Chicago Defender*, 24 Dec. 1921, 7.

Gray, Eddie. "An Epistle." *Chicago Defender*, 3 Feb. 1917, 7.

"New York Society." *Chicago Defender*, 7 July 1923, 8.

"New York Society." *Chicago Defender*, 14 Mar. 1931, 11.

"New York Society." *Chicago Defender*, 30 Aug. 1930, 11.

"Obituary: Tony Jackson." *Chicago Defender*, 30 Apr. 1921, 8.

"On and Off the Stroll." *Chicago Defender*, 10 Oct. 1914, 6.

"Opens With Creole Jass Band at 11 O'Clock Each Night." *Chicago Defender*, 25 May 1918, 6.

"Pekin Beaux Arts Club Has Three Song Birds." *Chicago Defender*, 27 Apr. 1918, 6.

Rose, Al. *Storyville, New Orleans: Being an Authentic, Illustrated Account of the Notorious Red-Light District*. Tuscaloosa: University of Alabama Press.

Shapiro, Nat, and Nat Hentoff, eds. *Hear Me Talkin' to Ya: The Story of Jazz as Told by the Men Who Made It*. Mineola, N.Y.: Dover Publications, 1966.

Waters, Ethel. *His Eye Is on the Sparrow*. New York; Doubleday, 1951.

## Chapter 11. Powder Puffs

Bulmer, Martin. *The Chicago School of Sociology: Institutionalization, Diversity, and the Rise of Sociological Research.* Chicago: University of Chicago Press, 1984.

Cassidy, Claudia. "On the Aisle: Mae West as a Connoisseur, Pronounced Sewer, of Amour." *Chicago Tribune*, 13 Mar. 1945, 13.

Ernest Burgess Collection. University of Chicago. Source of reports by Burgess's students unless otherwise indicated.

Gregory Sprague Collection. Chicago History Museum, Chicago.

"Powder Puffing Men Lauded by Beauty Doctors." *Chicago Tribune*, 3 Aug. 1926, 2.

"Pansy Parlors—Tough Chicago Has Epidemic of Male Butterflies." *Variety*, 10 Dec. 1930, n.p.

"Pink Powder Puffs." *Chicago Tribune*, 18 July 1926, 10.

Provines, June. "Front Views and Profiles." *Chicago Tribune*, 9 July 1934, 15.

———. "Front Views and Profiles." *Chicago Tribune*, 20 July 1934, 21.

Shaffer, Rosalind. "Souvenir Fiends Loot Sennett Lot." *Chicago Tribune*, 13 May 1928, G6.

Sprague, Gregory. "Chicago's Past: A Rich Gay History." *Advocate*, 18 Aug. 1983, n.p.

Tinee, Mae. "Fleeting Glimpses of Sacred Son of Italy in This Film." *Chicago Tribune*, 11 Feb. 1923, D1.

Valentino, Rudolph. "To the Man (?) Who Wrote the Editorial Headed 'Pink Powder Puffs'" in Sunday's *Tribune*." *Chicago Herald-Examiner*, 19 July 1926.

"Valentino Seeking Fight with Editor." *New York Times*, 21 July 1926.

Wolfe, W. Beran. "The Riddle of Homosexuality." *Modern Thinker*, Apr. 1932.

"Writer of Plays Casts Himself in Real Life Role." *Chicago Tribune*, 4 Apr. 1931, 19.

## Chapter 12. Gay Life in the 1930s

The primary sources include the author's interviews with Jim Wickliff, Sam, Charles B., and others. Some sections of the interviews appeared in the column "Chicago Whispers" in *Outlines* between 3 Dec. 1997 and 13 Sep. 2000 and in *Windy City Times* between 20 Sep. 2000 and 28 Jan. 2004.

Asbury, Herbert. *Gem of the Prairie: An Informal History of the Chicago Under-world.* 1940. Reprint, Dekalb: Northern Illinois University Press, 1986.

"Ban 'Children's Hour' by Direction of Mayor." *Chicago Daily News*, 9 Jan. 1936, 1.

"City Fights Vice Dens Masked as Massage Shops." *Chicago Tribune*, 26 Oct. 1933, 9.

Curtin, Kaier. *We Can Always Call Them Bulgarians: The Emergence of Lesbians and Gay Men on the American Stage.* Boston: Alyson, 1987.

Donaghey, Frederick. "This Thing and That Thing of the Theater." *Chicago Tribune*, 28 Feb. 1926, F1.

———. "This Thing and That Thing of the Theater." *Chicago Tribune*, 14 Nov. 1926, E1.

Ernest Burgess Collection. University of Chicago. Source of reports by Burgess's students unless otherwise indicated.

"Freeman Opens Final Institute Benefit Tonight." *Chicago Tribune*, 11 Mar. 1934, W2.

Gregory Sprague Collection. Chicago History Museum, Chicago.

Joseph, John. "*Sin of Sins* Brings Strange Fish into Adelphi Aquarium." *Chicago Herald-Examiner*, 9 Nov. 1926, n.p.

"Launch Tavern Cleanup War to Stamp Out Vice." *Chicago Tribune*, 9 Dec. 1934, 1.

Mantle, Burns. "Lillian Hellman Causes Second Dramatic Stir." *Chicago Tribune*, 26 Feb. 1939, E2.

Pick, Grant. "Tempo: Paul Goldman; Fifty Years of Defending Gays." *Chicago Tribune*, 17 Nov. 1979, S15.

"Revoke License of Bath House on Morals Charge." *Chicago Tribune*, 13 Mar. 1936, 4.

"Search in Banks Yields $110, 860 in 'Modest' Estate." *Chicago Tribune*, 22 Apr. 1947, 20.

Tinee, Mae. "Here's a Film That Anybody Should Like: Maedchen in Uniform." *Chicago Tribune*, 15 Nov. 1932, 17.

## Chapter 13. Bronzeville

The primary sources include the author's interviews with an anonymous African American playwright, Tony "Toni" Midnite, and others. Some sections of the interviews appeared in the column "Chicago Whispers" in *Outlines* between 3 Dec. 1997 and 13 Sep. 2000 and in *Windy City Times* between 20 Sep. 2000 and 28 Jan. 2004.

"37th Annual Finnie Ball Attracts Thousands." *Chicago Defender*, 11 Nov. 1972, 14.

Akins, Doug. "Now You See HER—Now You See HIM!" *Chicago Defender*, 7 Nov. 1974, 20.

"The Architect's Conception of Rev. Cobbs's New $55,000 Church." *Chicago Defender*, 8 July 1939, 9.

"Big Benefit." *Chicago Defender*, 26 Feb. 1921, 4.

"Bishop, Convicted On Morals Charge, Freed." *Chicago Defender*, 21 Dec. 1940, 1.

"Bishop, Facing Morals Charge, Tells Crowded Court Jesus Is His Lawyer." *Chicago Defender*, 9 Mar. 1940, 3.

"Bishop Threatens Suicide." *Chicago Defender*, 2 Mar. 1940, 1.

"Boy Changes Story About 'Queer St.'" *Chicago Defender*, 10 Feb. 1951, 1.

"Boy Meets 'Girl' at Hallowe'en Ball." *Chicago Defender*, 10 Nov. 1951, 3.

Bragg, Columbus. "On and off the Stroll." *Chicago Defender*, 10 Oct. 1914, 6.

"'Bullfrog Shorty' To Be Married at the Cabin Inn." *Chicago Defender*, 3 Oct. 1935, n.p.

Burley, Dan. "Bares New Moves in Vice System Operating in City." *Chicago Defender*, 24 Jan. 1959, 9.

"Cabin Inn's Revue Still Town's Talk." *Chicago Defender*, 4 Nov. 1939, n.p.

"Classifying a 'Sissy.'" *Chicago Defender*, 20 Jun. 1914, 3.

"Cobbs Settles Libel Case." *Chicago Defender*, 22 Mar. 1941, 1.

"Cocktails Get Female Impersonator in 'Dutch.'" *Chicago Defender*, 15 July 1939, 24.

"Continuances Granted in Vice Case." *Chicago Defender*, 15 Mar. 1966, 5.

Dancer, Maurice. "'Gloria Swanson' Buried in Harlem." *Chicago Defender*, 4 May 1940, 21.

Drake, St. Clair, and Horace R. Clayton. *Black Metropolis: A Study of Negro Life in a Northern City*. New York: Harcourt Brace, 1945.

Duckett, Alfred. "'Third Sex' Starts This Issue." *Chicago Defender*, 9 Feb. 1957, 1.

———. "'Third Sex' Starts This Issue." *Chicago Defender*, 16 Feb. 1957, 1.

———. "'Third Sex' Starts This Issue." *Chicago Defender*, 23 Feb. 1957, 11.

———. "'Third Sex' Starts This Issue." *Chicago Defender*, 2 Mar. 1957, 7.

———. "'Third Sex' Starts This Issue." *Chicago Defender*, 9 Mar. 1957, 11.

"Female Impersonators Hold Costume Ball." *Ebony*, Mar. 1952, 62–67.

"Finnie's Ball Is Slated for Halloween." *Chicago Defender*, 28 Oct. 1967, 20.

"Finnie's Club Ball at Coliseum Oct. 31." *Chicago Defender*, 20 Oct. 1960, A20.

"Finnie's Club Plans Masquerade Ball." *Chicago Defender*, 21 Oct. 1957, 17.

"Gala Extravaganza Features 25 Men and One Woman." *Chicago Defender*, 2 Apr. 1960, 26.

"GIs Like All-Girl's Band." *Chicago Defender*, 15 Dec. 1945, 14.

"Grand Masque Ball." *Chicago Defender*, 30 Nov. 1912, 5.

"Here from Kansas City." *Chicago Defender*, 17 May 1930, 6.

"Hold Bishop on Immorality Charge of Boy." *Chicago Defender*, 24 Feb. 1940, 12.

"Impersonators Have Their Night amid Pumpkins, Music, Noise." *Chicago Defender*, 14 Nov. 1953, 20.

"'Jewel Box Revue' Awes Theatre Goers." *Chicago Defender*, 10 Sep. 1960, 19.

"Jewel Box Revue Has Wo-Man Star." *Chicago Defender*, 21 Oct. 1961, 10.

"Jewel Box Revue Hits Tivoli Stage April 1." *Chicago Defender*, 8 Mar. 1960, A16.

"Jewel Box Revue in Last 'Regal' Week." *Chicago Defender*, 17 May 1966, 10.

"Joe's Deluxe Club Gets Praise for New Number." *Chicago Defender*, 3 Oct. 1943, n.p.

"'Mae West' to Invade the Coast." *Chicago Defender*, 19 Oct. 1935, 9.

McKay, Clifford W. "Going Backstage With the Scribe." *Chicago Defender*, 23 May 1931, 5.

"'Midget Shorty' Bunch to Wed Oct. 15 at Cabin Inn." *Chicago Defender*, 12 Oct. 1935, n.p.

"The Monogram." *Chicago Defender*, 23 Dec. 1911, 7.

"Night Club Parade Gay with Music, Song." *Chicago Defender*, 23 Feb. 1952, 22.

"Opens with Creole Jass Band at 11 O'Clock Each Night." *Chicago Defender*, 25 May 1918, 6.

"Original Finnie's Club." *Chicago Defender*, 21 Oct. 1972, 14.

Orro, David. "Six Sleuths Put on Trail of Shocking Rumors in Rev. Cobbs 'Scandal.'" *Chicago Defender*, 2 Dec. 1939.

"Pekin Beaux Arts Club Has Three Song Birds." *Chicago Defender*, 27 Apr. 1918, 6.

"Petite Swanson at Ritz Cafe in Pittsburgh." *Chicago Defender*, 26 Mar. 1938, 18.

"Prize Winning Hallowe'en Impersonators." *Chicago Defender*, 9 Nov. 1957, 18.

"'Queer St.' Den Found by Police." *Chicago Defender*, 3 Feb. 1951, 1.

"Radio Pastor Sues *Defender* for $250,000; Says 'Virtue and Integrity Were Injured.'" *Chicago Defender*, 9 Dec. 1939, 9.

"Rev. Cobb [*sic*] Denies Scandal; Defends Self against Rumors in Broadcast." *Chicago Defender*, 18 Nov. 1939, 1.

"Rev. Cobbs Breaks Ground for New Church." *Chicago Defender*, 3 June 1939, 7.

"Rev. Cobbs Halts Service to Oust *Defender* Scribe." *Chicago Defender*, 26 Oct. 1940, 7.

"Rev. Taylor Trial Oct. 7." *Chicago Defender*, 5 Oct. 1940, 9.

Roy, Robert. "Behind the Scenes." *Chicago Defender*, 8 Nov. 1960, 23.

See, Hilda. "Female Impersonators' Rule Many Floor Shows." *Chicago Defender*, 12 Sep. 1936, 21.

"See Jam for Finnie's Big Ball Tonight." *Chicago Defender*, 31 Oct. 1960, A17.

"Sepia Mae West Returns." *Chicago Defender*, 14 July 1934, 9.

Shirley, Thelma Hunt. "Death Breaks Strong Bond." *Chicago Defender*, 16 Jan. 1965, 1.

"State's Attorney Probes Scandal on Rev. Cobb." *Chicago Defender*, 25 Nov. 1939, 1.

Ston, Ted. "Jewel Box Revue Back at Roberts by Demand." *Chicago Defender*, 24 Feb. 1958, A18.

Thompson, Nathan. *Kings: The True Story of Chicago's Policy Kings and Numbers Racketeers: An Informal History.* Chicago: Bronzeville, 2003.

"Tid-Bits of New York Society." *Chicago Defender*, 16 Nov. 1929, 11.

"Tid-Bits of New York Society." *Chicago Defender*, 22 Mar. 1930, 11.

"The Truth about 'Sin Corner.'" *Chicago Defender*, 2 Mar. 1961, 1.

"Weber's Theatre." *Chicago Defender*, 18 Feb. 1911, 4.

## Chapter 14. World War II and
## the 1940s

The primary sources include the author's interviews with LeRoi, Charles B., Jacqui O'Shea, Frank W., and others. Some sections of the interviews appeared in the column "Chicago Whispers" in *Outlines* between 3 Dec. 1997 and 13 Sep. 2000 and in *Windy City Times* between 20 Sep. 2000 and 28 Jan. 2004.

"2 Taverns Stripped of Permits; Report Sex, Dope Violations." *Chicago Tribune*, 29 July 1949, 9.
"2 North Side Taverns Lose Licenses after Police Cleanup Drive." *Chicago Tribune*, 13 Jan. 1949, 18.
"3 Bartenders Fined as Result of Raid on Windup Bar." *Chicago Tribune*, 5 Feb. 1949, A4.
"6 Arrested in Vice Raid on N. State St. Demand Jury Trials." *Chicago Tribune*, 22 Jan. 1949, 9. "Bartender Seized by Police in Morals Raid Is Fined $100." *Chicago Tribune*, 3 Feb. 1949, B3.
"Bath House Inmate Gets 90 Days and $100 Fine: 2 Others Freed." *Chicago Tribune*, 1 Mar. 1949, 14.
Bérubé, Allan. *Coming Out under Fire: The History of Gay Men and Women in World War Two*. New York: Free Press, 1990.
"Capt. Harrison Jails 24 in War on Degenerates." *Chicago Tribune*, 17 Jan. 1949, 31.
"Connelly, Tom, and Bill Drury. "Vice Dive Owner." *Chicago Herald-American*, 10 Jan. 1949, n.p.
"Continue Hearings of 86 Men Arrested in Police Vice Raid." *Chicago Tribune*, 11 Jan. 1949, 19.
"Dive Keepers on N. Clark St. Get Warnings." *Chicago Tribune*, 14 Nov. 1948, 15.
Duis, Perry, and Scott La France. *We've Got a Job to Do: Chicagoans and World War II*. Chicago: Chicago Historical Society, 1992.
"File Charges against 87 in Vice Net." *Chicago Tribune*, 10 Jan. 1949, 1.
"Homosexuals in Uniform." *Newsweek*, 9 June 1947, n.p.
"Inmate Gets 90 Days and $100 Fine: 2 Others Freed." *Chicago Tribune*, 1 Mar. 1949, 14.
Lait, Jack, and Lee Mortimer. *Chicago: Confidential!* New York: Crown, 1950.
Olkon, D. M., and Irene Case Sherman. "Eonism with Added Outstanding Psychopathic Features: A Unique Psychopathological Case." *Journal of Nervous and Mental Disease* 99, no. 2 (1944): 159–67.
"Primrose Path Tavern Sold by U.S. for $8,550." *Chicago Tribune*, 6 Feb. 1948.
"Tower Ticker." *Chicago Tribune*, 14 Jan. 1949, 23.
"Tower Ticker." *Chicago Tribune*, 17 Feb. 1949, 21.
"Tower Ticker." *Chicago Tribune*, 29 June 1949, 23.

"Woman Tavern Owner Slugged, Robbed of $200." *Chicago Tribune*, 8 Jan. 1945, 21.

## Chapter 15. The Cold War

"Chicago Woman Held for Quiz in 'Dahlia' Case." *Chicago Tribune*, 5 Mar. 1947, 32.

"Dirksen Tells of 'Destroyers' in Federal Jobs." *Hollywood Citizen-News*, 23 Sep. 1954, n.p.

"Doctors Doubt Sex Perversion Senate Figures." *Chicago Tribune*, 21 May 1950, 4.

Doherty, James. "Expert Debunks Reasons Given for Sex Crimes." *Chicago Tribune*, 28 Nov. 1949, 20.

Edwards, Willard. "Assert Truman 'Gag' Is Hiding Moral Laxities." *Chicago Tribune*, 26 Mar. 1950, 5.

———. "Senators Told of Immorality in Washington." *Chicago Tribune*, 30 Mar. 1950, 1.

———. "Sen. McCarthy Marries His Ex-Secretary as FBI Watches 2,500 Cheer in Streets." *Chicago Tribune*, 30 Sep. 1953.

"FBI Secret Files Tell Tales of Sex and Politics." *Chicago Tribune*, 13 Dec. 1983, C10.

"Gays Win Big Round in U.S. Jobs Equality." *Chicago Tribune*, 4 July 1975, 11.

Greenspun, Hank. "The Secret Lives of Joe McCarthy." *Rave*, June 1954, 58–72.

———. "Where I Stand." *Las Vegas Sun*, 25 Oct. 1952, n.p.

Gregory Sprague Collection. Chicago Historical Museum. Source of Civil Service Commission: reports about and interview with Bruce Chardon Scott, 1962; Scott's police arrest report, October 1951; appeal of decision by CSC not to hire Scott, 1962; *Scott v. Macy* [CSC], 1963–65.

"History of the Mattachine Society." *Mattachine Review* 1, no. 2 (Mar.–Apr. 1955).

Hoey, Sen. Clyde. *Employment of Homosexuals and Other Sex Perverts in Government*. Washington, D.C.: U.S. G.P.O.

Holley, Val. *Mike Connolly and the Manly Art of Hollywood Gossip*. Jefferson, N.C.: McFarland & Co., 2003.

Hoover, J. Edgar. "How Safe Is Your Daughter?" *American Magazine* 144 (July 1947): 32–33, 102–4.

Johnson, David K. *The Lavender Scare: The Cold War Persecution of Gays and Lesbians in the Federal Government*. Chicago: University of Chicago Press, 2004.

"National Affairs: The Alger Hiss Issue." *Time*, 3 Nov. 1952, n.p.

Pearson, Drew. "The Washington Merry-Go-Round." *Washington Post*, 15 Dec. 1953.

"Sex Offenders in Majority, Board Reports." *Chicago Tribune*, 22 Apr. 1953, 14.

Stevenson, Adlai. Speech in opposition to the Broyles bill of 1950. In *The Papers of Adlai E. Stevenson*, vol. 3, ed. Walter Johnson (Boston: Little, Brown, 1973), 412–18.

Swearingen, M. Wesley. *FBI Secrets: An Agent's Exposé*. Boston: South End Press, 1994.

Thompson, John H. "Doctors Agree Sex Offense not Increasing." *Chicago Tribune*, 9 Apr. 1950, 42.

## Chapter 16. Masculinity and the Physique Culture

The primary sources include the author's interviews with G. F. H., Charles "Chuck" Renslow, and others. Some sections of the interviews appeared in the column "Chicago Whispers" in *Outlines* between 3 Dec. 1997 and 13 Sep. 2000 and in *Windy City Times* between 20 Sep. 2000 and 28 Jan. 2004.

"5 Sentenced in Mail Club Case; 2 to Jail." *Chicago Tribune*, 3 Mar. 1962, A2.

"12 Plead Not Guilty to 'Pen Pal' Obscenity." *Chicago Tribune*, 7 Feb. 1961, B13.

"13 in Smut Club Plead: Guilt Admitted by 1." *Chicago Tribune*, 16 Feb. 1961, 16.

"16 Are Given New Trials on Smut Charges." *Chicago Tribune*, 20 Jan. 1960, B3.

"Bakery Worker Pleads Guilty to Smut Charge." *Chicago Tribune*, 22 Mar. 1961, 15.

"Ballet Company Will Perform in Woodstock." *Chicago Tribune*, 23 Apr. 1967, 3.

"Ballet Group Will Present 'Snow White.'" *Chicago Tribune*, 1 Dec. 1960, N9.

"Ballet Guild to Present Original Program May 19." *Chicago Tribune*, 5 May 1957, E14.

"Bans 'Adults Only' Tag on Films in City." *Chicago Tribune*, 25 Mar. 1959, A7.

"Books Seized in Smut Raid." *Chicago Tribune*, 24 July 1965, W7.

"Charges of Obscenity Dropped against Four." *Chicago Tribune*, 21 May 1966, 4.

"Communities Waging Fight against Smut." *Chicago Tribune*, 26 Mar. 1959, N6.

"Convict Three in Adonis Club; Two Teachers." *Chicago Tribune*, 2 Feb. 1962, 8.

Cromie, Robert. "Toklas Alone, Alive and Gossiping." *Chicago Tribune*, 10 Feb. 1974, F9.

"Dance Notes." *Chicago Tribune*, 26 Apr. 1970, G4.

"The Dance That Explores Man's Mind." *Chicago Tribune*, 6 Jan. 1963, C6.

"Debut of Martinus Sieveking." *Chicago Tribune*, 16 Nov. 1896, 1.

"Dom Orejudos Ballets to Be Given Friday." *Chicago Tribune*, 6 Jan. 1963, F8.

"Grab 253 Books, Magazines in Raid on Firm." *Chicago Tribune*, 15 Jan. 1960, 8.

"Gymnastics." *Chicago Tribune*, 7 Mar. 1864, 4.

Hooven, F. Valentine, III. *Beefcake: The Muscle Magazines of America, 1950–1970*. Cologne: Benedikt Taschen, 1995.

"Illinois Ballet Will Introduce 3 New Numbers." *Chicago Tribune*, 19 June 1960, D12.

Kennedy, Hubert. *The Ideal Gay Man: The Story of Der Kreis*. New York: Harrington Park, 1999.

Kinsey, Alfred C., Wardell B. Pomeroy, and Clyde E. Martin. *Sexual Behavior in the Human Male*. Philadelphia: W.B. Saunders Company, 1948.

Kling, William. "Chicago Gains in Its War on Smutty Books." *Chicago Tribune*, 27 July 1965, B15.

———. "Smut Sells Here Openly and Cheaply." *Chicago Tribune*, 25 July 1965, 3.

———. "Supreme Court's Liberality Paves Way for Peddlers of Smut." *Chicago Tribune*, 26 July 1965, 12.

"Manly Beauty." *Chicago Tribune*, 25 Feb. 1894, 14.

"Music and Drama." *Chicago Tribune*, 24 Oct. 1893, 6.

"News Agency Raided; Take 56 Magazines." *Chicago Tribune*, 18 Aug. 1959, 20.

"Notes of Dance World." *Chicago Tribune*, 2 May 1965, G8.

"Obscenity Law Held Illegal." *Chicago Tribune*, 11 Mar. 1960, 1.

Paschall, Harry B. "Let Me Tell You a Fairy Tale." *Strength and Health*, June 1957, n.p.

"Physical Culture." *Chicago Tribune*, 13 June 1860, o_1.

"Police Call a Magazine Lewd; Nab 5." *Chicago Tribune*, 27 Feb. 1959, 8.

"Police Probe Pornography." *Chicago Tribune*, 3 Mar. 1960.

"Police Seize 3 in Sale of Obscene Magazines." *Chicago Tribune*, 9 July 1959, 3.

"Police Seize Books in Raid on Publisher." *Chicago Tribune*, 5 Jan 1960, 12.

"Puts Pen Pal of Smut Ring on Probation." *Chicago Tribune*, 11 Apr. 1961, 12.

"Press, Public Barred from Sex Club Trial." *Chicago Tribune*, 19 Jan. 1962, 14.

"Sandow Says Her Figure Is the Most Perfect in the World." *Chicago Tribune*, 26 Mar. 1905, G1.

"Smut Is Feared as a Peril to Social Beliefs." *Chicago Tribune*, 28 July 1965, 19.

Sparrow, Phil [Samuel Steward]. "Letter to the Editor." *Chicago Tribune*, 14 Sep. 1959, 16.

Spring, Justin. *Secret Historian: The Life and Times of Samuel Steward, Professor, Tattoo Artist and Sexual Renegade*. New York: Farrar, Straus and Giroux, 2010.

Steward, Samuel M. *Chapters from an Autobiography*. San Francisco: Grey Fox Press, 1981.

———. *Dear Sammy: Letters from Gertrude Stein and Alice B. Toklas*. Boston: Houghton Mifflin, 1977.

"Stronger than Samson: A London Audience Amazed at an 'Unknown's' Feats of Strength." *Chicago Tribune*, 30 Oct. 1889, 1.

"Strongest Man in Greece." *Chicago Tribune*, 13 Mar. 1898, 43.

"Tattoo." *Chicago Tribune*, 11 July 1958, 12.

"Tattoo." *Chicago Tribune*, 27 Aug. 1959, 16.
"Teacher Gets Suspended on 'Smut' Charge." *Chicago Tribune*, 18 Jan. 1961, 21.
"Tell of Part in Club Facing Smut Charge." *Chicago Tribune*, 5 Jan. 1962, 10.
"They'll Dance 'Façade.'" *Chicago Tribune*, 1 Nov. 1959, F10.
"Thoughts and Afterthoughts." *Strength and Health*, May 1961, 15.
"Tieken Freed of Libel Suit in Adonis Case." *Chicago Tribune*, 21 Mar. 1962, A4.
"U.S. Indicts 53 in Breakup of 'Smut' Club." *Chicago Tribune*, 17 Jan. 1961, B2.
*U.S. v. Zuideveld*. C.A. Ill. 316 F.2d 873 (1963).
"Wife to Serve Term in Jail, Then Husband." *Chicago Tribune*, 11 Mar. 1964, B11.
"Woman Editor Seized in Book Raid Is Freed." *Chicago Tribune*, 16 Dec. 1960, D3.
Zuideveld, Jack. "Homosexuality . . . on the Increase." *Gym*, Apr. 1960, n.p.

## Chapter 17. Lesbian Pulp Paperbacks and Literature

Foster, Jeanette H. "Ann of 100,000 Words Plus." *The Ladder* 4, no. 11 (Aug. 1960), 7.
———. *Sex Variant Women in Literature*. 1956. Reprint, Tallahassee, Fla.: Naiad, 1985.
"Judge Stops Obscene Books Trial to Read Them." *Chicago Tribune*, 13 June 1952, 7.
Kotulak, Ronald. "Unique Colony in South Shore Due to Close." *Chicago Tribune*, 16 Aug. 1959, S2.
"Lesbiana" [review of *Evil Friendship* by Vin Packer]. *The Ladder* 3, no. 4 (Jan. 1959): 16.
Martin, Del. "Open Letter to Ann Aldrich." *The Ladder* 2, no. 7 (Apr. 1958): 4–6.
Meeker, Martin. "A Queer and Contested Medium: The Emergence of Representational Politics in the 'Golden Age' of Lesbian Paperbacks, 1955–1963." *Journal of Women's History* 17, no. 1 (2005): 165–88.
Passet, Joanne Ellen. *Sex Variant Woman: The Life of Jeannette Howard Foster*. New York, Da Capo, 2008.
Petersen, Clarence. "Paperbacks: Closing Up Shop." *Chicago Tribune*, 28 Aug. 1966, K9.
Stryker, Susan. *Queer Pulp: Perverted Passions from the Golden Age of the Paperback*. San Francisco: Chronicle, 2001.
Taylor, Valerie. *The Girls in 3-B*. New York: Gold Medal Books, 1959.
———. *Whisper Their Love*. Greenwich, Conn.: Fawcett Publications, 1957.
Terkell, Studs. *Coming of Age: The Story of Our Century by Those Who've Lived It*. New York: New Press, 1995.
Valerie Taylor Collection. Cornell University, Ithaca, N.Y.

## Chapter 18. Negro Arts and Literature

"About Gertrude Stein in Chicago for 'Four Saints in Three Acts.'" *Chicago American*, 7 Nov. 1934, n.p.

"About Gertrude Stein in Chicago for 'Four Saints in Three Acts.'" *Chicago American*, 8 Nov. 1934, n.p.

Algren, Nelson. "Motley Novel Tackles the Dope Problem." *Chicago Tribune*, 17 Aug. 1958, B1.

Atkinson, Brooks. "The Theatre: 'A Raisin in the Sun'; Negro Drama Given at Ethel Barrymore Theatre." *New York Times*, 12 Mar. 1959.

"Baldwin Discusses Hansberry's Works." *Chicago Defender*, 19 Nov. 1969, 15.

Berry, Faith. *Langston Hughes: Before and Beyond Harlem*. 1983. Reprint, New York: Carol Publishing Group, 1992.

"Bogart Will Introduce New Players in 'Knock on Any Door.'" *Chicago Defender*, 4 Sep. 1948, 9.

"Bontemps-Hughes Play Presented." *Chicago Defender*, 2 May 1936, 4.

Calloway, Earl. "'Raisin' is Fabulous." *Chicago Defender*, 27 Oct. 1973, 17.

———. "'To Be Young, Gifted and Black' Dramatic Fire Flickers and Dies." *Chicago Defender*, 25 Feb. 1974, 12.

Carter, Art. "'Raisin' Makes Broadway History." *Chicago Defender*, 27 Apr. 1974, B14.

Cassidy, Claudia. "On the Aisle." *Chicago Tribune*, 21 Mar. 1965, A16.

Chapman, John. "'A Raisin in the Sun' a Glowingly Lovely and Touching Little Play." *New York Daily News*, 12 Mar. 1959.

"Chicago Author Said near Death in Mexico." *Chicago Defender*, 3 Mar. 1965, 3.

"Chicago Will See Hughes New Play." *Chicago Defender*, 5 Nov. 1938, 5.

"Columbia to Film Another Motley Story." *Chicago Defender*, 2 Apr. 1958, 17.

Cullen, Countee. "Poet on Poet." Review of *The Weary Blues* by Langston Hughes. *Opportunity* 4 (Feb. 1926): 73.

Duckett, Alfred. "Langston Hughes' 'Simply Heavenly' Gay, Tuneful and Comic-Crazed Hit." *Chicago Defender*, 1 June 1957, 9.

Dumetz, Louise P. "Lush!" *Chicago Defender*, 27 Mar. 1965, 10.

Ewald, William. "Lorraine Hansberry to Write TV Script." *Chicago Defender*, 20 June 1959, 18.

Gaver, Jack. "'Raisin in the Sun' Author Has Her Say about Route to Broadway." *Chicago Defender*, 4 Apr. 1959, 18.

"Hit Play 'A Raisin in the Sun' Back in Chicago for Repeat Run." *Chicago Defender*, 25 Feb. 1961, 18.

"'Honey' Drawing Throngs to Cinema Theatre." *Chicago Defender*, 24 July 1962, 16.

Hughes, Langston. "Conversation after Midnight." *Chicago Defender*, 13 Feb. 1943, 14.

———. "Here to Yonder." *Chicago Defender*, 21 Nov. 1942, 1.

———. "Negro Amateur Theatres Have Developed Talent." *Chicago Defender*, 9 May 1953, 11.

———. "Week By Week." *Chicago Defender*, 14 Mar. 1959, 10.

Klinkowitz, Jerome, ed. *The Diaries of Willard Motley*. Ames: Iowa State University Press, 1979.

"'Knock on Any Door' Is Expected to Really Hit the Jack Pot." *Chicago Defender*, 13 Nov. 1948, 17.

"'Knock on Any Door' Purchased for Film." *Chicago Defender*, 11 Oct. 1947, 19.

"Langston Hughes Driven Out of Japan." *Chicago Defender*, 29 July 1933, 1.

"Langston Hughes Extols Communist Party." *Chicago Defender*, 25 June 1932, 2.

"Langston Hughes' Play to Broadway." *Chicago Defender*, 19 Oct. 1935, 9.

LHN [Lorraine Hansberry]. "Letter to the Editor." *The Ladder* 1, no. 8 (May 1957): 27–28.

"Lorraine Hansberry, 34, Dies: Penned 'Raisin.'" *Chicago Defender*, 13 Jan. 1965, 1.

"Lorraine Hansberry Guest at WSA of Roosevelt Achievement Fete." *Chicago Defender*, 14 May 1959, 17.

"Lorraine Hansberry Near Death." *Chicago Defender*, 24 Oct. 1964, 1.

Monroe, Al. "'Raisin in the Sun' Brighter in Homecoming." *Chicago Defender*, 11 Mar. 1961, 18.

Millender, Naomi. "Great Black Women: Hansberry: Playwright." *Chicago Defender*, 13 Aug. 1970, 18.

Motley, Willard. "First Bud Billiken Tells about Himself after 15 Years." *Chicago Defender*, 17 Feb. 1940, 19.

———. "Hull House Neighborhood." *Hull House* magazine, Nov. 1939, n.p.

———. *Knock on Any Door*. New York: Appleton-Century-Crofts, Inc., 1947.

"Motley Balks Plan to Rewrite His 'Knock on Any Door' for Films." *Chicago Defender*, 13 Mar. 1948, 8.

"Motley's Cyst." *Chicago Defender*, 25 Mar. 1965, 12.

"New Englanders Hail 'A Raisin in the Sun.'" *Chicago Defender*, 27 Jan. 1959, 42.

"New Hansberry Play Coming." *Chicago Defender*, 2 Nov. 1963, 10.

Patterson, Lindsay. "Personalities in the News: Lorraine Hansberry's Loves." *Chicago Defender*, 19 Jan. 1965, 9.

Perry, Shauneille. "How 'Raisin' Got Started to Stage." *Chicago Defender*, 21 Feb. 1959, 1.

———. "Miss Hansberry Makes History." *Chicago Defender*, 14 Feb. 1959, 1.

"'Raisin in Sun' at Carver High Fri., May 11." *Chicago Defender*, 9 May 1962, 16.

"'Raisin in Sun' Moves to New Broadway House." *Chicago Defender*, 24 Oct. 1959, 18.

"'A Raisin in the Sun' Opens at Blackstone Night of February 10." *Chicago Defender*, 2 Feb. 1959, 19.

"Robeson Gives Eulogy at Hansberry Rites." *Chicago Defender*, 18 Jan. 1965, 8.

Saunders, Doris. "Friends Remember Langston Hughes at S. S. Art Center." *Chicago Defender*, 1 June 1967, 22.

Saunders, Doris E. "Hansberry Work Off-Broadway Author Tribute." *Chicago Defender*, 4 Feb. 1969, 17.

"Schedule Mass Here for Author Willard Motley." *Chicago Defender*, 8 Mar. 1965, 7.

Scott, Lillian. "Motley's 'Knock on Any Door': Acting Is Great, Pix Mediocre." *Chicago Defender*, 5 Mar. 1949, 16.

"Secret Divorce Revealed by Hansberry Will." *Chicago Defender*, 10 Feb. 1965, 13.

"Short Story." *Chicago Defender*, 23 Sep. 1922, 14.

"'Sign' to Open Friday at Studebaker Theater." *Chicago Defender*, 20 Mar. 1965, 10.

"Skylofters' Drama Will Honor Langston Hughes." *Chicago Defender*, 27 Mar. 1948, 8.

"Skylofters Polish Up 2nd Play." *Chicago Defender*, 18 Nov. 1950, 21.

Smith, Homer. "Race Prejudice Finds No Sanctuary in Russia." *Chicago Defender*, 4 Mar. 1933, 10.

Stamper, "Steam." "Langston Hughes Play Not Wanted in Quaker Town." *Chicago Defender*, 20 Feb. 1937, 21.

Stephens, Louise. "$64 Question? Is 'Knock on Any Door' Too Hot for Hollywood!" *Chicago Defender*, 7 Mar. 1948, 1.

"'Taste of Honey' to Feature New Negro Star." *Chicago Defender*, 30 Nov. 1963, 10.

"'To Be Young, Gifted and Black' Booked for Goodman." *Chicago Defender*, 8 Dec. 1973, 18.

Watkins, Robert [Bud Billiken]. "Young Folks." *Chicago Defender*, 2 Apr. 1921, 5.

Watson, Steven. *Prepare for Saints: Gertrude Stein, Virgil Thompson, and the Mainstreaming of American Modernism.* New York: Random House, 1998.

Weaver, Audrey. "City Plays Host to 'Raisin'" Cast. *Chicago Defender*, 11 July 1960, A2.

"Willard Motley Still Critical." *Chicago Defender*, 4 Mar. 1965, 4.

## Chapter 19. The Night Life

The primary sources include the author's interviews with Blondina, Mame, Bic Carrol, Tessie, Cab Driver Joey, Vicki St. John, Ron "Polish Princess" Helizon, Old Marlene, and others. Some sections of the interviews appeared in the column "Chicago Whispers" in *Outlines* between 3 Dec. 1997 and 13 Sep. 2000 and in *Windy City Times* between 20 Sep. 2000 and 28 Jan. 2004.

"2 Ask Damages for Beating in Rush St. Club." *Chicago Tribune*, 5 Mar. 1963, 2.

"2 Captains Face Quiz Today." *Chicago Tribune*, 30 Jan. 1953, 1.

"2 More Teachers in Raid Quit; Others off Duty." *Chicago Tribune*, 28 Apr. 1964, A6.

"3 Patrolmen and Sergeant Are Suspended." *Chicago Tribune*, 4 Nov. 1949, 9.

"3 Shot in Bar on North Side; Hunt Suspect." *Chicago Tribune*, 15 Nov. 1962, C4.

"3 Women, 6 Men Seized in Vice Raids." *Chicago Sun-Times*, 29 Apr. 1964, 58.

"5 Bar Owners, Defy Jury in Rush St. Quiz." *Chicago Tribune*, 9 Oct. 1959, 20.

"5 Shotgun Blasts Break Bellwood Bar Windows." *Chicago Tribune*, 2 Nov. 1949, B9.

"32 Seized in Raid on North Side Bath." *Chicago Tribune*, 6 Mar. 1966, 7.

"33 Men Seized thru Vice Raid on Bathhouse." *Chicago Tribune*, 14 June 1964, 22.

"98 Arrested in Fun Lounge Raid Are Freed." *Chicago Tribune*, 16 May 1964, S7.

"Area Teachers among 109 Seized in Raid on Vice Den." *Chicago Sun-Times*, 26 Apr. 1964, n.p.

Beckman, Aldo, and Sandy Smith. "Vice Thriving on Clark St." *Chicago Tribune*, 9 Oct. 1961, 1.

"Bellwood Raids and Closes Bar Twice in a Day." *Chicago Tribune*, 9 Oct. 1949, A11.

"Boards to Get Vice Raid Data on 8 Teachers." *Chicago Tribune*, 27 Apr. 1964, 3.

"Boyles Aids Raid Leyden Township Tavern: Seize Owner." *Chicago Tribune*, 23 Oct. 1949, 9.

Bronté, Patricia. "Chicago's Fabulous Village." *Chicago Tribune*, 14 Dec. 1952, D7.

———. *Vittles and Vice*. Chicago: Henry Regnery, 1952.

Buck, Thomas. "Tour Finds Vice Booming, Bold on Near N. Side." *Chicago Tribune*, 13 Apr. 1951, 13.

"Captain New, But It's Still N. Clark." *Chicago Sun-Times*, 8 July 1951, 3.

"Charge Former Court Officer with Robbery." *Chicago Tribune*, 26 Dec. 1954, 24.

"City Revokes 8 Licenses; 6 Are Taverns." *Chicago Tribune*, 7 June 1968, 20.

"Cop Arrests 5 in Raid at 7 W. Division." *Chicago Tribune*, 6 July 1962, 13.

"Crime Group Assails Honky Tonks 'Graft.'" *Chicago Tribune*, 9 May 1950, 1.

"Double Blast Kills Barkeep, Injures Two." *Chicago Tribune*, 29 Jan. 1960, A1.

"Fined $50 as Keeper of Disorderly House." *Chicago Tribune*, 24 July 1964, 15.

"Five Fined a Total of $300 and Costs in Gambling Cases." *Chicago Tribune*, 26 Aug. 1948, B8.

"Four Taverns Lose Licenses to Sell Liquor." *Chicago Tribune*, 27 Mar. 1964, C9.

"Fun Lounge Finds Things Get Unhappy." *Chicago Tribune*, 9 Oct. 1962, A9.

"Hear Bedwell Extradition Case March 25." *Chicago Tribune*, 12 Mar. 1957, A8.

"Hint Gang Link in Barkeep's Slaying in Car." *Chicago Tribune*, 9 Nov. 1961, A6.

"Keeper Fined in Vice Raid on Lincoln Baths." *Chicago Tribune*, 20 Apr. 1966, A11.

"Lie Test Clears Business Man in Rinearson Case." *Chicago Tribune*, 17 Dec. 1949, 2.

"Mayor Takes Licenses from Two Taverns." *Chicago Tribune*, 9 Jan. 1954, A7.

"Nab 4 Women in Rush St. Raid." *Chicago Tribune*, 5 Mar. 1964, 17.

"Nab 36 Women, 28 Men in Vice Raid on Tavern." *Chicago Tribune*, 17 Feb. 1952, 39.

"Nab Women in Raid." *Chicago Tribune*, 8 Nov. 1964, 3.

"Ogilvie Says He'd Padlock Fun Lounge." *Chicago Tribune*, 8 Oct. 1962, B14.

"Plan to Curb B-Girls Wins Council Test." *Chicago Tribune*, 20 Mar. 1964, B11.

"Police Arrest 17 Persons in 4 Vice Raids." *Chicago Tribune*, 8 Jan. 1965, A8.

"Police Clerk Arrested in Vice Raid Resigns." *Chicago Tribune*, 7 May 1964, D2.

"Police Focus Interest on 20 Recent Killings. *Chicago Tribune*, 30 Oct. 1951, B9.

"Police Puzzled by Park Murder of Choir Singer." *Chicago Tribune*, 14 Apr. 1951, 11.

"Police Raid Tavern Giving Indecent Show." *Chicago Tribune*, 4 July 1954, 9.

"Police Seize 40 in Raid at Rush St. Inn: Witness Two Men Kissing and Move In." *Chicago Tribune*, 27 Mar. 1962, B5.

Powers, Thomas. "New Rush Street Cop Pledges to Reduce Vice, Gaming in Area." *Chicago Tribune*, 8 May 1966, 3.

"Professor Assails Wholesale Vice Arrests." *Chicago Daily News*, 11 May 1964, n.p.

"Raid Reveals Big Vice Bar Profit." *Chicago Tribune*, 17 Mar. 1966, A2.

"Revoke Permits of 5 Taverns in Hudson District." *Chicago Tribune*, 25 Feb. 1953, 21.

"School Districts Acting against 9 Teachers Seized in Narcotics Raid." *Chicago Daily News*, 27 April 1964, n.p.

"Seize 10 Men, 3 Women in Vice, Gaming Raids." *Chicago Tribune*, 29 Apr. 1964, C14.

"Seven Men Sentenced for Moral Offenses." *Chicago Tribune*, 1 July 1964, C16.

"Sex Party—58 Are Seized, Including Two Juveniles." *Chicago Tribune*, 4 May 1964, 2.

"Shot Fighting Policeman in Jackson Park." *Chicago Tribune*, 11 Aug. 1951, 3.

Smith, Sandy. "Wilson Backs His Captain in Vice Scandal." *Chicago Tribune*, 12 Oct. 1961, A8.

"Sues over Fun Lounge Arrest." *Chicago Tribune*, 12 June 1964, 14.

"Teacher, 1 of 8 Seized in Vice Raid, Quits." *Chicago Tribune*, 26 Apr. 1964, 1.

"Tells How Mob Is Preying on Sex Deviates." *Chicago Tribune*, 15 Mar. 1966, 7.

"Trace Actions of Choir Singer before Slaying." *Chicago Tribune*, 15 Apr. 1951, 26.

"Two Taverns Lose Licenses, Two Suspended." *Chicago Tribune*, 4 Mar. 1964, 2.

"Vice Charges Filed against 58 in Bar Raid." *Chicago Tribune*, 31 Dec. 1951, B7.

"Voids Licenses of Club 51 and Magic Lounge." *Chicago Tribune*, 5 Feb. 1963, 22.

Wiedrich, Robert. "Nab 14 in Raid on Near North Side Lounge." *Chicago Tribune*, 29 Jan. 1968, C8.

"Wilson Wars on B-Girls; 3 Bars Shut." *Chicago Tribune*, 3 Mar. 1964, 1.

"Zuckerman Gets 1–5 Yrs. in Hot Bonds Case." *Chicago Tribune*, 4 July 1962, 8.

## Chapter 20. Trouble with the Law

"2 Ex-Police Aides Talk before Jury." *Chicago Tribune*, 21 July 1972, 13.
"2 Found Guilty in Chicago in Extortion of Homosexuals." *New York Times*, 9 Dec. 1966, n.p.
"14 Cops in Graft Quiz Sue on Suspension." *Chicago Tribune*, 31 Jan. 1973, A13.
"20 Are Arrested in 5 N. Side Night Spots." *Chicago Tribune*, 26 Sep. 1973, 4.
"Blackmail Lawmaker in Homosexual Ring." *Chicago Tribune*, 17 May 1967, A11.
"Blackmailer Gets Five-Year Sentence in Homosexual Case." *New York Times*, 17 Aug. 1966, 23.
"Braasch, 17 Other Cops Get Prison Terms Cut." *Chicago Tribune*, 14 Oct. 1975, 3.
"Braasch Working as Freight Pusher." *Chicago Tribune*, 24 Jan. 1974, C15.
"Captures 'Cop'; Tells Story of Extortion Plot." *Chicago Tribune*, 8 June 1949, B6.
"Court Upholds Conviction of 2 for Extortion." *Chicago Tribune*, 16 July 1968, 17.
Davis, Robert. "3 More Taverns Tell of Payoffs." *Chicago Tribune*, 1 Sep. 1973, S3.
———. "5 Ex-Cops Guilty in Payoffs." *Chicago Tribune*, 30 Oct. 1973, 1.
———. "Angelos Admits Making Payoffs to Police Vice Club." *Chicago Tribune*, 7 Sep. 1973, 4.
———. "Angelos Paid Me: Ex-Cop." *Chicago Tribune*, 5 Sep. 1973, 1.
———. "Braasch Denies Any Role in Shakedown of Taverns." *Chicago Tribune*, 25 Sep. 1973, 1.
———. "Braasch Is Called Sophisticated and Educated Con Man." *Chicago Tribune*, 2 Oct. 1973, B7.
———. "Braasch's Share of Payoff Is Put at $3,710 Monthly." *Chicago Tribune*, 11 Sep. 1973, 1.
———. "Braasch Trial, Witness." *Chicago Tribune*, 6 Sep. 1973, 3.
———. "Cop Who Joined Prosecution in Payoff Case Gets Probation." *Chicago Tribune*, 21 Dec. 1973, 8.
———. "Court Upholds Use of Federal Statute to Prosecute Police in Payoff Cases." *Chicago Tribune*, 27 Oct. 1973, S5.
———. "Denies Taking Money." *Chicago Tribune*, 22 Sep. 1973, 2.
———. "Ex-City Aide Tells Role in Cop Bribes." *Chicago Tribune*, 31 Aug. 1973, 1.
———. "Ex-Cop Tells How He Collected Vice Cash." *Chicago Tribune*, 14 Aug. 1973, 1.
———. "Ex-Deputy Chief Is Linked to Shakedown of Taverns." *Chicago Tribune*, 12 Sep. 1973, 1.
———. "Fake Charges Made to Cover Vice: Ex-Cop." *Chicago Tribune*, 14 Sep. 1973, 3.
———. "In Police Bribery Trial." *Chicago Tribune*, 17 Aug. 1973, 8.

———. "In Shakedown Trial." *Chicago Tribune*, 8 Sep. 1973, N2.

———. "Paid Vice Club Cops and Others—Witness." *Chicago Tribune*, 18 Aug. 1973, S2.

———. "Police Shakedown Trial." *Chicago Tribune*, 16 Aug. 1973, 2.

———. "Reporter Testifies." *Chicago Tribune*, 27 Sep. 1973, A7.

Davis, Robert, and John O'Brien. "Bribe Trial Figure Indicted for Lying." *Chicago Tribune*, 25 May 1973, 14.

"Gets 3 Year Sentence for Extortion Plot." *Chicago Tribune*, 14 Dec. 1967, 2.

"Ill Ex-Cop Freed in Payoff Case." *Chicago Tribune*, 20 Nov. 1973, 13.

"Judge Orders Cop to Face Charge in N.Y." *Chicago Tribune*, 14 July 1966, D13.

Kelley, William B. "Eye on the News." *Chicago Gay Crusader*, June 1973, 10.

McCaughna, Daniel, and Robert Davis. "Braasch—Ever a Man Apart." *Chicago Tribune*, 6 Oct. 1973, S1.

"Nab 5 in Bus Depot Shakedown." *Chicago Tribune*, 22 Mar. 1963, 7.

"Obituary: Ralf L. Johnston." *Chicago Tribune*, 29 June 1986, B11.

"Obituary: Dean T. Kolberg." *Journal Star* (Peoria, Ill.), 17 Oct. 1997, C11.

O'Brien, John. "Take Set at 'Hundreds of Thousands.'" *Chicago Tribune*, 31 Dec. 1972, 1.

Phillips, Richard. "4 Police Captains Indicted in Austin Bar Extortion Case." *Chicago Tribune*, 17 Oct. 1974, 1.

———. "Ex-Cop Gets 3½-Year Term in Austin Tavern Extortion." *Chicago Tribune*, 12 Feb. 1974, 9.

———. "Indictment Cites Moorings Payoffs." *Chicago Tribune*, Jan. 23, 1976, 6.

"Policeman Gets 2 Years in Graft." *Chicago Tribune*, 28 Mar. 1973, 3.

Ranzal, Edward. "3 Indicted Here as Sex Extorters; U.S. Charges Ex-Convicts Preyed on Homosexuals." *New York Times*, 1 June 1966, 95.

Sneed, Michael. "Carey Says Daley Perils Bars in Bribe Quiz." *Chicago Tribune*, 15 Sep. 1973, S7.

"Two Former Cops Sentenced." *Chicago Tribune*, 22 May 1974, B7.

"Victim Tells of Extortion Plot." *Chicago Tribune*, 18 May 1967, B3.

Wattley, Philip. "Police Indicted in Tavern Shakedowns Are Suspended." *Chicago Tribune*, 1 Jan. 1973, 1.

Wiedrich, Robert. "10 More Policemen Subpoenaed by Jury." *Chicago Tribune*, 7 July 1972, 1.

———. "More Corruption That Went Unseen." *Chicago Tribune*, 19 Dec. 1973, 18.

Zullo, Joseph. "Enters Guilty Plea in Sex Extortion." *Chicago Tribune*, 7 Feb. 1967, B7.

———. "Orders Ex-Cop Seized in Sex Extortion Ring." *Chicago Tribune*, 1 July 1966, A6

## Chapter 21. Trans-Forming Drag

The primary sources include the author's interviews with Tony "Toni" Midnite, Dee LoBue, and others. Some sections of the interviews appeared in the column "Chicago Whispers" in *Outlines* between 3 Dec. 1997 and 13 Sep. 2000 and in *Windy City Times* between 20 Sep. 2000 and 28 Jan. 2004.

"Bather Seized in Female Garb Is FBI Suspect." *Chicago Tribune*, 27 June 1953, 5.

"Carl, after Surgery, Is Miss Hedy Jo Star." *Chicago Tribune*, 24 Oct. 1962, A9.

"Christine Arrives back Home a New Woman and with Mink." *Chicago Tribune*, 13 Feb. 1953, A14.

"Clear Female Impersonator in Strangling." *Chicago Tribune*, 26 Sep. 1950, 14.

"Cops Seize Female Impersonator, 29, for Quiz in Slaying." *Chicago Tribune*, 25 Sep. 1950, 16.

"Cross-Sex Dress Ban Overruled." *Chicago Tribune*, 21 Sep. 1973, 17.

*Easy Life Club, Inc. v. License Appeal Commission of City of Chicago, Ill.* 18 Ill. App.3d 879, 310 N.E.2d 705 (App. 1974).

"Ex-GI Becomes Blonde Beauty; Operations Transform Bronx Youth." *New York Daily News*, 1 Dec. 1952, 1.

"Fiancé Tells of His Love for Christine." *Chicago Tribune*, 1 Apr. 1959, 14.

"Helga, Great 'Girl' Athlete, Becomes Boy." *Chicago Tribune*, 14 Dec. 1952, 1.

Jorgensen, Christine. *Christine Jorgensen: A Personal Autobiography*. New York: P.S. Eriksson, 1967.

Newton, Esther. *Mother Camp: Female Impersonators in America*. Englewood Cliffs, N.J.: Prentice-Hall, 1972.

*Night Life in Chicago*, 12–19 July 1963; 14–21 Feb. 1964, 1–8 Jan. 1965.

Nite Life [article about raid]. *Chicago Sun-Times*, 29 Apr. 1964, n.p.

Park, Jordan. *Half*. New York: Lion Books, 1953.

"Putting Men into Skirts." *Chicago Tribune*, 20 Mar. 1895, 6.

Raven, Seymour. "T. C. Jones Show a Too-Too Revue." *Chicago Tribune*, 25 Sep. 1958, C7.

"Seize Female Impersonator for Robbery." *Chicago Tribune*, 21 Nov. 1960, B3.

"Seven Men Sentenced for Morals Offenses." *Chicago Tribune*, 1 July 1964, 16.

Sherman, Gayle. "I Want to Be a Woman." *National Insider*, 27 Oct. 1963, 1.

Star, Hedy Jo. *I Changed My Sex*. New York: Novel Books, 1963.

"Surgery Makes Him a Woman, Ex-GI Writes." *Chicago Tribune*, 1 Dec. 1952, 1.

"T. C. Jones Bringing 'Mask and Gown' on Wednesday." *Chicago Tribune*, 21 Sep. 1958, G10.

"Transvestite Law Upheld by U.S. High Court." *Chicago Tribune*, 28 Mar. 1967, B8.

Wiedrich, Robert. "Christine Finds Her Career Has Talking Points." *Chicago Tribune*, 4 July 1956, 11.
"Woman Who Was Man Admits She Hopes to Marry." *Chicago Tribune*, 6 Dec. 1952, 11.

## Chapter 22. The Sodomy Laws

Illinois Criminal Code of 1961. Enacted 28 July 1961, effective 1 Jan. 1962. *Laws of Illinois 1961*, p. 1983.
*Fitzgibbons v. People.* 179 N.E. 106 17 (17 Dec. 1931).
*Honselman v. People.* 48 N.E. 304 (1 Nov. 1897).
*Kelly v. People.* 61 N.E. 425 (24 Oct. 1901).
Kinsey, Alfred C., Wardell B. Pomeroy, and Clyde E. Martin. *Sexual Behavior in the Human Male*. Philadelphia: W.B. Saunders Company, 1948.
Martin, Del. "New Illinois Penal Code—What Does It Mean?" *The Ladder* 6, no. 6 (March 1962): 14–15.
"New Criminal Code in Effect Jan. 1." *Chicago Sun-Times*, 21 Dec. 1961, 43.
"New Penal Code in Illinois." *Mattachine Review* 8, no. 1 (Oct. 1962).
Sheedy, Rev. Charles. "Law and Morals." *Chicago Bar Record*, vol. 43–44 (1961).
*Smith v. People.* 101 N.E. 957 (19 Apr. 1913).
Wexler, Morris J. "Sex Offenses under the New Criminal Code." *Illinois Bar Journal*, October 1962, 152–54.

## Chapter 23. The Gay Pioneers

"3 Deviates Invite Exclusion by Bars." *New York Times*, 22 Apr. 1966, 43.
"400 at Meeting Here in Behalf of Rosenbergs." *Chicago Tribune*, 9 Jan. 1953, 14.
Akers, Milburn P. "For Judge, a Fighter, Pearl Hart." *Chicago Sun*, 26 Oct. 1947, 34.
"Ask $50,000 for Auto Hurts." *Chicago Tribune*, 2 Aug. 1911, 2.
Basker, Robert. Letter. *Chicago Tribune*, 28 May 1964, 12.
———. Letter. *Chicago Tribune*, 13 Feb. 1965.
"'Baby Hands' Reunion Fails to Prove Lasting." *Chicago Tribune*, 6 Aug. 1915, 1.
"Bob Basker, Portrait of a Pioneer." *GayLife*, 25 June 1982, n.p.
Bullough, Vern L. *Before Stonewall: Activists for Gay and Lesbian Rights in Historical Context*. New York: Harrington Park, 2002.
Chicago Mattachine. *Newsletter*, July 1954.
"Children Unite the Churans." *Chicago Tribune*, 11 July 1911, 5.
Cory, Donald Webster. *The Homosexual in America*. New York: Greenberg, 1951.
"Drama's Role in Radio Visioned by Rawlinson." *Chicago Tribune*, 6 Dec. 1931, F6.

"Easy Aces, New Bridge Feature, Coming to W-G-N." *Chicago Tribune*, 4 Oct. 4, 1931, D6.

Gregory Sprague Collection. Chicago Historical Museum, Chicago.

"Jewish Women to Hear Talk on the 'Alien': Pearl Hart to Lecture before Auxiliary." *Chicago Tribune*, 7 Apr. 1940, N4.

Kleiman, Carol. "Legal Help for Harassed Sisters." *Chicago Tribune*, 6 Feb. 1972, E4.

Komisar, Lucy. "Three Homosexuals in Search of a Drink." *Village Voice*, 5 May 1966, 15.

"Natalie Alt to Be Featured in New Music Hour." *Chicago Tribune*, 21 June 1931, C6.

"News of the Society World." *Chicago Tribune*, 19 Apr. 1903, 59.

"Northwestern U. Prof Will Speak to Nurses." *Chicago Tribune*, 27 Nov. 1956, B6.

"Obituary: Pearl Hart." *Chicago Tribune*, 23 Mar. 1975, B18.

Pearl Hart Collection. Chicago History Museum, Chicago.

"Pearl Hart Progressive Chief Justice Candidate." *Chicago Tribune*, 18 Apr. 1948, 3.

"Placard Waving Students Picket Red Tinged Meeting." *Chicago Tribune*, 1 Jan. 1961, 6.

"Says Churan Had Affinity." *Chicago Tribune*, 2 July 1911, 7.

Schofler, Patricia. "At 81, Woman Lawyer Continues Work." *Chicago Tribune*, 3 Jan. 1971, W4.

"Society." *Chicago Tribune*, 20 Aug. 1895, 12.

"Society, Clubs, Entertainments." *Chicago Tribune*, 27 Aug. 1910, 8.

Tobin, Kay, and Randy Wicker. *Gay Crusaders*. New York: Paperback Library, 1972.

"Unite to Fight Social Diseases in Two 'U' Cities." *Chicago Tribune*, 24 Oct. 1937, 11.

"Wed by Trick, Doctor Says; Asks Freedom." *Chicago Tribune*, 11 Oct. 1934, 13.

"W-G-N Opera Company." *Chicago Tribune*, 26 Apr. 1931, G11.

"Woman and Daughter Injured in Automobile Accident." *Chicago Tribune*, 23 Feb. 1911, 5.

"Woman Lawyer to Defend Girls in Morals Court." *Chicago Tribune*, 19 July 1931, 13.

"Women Who Fall for Lesbians." *Jet*, 25 Feb. 1954, 22.

## Chapter 24. Mattachine Midwest and the Struggle toward a Greater Visibility

Beck, Joan. "The Boys Who Don't Grow into Men: A Danger." *Chicago Tribune*, 13 Aug. 1968, B2.

Chicago Mattachine. *Newsletter*, Apr. 1955.

Cunningham, Bill. "Plumage for Male Peacocks." *Chicago Tribune*, 21 Mar. 1967, B1.

"Douglas Dissents as Tribunal Upholds Ouster of Homosexual." *Chicago Tribune*, 23 May 1967, 4.

Dreiske, John. "Senate Votes Study of Sexual Deviation in State." *Chicago Sun-Times*, 9 June 1967, 25.

Elliot, Nell. "The Apostles of the Streets." *Chicago Tribune*, 1 Dec. 1968, N19.

Forsythe, Ronald. "Why Can't 'We' Live Happily Ever After, Too?" *New York Times*, 23 Feb. 1969, n.p.

Foster Gunnison Papers. Thomas J. Dodd Research Center, University of Connecticut, Stores, Conn.

Gallo, Marcia M. *Different Daughters: A History of the Daughters of Bilitis and the Rise of the Lesbian Rights Movement*. New York: Carroll & Graf, 2006.

"'Gay' President Quits; 25-Year-Old Takes Post." *Chicago Defender*, 8 Aug. 1970, 41.

Gould, Robert E. "Will They Grow Out of It?—A Psychiatrist's View." *Chicago Tribune*, 19 Feb. 1967, I33.

Gowran, Clay. "Repeat: TV No Spot to Unload Garbage." *Chicago Tribune*, 8 Mar. 1967, D4.

Gustav-Wrathall, John Donald. *Take the Young Stranger by the Hand: Same-Sex Relations and the YMCA*. Chicago: University of Chicago Press, 1998.

Hacker, Helen. "Homosexuals: Should They Have Equal Rights?" *The Ladder* 14, no. 1/2 (Oct./Nov. 1969): 14–16.

Hirsley, Michael. "'Vice Versa' Squad Fights Male Hookers." *Chicago Tribune*, 25 July 1976, 38.

"Homosexual Bill of Rights." *Kaleidoscope*, 22 Nov.–5 Dec. 1968.

"Homosexuals Ask Candidates' Ideas; Seek Views on Penalties." *New York Times*, 19 Aug. 1968, n.p.

"I'm Glad You Asked That . . ." *New Republic*, 7 Sep. 1968, 14.

Jones, Malden. "Senate OK's Bill for Commission to Study Homosexuals." *Chicago American*, 8 June 1967, 12.

Leonard, William. "'Boys in the Band' a Smash." *Chicago Tribune*, 3 Dec. 1969, C9.

———. "Good Taste, Humor Help as Taboo Theme Comes to Stage." *Chicago Tribune*, 13 Mar. 1968, C2.

———. "Theater: 'Staircase.'" *Chicago Tribune*, 2 May 1969, B14.

*Mattachine Midwest Newsletter*, Aug.–Nov. 1965, Feb.–Oct. 1966, Dec. 1966, Jan. 1967, Apr.–July 1967, Oct. 1967, May–Dec. 1968, Jan.–July 1969.

Moss, Ruth. "Are Sexes Depolarizing?" *Chicago Tribune*, 15 Nov. 1968, B19.

Rankin, Jim. "NACHO Upside Down." *Gay Sunshine*, October 1970.

Ridgeway, James. "The Cops & the Kids." *New Republic*, 7 Sep. 1968, 11.

Taylor, Valerie. "The Early Years of Mattachine Midwest." *Mattachine Midwest Newsletter*, Apr./May 1980.

Terry, Clifford. "'Detective' Mugged by Script." *Chicago Tribune*, 12 July 1968, B19.

"Trends: Where the Boys Are." *Time*, 28 June 1968, n.p.

Weimhoff, Henry. "Roommates Wanted Ad." *Maroon*, 3 Oct. 1969, n.p.

Wiedrich, Robert. "Tells How Mob Is Preying on Sex Deviates." *Chicago Tribune*, 15 Mar. 1966, 7.

———. "Raid Reveals Big Vice Bar Profit." *Chicago Tribune*, 17 Mar. 1966, A2.

Wille, Lois. "Chicago's Twilight World—The Homosexuals—A Growing Problem." *Chicago Daily News*, 20–23 June 1966, n.p.

"Your Legal Rights." *The Ladder* 1, no. 11 (Aug. 1957): 9.

Zubro, Mark. "Bradford Was There Fighting in the Early Days of Mattachine." *GayLife*, 14 Mar. 1980.

# Index

313